Modeling Business Processes

Cooperative Information Systems

Michael P. Papazoglou, Joachim W. Schmidt, and John Mylopoulos, editors

Modeling Business Processes

A Petri Net–Oriented Approach

Wil van der Aalst and Christian Stahl

The MIT Press
Cambridge, Massachusetts
London, England

For information about special quantity discounts, please email special_sales@mitpress.mit.edu

This book was set in Stone Sans and Stone Serif by Westchester Book Composition. Printed and bound in the United States of America.

Library of Congress Cataloging-in-Publication Data

Aalst, Wil van der.
Modeling business processes : a petri net-oriented approach / Wil van der Aalst and Christian Stahl.
    p. cm. — (Cooperative information systems series)
Includes bibliographical references and index.
ISBN 978-0-262-01538-7 (hardcover : alk. paper)
1. Business—Data processing. 2. Management information systems. 3. Petri nets. I. Stahl, Christian, 1978–. II. Title.
HF5548.2.A227 2011
658.4′0380151135—dc22

                                                    2010036474

10 9 8 7 6 5 4 3 2 1

Contents

Foreword

The development of enterprise information systems is challenging. These systems are complex and possess concurrency and nondeterminism, which makes it difficult to envision all possible execution paths and therefore difficult to design and configure them. As a result, enterprise information systems often malfunction or are misaligned, leading to business processes that have poor performance. The traditional focus on data modeling is too limited, and more attention needs to be paid to the business processes these systems support. Therefore, it is my pleasure to write the foreword of this book on business process modeling.

Business process modeling has evolved into one of the most important application domains of Petri nets. This book uses colored Petri nets (CPNs) to model enterprise information systems and the business processes they support. Petri nets provide the foundation of the graphical notation and the basic primitives for modeling concurrency, communication, and synchronization. The extension of these basic primitives with data (color), time, and hierarchy (modules) makes it possible to model and analyze complex artifacts, as is demonstrated in this book. The book is supported by CPN Tools, developed in Aarhus, Denmark. CPN Tools supports the editing, simulation, state-space analysis, and performance analysis of CPNs. This makes the approach described directly applicable. Students can quickly model simple systems and business processes to test their understanding of important concepts. Practitioners can use CPN Tools to model complex information systems and evaluate them using interactive simulation and state-space analysis. It is also possible to compare the performance of different business process designs.

The authors are experts in business process management and the application of formal methods such as Petri nets. Eindhoven University of Technology is one of the leading universities in the field. In 2010, Wil van der Aalst's group was rated as one of the best computer science groups in the Netherlands. Moreover, Van der Aalst is one of the most prolific academics in computer science, and his work is influential, as his h-index (more than 70 according to Google Scholar) shows. Christian Stahl is a young and promising researcher who recently completed his PhD in the context of the

Berlin–Rostock–Eindhoven Service Technology Program. He is an expert on Petri nets, focusing on the design and the analysis of services.

The book is based on many years of teaching, which makes it a reliable and mature source of information. It provides a comprehensive introduction to business process modeling using rigorous modeling and analysis techniques and manages to explain these challenging concepts in a clear and intuitive way. Moreover, there are many exercises with solutions. The presentation makes CPNs accessible to a wide audience ranging from students majoring in computer science, industrial engineering, or management science to practitioners involved in the development of enterprise information systems or the management of business processes.

I hope (and expect) that the reader will enjoy this book.

Kurt Jensen
Professor at Aarhus University, Denmark
Head of the Steering Committee for the International Petri Net Community

Preface

This book is the result of two decades of experience in teaching business process modeling to different audiences ranging from undergraduate and graduate students to system designers and business consultants. In the early nineties, the first author developed a course on specification of information systems (SIS). This aimed to teach undergraduates at Eindhoven University of Technology the basics of information systems modeling. This course consisted of two main parts: one part on object modeling and one part on process modeling. Over time, the course focused more and more on process modeling. This shift was motivated by the increasing emphasis on business processes in industry and the availability of more and more process-aware information systems. Today, it is widely acknowledged that process orientation is important for creating enterprise information systems that are aligned with the actual business processes. However, two decades ago, technology and information modeling served as the predominant starting point for IT (information technology) systems development.

From the start, Petri nets were used to provide a system-independent foundation for business process modeling in the SIS course. While industry standards come and go, this foundation proved to be remarkably stable. This fits well with the goal of this book: to provide a comprehensive and foundational approach to business process modeling that is timeless but highly relevant for anyone involved in the development or analysis of enterprise information systems.

Initially, ExSpect was used as a system to support the different courses given by the first author. Later, ExSpect was replaced by CPN Tools because colored Petri nets had become the standard for practical modeling based on Petri nets. Moreover, CPN Tools provided didactic advantages through the direct manipulation of the model, incremental checking, and interactive simulation. As a result of these developments and new insights, the current book has little overlap with the syllabus initially developed for the SIS course in 1992.

Many people have been involved in courses such as business information systems (BIS), specification of information systems (SIS), process modeling (PM), workflow management (WFM), and business process management systems (BPMS) given by the first author. Their efforts resulted in continuous improvements of the material and a vast number of exercises. Moreover, several people provided feedback on earlier drafts of the book. Therefore, we would like to thank Ad Aarts, Jacques Bouman, Søren Christensen, Boudewijn van Dongen, Jan Goossenaerts, Judith Gordebeke, Kees van Hee, Monique Jansen-Vullers, Kurt Jensen, Herman Koppelman, Niels Lohmann, Arjan Mooij, Hajo Reijers, Ella Roubtsova, Robert Schuwer, Eric Verbeek, Marc Voorhoeve, Gerd Wagner, Lisa Wells, and Jaap van der Woude. Moreover, we thank the CPN Group at the University of Aarhus for their work on CPN Tools.

1 Information Systems: Introduction and Concepts

Information systems have become the backbone of most organizations. Banks could not process payments, governments could not collect taxes, hospitals could not treat patients, and supermarkets could not stock their shelves without the support of information systems. In almost every sector—education, finance, government, health care, manufacturing, and businesses large and small—information systems play a prominent role. Every day work, communication, information gathering, and decision making all rely on information technology (IT). When we visit a travel agency to book a trip, a collection of interconnected information systems is used for checking the availability of flights and hotels and for booking them. When we make an electronic payment, we interact with the bank's information system rather than with personnel of the bank. Modern supermarkets use IT to track the stock based on incoming shipments and the sales that are recorded at cash registers. Most companies and institutions rely heavily on their information systems. Organizations such as banks, online travel agencies, tax authorities, and electronic bookshops can be seen as IT companies given the central role of their information systems.

This book is about modeling business processes. A business process describes the flow of work within an organization. It is managed and supported by an information system. In this chapter, we first introduce information systems (section 1.1) and discuss different types of information systems and their roles in organizations (section 1.2). After introducing information systems, we look at the life cycle of these systems and concentrate on the important role that models play in this life cycle (section 1.3). Next, we show how to describe information systems in terms of states and state transitions (section 1.4). Although transition systems are not suitable for modeling industrial information systems and business processes, they illustrate the essence of modeling. Finally, we discuss the role of modeling and provide an outlook on the next chapters (section 1.5).

1.1   Information Systems

Organizations offer products to customers to make money. These products can be goods
or services. In most organizations, huge volumes of data accumulate: data of products,
data of customers, data of employees, data of the delivery of products, and data of other
sources. These data therefore play an important role in contemporary organizations and
must be stored, managed, and processed, which is where *information systems* come into
play. Because there is no unique understanding of what an information system is, we
develop a definition of an information system in this section by considering an example
organization everybody should be familiar with: a family doctor.

Example 1.1   A patient who consults a family doctor usually first tells the doctor about
the symptoms. With this information, the doctor examines the patient and makes a
diagnosis. Afterward, the doctor determines the treatment to heal the patient. For example, based on the diagnosis, the doctor may write the patient a prescription for some
medication. Finally, the doctor must document the symptoms, the diagnosis, and the
treatments. Today, most doctors use a software system to record this information.

Before we provide our definition of an information system, we first explain the term
"information," which can mean any of the following:

1. The *communication act* of one agent—the term "agent" may refer to any entity ranging from a person or a software component to an organization—informing another
agent (e.g., by exchanging messages);
2. The *knowledge* or *beliefs* of agents as a part of their mental state; or
3. (Data) *objects* that represent knowledge or beliefs.

Example 1.2   In the example of the family doctor, the situation in which a patient
informs the doctor about the symptoms is an example of a communication act. The
patient and the doctor are the agents in this example. The doctor uses her knowledge
and the symptoms described by a patient to examine the patient. The doctor may
have beliefs about possible causes based on earlier interactions with the patient. Based
on the outcomes of the examination and on prior knowledge, the doctor makes a
diagnosis. The documentation of the symptoms, of the diagnosis, and of the treatments
in a software system leads to the creation of data objects. These data objects represent
the new knowledge and may be used for various purposes—for example, for billing the
insurance company of the patient.

There are textbooks in which the authors distinguish between data, information,
and knowledge. In these textbooks, the term "data" refers to the syntax, "information"

refers to the interpretation, and "knowledge" refers to the way information is used. The data element "29-01-1966," for example, may be seen as a string; in a particular context it may, however, be interpreted as the birthdate of a person, and people may use this information to congratulate this person on the twenty-ninth of January each year. In this chapter, we use the term "information" in a broader sense, as described earlier.

Having explained "information," we can define the term "information system." The standard definition is that *an information system manages and processes information*. This definition is general and allows different interpretations. For example, it is not clear whether "information system" refers only to software systems or also to humans, such as a family doctor who manages and processes information. For this reason, we develop a more refined definition.

The reason for "information system" having several meanings becomes clear when we consider Alter's framework for information systems (Alter 2002) in figure 1.1. It shows an integrated view of an information system encompassing six entities: customers, products (and services), business processes, participants, information, and technology. Customers are the actors that interact with the information system through the exchange of products or services. These products are being manufactured or assembled in business processes that use participants, information, and technology. Participants are the people who do the work. Information may range from information about customers to information about products and business processes. Business processes use technology, and new technologies may enable new ways of doing work.

Customers and participants are examples of *agents*. As figure 1.1 shows, business processes play a central role in larger information systems. A business process describes the flow of work within an organization. In this book, we use the following definition of a business process adapted from work by Weske (2007).

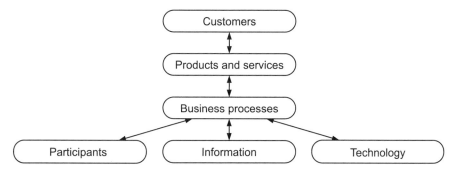

Figure 1.1
An integrated view of an information system.

Definition 1.3 (Business process)   A *business process* consists of a set of activities that is performed in an organizational and technical environment. These activities are coordinated to jointly realize a business goal. Each business process is enacted by a single organization, but it may interact with business processes performed by other organizations.

According to this definition, a business process consists of coordinated activities. Typically, these activities must be performed in a particular order. For example, the family doctor first examines a patient and then makes a diagnosis. Although a business process is enacted by a single organization, it may interact with other business processes within and across organizational boundaries. For example, the family doctor may bill the insurance company of the patient.

Diagrams like the one in figure 1.1 illustrate why it is difficult to provide a standard definition of an information system. Some researchers and practitioners hold a view that all six elements constitute an information system; other researchers and practitioners argue that only a subset (e.g., just business processes, information, and technology) constitutes an information system.

Example 1.4   Let us pick up again the example of the family doctor. A patient serves as a customer, according to figure 1.1, and the product is health care. The business process describes the procedure of the medical treatment. It has five activities: a patient informs the doctor about the symptoms, then the doctor examines the patient, makes a diagnosis, determines the treatments, and finally the doctor enters the data into the software system. The doctor is a participant, pieces of information are the symptoms of the patient and the data added to the software system, and the doctor's software system is the technology involved.

Given these considerations, we present the following definition of an information system, which is adapted from Alter's definition (Alter 2002).

Definition 1.5 (Information system)   An *information system* is a software system to capture, transmit, store, retrieve, manipulate, or display information, thereby supporting people, organizations, or other software systems.

In contrast to other definitions, we consider an information system to be a software system. A family doctor is, hence, not part of an information system. Furthermore, an information system may support not only an organization or a person but also other software systems and, hence, information systems. In addition, our definition of an information system does not require the existence of a business process; a text editor is an example of an information system that has no business process. In this book, however, we concentrate on information systems in which business processes play a central role.

Example 1.6 In the example of the family doctor, the information system is the software system that stores the data of the patient. This information system supports a person: the doctor.

1.2 Types of Information Systems

In the previous section, we defined "information system." Many types of information systems exist on the market. To illustrate this, this section first provides a broad classification of information systems. We then narrow our view to enterprise information systems and present for this class of information systems an overview of existing types of software systems. Moreover, we provide examples of typical enterprise information systems in various industries.

1.2.1 Classifying Information Systems

It is ambitious to classify the many types of information systems that have emerged in practice. Many classifications for information systems exist in the literature; see classifications by Alter (2002), Dumas, Van der Aalst, and Ter Hofstede (2005), and Olivé (2007), for instance. The problem is that classification is in flux; that is, a classification developed a few years ago is not necessarily current. As another and main limiting factor, the categories of a classification are typically not disjointed: one type of information system belongs to multiple categories. Given these problems, we present a high-level classification that distinguishes three classes of information systems.

The first class of information systems is *personal information systems*. Such an information system can manage and store information for a private person. Examples are an address book or address database and an audio CD collection.

Enterprise (or organizational) *information systems* are the second class of information systems. An enterprise information system is tailored toward the support of an organization. We distinguish between *generic* types and technologies of information systems and information systems for *certain* types of organizations. The former class of enterprise information systems supports functionality that can be used by a wide range of organizations. Examples are workflow management systems, enterprise resource planning systems, data warehouse systems, and geographic information systems. In contrast, information systems for certain types of organizations offer functionality that is tailored toward certain industries or organizations. Examples are hospital information systems, airline reservation systems, and electronic learning systems.

The third class of information systems is *public information systems*. Unlike personal information systems, public information systems can manage and store information that can be accessed by a community. Public libraries, information systems for museums, Web-based community information systems, and Web-based stock-portfolio information systems are examples of public information systems.

In this book, we concetrate on enterprise information systems. These systems play a crucial role in a wide variety of organizations and have an enormous economic value. The complexity and importance of such systems provide serious challenges for IT professionals ranging from software engineers to management consultants. Business processes and business process models play a dominant role in enterprise information systems. This explains why business process modeling is the focus of later chapters.

1.2.2 Types of Enterprise Information Systems

There are many types of enterprise information systems in practice. This section gives an overview of the most important types.

Enterprise Resource Planning Systems   An *enterprise resource planning* (ERP) *system* is an information system that supports the main business processes of an organization—for example, human resource management, sales, marketing, management, financial accounting, controlling, and logistics. In the past, each business process was encapsulated in a separate information system. As most of these business processes use related data, much redundant data had to be stored within the respective information systems. The increasing number and complexity of information systems forced organizations to spend much effort in synchronizing the data of all information systems.

An ERP system is a solution to overcome these synchronization efforts by integrating different information systems. It is a software system that is built on a distributed computing platform including one or more database management systems. The computing platform serves as an infrastructure on which the individual business processes are implemented. First-generation ERP systems now run the complete back office functions of the world's largest corporations.

ERP systems run typically in a three-tier client/server architecture consisting of a user interface (or presentation) tier, an application server tier, and a database server tier. ERP systems provide multi-instance database management, configuration management, and version (or customization) management for the underlying database schema, for the user interface, and for the many application programs associated with them. As ERP systems are typically designed for multinational companies, they have to support multiple languages, multiple currencies, and country-specific business practices. The sheer size and the tremendous complexity of these software systems make them complicated to deploy and maintain.

ERP systems are large and complex software systems that integrate smaller and more focused applications; for example, most ERP systems include functionality that is also present in other enterprise information systems, such as procurement systems, manufacturing systems, sales and marketing systems, delivery systems, finance systems, and workflow management systems. We introduce these systems in the following discussion.

The market leader in the ERP market is SAP, with 43,000 customers for its system SAP ERP (data from 2009). Other important vendors are Oracle, Sage Company, and Microsoft.

Procurement Systems   A *procurement system* is an information system that helps an organization automate the purchasing process. The aim of a procurement system is to acquire what is needed to keep the business processes running at minimal cost. With the available inventory, the expected arrival of ordered goods, and forecasts based on sales and production plans, the procurement system determines the requirements and generates new orders. At the same time, it tracks whether ordered goods arrive. The key point is to order the right amount of material at the right time from the right source. If the material arrives too early, money for buying the material and warehouse space to store the material will be tied up. If, in contrast, the material arrives too late, then production is disrupted. Hence, the goal is to balance reducing inventory costs with reducing the risk of out-of-stock situations.

Procurement is an important ingredient of *supply chain management* (SCM), in which coordination of the purchasing processes is not limited to two actors. Instead, SCM aims at closely coordinating an organization with its suppliers so that inefficiencies are avoided by optimizing the entire purchasing process. For example, by synchronizing the production process of an organization with its suppliers, all parties may reduce their inventories. The market leader in the SCM market is SAP with SAP SCM; competitors are Oracle and JDA Software (data from 2007).

Procurement is related to *electronic data interchange* (EDI), the electronic exchange of information based on a standard set of messages. EDI can be used to avoid delays and errors in the procurement process as a result of rekeying information. In the classical (pre-EDI) situation, a purchase order is entered into the procurement system of one organization, it is printed, and the printed purchase order is sent to the order processing department or to another organization. The information on the printed purchase order is then reentered into the procurement system. By using EDI or technology such as Web services, organizations can automate these parts of the procurement process. The purchase order is electronically sent to the processing department or to the other organization. This automation makes the overall procurement process faster and less error-prone, thereby reducing the costs for each purchase order.

Manufacturing Systems *Manufacturing systems* support the production processes in organizations. Driven by information, such as the bill of materials (BOM), inventory levels, and available capacity, they plan the production process. With increasing automation of production processes, manufacturing systems have become more and more important. For example, most steps in the production line of a car, such as welding the auto body, are performed by robots. This requires precise scheduling and material movement and, hence, a manufacturing system that supports these processes.

Material requirements planning (MRP) is an approach to translate requirements (i.e., the number of products for each period), inventory status data, and the BOM into a production plan without considering capacities. Successors, such as *manufacturing resources planning* (MRP2), also take capacity information into account. Software based on MRP and MRP2 has been the starting point for many ERP systems.

Consider an organization that produces different flavors of yogurt (e.g., strawberry, peach, and pear). The organization has several machines to produce yogurt; each machine can produce any flavor. Production planning means scheduling each machine for the flavor of yogurt it must produce. The production plan depends on the demand for each flavor and on the delivery of ingredients. Furthermore, each machine has to be cleaned at regular intervals and when the production changes to a new flavor. Calculating a production plan is a complex optimization problem, often depending on several thousand constraints. Consequently, the aim is to find a good solution rather than an optimum solution.

Sales and Marketing Systems *Sales and marketing systems* need to process customer orders by taking into account issues such as availability. These systems are driven by software addressing the four *p*'s: product, price, place, and promotion. Organizations undertake promotional activities and offer their products at competitive prices to boost sales, but a product that is not available or not at the right location cannot be sold. One prominent example of a promotional activity is a bonus card in supermarkets. Customers who register for a bonus card get a discount or a voucher. Bonus cards are an instrument for organizations to obtain personal data about their customers (e.g., age, address) and data about the buying behavior of customers (i.e., what they buy and when they buy it). These data are collected and processed by an information system. The information extracted from these data can help to improve marketing and to determine the range of products to offer.

New technologies are increasingly used to support sales over the Internet. *Electronic commerce* uses the Internet to inform (potential) customers, to execute the purchase transaction, and to deliver the product. Again, this functionality is typically embedded in an ERP system. To manage the contact with their customers, organizations use dedicated *customer relationship management* (CRM) *systems*. A CRM system has a database to store all customer-related information, such as contact details and past purchases.

This information helps tailor the marketing efforts to expected customer needs. As an example, a car dealer does not need to send information about a new expensive sports car to customers who recently bought a van or a compact car.

Delivery Systems   A *delivery system* is an information system that supports the delivery of goods to customers. The task of these systems is to plan and schedule when and in what order customers receive their products. Consider, for example, a transportation company with hundreds of trucks. The planning of trips, the routing of these trucks, and reacting to on-the-fly changes require dedicated software. Creating an optimal schedule is a complex optimization problem. As circumstances—for example, traffic jams and production problems—may force rescheduling, contemporary delivery systems aim to find a good solution rather than a theoretical optimum solution. More and more delivery systems offer tracking-and-tracing functionality; for example, customers of package delivery companies, such as UPS, can track down the location of a specific parcel via the Internet.

Finance Systems   Among the oldest information systems are *finance systems*. These systems support the flow of money within and between organizations. Finance systems typically provide accounting functionality to maintain a consistent and auditable set of books for reporting and management support. Another important application of finance systems is the stock market. At a stock market, dedicated information systems are essential to process the operations. Again, the functionality of finance systems is absorbed by ERP systems. The origin of the SAP system, for example, was in finance rather than production planning.

Product Design Systems   Enterprise information systems not only support the production of products, they also support the design of products. Examples are *computer-aided design* (CAD) *systems* and *product data management* (PDM) *systems*. CAD systems support the graphical representation and the design of product specifications. PDM systems support the design process in a broader sense by managing designs and their documentation. Typically, there are many versions of the same design, and designs of different components need to be integrated. To support such complex concurrent engineering processes, PDM systems offer versioning functionality.

Workflow Management Systems   Many organizations aim to automate their business processes. To this end, they have to specify in which order the activities of a business process must be executed and which person has to execute an activity at which time. A *workflow* refers to the automation of a business process, in whole or in part. Each activity of the workflow is implemented as software. The workflow logic specifies the order of the activities. A *workflow management system* (WfMS) is an information system that defines, manages, and executes workflows. The execution order of the workflow's activities is driven by a computer representation of the workflow logic. The ultimate goal of workflow management is to make sure that the proper activities are executed by the right people at the right time (Aalst and Hee 2004).

Not every business process corresponds to a single workflow. Workflows are case-based; that is, every piece of work is executed for a specific case. One can think of a case as a workflow instance, such as a mortgage, an insurance claim, a tax declaration, a purchase order, or a request for information. Each case is handled individually according to the workflow definition (often referred to as the workflow schema). Examples of business processes that do not correspond to a single workflow are stock-keeping processes; for example, in *make-to-stock* and *assemble-to-order* processes, end products or materials already exist before the order is placed (i.e., before the case is created, manufacturing or assembly activities have already occurred). For this reason, only fragments of such business processes (i.e., in-between stocking points) are considered to be workflows.

Interestingly, WfMSs are embedded in some of the enterprise information systems already mentioned; for example, most ERP and PDM systems include one or more WfMS components. Besides enterprise information systems, middleware software (e.g., IBM's WebSphere) and development platforms (e.g., the .NET framework) embed workflow functionality; see the WebSphere Process Server and the Windows Workflow Foundation. Examples of stand-alone WfMSs are BPM|one, FileNet, and YAWL.

Data Warehouses A *data warehouse* is a large database that stores historical and up-to-date information from a variety of sources. It is optimized for fast query answering. To allow this, there are three continuous processes: The first process extracts data at regular intervals from its information sources, loads the data into auxiliary tables, and then cleans and transforms the loaded data to make it suitable for the data warehouse schema. Processing queries from users and from data analysis applications is the task of the second process. The third process archives the information that is no longer needed by means of tertiary storage technology.

Nowadays, most organizations employ information systems for financial accounting, purchasing, sales and inventory management, production planning, and management control. To efficiently use the vast amount of information that these operational systems have been collecting over the years for planning and decision-making purposes, the information from all relevant sources must be merged and consolidated in a data warehouse.

Whereas an operational database is accessed by *online transaction processing* (OLTP) applications that update its content, a data warehouse is accessed by ad hoc user queries and by special data analysis programs, referred to as *online analytical processing* (OLAP) applications. In a banking environment, for example, there may be an OLTP application for controlling the bank's automated teller machines (ATMs). This application performs frequent updates to tables storing current account information in a detailed format. There may also be an OLAP application for analyzing the behavior of bank customers. A typical query that could be answered by such a system would be to calculate the average amount that customers of a certain age withdraw from their accounts by using ATMs in a certain region. To minimize response times for such complex queries, the bank would maintain a data warehouse into which all relevant information (including historical account data) from other databases is loaded and suitably aggregated.

Queries in data warehouses typically refer to business events, such as sales transactions or online shop visits that are recorded in event history tables (i.e., fact tables) with designated columns for storing the time and the location at which the event occurred. An event record usually has numeric parameters (e.g., an amount, a quantity, or a duration) and additional parameters (e.g., references to the agents and objects involved in the event). Whereas the numeric parameters are the basis for forming statistical queries the time, location, and reference parameters are the *dimensions* of the requested statistics. There are *multidimensional databases* for representing and processing this type of multidimensional data. The leader in the data warehouse market is Oracle (data from 2009).

Business Intelligence Systems   A *business intelligence system* provides tools to analyze the performance—that is, the efficiency and the effectiveness—of *running* business processes. These tools extract information on the business processes from the data available in an organization. Different tools and techniques exist, among them business performance management, business activity monitoring, querying and reporting, data mining, and process mining.

Business performance management concentrates on improving the performance of business processes. The goal is to extract information from the history of running business processes and to display this information on a management dashboard. For example, one could monitor a credit approval process to get insight into the length of time required to make the decision.

In contrast to business performance management, *business activity monitoring* aims at providing real-time information on business processes and the activities in these business processes. The goal is to support decision making at runtime. Such a tool may monitor inventory levels, response times, or queues and take action whenever needed.

Querying and reporting tools explore data (e.g., stored in a data warehouse) to provide insight into efficiency and effectiveness of business processes and trends in the environment. Typically, statistical analysis is applied to the data to distinguish between trends and isolated events.

The term *data mining* refers to a collection of techniques to extract patterns from examples. Originally, the term "data mining" had a negative connotation (i.e., data dredging, data snooping, and data fishing), but nowadays data mining is an established research domain with a huge impact. Examples of classical data mining tasks are *classification* (which arranges the data into predefined groups), *clustering* (like classification, but the groups are not predefined), *regression* (which attempts to find a function that models the data with the least error), and *association rule learning* (which searches for relationships between variables). Data mining techniques can be applied to any type of data and do not explicitly consider business processes.

Process mining looks at data from the viewpoint of a particular business process. Information systems usually log the occurrences of events—for example, accepting an order, sending an invoice, or receiving a payment. The availability of such *event logs*, which contain footprints of a business process, enables the discovery of models describing reality. The resulting business process model can be compared with the specification of the business process and used for simulation and performance analysis. Process mining is discussed in section 8.5.

Business intelligence is still a young discipline that will receive more acceptance and attention soon. Most commercial tools support business performance management, business activity monitoring, and querying and reporting rather than the more sophisticated techniques of data and process mining. Business intelligence is so far restricted to reporting information on running business processes and offers little support in terms of how a business process can be improved. The market leader in business intelligence is SAP (data from 2008) with SAP BusinessObjects; other main vendors are SAS, IBM, Oracle, and Microsoft. Examples of open-source projects providing data and process mining software are WEKA (Witten and Frank 2005) and ProM (Aalst, Reijers, et al. 2007).

1.2.3 Enterprise Information Systems in Different Industries

The various types of enterprise information systems have different levels of granularity. For example, SAP Business Workflow is just one component in the large SAP ERP system, but its functionality is comparable to many stand-alone WfMSs. Functionality of software systems is more and more wrapped into services that can be accessed over the Internet, which allows software systems to be viewed at different levels of granularity. Organizations do not develop their enterprise information systems from scratch; they instead purchase large software suites that must to be customized, or they assemble a software system from components. Configuration corresponds to specifying information about the organization and its business processes and to switching functionality on or off. Organizations typically use only a small percentage of the functionality provided by software vendors, such as SAP. Similarly, few hospitals use all of the functionality provided by software vendors, such as ChipSoft and Siemens.

The abundance of functionality in today's enterprise information systems can be explained by looking at the cost of software. Development of enterprise information systems is extremely expensive, because these systems are—from an engineering point of view—highly complicated. However, once developed, software can be copied without much effort. This development cycle is completely different from that of physical products. For this reason, software vendors are tempted to provide an abundance of functionality that can be adapted to the customer's specific requirements. As a result, software vendors shift efforts from software implementation to configuration of enterprise information systems.

The application of a particular enterprise information system and its configuration depends on the industry an organization is operating in. For example, a hospital, a bank, a manufacturer, and a municipality may all use an ERP system, such as SAP, but the configurations will vary. Although all four organizations may use the financial component or the procurement component of SAP, it is likely that only the manufacturer is using the MRP component for production planning. In addition to standard components, these organizations will use industry-specific enterprise information systems. For example, the hospital may use a dedicated radiology information system and an information system to create and maintain electronic patient records. The bank will have software to make calculations related to interest and mortgages, and the municipality will have software to access governmental administrations.

The hospital, the bank, the manufacturer, and the municipality in this example may use the same WfMS (e.g., BPM|one or YAWL), but the workflow schemas that are used to configure the systems of the four organizations are different. For example, the municipality will need to specify the business process for registering a newborn. This business process is irrelevant for the other three organizations.

Given the various types of enterprise information systems and the many ways they can be configured, this chapter does not target specific industries or specific types of enterprise information systems. Instead, we concentrate on general principles of (enterprise) information systems.

1.3   The Life Cycle of an Information System

There are various ways to develop an enterprise information system. Accordingly, the most important question a designer of such a system has to deal with is: how do I develop an enterprise information system? To answer this question, we introduce a *life cycle model* of enterprise information systems. This life cycle model covers the phases of the development process of an enterprise information system. Enterprise information systems are complex software systems that are modified to reflect organizational needs and changes rather than developed from scratch. For this reason, the life cycle model includes phases that address change and redesign of existing enterprise information systems. In this section, we aim at being more generic and consider information systems rather than enterprise information systems.

1.3.1 Introduction to the Life Cycle Model

According to the integrated view of an information system shown in figure 1.1, an information system may include each of the six entities. In definition 1.5, we restricted information systems to software systems, thereby requiring the presence of the technology of figure 1.1. When considering the development process of an information system, however, we interpret the information system in a more narrow sense in which just the software is taken into account. Information systems typically have two development processes. In the first development process, a generic information system is implemented; in the second development process, this system is customized. For example, for an ERP system, software vendors, such as SAP, implement new releases of their ERP system for other organizations. The implementation of the ERP system is guided by the development process of the software vendor. After an organization purchases an ERP system, this ERP system passes through the development process of the organization. In this second development process, the ERP system needs to be installed, configured, customized, and introduced in the organization.

There can be mixtures of these two development processes. For example, the information system of a bank may be composed of selected components of an ERP system and of self-developed software components that provide specific functionality. In this case, the development process for building the information system for the bank includes a software development process similar to that of software vendors. Because of their tremendous complexity, existing information systems are usually redesigned and iteratively improved rather than replaced by a new system. As a consequence, the development process of an information system contains phases, such as maintenance and improvement. For example, in the information system of a bank, the ERP system may be reconfigured or upgraded to a newer version.

Organizations develop and run information systems, which may involve software components purchased from other organizations. People who are going to use the information system are the *users* or *participants*. People who design the information system or the products that are used to assemble the information system are the *designers*. In this section, we concentrate on the work of designers.

Many life cycle models are described in the literature and used in practice. Some aim at the software development process (e.g., within companies), and others aim at the development of an information system in an organization (e.g., a bank). Our life cycle model, depicted in figure 1.2, is a mixture of both. Each rectangle illustrates a phase in the life cycle, and arcs represent the order of the phases. The main cycle models the development process of a new information system. It takes into account the development process of generic software, the development process of information systems that are customized from generic software, and a mixture of these development processes. The two smaller cycles, which contain shaded rectangles, model the development process of existing information systems—that is, the maintenance and the improvement

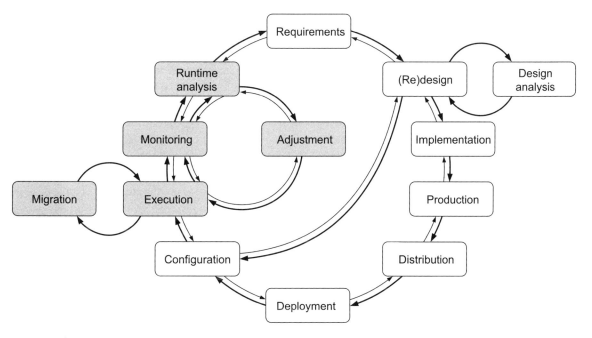

Figure 1.2
The life cycle model of an enterprise information system.

of running information systems. In the following sections, we discuss the life cycle model of figure 1.2 in more detail.

1.3.2 A Software Development–Oriented Life Cycle

The life cycle model in figure 1.2 is based on the observation that information systems are complex, customized (i.e., made-to-order) software systems whose development requires many man-years. Developing an information system can be compared to constructing a tunnel or manufacturing a car. It is usually organized in the form of a project. The main cycle in figure 1.2 specifies the development process of a new customized information system, which is the focus of this section.

We distinguish the following eleven phases for customized information systems: *requirements phase, design phase, design analysis phase, implementation phase, production phase, distribution phase, deployment phase, configuration phase, execution phase, monitoring phase,* and *runtime analysis phase.* Not all of these phases are relevant for all information systems; for example, production, distribution, and deployment phases are only relevant in the case of generic (i.e., made-to-stock) information systems, such as ERP systems, Microsoft Office tools, or database management systems.

Models play an important role in the development process of an information system. A model describes the information system to be designed in a certain form (e.g., textual or graphical). Models can be displayed in many ways, but they are always intended to describe the information system or the business processes supported by it. The way in which such a description is expressed depends on the point of view from which we want to look at the information system and is determined by the purpose of the description. A model abstracts away from aspects that are considered not relevant for the model. There are countless modeling formalisms. Most of them are grounded in logic, set theory, algebra, or graph theory.

Example 1.7 A bicycle map is a model of a geographic area and is intended to support cyclists. Not all aspects of the real landscape are present in the model. The bicycle map represents only those aspects that are important to the cyclists, that is, an overview of all bicycling tracks in the designated area. The map may display the bicycling tracks as blue, even though they have a different color in reality. Only the purpose of the model is important: cyclists want to see bicycling tracks on the map. A map of the same area designed for another means of transport (e.g., car or boat) would look different.

Models may serve as an *abstract description* or as a *specification*. An abstract description model describes an already existing information system. This model allows us to analyze the information system. In contrast, a specification model serves as a specification of what an information system is supposed to do. Such a model is intended to be used for constructing a new information system. The modeling of existing information systems and of information systems to be developed are considered in this book. We investigate business process–related aspects of information systems and use Petri nets extended with data, time, and hierarchy as a modeling formalism.

In the following sections, we discuss the eleven phases of the main life cycle in figure 1.2. The requirements phase and the design phase are of particular interest, because developing models is an essential part of these two phases. We further concentrate on the software development process of information systems. The configuration-oriented life cycle (e.g., configuring a customized information system) is discussed in section 1.3.3.

Requirements Phase The *requirements phase* is the first phase in the main life cycle in figure 1.2. It involves collecting the various requirements for the information system and assembling a coherent requirements specification. In many cases, there is an existing information system that does not satisfy all requirements. It is then wise to analyze thoroughly what the existing information system does for its environment. The result of this analysis will inform which functionality of the existing information system should be preserved in the new one. We can also obtain valuable insights by analyzing the deficiencies of the existing information system and the reasons why a new information system is being developed. After this analysis, we can formulate the requirements of the new information system.

Example 1.8   The requirements phase in the development of a new (simplified) ATM leads to the following requirements. The ATM should allow its clients to query their current account balances and to withdraw money. If clients want to withdraw money, then the ATM should offer them several amounts, but it should also allow them to choose an amount of money. There are several restrictions. For example, the amount of money clients withdraw should be less than a maximum amount (e.g., 500 euros for each day), and it should not lower the client's account balance below a predefined lower bound. Furthermore, if clients just query their current account balance, then their account balance should not change.

The requirements refer to the functionality of the new information system and also to other (nonfunctional) aspects, such as costs, maintenance, and reliability. In the early requirements phase, requirements are expressed in ordinary language. This is important, because key users should be able to understand the requirements. Users typically express requirements in cooperation with designers. In the late requirements phase, requirements are expressed by specification languages and by models resulting in a *domain model* that captures the concepts of the domain under study. The development of requirements specifications is known as *requirements engineering* (Hull, Jackson, and Dick 2004).

Exercise 1.1   Express the main requirements for an information system that advises travelers about a travel scheme (route and time) when they want to make a holiday trip.

Design Phase   The purpose of the *design phase* is to develop two models that are suitable to communicate with the users and the software developers of the information system. First, designers derive a *functional design model* from the domain model. The functional design model is expressed in terms of general software modeling constructs, but it still abstracts away from specific implementation. Second, designers derive an *implementation model* from the functional design model by taking the target programming language or implementation framework into account.

A functional design model captures the functionality of the information system. This model typically consists of several diagrams that visualize (static) data models and (dynamic) business process models. It abstracts away from implementation details. This is especially important for the communication between users and designers. Users are laymen and should not be confronted with all details of the information system; instead, end users must understand relevant parts of the model to investigate whether the designer has correctly taken their requirements into account.

Designers can construct a functional design model for an information system in the form of an *executable specification* providing a formal description and a *prototype* of the information system. A prototype is an experimental first version that is used for testing a design and for gaining more insight into the requirements of the information system to be built. It does not normally implement the entire functionality of the information system. For instance, it may lack an ergonomic user interface, it may not provide the necessary security mechanisms, or it may not provide the required performance. At the beginning of the design process, the requirements of an information system are often incompletely and ambiguously specified. By constructing a model and doing experiments with a prototype, ambiguities and hidden requirements may be discovered. This helps ensure that the final information system satisfies the requirements of its users and avoids costly and time-consuming revisions at a later stage.

The second model, which designers construct during the design phase, is an *implementation model*. It is a detailed work design for the software developers who are going to implement the information system. There are usually several work designs, each reflecting a certain aspect or detail of the information system. Because it is essential that the implementation model conforms to the functional design model, the designer has to verify that these models match.

Example 1.9 In the example of the ATM, the designer constructs a functional design model of the ATM on the basis of the previously developed domain model. The functional design model can be an algebraic specification of the static information (e.g., querying the current account balance returns an account balance in euros) and a business process model describing the order of activities (e.g., clients choose to withdraw money, next they can choose between a standard amount or a customized amount, and so on). In addition, the functional design model can contain a prototype showing the user the possible interactions with the ATM. With this model, the user and designer can discuss all open issues of the final design of the ATM.

In the next step, the designer develops an implementation model based on the functional design model. This model may contain detailed information about how the database of the bank must be queried, how the chosen security mechanisms must be implemented, and how the interplay of the information system with the hardware of the ATM must be implemented. The implementation model serves as a basis for discussion between the designer and the software developer to identify the way in which the ATM should be implemented.

In the ATM example, the mediator role of the designer and the benefit of the two models becomes clear. The designer uses the functional design model to communicate with the user and the implementation model to communicate with the software developers.

In the software development process, usually one person or a group of people plays the role of the designer and of the software developer. The distinction between the functional design model and the implementation model may then become blurred. In these circumstances, often the user cannot understand the model because it is too detailed, or the model does not sufficiently support the implementation because it is unclear or incomplete.

Design Analysis Phase The role of the functional design model and the implementation model is not only to serve as a basis for discussion between the designer and the user and between the designer and the software developer. Models abstract away from facts that are considered not relevant for the model, are less complex than the information system, and can, therefore, be analyzed. Analyzing the functional design model and the implementation model is the subject of the third phase of the life cycle, the *design analysis phase*.

The goal of this phase is to gain insight into the model and, hence, into the information system to be implemented. If the model is an abstract description to be used to analyze an existing information system, the model must first be validated. *Validation* checks whether the model correctly reflects the information system. A validated abstract description model and a specification model can be analyzed. There are several ways to analyze a model. *Verification* is an analysis technique to *prove* that the model conforms to its specification. A specification can be another more abstract model or a set of properties that the model must satisfy. Most verification techniques must explore (parts of) the states of the model and analyze whether the desired properties hold in every state. As the functional design model and the implementation model of an information system typically have many states, verification is often hard to achieve. For this reason, another analysis technique is used more frequently: *simulation*. The idea of simulation is to make the model executable and to run certain *experiments* (known as runs or scenarios). A model may allow infinitely many scenarios. Because only a finite number of scenarios can be executed, simulation does not typically visit all states of a model. Consequently, unlike verification, simulation can be applied to verify only the presence of errors but not their absence. Simulation is often applied for *performance analysis*. Performance analysis assesses key performance indicators, such as response time and flow time, to detect possible bottlenecks in the system during the design.

Example 1.10 Using the ATM example, we can specify a scenario of a client who first queries an account balance and afterward withdraws 100 euros. By using simulation, we can execute this scenario on the model and check whether this model behaves as expected. Simulation also allows performance analysis; for example, we could check whether the database system can retrieve the current account balance within a certain time interval. It would be important to verify that clients cannot crash the ATM.

An overview of existing analysis techniques is provided in chapter 8.

Implementation Phase   The fourth phase in the life cycle model is the *implementation phase*. In this phase, the information system is constructed. Because an information system is a software system, construction means either programming the entire functionality from scratch or extending or reimplementing existing functionality. Nowadays, software projects increasingly develop generated code. Development tools, such as Eclipse, may generate template code to create a graphical user interface, for instance. The programmer can later modify and refine this generated code. This significantly increases a programmer's productivity.

Production Phase   The fifth phase is the *production phase*, in which software of an information system in prepared for distribution. Unlike classical manufacturing processes, it is relatively easy to produce software, because this boils down to copying and downloading. For widely used standard products, such as database management systems and the Microsoft Office tools, however, the production of manuals, CDs, and so forth may be nontrivial. For product software, licensing issues may also require effort.

Distribution Phase   In the case of mass production, there is a sixth phase, the *distribution phase*. The goal of this phase is to make the information system available to its future users. The marketing for the information system is also a part of this phase. The production and distribution phases do not apply to customized information systems.

Deployment Phase   In the *deployment phase*, the information system is installed in its target environment, and the users of the information system are trained to use it or to work with it. For example, in the case of a health care system in a hospital, professionals must be trained. Training is important in other domains as well, because information systems, such as ERP systems and database management systems, provide a multitude of functionality. The deployment phase is the seventh phase in the life cycle model.

Configuration Phase   Many organizations do not implement their information systems from scratch but instead buy standard software, which is often referred to as *commercial off-the-shelf* software or *product* software. In this case, the information system needs to be configured and customized to the organization and its business processes. Even when organizations develop their own software, there is often the need for configuration. This is the subject of the eighth phase in the life cycle model, the *configuration phase*.

For sectors such as financial accounting, inventory management, or production planning, there are customizable standard software packages: ERP systems. These packages have many adjustable parameters, among them the standard currency and the date display format to be used (e.g., 1-Jan-2001, 01/01/2001, or 20010101). The customization of an ERP system can be viewed as a kind of programming in a special language. The difference from conventional programming is that the entire functionality does not need to be programmed. Much of the standard functionality provided can be used instead. Nevertheless, adapting standard business processes to specific organizations may require substantial effort and should not be underestimated. It may even be the case that the standard functionality provided is inadequate, and parts need to be reimplemented.

Execution Phase   After the deployment and configuration, organizations can finally run their information systems. In an ideal world, this *execution phase*—the ninth phase in the life cycle model—would be the final phase of the development process, with maintenance consisting of the organization keeping the data up to date and making backups. Because of its complexity, however, it is unlikely that an information system meets all requirements and performs in a way it is expected at the start of this phase. Moreover, the environment of the information system is changing over time. To simplify error detection and to get insight into what functionality is actually used (and also how it is used), information systems log an enormous number of events. These event logs provide detailed information about the activities that have been executed. Event logs play an important role in the successive phases of the life cycle model.

Monitoring Phase   In the tenth phase, the *monitoring phase*, organizations extract real-time information about how their information systems perform. Monitoring provides information on the current state of each business process instance and on the performance of the previously executed activities. In a way, the monitoring phase is a simulation of the running business processes in practice. The extracted information can be compared with the domain model (i.e., the requirements) and the functional design model. Unlike the process shown in figure 1.2, the execution phase and the monitoring phase typically run in parallel. The monitoring phase is using data from the execution phase, but it can also influence execution through the adjustment phase (see section 1.3.4).

Runtime Analysis Phase   Monitoring is performed while the information system is running, but it is not intended to change information systems or redesign business processes. Monitoring provides relatively simple types of diagnostic information. More advanced analysis techniques are possible and are performed in the *runtime analysis phase*.

   In contrast to the design analysis phase in which information system models are analyzed, the runtime analysis phase analyzes whether the implemented information system conforms to its specification. Event logs play an important role in this phase.

These event logs can be analyzed—for example, to figure out whether requirements of the information system are violated—or replayed on the functional design model and the implementation model. Process mining techniques allow information to be extracted from the event logs to provide designers with more insights into the running information system and the supported business processes. Because of the complexity of contemporary information systems and rapidly changing circumstances (e.g., new laws and changing regulations), the importance of the runtime analysis phase is increasing.

1.3.3   A Software Configuration–Oriented Life Cycle

The focus of the previous section was on the development process of information systems that either are generic software systems or contain at least some self-developed software components. The life cycle of these information systems includes, among other phases, an implementation phase and a deployment phase. The production phase and the distribution phase are, in contrast, relevant only for the development process of generic software systems. There are many organizations that do not implement an information system; instead, they construct it from predefined generic software systems, such as ERP systems. In this section, we discuss the life cycle of *customized information systems*, which consists of seven phases of the main life cycle of figure 1.2: *requirements phase, design phase, design analysis phase, configuration phase, execution phase, monitoring phase,* and *runtime analysis phase*.

As for generic information systems, the development process of a customized information system starts with the requirements phase. The designer expresses the identified requirements as a domain model. In the subsequent design phase, the designer derives a functional design model from the domain model and constructs an implementation model. The models are then analyzed in the design analysis phase. In contrast to the development process of a generic information system, the designer uses the implementation model to identify which software components are necessary to create the information system. The purchase of these software components, including actions such as tender procedures, is a process that is orthogonal to the phases of the life cycle. In the life cycle model, we therefore assume that an organization has purchased all necessary software components to design an information system. In the following configuration phase, the designer (supported by software developers) configures and customizes these software components. Recall that configuration refers to choosing between existing predefined parameters and reimplementing some of the standard functionality to adapt it to the requirements of the organization.

The subsequent execution, monitor, and runtime analysis phases are as described section 1.3.2. The monitor and runtime analysis phases are intended to verify that the configuration yields an information system that conforms to the requirements and, hence, to the specification, rather than to verify whether the implemented software components are correct (although these components may contain bugs, like any software). Although generic information systems offer functionality that organizations of different industries can use, configuring an information system such that it perfectly satisfies the requirements of an organization can be time-consuming.

In figure 1.2, it is assumed that the smaller software configuration–oriented life cycle does not include a deployment phase. Deployment is typically not needed if existing information systems are reconfigured; however, if an organization introduces a new enterprise information system, then it must perform the activities mentioned in the deployment phase.

1.3.4   A Runtime-Oriented Life Cycle

Ever-changing market conditions, regulations, and further customizations require organizations to be flexible and to adapt to changing circumstances. As a result, business processes are subject to change. This requires that we adapt the information systems that support these business processes to the new requirements. For this reason, the life cycle model in figure 1.2 includes phases that need to be passed through to change and redesign existing information systems. Shaded rectangles in figure 1.2 resulting in two smaller cycles depict these phases. The first cycle consists of four phases: *execution phase, monitor phase, runtime analysis phase,* and *adjustment phase.* It models that new requirements result in *adjusting* the information system. The second cycle takes this idea of adjusting the information system a step further and addresses the *replacement* of a (part) of the information system with a newer one. This cycle consists of an *execution phase* and a *migration phase.*

Adjustment Phase   Monitoring and analyzing a running information system is a continuous process. In the *adjustment phase,* a running information system is adapted to changing circumstances. For example, there may be a new law that clients of a bank are not allowed to withdraw money more than three times a day. Other causes for adjusting an information system are detected errors or performance bottlenecks. In a customized information system, adaptation may change some adjustable parameters. The adjustment phase uses predefined runtime configuration possibilities; that is, the information system is reconfigured but not changed. The cycle in figure 1.2 illustrates that adjusting an information system is also a continuous process. The information system is changed and then again monitored and analyzed.

Migration Phase   It is not always possible to adapt a running information system by a reconfiguration at runtime. Changes in the environment may require the replacement of (a part of) an old information system with a new information system. The new information system is developed according to the main life cycle in figure 1.2, as described in sections 1.3.2 and 1.3.3. At a certain point in time, the replacement has to take place. One of the challenges is the migration of data from the old information system to the new one. An example is the business process of a life insurance company.

A new legal regulation may cause a business process to change, while instances of this business process have been running for decades. In this case, each running instance of the old business process has to be migrated to the new business process. This is the subject of the *migration phase*.

1.3.5 Reflection

The development of an information system is, in practice, not as straightforward and well defined as the life cycle model in figure 1.2 may suggest. Typically, we have to revisit previous phases or start over with analysis; that is, the development process is *iterative*. In figure 1.2, this is illustrated by the counterclockwise arcs. In each iteration, the current models are being further refined and extended. As a consequence, the development process is also *incremental*. Phases of the life cycle can overlap with one another. We can construct an implementation model for parts of the information system, even if other parts have already been implemented. This book focuses on the analysis and design phases.

1.4 System Models

In the previous section, we presented a life cycle model of information systems. We explained that, in particular, in the early phases of this life cycle—in the requirements, design, and design analysis phases—models play an important role for specifying existing information systems and for implementing new information systems. In this section, we show that an information system can be viewed as a discrete dynamic system whose behavior can be modeled as a transition system.

1.4.1 Discrete Dynamic Systems

To clarify the most important system concepts, we look at several systems: a laptop computer, a washing machine, a railroad network, a car engine, a turning wheel, a wheel of fortune, a digital alarm clock, and the membership administration of a tennis club. All of these systems possess a state that is subject to change. We refer to them as *dynamic systems*. Dynamic systems can have *discrete* or *continuous* state changes, as described in the following examples.

A laptop computer can switch between four modes: on, hibernate, sleep, and off. A washing machine is washing at one moment and rinsing the next. At the railroad network, a signal is red at one moment, and, a little later, it is green. These three dynamic systems seem to change states in *discrete* jumps.

A car engine consumes fuel continuously and not in discrete quantities; the engine is a *continuous* dynamic system. The rate at which the state changes (e.g., the fuel level) depends on the way the engine is used. A turning wheel of a car is another example of a continuous dynamic system: the wheel turns continuously and not in discrete jumps.

It is a matter of conceptualization whether we consider a system to be continuous or discrete. We can view continuous systems in a discrete manner and vice versa. For example, the state changes of a wheel of fortune seem to be continuous, but only a limited number of states of the wheel matter; namely, those in which the wheel can stop. We can therefore treat the wheel of fortune as a dynamic system with a finite number of discrete states. Similarly, a washing machine can be described as a continuous dynamic system in which the water level is gradually increasing.

We tend to consider the passage of time as a continuous process. Nevertheless, a digital alarm clock is a system that changes states in discrete jumps. The alarm clock halts for a minute at 8:20 a.m. and then jumps to 8:21 a.m. For the function of an alarm clock, it is sufficient to display the time in hours and minutes. In the context of an alarm clock, we may treat the passage of time as a discrete process. This is also the case in other situations—for example, when measuring time at a sports event. For a sports event, we may measure time with higher accuracy (e.g., in milliseconds).

Systems that change states in discrete jumps are *discrete systems*. In mathematics, "discrete" means "distinct" and "noncontinuous." Likewise, systems that change states in continuous jumps are *continuous systems*. Examples of continuous systems are a river, a turning wheel, a chemical reaction, and a flying bullet. A continuous system is typically described using differential calculus. In this book, we do not consider continuous systems; instead, we conceptualize continuous systems as discrete (as with the wheel of fortune example). In the remainder of this book, we refer to a discrete dynamic system as a *system*.

Example 1.11 The membership administration of a tennis club is a system. At any moment, 120 members may be registered. When a new member enters the club, there will be a change in the membership state: the number of members increases to 121. This is a discrete change, even if the secretary of the club does not immediately import the data of the new member.

Exercise 1.2 Consider a bank where we are only interested in the balances of all bank accounts. Explain why this is a system.

There are two important concepts for describing a system: *state* and *state change*. Between two successive instantaneous changes, nothing happens in a system. We say that the system is in a certain state. A state change is a *state transition* or *transition*.

Example 1.12 A fan is a system with two states (off and on) and two transitions. One transition changes from off to on and the other from on to off.

1.4.2 State and State Space

We now take a closer look at the state concept of a system using an example. The medicine cabinet of a hospital department contains three kinds of drugs: painkillers, sleeping pills, and antipyretics. Nurses supply these drugs to patients as needed, so the stock decreases each time medication is administered. From time to time, the stock is replenished. Each moment, the medicine cabinet is in a certain state; that is, it contains a certain amount of each of the three drugs. We can record the actual stock in a table, such as table 1.1.

Table 1.1 gives a description of the state of the medicine cabinet at a particular moment. Two things are important for such a state description. First, we only include information in a state description that is relevant for the system. Second, there can be several descriptions of a state.

There is information that is not represented in the state description of the medicine cabinet—for example, the current temperature in the cabinet, the size of the cabinet, and whether the painkillers are on the first or the second shelf. What is relevant depends on the purpose of the system and on the needs of the users of the system. For the nurses, it is not interesting to know where a drug is exactly stored in the medicine cabinet. Because only three kinds of drugs are stored, it is possible to quickly see where each drug is. For a hospital pharmacy, which stores thousands of drugs, on the other hand, drug location would be important.

Depending on the needs of the users, there are several ways to describe the possible states of a system. Table 1.2 shows an alternative description of the contents of the medicine cabinet. For each drug, we define a desirable minimum number—that is, its *base stock*—and represent the difference of the actual stock from this number. The sum of these numbers equals the actual stock.

A state description should represent all things that may change and whose change is relevant for the system. The state description of the medicine cabinet, for instance, provides the number of drugs in stock. This is the only relevant information for this system. Other aspects of the medicine cabinet, such as the history of a drug stock, are not relevant and are abstracted away.

Table 1.1
The Contents of the Medicine Cabinet

Type of drug	Actual stock
Painkiller	14
Sleeping pills	9
Antipyretics	8

Table 1.2
An Alternative Representation of the State of the Medicine Cabinet

Type of drug	Base stock	Difference
Painkiller	10	4
Sleeping pills	10	−1
Antipyretics	5	3

Exercise 1.3   A hobbyist made a wheel of fortune from the wheel of a bicycle with 36 spokes. A simple but smart mechanism makes sure that the wheel can be stopped between each two spokes that are next to each other. Describe all possible states of this wheel.

In the following discussion, we assume that we always deal with state descriptions that represent states in an adequate way (corresponding to the interests of the users of the system and at the right abstraction level). We use the term "state" without explicitly mentioning that a certain description is involved.

A system can be in several states. The set of all possible states is the *state space*. The number of possible states of a system can be large. If the maximum stock of the medicine cabinet were 19 painkillers, 19 sleeping pills, and 19 antipyretics, there would be $20 \cdot 20 \cdot 20 = 8,000$ possible states.

To specify a state space, we use the notation of mathematical set theory. The fan in example 1.12 can be in states off and on. Accordingly, we formally represent the state space S of the fan as the set:

$S = \{\text{off}, \text{on}\}$.

For the possible states of the medicine cabinet, only the actual stock of the drugs is relevant. We can represent the actual stock as a triple (i.e., a sequence of three elements). The state displayed in table 1.1 is then represented as $(14, 9, 8)$. The state space is too large to be easily enumerated, but we can define it as:

$S = \{(x, y, z) \mid x, y, z \in \{0, \ldots, 19\}\}$.

Recall that, in a set expression, the order of elements does not matter. From the previous expression of state space S, we can conclude nothing about the order in which the states occur.

Exercise 1.4   Describe the state space of the wheel of fortune in exercise 1.3. How can you formally represent the state space?

1.4.3 Transitions and Transition Systems

A system can stay in the same state for a short or a long time, but it normally changes from one state to another after a certain time. The state change is performed instantaneously. For example, when a nurse takes drugs from the medicine cabinet, the stock decreases. The state of the medicine cabinet changes through such an *atomic* (i.e., indivisible) action.

For the time being, we abstract away from the time that is needed for a transition. This is not a problem for industrial applications. In the case of the medicine cabinet, we are interested in the changing stock of drugs and not in the time necessary to take out drugs from the cabinet. In the case of the fan (see example 1.12), we are interested in whether the fan is on or off and not in the relatively short time it takes to change from one state to another. If state changes take considerable time (i.e., they are nonatomic), then we can split the state change into two state changes: one indicating the start of the state change and the other indicating the completion of the state change. For example, we can split a transition "repair_car," indicating a car repair, into transitions "start_repair_car" and "end_repair_car," indicating the start and the completion of the car repair.

During a *transition*, a system changes from one state to another. We are not interested in what exactly happens during this change. For this reason, we can write a transition as an ordered pair:

(old_state, new_state).

Assume that the fan is switched on. The ordered state pair

(off, on)

describes exactly what is going on. First, we mention the old state and then the new state. The pair (on, off) represents the transition when the fan is switched off.

Definition 1.13 (Transition) A *transition* is an ordered pair (x, y) in which x and y are elements of the state space S—that is, $x, y \in S$.

Exercise 1.5 At a certain moment, the medicine cabinet contains three painkillers, five sleeping pills, and eight antipyretics. Then a nurse takes two sleeping pills and three antipyretics from the cabinet. Express this transition as an ordered pair of states.

For every system, we can record each transition with an ordered pair of states. If we consider all possible transitions of a system, then we obtain a set of ordered pairs of states.

Example 1.14 Consider the model of the ATM that we described in example 1.8. The state space is represented as:

$S = \{$idle, card, pin, balance, money,
         offer, choice, payout, violation, output_card$\}$.

The following set of transitions is possible:

$TR = \{$(idle, card), (card, pin), (pin, balance), (pin, money), (money, offer),
         (money, choice), (offer, payout), (offer, violation), (choice, payout),
         (choice, violation), (violation, money), (violation, output_card),
         (balance, output_card), (payout, output_card), (output_card, idle)$\}$.

The ATM is initially in state idle. A client then inserts a bank card (yielding state card) and keys a pin (pin). Next, a client can either query an account balance yielding state balance or withdraw money yielding state money. In state money, a client can either choose an amount of money (choice) or select an offered amount of money (offer). If the chosen amount of money is not too high, the money is paid out (payout), and the ATM returns the card to the client (output_card). Otherwise, the ATM enters state violation, from which the menu can be reached (state money), or the client asks the ATM to return the card (output_card). From state output_card, the ATM moves to state idle from which it can serve the next client.

In mathematics, a set of ordered pairs is a (binary) *relation*. Accordingly, each system has a *transition relation*, which contains all possible transitions of the system. The identifier TR denotes the transition relation. A transition relation usually does not contain all ordered pairs of states that can be formed by combining two states, because some pairs are not possible. In the case of the ATM, for example, state pairs (card, idle) and (money, balance) do not represent possible transitions.

We obtain the set of all ordered pairs of states of a state space S by forming the Cartesian product $S \times S$. For a state space $S = \{a, b, c\}$, the Cartesian product consists of $3 \cdot 3 = 9$ elements. We write:

$S \times S = \{ (a, a), (a, b), (a, c), (b, a), (b, b), (b, c), (c, a), (c, b), (c, c) \}$.

For the ATM, the Cartesian product of the state space with itself has $10 \cdot 10 = 100$ elements, but not all of these elements correspond to a possible transition. The transition relation TR is consequently a subset of the Cartesian product:

$TR \subseteq S \times S$.

By specifying the state space S, the transition relation TR, and an initial state, we can describe a system. The *initial state* of a system is the state in which a system starts its operations.

Definition 1.15 (Transition system)   A *transition system* is a triple (S, TR, s_0) where S is a finite state space, $TR \subseteq S \times S$ is a transition relation containing all possible state changes, and $s_0 \in S$ is the initial state.

The notion of a transition system in definition 1.15 is similar to the definition of a finite automaton (Hopcroft and Ullman 1979). A finite automaton is a transition system in which every transition is labeled by a symbol from a given alphabet. For simplicity, we do not label transitions, but it is easy to add a labeling function to (S, TR, s_0) assigning a label to all elements in *TR*.

In definition 1.15, we restricted ourselves to transition systems with a finite set of states. If this set does not contain too many states, state space and transition relation can be depicted in a diagram. We draw for each possible state a rectangle with rounded corners and for each transition an arrow from the old state to the new state. Figure 1.3 shows the transition system of the ATM. Such a diagram is the *state-transition diagram* of a transition system. An incoming transition without source pointing to state idle denotes that the ATM is initially in state idle (i.e., $s_0 = $ idle). The notion of a state-transition diagram is similar to the notion of a state diagram in other notations, such as the Unified Modeling Language (UML) (Rumbaugh, Jacobson, and Booch 1998; Object Management Group 2005).

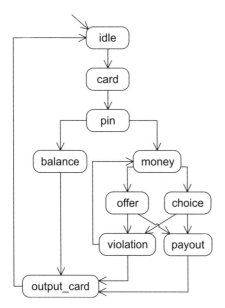

Figure 1.3
A state-transition diagram of the ATM.

The general concept for structures, such as state-transition diagrams, is a directed *graph*. A directed graph consists of nodes that are connected by directed edges.

Definition 1.16 (State-transition diagram) A *state-transition diagram* is a directed graph in which the nodes represent the states of the transition system, and the directed edges represent the possible transitions.

Exercise 1.6 A simple elevator system serving a building with five floors can be considered to be a discrete dynamic system. Reason why the elevator can be seen as a discrete dynamic system, define its transition system, and draw the state-transition diagram. Assume that the elevator is initially at the ground level.

In the example of the medicine cabinet, for which we must deal with 8,000 possible states, it is not feasible to depict the transition system as a state-transition diagram. The diagram would be too large and unmanageable. There are techniques to visualize large transition systems, but these techniques provide only an impression of the topology of the state space.

1.4.4 Transition Sequences and the Behavior of a System

Thus far, we have considered single transitions in isolation. To study the behavior of a system, we must consider possible sequences of transitions and the states visited by these sequences. It is important to determine which states can be reached from a given initial state of the system.

Definition 1.17 (Reachable state) A *reachable state* is a state that the system can reach from the initial state after zero or more transitions.

Question 1.18 The initial state of the ATM in example 1.14 is state idle. Are all states reachable?

We can determine reachability by following the arrows in the state-transition diagram in figure 1.3. State idle can be reached after zero transitions. From state idle we can go to state card, next to state pin, to state balance, to state output_card, and to state idle again.

A sequence of states reached by following the arrows in figure 1.3 is a *transition sequence*. For example,

⟨idle, card, pin, money, choice, payout, output_card, idle⟩

is a transition sequence that represents withdrawing money by selecting a specific amount of money. The transition sequence for querying the account balance is:

⟨idle, card, pin, balance, output_card, idle⟩.

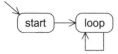

Figure 1.4
A self-loop: State loop can change to itself.

Transition sequences give us insight into the dynamics of a system. On the basis of the transition sequences, we can see how the system behaves. The set of all possible transition sequences from a given initial state specifies the *behavior* of the system.

In the behavior of a transition system, two special cases are possible. The first case is a state in which no further transition is possible. Such a state is a *terminal state*, often referred to as deadlock. The state-transition diagram of the ATM in figure 1.3 does not have a terminal state, but if we remove transition (output_card, idle), then state output_card becomes a terminal state. A terminal state should not be confused with a state that can only change to itself, known as a *self-loop*, as shown in figure 1.4. In the state-transition diagram in figure 1.3, there is no self-loop.

The second special case is the situation in which, from every state, at most one transition is possible. This means that, in the state-transition diagram, each node has at most one outgoing arrow. Such a system is *deterministic*, whereas a system with multiple options for a successor state is *nondeterministic*. The transition system of the fan (see example 1.12) is an example of a deterministic system. The ATM is a nondeterministic system, because from state pin a client can choose state balance or state money.

Exercise 1.7   Describe why the medicine cabinet is a nondeterministic system.

1.5   Roles of Models

A model of an enterprise information system can serve different purposes. We identify two dimensions to characterize models of enterprise information systems. First, a model may be *design oriented* or *analysis oriented*. Second, a model may be *information system oriented* or *business process oriented*. Table 1.3 shows that these two dimensions are orthogonal, and therefore we have to distinguish four kinds of models.

The role of a *design/information-system-oriented model* is to create a new enterprise information system or to adapt an existing one. An example is a specification model and an implementation model. The purpose of such a model is to specify desired functionality, to document requirements and design decisions, to guide implementation efforts, or to prescribe a configuration.

An *analysis/information-system-oriented model* focuses on the analysis of an enterprise information system. The purpose of such a model is to gain insight into an existing

Table 1.3
The Different Roles That Models Play

	Design	Analysis
Information system	Specification	Verification
	Requirements	Performance analysis
	Design decisions	
	Implementation	
	Configuration	
Business process	Business process reengineering	Performance analysis
	Continuous process improvement	Gaming

enterprise information system or into an enterprise information system after it has been created. For example, we can verify models to discover design flaws in new or existing enterprise information systems, and simulation can predict performance under different circumstances.

In contrast to the two previous kinds of models, a *design/business-process-oriented model* focuses on the (re)design of business processes supported by an enterprise information system (and not on the enterprise information system). The goal is to improve the performance of business processes by redesigning them. Business process reengineering (BPR) (Hammer and Champy 1993) aims at a radical redesign of business processes. New enterprise information systems may be needed to achieve such a redesign. Consequently, BPR initiatives may trigger enterprise information system development. Continuous process improvement (CPI) (Harrington 1991) aims at less radical change. Business processes are continuously reviewed to search for gradual improvements. Continuous monitoring can, for example, support CPI initiatives.

An *analysis/business-process-oriented model* focuses on the analysis of business processes supported by an enterprise information system. The goal is to evaluate existing business processes or to judge alternative business process designs obtained through BPR/CPI initiatives. Simulation is the primary analysis technique used here. It can evaluate the performance of business processes (e.g., response times, flow times, inventory levels, costs, and service levels). Furthermore, interactive simulation models can create management games that help users to spot inefficiencies and understand new ways of working.

In some cases, it may not be clear whether a model is intended to be used for information system analysis and design or for business process analysis and design. Later in this book, we shall see examples of models that are used to analyze the performance of business processes using simulation but that also serve as a specification or configuration model for an information system. To simulate a system, additional information about times and probabilities is necessary. For example, we need to know the time a system stays in each of its states. Without time information, we cannot analyze the performance of the system. If the system is nondeterministic, we need information about the *probability* that the system chooses a particular successor state. Such information can be easily added to a system model or can be extracted from historical data.

Example 1.19 The state-transition diagram in figure 1.3 models the functional design of an ATM. To simulate this model, we need to add time information and probabilities. As an example, reading the bank card in state idle may take two seconds, checking the pin code in state card five seconds, and returning the bank card to the client in state payout three seconds. In state pin, the client may choose in 70% of the cases withdrawal of money and in 30% an account balance. After adding probabilities to all transitions, we can simulate this model and, for example, calculate the probability that the ATM enters state violation.

Markov models (Marsan et al. 1995; Haas 2002; Haverkort 1998) extend transition systems with time and probabilities. Like transition systems, Markov models suffer from the *state explosion problem* (Valmari 1998); that is, even small industrial systems have far more states than a computer can handle and therefore cannot be verified. For this reason, we must use higher-level models and simulation techniques (Buzacott 1996; Marsan et al. 1995).

Exercise 1.8 A wristwatch is an example of a simple information system. Give an estimation of the number of possible states and transitions of a watch that contains only information about the present time. A possible state of this watch is, for example, 23:11:55.

It is unrealistic to model enterprise information systems in terms of a transition system (S, TR, s_0). The state space is too large to be enumerated or to be captured in a simple mathematical set expression. Finding a suitable representation for the transition relation is even more difficult. Accordingly, we need more powerful notations.

The state space S is typically captured using complex data types or database tables. To model the structure of the state space, *data models* are used. Examples are class diagrams in UML (Rumbaugh, Jacobson, and Booch 1998; Object Management Group 2005), entity-relationship (ER) models, crow's foot diagrams, and natural language information analysis method/object role modeling (NIAM/ORM). Data modeling is concerned with the identification of the relevant types of data entities and their relationships. Beside *data modeling*, terms such as *information modeling* and *object modeling* are in use.

Data models do not capture behavior. We therefore need *process models* to describe the transition relation *TR*. Examples of process modeling techniques are Petri nets, UML activity diagrams, BPMN, and EPCs. In this book, we concentrate on process modeling and use Petri nets extended with data, time, and hierarchy as a formalism.

A *system model* refers to the state space and to the transition relation. Consequently, data and process modeling are required to create such models.

1.6   Test Yourself

1.6.1   Solutions to Exercises

1.1   The information system should allow the specification of a journey from one location (home) to a holiday destination. It should be possible to make the trip by bicycle, boat, car, train, airplane, or bus (or a combination of these modes of transport). The traveler should be able to indicate when the journey should start and end. Given the preferences of the traveler, the information system should propose several alternatives for the travel scheme, such as the cheapest, the fastest, the shortest, and the easiest possibilities.

1.2   This system is dynamic, because it is subject to state changes in the form of changing balances through money transfers. It is discrete, because the changes happen instantaneously; that is, a money transfer is an instantaneous event.

1.3   The spokes of the wheel could be numbered 1 to 36 in such a way that there is always one number between two spokes. When the wheel stops between two spokes, its state can be identified by its number.

1.4   The state space consists of 36 states in which the wheel can stop. These states are numbered 1 to 36. In addition, there is one more state the wheel can be in: the wheel could be turning and not in one of the states 1 to 36. Formally, we denote this as:

$S = \{turning, 1, 2, 3, 4, \ldots, 36\}.$

We could also represent state *turning* as a number—for example, as 0.

1.5   We can describe the old and the new state by the triple $(3, 5, 8)$ and $(3, 3, 5)$, respectively. The pair $((3, 5, 8), (3, 3, 5))$ represents the transition.

1.6   The elevator system is dynamic, because it does not stay in one state but jumps from one floor to the next. The system is discrete, because the elevator goes step-by-step from one floor to the next. The state space of the elevator system is a set with five states, one for each floor:

$S = \{0, 1, 2, 3, 4\}.$

If we assume that the elevator may go up or down one floor at a time, then the transition relation TR is as follows:

$TR = \{(0, 1), (1, 2), (2, 3), (3, 4), (4, 3), (3, 2), (2, 1), (1, 0)\}.$

Assuming that the initial state is $s_0 = 0$, figure 1.5 depicts the state-transition diagram.

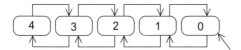

Figure 1.5
State-transition diagram for the elevator system.

1.7 The medicine cabinet is a nondeterministic system, because it is composed of states from which more than one transition is possible. Drugs can be removed from the cabinet or replenished in various numbers and combinations.

1.8 The state 23:11:55 corresponds to the point of time five seconds before twelve minutes past eleven at night. The number of possible states of the wristwatch is equal to the number of points of time (counted in seconds) in one day. The number of possible states is $24 \cdot 60 \cdot 60 = 86,400$. Because there is exactly one transition possible from each state, the number of transitions is also equal to 86,400.

1.6.2 Further Exercises

Exercise 1.9 Explain the terms "business process" and "information system."

Exercise 1.10 List as many types of enterprise information systems as you can and give one characteristic feature or an example for each of them.

Exercise 1.11 Explain the life cycle of developing a new information system and the life cycle of redesigning an existing information system. Use the life cycle model in figure 1.2.

Exercise 1.12 Draw the state-transition diagram for a washing machine with state space

$S = \{$off, defective, pre-wash, main_wash, rinse, whiz$\}$

with $s_0 =$ off and transition relation

$TR = \{$(pre-wash, defective), (main_wash, defective), (rinse, defective),
       (whiz, defective), (off, pre-wash), (pre-wash, rinse),
       (rinse, main_wash), (off, main_wash), (main_wash, rinse),
       (rinse, off), (rinse, whiz), (whiz, off)$\}$.

Exercise 1.13 The behavior of the washing machine in exercise 1.12 is not completely realistic, because transition sequences

⟨off, pre-wash, rinse, off⟩

and

⟨off, main_wash, rinse, main_wash, rinse, main_wash, rinse, . . .⟩

are possible. Adjust the state space and the transition relation such that these transition sequences are no longer possible. Draw the improved state-transition diagram.

Exercise 1.14   A Dutch traffic light is an example of a system with three possible states: R (red), G (green), and O (orange). Model a T-junction with three traffic lights (see figure 1.6) as a transition system and draw the state-transition diagram. The traffic lights are programmed in such a way that at least two lights are red at the same time—that is, for at most one direction of the traffic, the traffic light can be green or orange. (Hint: Represent each state by a combination of three colors.)

Exercise 1.15   To improve the traffic flow, the traffic light system of exercise 1.14 is upgraded to a situation with five lights; see figure 1.7. The goal is to program the traffic light system such that crossing cars coming from different directions cannot have a green light at the same time. Furthermore, if at any point lights turn orange, they must first turn red before other lights can change. Model this system as a transition system and draw the state-transition diagram.

Exercise 1.16   The score in a game of tennis is calculated as follows. The first player who wins four rallies in total and at least two rallies more than the opponent wins the

Figure 1.6
A T-junction with three traffic lights.

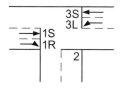

Figure 1.7
A T-junction with five traffic lights.

game. If both players have won three rallies (40–40), then the player who wins the next rally gets the advantage. If this player wins another rally, she wins the game. If she loses the next rally, she loses the advantage, and the score is equal to the situation in which both players have won three rallies (40–40). Model this system as a transition system and draw the state-transition diagram.

Exercise 1.17   Consider the process in a restaurant. After customers enter the restaurant, a waiter assigns them a table and gives them the menu. The customers then order, and the waiter writes down this order, takes the menu, and delivers the order to the kitchen. A cook prepares the order, and the waiter brings it to the customers who then consume it. If the appetite of the customers is not yet satisfied, they can call the waiter and ask for the menu again (after which the entire process repeats itself). If the customers are satisfied, they call the waiter and ask for the check. When that check arrives, they pay and leave.

1. Give the transition system that models the behavior of a customer and the transition system that models the behavior of a waiter. Draw both state-transition diagrams.
2. If you want to make one state-transition diagram in which you describe the behaviors of a customer and a waiter, how many states do you need?

Exercise 1.18   Figure 1.8 depicts a simplified remote control of a TV. It has six buttons to choose a channel, one button to regulate the volume, one button to mute the sound (and to turn it on again), and one button to switch the TV on or off. We consider the remote control and the corresponding TV as a system and assume that the possible states of this system are controlled by the buttons on the remote control.

1. Is this system a discrete dynamic system?
2. Describe all possible states of this system.

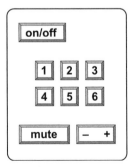

Figure 1.8
The remote control of a TV.

3. The transition relation is too large to be depicted as a state-transition diagram. Give examples of possible and impossible transitions. Pay attention to switching the TV on and using the volume button in combination with the mute button.

Exercise 1.19   Consider a transition system with state space

$\{0, 1, 2, 3, 4, 5, 6, 7, 8\}$

and with transition relation

$\{ (0, 1), (1, 2), (2, 3), (3, 4), (3, 5), (5, 0), (5, 4), (4, 4), (6, 7), (7, 6), (7, 8) \}$.

1. Draw the state-transition diagram.
2. Which states are reachable from the initial state 0?
3. List three transition sequences that start in state 0.
4. Does the system have a terminal state?

1.7   Summary

In this chapter, we introduced information systems in general, took a more detailed look at enterprise information systems, and characterized important types of enterprise information systems. We described the different phases in the life cycle of developing and maintaining information systems. We then showed that an information system is a discrete dynamic system whose behavior can be modeled as a transition system. Finally, we discussed the four roles that models play.

We also introduced transition systems as the simplest technique to model discrete dynamic systems and business processes. In the next chapters, we present more advanced modeling techniques that facilitate the modeling of complex enterprise information systems and the business processes they support.

After studying this chapter, you should be able to:

- Explain the terms "information system" and "business process."
- List the most important types of enterprise information systems and briefly characterize them.
- Describe which life cycle phases are required to develop and to maintain an information system.
- Explain the terms "discrete dynamic system," "state," "state space," "transition," "state-transition diagram," "transition sequence," "deterministic system," and "non-deterministic system."
- Describe a system as a transition system and represent it in the form of a state-transition diagram.
- Determine the transition sequences of a simple transition system.
- Explain the difference between a data model and a process model.
- Explain the four roles that a model of an enterprise information system can play.

1.8 Further Reading

There are many books on information systems in the literature. Alter (2002) introduces information systems, their development, and modeling of information systems from a business perspective. Weske (2007), in contrast, concentrates on business processes and business process management. Van Hee (2009) investigates formalization aspects and the integration between data and process modeling.

In this book, we emphasize the role of process models in the realization of enterprise information systems. WfMSs are information systems that are directly driven by business process models. We therefore reference several books on workflow management systems—see work by Van der Aalst and Van Hee (2004), Dumas, Van der Aalst, and Ter Hofstede (2005), Ter Hofstede et al. (2010), Jablonski and Bussler (1996), and Leymann and Roller (1999)—and elaborate more on this in the next chapter.

There are many life cycle models for devloping an information system. Two classical life cycle models are the *waterfall model* and the *spiral model*. The waterfall model, presented by Royce (1970), was the first publicly documented life cycle model. The model was developed to cope with the increasing complexity of aerospace products. The model's focal point is on documentation. The spiral model was introduced by Boehm (1988) to address problems associated with the waterfall model. Alter (2002) introduced a life cycle model that concentrates more on the management perspective and less on the software.

The final topics addressed in this chapter are discrete dynamic systems and transition systems. Hopcroft and Ullman (1979) provide a good overview of this topic. For a deeper study of data modeling, we refer to ER modeling of Chen (1976) and UML (Rumbaugh, Jacobson, and Booch 1998; Object Management Group 2005).

2 Business Processes and Information Systems

Information technology has changed business processes within and between organizations. More and more business processes are being conducted under the supervision of enterprise information systems that are driven by the business processes they support. Examples are WfMSs, such as BPM|one and FileNet; ERP systems, such as SAP ERP and Oracle's JD Edwards EnterpriseOne; and include many domain-specific information systems—for example, hospital information systems, such as ChipSoft and Siemens Soarian. It is hard to imagine enterprise information systems that are unaware of the business processes they support.

The goal of this chapter is to make clear the omnipresence of business processes and business process models in the field of information systems. First, we describe how business processes, information systems, and models relate (section 2.1). We show that models play a crucial role in developing and executing business processes and information systems. Next, we introduce *process-aware information systems*, a class of information systems that is aware of the business processes it supports (section 2.2). Almost every enterprise information system is process aware. We illustrate this by describing the role of business process models in several concrete enterprise information systems (section 2.3). Finally, we discuss the role of data modeling in relation to process modeling (section 2.4).

2.1 The Relationships between Business Processes, Information Systems, and Models

In chapter 1, we explained that information systems play a crucial role in supporting business processes. We introduced a life cycle model for the development and redesign of information systems and showed that models play an important role in this life cycle model, because they provide a simplified picture of reality to help us understand it. In addition to designing information systems, models are also important for the execution of information systems; for example, a business process model can be used to configure an information system. For this reason, we describe the relation of business processes,

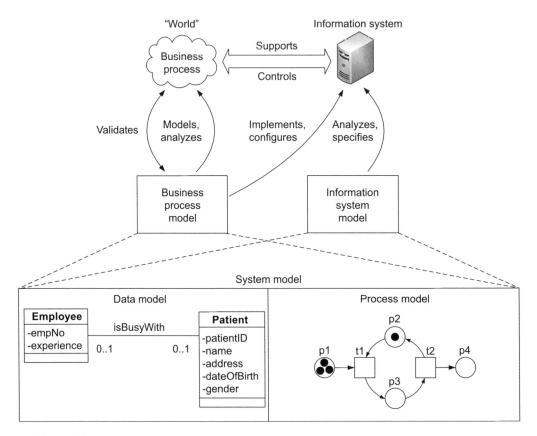

Figure 2.1
The relation of business processes, information systems, and models.

information systems, and (business process and information system) models in this section.

   An information system usually controls and supports business processes. As a result, information systems and business processes interact with each other. Figure 2.1 shows this relation. Four characteristic situations describe the scope of an information system in relation to the business processes it supports.

• The information system plays a minor role in one business process (see figure 2.2(a)). For example, the information system supports only one of the activities of the business process, such as an interest calculation in a mortgage process.

• The information system supports one business process end-to-end; that is, all activities in the business process are supported by the information system, but the scope of the information system is limited to a single business process (see figure 2.2(b)).

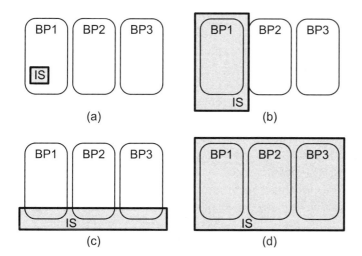

Figure 2.2
The scope of an information system *IS* relative to business processes *BP1*, *BP2*, and *BP3*.

• The information system takes care of the interaction between several business processes (see figure 2.2(c)). In this case, the focus is on interbusiness process communication and not on the activities in the business processes themselves. For example, EDI-based communication software can connect several organizations.
• The information system supports and integrates several business processes (see figure 2.2(d)). For example, an ERP system not only supports complete business processes but also the interaction between these business processes.

Example 2.1 The information system of the family doctor, as introduced in chapter 1, supports only a single activity of the business process; namely, adding the data of patients to the software system. All other steps—for example, examining patients, billing the patients' insurance companies, and replenishing bandages—need to be performed by the doctor herself. A monitoring system collects data for every activity of the business process, thus supporting the whole business process. An example of an information system that connects several business processes is the information system of a city tax office, which also supports the business process of the ministry of finance. Finally, an ERP system is an example of an information system that integrates standard business processes of an organization.

In the past, it was common for information systems to support only small parts of business processes, with the remaining portion handled outside the information system. Because of the automation of business processes, the overlap between information systems and business processes is increasing. Furthermore, because of the omnipresence of the Internet, business processes in different organizations are connected, and there has been a shift from the situation shown in figure 2.2(a) to the situation shown in figure 2.2(d), in which business processes are supported and integrated end-to-end.

Let us first describe the relation between information systems and models. In the previous chapter, we made the implicit assumption that information systems are discrete dynamic systems, and we presented transition systems as a basic modeling technique for discrete dynamic systems. An information system has a state space and a transition relation. We can structure the state space using a data model (e.g., a UML class diagram (Rumbangh, Jacobson, and Booch 1998; Object Management Group 2005)), and we can specify the transition relation using process modeling techniques, such as Petri nets. Data models and process models abstract from the "real world", the information system. These abstractions can be very high level but also very detailed (e.g., the source code of a software program). The abstractions allow us to analyze the information system model and to gain insight into the information system. Typically, these models serve as a specification of an information system to be built (see figure 2.1).

In addition to modeling the information system, we can also model the business processes supported by this information system; see section 1.5. Similar to the information system, a business process is a discrete dynamic system that can be modeled using a data or process model. Again, we analyze a business process model to gain insight into the business process and to understand it. Validating the business process and the business process model helps to confirm that the model correctly reflects the business process; validation also allows us to check that the business process actually has the expected functionality (see figure 2.1).

Although the purpose of models of the information system and models of the business processes supported by the information system is different, there is considerable overlap between these models. Some of the entities that exist in the business process model also exist in the information system model, and transitions taken in the business process model may be triggered or monitored by the information system model. The information system and its business processes are discrete dynamic systems with many things in common.

Example 2.2 Consider the information system of a car rental company. The information system "knows" about customers and cars. Entity "car" exists in the business process as a physical object, but it also exists inside the information system as an information element. Similarly, related events exist in the business process and inside the information system of the car rental company; for example, the event "customer returns car" occurs in the business process but is registered by the information system. Sometimes an event in the business process is followed by an event inside the information system (e.g., a customer reserves a car), and sometimes an event inside the information system is followed by an event in the business process (e.g., send bill).

Many information systems are driven by the models of the business processes they support. For example, the database management system of an information system that supports a travel agency is configured on the basis of a data model of the business process of the travel agency, and a voice response system of a customer care center is configured on the basis of a process model of the customer care center's business process. There are two possibilities to implement a business process model: The business process model is *hard-coded* into the information system, or it *configures* the information system. If it is hard-coded, then the business process model can be seen as a specification of the information system. Typically, predefined information systems, such as ERP systems, need to be adjusted such that they fit the needs of an organization. If the business process model configures the information system, the information system can be changed without recoding—only the business process model has to be changed. This approach is used in WfMSs and allows for high flexibility and fast changes; see work by Van der Aalst and Van Hee (2004), Dumas, Van der Aalst, and Ter Hofstede (2005), Ter Hofstede et al. (2010), Jablonski and Bussler (1996), and Leymann and Roller (1999).

We have seen that business processes, information systems, and models are strongly related and that models play a crucial role. In this book, we concentrate on process models rather than data models. Process models can be used for:

1. *Insight.* Process modeling forces the designer and the analyst to make the structures and rules of business processes and information systems explicit. As a result, new ideas arise, and inconsistent or flawed design decisions are exposed.
2. *Analysis.* Process models serve as a starting point for all kinds of analysis, ranging from validation to verification and performance analysis.
3. *Realization.* Models can specify or configure information systems.

2.2 On the Process Awareness of Information Systems

Figure 1.1 illustrates that business processes are the core of most information systems. Organizations can only survive if they offer products to customers. This requires that organizations specify their flow of work—their business processes. These business processes orchestrate participants, information, and technology to produce useful products and services. Given the central role of business processes in information systems, we concentrate on the *process view* (i.e., the transition relation) of information systems.

2.2.1 Brief History of Information Systems

To understand the central role business processes play in information systems, it is interesting to put information systems into a historical perspective. In particular, we show some of the ongoing trends in information system development.

In the early stage of computer science—that is, in the 1960s—applications were implemented on top of an operating system. As storing and modifying data became more and more complicated, caused by the increasing amount of data, database management systems were introduced as a layer in between the operating system and the applications. Database management systems were consequently the first enterprise information systems used. In the 1970s and 1980s, information systems were devoted to storing, retrieving, and presenting data. As a result, data models played a dominant role during that time.

With increasing complexity of information systems, organizations demanded an optimization of their business processes. Here, the data-centric design of information systems was disadvantageous, because the flow of work was spread across many software applications, making optimization difficult. As a consequence, in the early 1990s, there was a trend from data orientation to process orientation. This trend was not only driven by the demand to optimize business processes but also by the shift from programming to assembling. Instead of building their information systems from scratch, organizations bought (large) software applications from other vendors. Integrating these software applications into an existing information system of an organization is known as *enterprise application integration* (EAI) (Hohpe and Woolf 2003). The main integration task is to keep the data sets consistent between the existing information system and the new software application. The order in which the software applications must be executed is specified by a workflow. A WfMS can then execute this workflow. This approach allows for high flexibility, because the business process logic (i.e., the workflow) is separate from the application logic (i.e., the software applications). As a consequence, only the workflow has to be adjusted if the execution order of the software applications changes. As information systems change from monolithic systems to distributed applications running on heterogenous platforms across organizational boundaries, EAI becomes more and more complex.

Closely related to the trend from programming to assembling is the trend from programming to configuration. This is the trend in which enterprise information systems offer their users much more functionality than is actually needed. Organizations buy large software systems in which functionality can be switched on or off. Examples are ERP systems, such as SAP ERP and FileNet, in which many organizations use only a fraction of the available functionality.

Because of the extensively growing acceptance of the Internet and Internet-related technologies, organizations must act dynamically and change and adapt their business processes whenever necessary. This causes the latest paradigm change from carefully planned designs of information systems to redesign and organic growth. Instead of designing an information system from scratch, existing information systems are redesigned and iteratively improved. *Service-oriented computing* (SOC) (Papazoglou 2007) is a computing paradigm that implements this trend. Business functionality (e.g., an application) is encapsulated within a *service* and can be accessed through a well-defined interface. The idea is to aggregate services to service compositions to implement a business process. Recently, *service-oriented architectures* (SOAs) have been introduced as a key technology to design and execute services according to the SOC paradigm. An SOA is an architectural style whose goal is to achieve loose coupling among interacting services. It provides an IT infrastructure for publishing services of an organization via the Internet. Using standardized interfaces and message protocols, these published services can then be automatically found and accessed by other organization. By using an SOA, it becomes easier to compose and to maintain information systems. As a consequence, EAI is simplified and, hence, becomes less expensive.

Service orientation is getting more and more important. Often the term "software as a service" (SaaS) is used to emphasize that organizations do not need to host and run their own information systems, and that they can subcontract parts of it to external parties. The vision is for IT to be supplied like electricity and water—that is, having it available on demand and using it without worrying how it is produced or supplied. Although this metaphor is not accurate—electricity and water can be produced to stock, whereas information is always made to order—it illustrates the advantages of sharing IT investments. In this context, the term *cloud computing* is also used. The idea is that enterprise information systems run in a "cloud," where an infrastructure is shared with many other organizations. For example, Google hosts e-mail accounts for many organizations; these organizations share a common infrastructure and do not need to worry about backups and other maintenance activities.

Figure 2.3 lists the four trends and sketches the architecture of an enterprise information system in the 1960s and compares it with a typical architecture of a contemporary enterprise information system. In the 1960s, enterprise information systems were built from scratch; that is, the whole enterprise information system was programmed without using generic software other than an operating system and programming tools. Today, enterprise information systems are assembled from smaller components and use configurable product software, such as ERP systems. An organization may use only a fragment of the ERP system and switch off the parts it does not need through configuration. The smaller components may be assembled by a WfMS. A WfMS can avoid hard-coding the business processes into tailor-made applications, thus supporting the shift from programming to assembling. Different parts of the system may be created by services provided by a third party. Figure 2.3 illustrates the complex and highly dynamic landscape of today's information systems. As business processes and technologies change, the IT infrastructure must adapt.

2.2.2 Process-Aware Information Systems

A trend toward information systems that support business processes has made the process view of information systems and, accordingly, business process modeling more and more important.

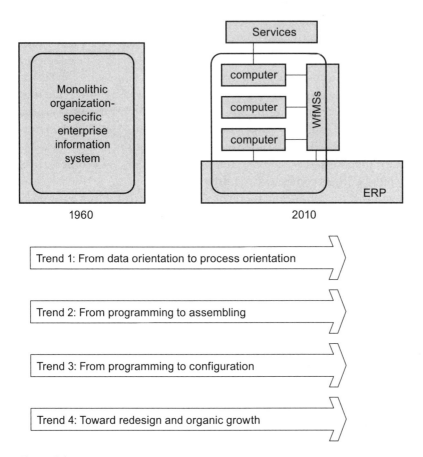

Figure 2.3
Four trends and the changes over 50 years of information systems development.

Despite the central role of business processes in information systems, there are only a few examples in which business processes are visible. One example is the production line of a car manufacturer, in which each step of the production line is visible for each car. Because of increasing automation, most business processes are hidden; for example, a business process can be hard-coded into a software system, or it exists only on paper—think of the flow of work of a clerk in a tax office. For this reason, the term "paper process" is often used. A paper process manifests itself by the order in which participants, information, and technology interact with each other.

Not only do information systems support business processes, many information systems are driven by the business processes they support. We refer to those information systems as *process-aware information system* (Dumas, Aalst, and Hofstede 2005).

Definition 2.3 (Process-aware information system)   A *process-aware information system* (PAIS) is a software system that manages and executes operational processes involving people, applications, or information sources on the basis of business process models.

According to this definition, a PAIS is an information system that supports a business process. Moreover, a PAIS is configured by a business process model, or it is an implementation of a business process model.

Example 2.4   A text editor is not process aware, because it just facilitates the execution of specific activities and can operate without any knowledge of the business processes at hand. The same is true of an e-mail program. An activity in a business process may result in sending an e-mail, but the e-mail program is unaware of the business process it is used in. At any point in time, one can send an e-mail without being restricted but also without receiving any support. Text editors and e-mail programs are applications supporting activities rather than business processes.

This book is about business process modeling; hence, we concentrate on information systems that are process aware. PAISs need to know about the business processes they support. This information can be hard-coded into applications, but it can also be used to configure applications, as described in section 2.1. In this book, we consider business process models serving as a specification of an information system and as the input of a configurable information system.

2.3   Tool Support for the Business Process Life Cycle

PAISs are driven by business process models. To illustrate this, we introduce several PAISs from practice and describe the role of business process models in these tools. We classify these tools by mapping them on the life cycle model for the development and the redesign of information systems (see figure 1.2).

The first class of tools we present are *business process modeling tools*. These tools support the design of business process models during the design phase in the life cycle model. The analysis of business process models takes place in the design analysis phase and is supported by *model-based analysis tools*. In the configuration phase in the life cycle model, business process models are refined to operational business processes. To this end, business process models configure PAISs and are—in the execution phase—executed. We refer to these tools as *business process enactment tools*. Finally, we look at tools that analyze running business processes. These tools support the maintenance of running business processes; that is, they support the monitoring and the runtime analysis phase in the life cycle model.

2.3.1 Business Process Modeling Tools

Business process modeling tools support the design phase in the life cycle model of information systems in figure 1.2. They support the modeling of business processes in some graphical notation. The reason for using a graphical notation instead of an algebraic notation is that a diagram is easier for people to understand. Comprehensibility of a business process model is important, because this model serves as a basis for discussion between, for example, the designer and the user. Business process modeling tools provide a palette of modeling constructs to design a graphical business process model. With the requirements determined in the requirements phase, the business process designer models the business process.

There are many industrial languages for modeling business processes. Examples are Business Process Modeling Notation (BPMN) (Object Management Group 2009), Event-driven Process Chains (EPCs) (Scheer 1994), UML (Rumbangh, Jacobson, and Booch 1998, Object Management Group 2005), and Web Services Business Process Execution Language (WS-BPEL) (Alves et al. 2007). Unfortunately, these languages offer different modeling constructs and, in addition, use different graphical notations for the same modeling constructs. Another drawback of industrial modeling languages is that they typically lack formal semantics. As business processes modeled in such a language need to be transformed into executable code, more rigorous interpretations have been added afterward. The UML, which is the de facto standard for software development, is an example of a language in which formal semantics have been added later. With the help of formal semantics, ambiguities can be detected and removed.

Examples of business process modeling tools are ARIS Business Architect from IDS Scheer, the Process Designer in BPM|one from Pallas Athena, and the Business Modeler from IBM's WebSphere Suite. These tools support the modeling of business processes using multiple views. The *process view* describes the control flow of a business process model (i.e., the ordering of activities). The *data view* describes the information elements that are used. The *organizational view* describes the structure of the organization and identifies resources, roles, and organizational units.

BPM|one is partly based on Petri nets; ARIS uses EPCs, but it also supports BPMN, UML, and WS-BPEL; and the Business Modeler supports modeling with a kind of UML activity diagram. Figure 2.4 depicts a screenshot of the Process Designer in BPM|one; this business process model illustrates a claims-handling procedure. The structure of the business process model, the process view, the data elements, and the organizational view of the business process model are shown.

2.3.2 Model-Based Analysis Tools

A business process model, constructed during the design phase of the life cycle model in figure 1.2, must conform to the requirements that have been determined in the requirements phase. The requirements are often incomplete, contradictory, or even

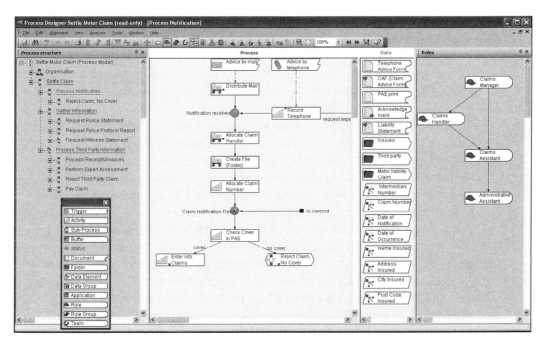

Figure 2.4
The Process Designer in BPM|one.

wrong. Because business process modeling is a difficult and error-prone process that requires much modeling experience, business process models must be analyzed. As business process models can be complex, tool support for analyzing these models is indispensable.

Most of the business process modeling tools provide limited support for analyzing business process models. These tools offer functionality to *simulate* the designed business process models. In contrast, verification of business process models—that is, a mathematical proof that desired properties, such as termination, hold (e.g., by exploring all reachable states of a business process model)—is usually not supported by industrial model-based analysis tools. For many of these commercial languages and tools, there are, however, translations into Petri nets (or other formal notations) such that academic or open source analysis software (e.g., Woflan (Verbeek, Basten, and Aalst 2001), ProM (Aalst, Dongen, et al. 2007), and LoLA (Wolf 2007)) can analyze the formal models.

Simulation tools have been available for decades. Traditionally, simulation tools were classified into two categories: *simulation languages* and *simulation packages*. Simulation languages are extensions of programming languages with facilities for timed and stochastic behavior. Examples of such languages are Simula, SLAM, and Must.

Simulation packages are graphical applications in which people can assemble a simulation model from predefined components (e.g., machines and buffers). Classical examples of such packages are Arena, Taylor, and Simfactory. Simulation languages are flexible but require implementation. In contrast, simulation packages allow for graphical modeling but are less flexible, because only predefined components can be glued together.

The basic idea of any simulation tool is to generate experiments (often referred to as scenarios or runs) on the basis of a business process model and by using a random generator. By aggregating the results of these experiments, it is possible to give estimates for many performance measures (e.g., waiting time and utilization). The application of simulation is not limited to performance analysis. Simulation can validate models and allow people to play with different ideas. Moreover, interactive simulation models can create management games that help users to spot inefficiencies and to understand new ways of working.

Figure 2.5 depicts a screenshot of the WebSphere Business Modeler. The upper left of the screenshot shows the structure of the business process model (i.e., the process tree). The lower left depicts the overall business process model, and the upper right of figure 2.5 shows a fragment of the overall business process model in more

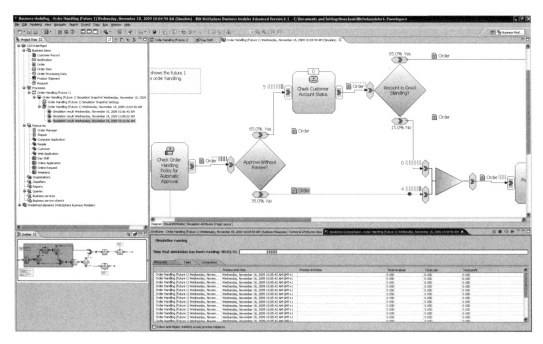

Figure 2.5
Simulation of a business process model in WebSphere Business Modeler.

detail. All transitions are annotated with probabilities, because the model is a simulation model. The lower right of figure 2.5 lists the events that have occurred in the simulation.

2.3.3 Business Process Enactment Tools

In the configuration phase of the life cycle model in figure 1.2, the analyzed business process model is refined to an operational business process. This operational business process can configure an information system, for example, by using a WfMS or an ERP system. However, it is still current practice that large parts of an enterprise information system are hard-coded using conventional programming language like Java, C, and C++. After developing the enterprise information system, the organization can execute the business process; see the execution phase in figure 1.2.

Although many enterprise information systems are still developed using conventional programming languages, we advocate the use of WfMSs to assemble enterprise information systems from smaller components or the use of ERP-like software to realize systems by configuration rather than by programming. In practice, a mixture of these approaches is often used.

The goal of WfMSs is to make sure that the right activity of a business process is executed at the right time by the right person. For this reason, the WfMS is driven by operational business process models. By modifying only the graphical model, a workflow can be changed. Examples of contemporary WfMSs are BPM|one, FileNet, and Tibco. Interestingly, ERP systems, such as SAP ERP, also contain several WfMSs, which can be employed to integrate existing applications.

In the case of an ERP system, parts of the operational business process typically must be hard-coded. Although ERP systems are configurable, the predefined solutions offered by ERP systems may only partially fit the business processes of an organization. In this case, extensive reconfiguration or even the reimplementation of parts of original solution may be needed. Examples of ERP systems are SAP ERP (which is part of the SAP Business Suite), Oracle's JD Edwards EnterpriseOne, Sage Pro ERP, and Microsoft Dynamics.

Business process models can be automatically configured and executed—for example, using the WebSphere Integration Developer. Once a business process is executed, tools such as IBM WebSphere's Business Process Choreographer can display its running instances and the current state of each instance. Figure 2.6 shows four running instances of the business process in figure 2.5.

2.3.4 Tools for Analyzing Running Business Processes

The goal of the monitoring and runtime analysis phase of the life cycle model in figure 1.2 is to diagnose running business processes and to figure out possibilities to improve them. Tool support for analyzing running business processes includes business

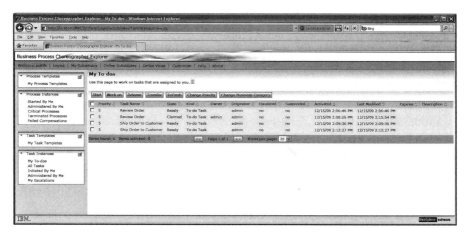

Figure 2.6
Visualization of running business process instances in WebSphere Business Process Choreographer.

intelligence systems, which mainly focus on process performance analysis and process monitoring. Such functionality is contained in tools, such as BPM|one (Pallas Athena), ARIS Business Simulator, and IBM WebSphere Business Monitor.

Figure 2.7 depicts a screenshot of the Business Monitor, which is part of IBM's WebSphere Integration Developer. In this figure, the Business Monitor provides five dashboards (upper part of figure) illustrating key performance indicators, such as average process duration, percentage of orders shipped, and shipped orders. It further provides reports in the form of bar charts and spreadsheets (lower part of figure) to illustrate analysis results. Dashboards like in figure 2.7 are common for contemporary business intelligence systems.

Similar to model-based analysis tools, contemporary tools for analyzing running business processes offer only limited analysis techniques. For example, data mining techniques to extract information from data are hardly supported. Furthermore, few tools make use of a business process model and the historical and runtime data of the business process. From historical data, stochastic data about routing and timing can be obtained, which is crucial to specify a simulation model. Runtime data allow for reconstructing the current state in a simulation model. Simulation based on the current state, historical data, and an adequate business process model offers high-quality information about potential problems in the near future (Rozinat, Wynn, et al. 2009). With this information, we can also provide recommendations when users of the business process must make decisions. In addition, historical data can be used for process mining (i.e., to discover a business process model). BPM|one is an innovative

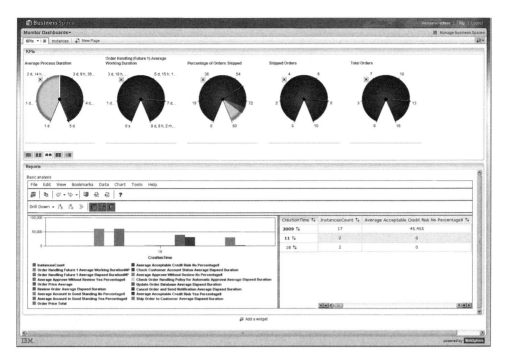

Figure 2.7
The Business Monitor of IBM's WebSphere Integration Developer.

product that, unlike most other tools, provides process mining techniques to customers.

Figure 2.8 shows a part of the process mining functionality offered by BPM|one. For a given event log file of a business process, the tool can automatically discover a model of this business process. Figure 2.8 depicts the discovered business process model, consisting of eleven activities. In addition, the tool generates an animation based on the event log. In this animation, the executed instances of the business process are replayed on the discovered business process model. For example, it is possible to create a five-minute movie showing all events in the past year. In figure 2.8, there are many tokens flowing through the process model. Each token represents one instance of the business process. The charts on the right side of the figure show the number of running instances of the business process and their average throughput times. Clearly, process mining can provide useful insights into running business processes of organizations. End users can see where business processes deviate from normative business processes, detect bottlenecks, and explore undesired phenomena.

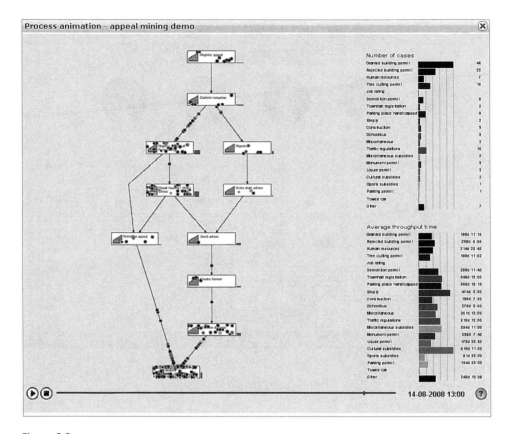

Figure 2.8
Process mining in BPM|one.

2.4   How about Data?

We explained in section 2.1 that models play a crucial role in developing and executing business processes and information systems. In section 1.5, we introduced the
term "system model" to refer to the combination of a process model that covers the
transition relation and a data model that covers the structuring of the state space of
a system. Figure 2.1 shows the distinction between these two models. Although this
book focuses on process models, data models are also important. When developing
enterprise information systems, substantial time must be devoted to data modeling. Some people prefer to talk about *information modeling* or *object modeling* rather
than *data modeling* to stress that the structuring of information is important not just
for implementation purposes but also for understanding the domain. Contemporary
business process modeling tools support the design of data models; see the data view

in the screenshot of BPM|one in figure 2.4. There are many notations for data modeling. Examples are ER models (Chen 1976), NIAM | ORM, and crow's foot diagrams. In this section, we use UML class diagrams (Rumbaugh, Jacobson, and Booch 1998; Object Management Group 2005) as a representation to illustrate the role of data modeling.

A data model aims at structuring the state space of a system. It defines the data structures of the system that are used to represent the basic entities and their inter-relationships. In a UML class diagram, an entity is a *class*. To structure an entity, a class may contain *attributes*. It is also possible to specify *operations* of an entity. In an implementation, an operation corresponds to a function. Typically, a system consists of several basic entities yielding a class each. Beside specifying the classes, a UML class diagram also defines the *interrelationship* between the classes. We introduce the basic concepts of UML class diagrams with the help of two examples.

In a hospital, there is a service desk where patients must have a punch card made. This punch card contains the name, address, date of birth, and gender of the patient. In addition, every patient receives an identifier. There is one employee working at the service desk. At any moment, this person can make a punch card for at most one patient. We assume that the time it takes to make a punch card depends on the experience (expressed in years of experience) of the employee. For this reason, employee numbers and years of experience of the service desk employee are recorded.

To determine the data model of this example, we first need to identify the entities. In this example, there are two entities: "patient" and "employee." Each entity corresponds to one class in the UML class diagram. According to the specification, we can distinguish between different patients. A patient is distinguished by an identifier, name, address, date of birth, and gender. Each of these five characteristics defines an attribute of a patient. Similarly, we define two attributes for an employee: employee number and years of experience. Because an employee can store the customer data on a punch card, the two classes are related. Figure 2.9 depicts the resulting UML class diagram. The "0..1" multiplicity of the Patient class specifies that one employee is busy with zero or one patients. Likewise, the "0..1" multiplicity of the Employee class specifies that one patient is helped by at most one employee. In this example, the relation should be read

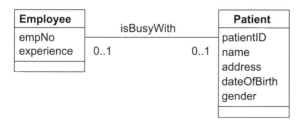

Figure 2.9
UML class diagram of the patient punch card service desk example.

Table 2.1
Instances of Class Patient

patientID	name	address	dateOfBirth	gender
12345	Peter	Kerkstraat 10, Amsterdam	13-Dec-1962	male
07234	John	Haagweg 3, Den Haag	17-Apr-1975	male
19222	Juliana	Kruisplein 11, Rotterdam	24-Mar-1943	female

Table 2.2
Instances of Class Employee

empNo	experience
641112	7
123456	12
235461	1

from left to right; that is, an employee is busy with a patient. Furthermore, we use the convention that the name of a class begins with a capital letter, whereas attributes (and also operations) begin with a lowercase letter.

Each class can be seen as a schema of a database table. A class defines an entity (i.e., the type of an object). In the system, instances of this entity exist. Such an instance corresponds to a data element in the database table of the entity. Table 2.1 shows possible instances of class Patient, and table 2.2 shows possible instances of class Employee.

Relationships between classes can be more involved. UML class diagrams support the concept of *inheritance*, which is well known from object-oriented programming languages; a class can inherit attributes and operations from another class. The following example illustrates inheritance.

A bank manages accounts for its customers. Each customer has at least one bank account. The bank stores an identifier, name, date of birth, and address of each account holder. A bank account has an account number and a balance and is for charge. Account holders can query the balance of a bank account and conduct transactions. A transaction has an identifier, specifies the amount of the transaction, and is related to one bank account. There are giro accounts and brokerage accounts. A giro account allows a customer to deposit money for which the bank pays a rate of interest, whereas a brokerage account allows a customer to hold stocks. Customers can withdraw money from a giro account and deposit money to a giro account. Customers who own a brokerage account may buy stocks. Likewise, customers may sell stocks from their brokerage accounts. For each kind of stock, the stock number and the quantity a customer owns is stored. Each customer has at least one giro account but does not necessarily have a brokerage account.

Question 2.5 What are the classes of the bank example?

There are seven classes: Bank, Customer, Transaction, BankAccount, GiroAccount, BrokerageAccount, and Stock. Figure 2.10 depicts the UML class diagram of the bank account example. Classes Bank, Customer, Transaction, and BankAccount and their attributes follow directly from the specification. According to the specification, there are two bank accounts: giro accounts and brokerage accounts. These two accounts inherit the three attributes and the operation to query the account balance from class BankAccount. The UML notation is a line with a closed arrow head from the *subclass* (i.e., class GiroAccount and class BrokerageAccount) to the *superclass* (i.e., class BankAccount). Class GiroAccount has an additional attribute, the rate of interest. It further offers operations to withdraw and deposit money. As every customer has a giro account but not every customer has a brokerage account, we relate class Customer to class GiroAccount

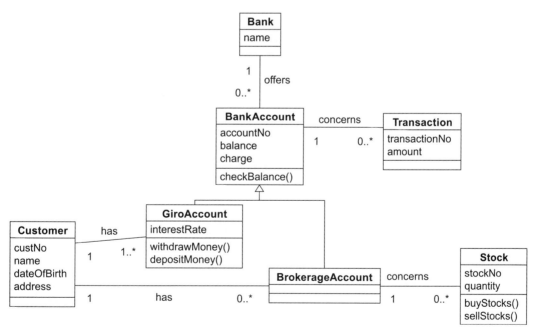

Figure 2.10
UML class diagram of the bank account example.

and class BrokerageAccount rather than to class BankAccount. A stock is characterized by an identifier and a quantity. As customers may buy and sell stocks, the respective operations are added to class Stock.

Exercise 2.1   Determine the UML class diagram for the following model of booking a train. A train has a number and several coaches. For each coach, the number of the coach and the number of seats is determined. A train may make several trips. Each trip has a departure day and time and an arrival day and time. It further has a departure station and an arrival station. A station is identified by a name and a postal code. Customers can make a reservation for a train trip. A seat reservation specifies a coach number and a seat number.

A data model shows the data entities of a system and their interrelationships. In the life cycle of an information system (see figure 1.2), data models play an important role as a domain model in the requirements phase and as a functional design model and implementation model in the design phase. Data models specified as a UML class diagram are general, because specific constraints cannot be expressed in UML. For example, it is not possible to specify that customers of a bank can only withdraw amounts less than 1,000 euros. For this reason, it is possible to create errors during the design of the system. To specify constraints of UML models, the Object Constraint Language (OCL) (Object Management Group 2003) can be used. By implementing the OCL constraints in a computer-aided software engineering (CASE) tool, we can analyze at design time whether the system satisfies these constraints. That way, data models can also be applied in the analysis phase (runtime analysis and design analysis).

In the remainder of this book, we concentrate on process modeling, using Petri nets extended with data, time, and hierarchy. The data aspect from such Petri nets can be structured using UML class diagrams or similar notations, as shown by Van Hee (2009).

2.5   Test Yourself

2.5.1   Solutions to Exercises
2.1   Figure 2.11 depicts the UML class diagram. It shows that the example has five classes: Train, Coach, Station, TrainTrip, and Reservation.

2.5.2   Further Exercises
Exercise 2.2   Explain the relation of business processes, information systems, and (business process) models.

Exercise 2.3   Name four trends in information systems development.

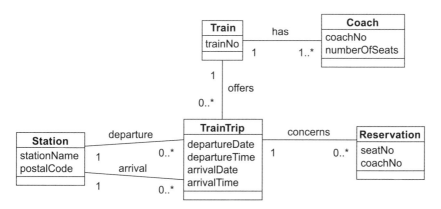

Figure 2.11
UML class diagram of exercise 2.1.

Exercise 2.4 Explain the term "process-aware information system."

Exercise 2.5 Describe the functionality of business process modeling tools, of model-based analysis tools, of business process enactment tools, and of tools for analyzing running business processes.

Exercise 2.6 Name examples of business process modeling tools, of model-based analysis tools, of business process enactment tools, and of tools for analyzing running business processes.

Exercise 2.7 Describe the role of process models in business process modeling tools, in model-based analysis tools, in business process enactment tools, and in tools for analyzing running business processes.

Exercise 2.8 Prepare a UML class diagram for the following example of a transportation company. Each shipment has an identifier, a departure day, and an arrival day. It further has a departure city and an arrival city. The name, postal code, and country specify a city. For each shipment, the company needs one truck. A truck is identified by a truck number. It pulls a trailer of a certain capacity. The trailer is also identified by a number. As the company has more trailers than trucks, not every trailer is in use at all times. Trailers are either of type tanker or cargo. A tanker trailer can load one sort of liquids, and a cargo trailer can load several solid products. The company receives orders. Each order has an identifier and relates to one product. A product has an identifier and a price. Solid and liquid products are distinguished; solid products are measured by weight, and liquid products are measured by volume. Each product can be loaded on one tanker or cargo trailer. Each order implies one shipment, but sometimes a truck has to drive to a city without a load. To save costs, trucks can deliver several shipments at once.

2.6   Summary

In this chapter, we described the relation of business processes, information systems, and models of business processes and information systems. We further discussed the role of business process models in existing business process modeling tools, model-based analysis tools, business process enactment tools, and tools for analyzing running business processes. The moment business process models are employed to specify or configure information systems, these models should be complete, precise, and un-ambiguous. Informal business process models that merely sketch the intended business processes are suitable only for communication but are not a solid basis for analysis or implementation. For this reason, we use Petri nets as a modeling language in this book. Petri nets are introduced in chapter 3.

After studying this chapter you should be able to:

- Describe the relation of business processes, information systems, and models.
- Explain the four paradigm changes in the history of information systems.
- Recognize business processes in PAISs.
- Describe the role of business process models in business process modeling tools, model-based analysis tools, business process enactment tools, and tools for analyzing running business processes.
- Understand the relation between data and process modeling.

2.7   Further Reading

The history of information systems is described in more detail by Van der Aalst and Van Hee (2004), Alonso et al. (2003), and Weske (2007). PAISs are discussed in detail by Dumas, Van der Aalst, and Ter Hofstede (2005). Moreover, Dumas, Van der Aalst, and Ter Hofstede (2005) present an overview of the main concepts and techniques for building PAISs. Van der Aalst (2009) surveys PAISs and reviews challenges in this field of research.

There are several books on workflow technology. Van der Aalst and Van Hee (2004), Jablonski and Bussler (1996), and Zur Muehlen (2004) explain the conceptual foundations of workflow management. Van der Aalst et al. (2003) developed the workflow patterns to evaluate WfMSs. Ter Hofstede et al. (2010) survey Yet Another Workflow Language (YAWL), a WfMS based on these workflow patterns. Leymann and Roller (1999) describe the conceptual foundations of IBM's workflow technology.

In this book, we concentrate on process modeling. There are many excellent textbooks on data modeling; for example, work by Hoberman (2009), Oppel (2009), Halpin and Morgan (2008), Olivé (2007), Ponniah (2007), Allen and Terry (2005), and Simsion and Witt (2004). Van Hee (2009) elaborates on the integration of data and process modeling. Also, in UML (Rumbaugh, Jacobson, and Booch 1998; Object Management Group 2005) data and process models can be related, but compared with work by Van Hee (2009), UML advocates a looser or coupling of these model types.

3 Basic Concepts of Petri Nets

Information systems typically control and support business processes. An information system and each business process it supports is a (discrete dynamic) system, which can be modeled as a transition system. As a modeling tool, however, transition systems are not suitable, because it is too cumbersome to describe a complex system in terms of a state space and a transition relation. More advanced modeling tools, such as data models and process models, are needed. Data models describe the state space of a system by classifying the possible data objects of the system and representing their relationships. Process models describe system behavior and specify the ways in which the system can change its state. This chapter introduces *Petri nets* as a process modeling technique.

Petri nets have several advantages. Like transition systems, Petri nets have a mathematical foundation. This allows us to apply various analysis techniques to Petri net models. Petri nets offer a formal but also graphical notation and are, therefore, accessible for nonexperts. Petri nets have many similarities with the modeling languages offered by the business process modeling tools presented in chapter 2; for this reason, Petri nets have been chosen as a formalism to develop formal semantics for languages such as EPCs, UML activity diagrams, and WS-BPEL. Another advantage is that there are many software tools that support modeling and analysis of Petri nets. The main advantage of using Petri nets rather than transition systems is that Petri nets do not explicitly represent the state space of a business process; instead, they model it in a more implicit and compact way. A small Petri net consisting of two nodes can represent a transition system with infinite state space.

In this chapter, we present the basic concepts of Petri nets, a formalism which was introduced by Carl Adam Petri in 1962. We first introduce this formalism by means of two examples (section 3.1). Then, we look at the structure of Petri nets in detail (section 3.2) and define the behavior of Petri nets (section 3.3). As every Petri net can be described by a transition system, we show the relation between these formalisms (section 3.4). Finally, we illustrate—with the help of two examples—how simple systems and business processes can be modeled as a Petri net (section 3.5).

3.1 An Introduction to Petri Nets

We introduce Petri nets using two examples. The first Petri net has a structure that is very close to the corresponding transition system. The second example shows why Petri nets are a more suitable process modeling formalism than transition systems.

3.1.1 A First Example of a Petri Net: Modeling an Elevator

We discuss Petri nets by using the elevator example of exercise 1.6. Figure 3.1 depicts a Petri net modeling the behavior of the elevator.

The elevator moves between five floors and can stop at any of these floors. We model each floor as a *place*. Graphically, a circle represents a place. There are five places in figure 3.1: floor0, floor1, floor2, floor3, and floor4. Place floor0 models the ground floor, place floor1 the first floor, and the other three places model the corresponding remaining floors.

At each floor, the elevator can go up or go down. The Petri net in figure 3.1 models each move of the elevator by a *transition*, which is represented by a square. The Petri

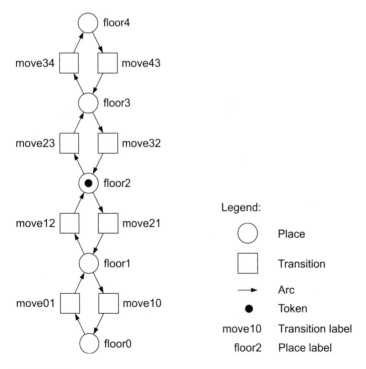

Figure 3.1
The elevator modeled as a Petri net.

net in figure 3.1 has eight transitions: move01, move12, move23, move34, move10, move21, move32, and move43. For example, at the second floor, the elevator can either go up to the third floor or go down to the first floor. Transition move23 models the move from the second to the third floor. The *directed arcs* connecting place floor2 to transition move23 and transition move23 to place floor3 show the direction of this move. Likewise, transition move21 models the change from the second to the first floor. The arcs connecting place floor2 to transition move21 and transition move21 to place floor1 again show the direction of the change.

A place may contain *tokens*. Graphically, a black dot represents a token. The state of a Petri net is a *marking* and determined by the number of tokens that are present in each place. In figure 3.1, only place p2 contains a token. This token indicates that the elevator is at the second floor.

The network structure of a Petri net—that is, the places, the transitions, and the arcs—is fixed, but transitions can change the distribution of tokens over the places. For example, transition move23 can take the token from place floor2 and put a new token in place floor3. The direction of the arcs connecting floor2 to move23 and move23 to floor3 determine the token flow. Transition move23 causes a change of the distribution of tokens that corresponds to the state transition in which the elevator moves from the second to the third floor. We call this the *firing* of transition move23. Figure 3.2 depicts the *effect* of the firing of transition move23.

The firing of transitions is subject to rules. To explain these rules, we must know the *input* and the *output places* of a transition. A place *p* is an input place of a transition *t* if there is an arc from *p* to *t*. Likewise, a place *p* is an output place of a transition *t* if there is an arc from *t* to *p*. In figure 3.1, place floor2 is the only input place of transition move23, and place floor3 is the only output place of transition move23.

Question 3.1   What are the input and output places of transition move01?

Transition t01 has only one input place, floor0, and only one output place, floor1.

A transition can fire only if there is at least one token in each of its input places. In the marking of figure 3.1, transition move01 cannot fire, because place floor0 is an input place of transition move01, and it does not contain a token. A transition that fires takes one token from each of its input places and puts one token in each of its output places. As illustrated in figure 3.2, transition move23 takes one token from its input place floor2 and puts one token in its output place floor3.

To summarize, a Petri net is a special kind of graph that consists of two types of nodes: places and transitions. These nodes can be connected by directed arcs. In graph theory, such a graph is known as a bipartite graph. In graphical notation, we represent a place by a circle and a transition by a square. An arc can only connect a place to a transition

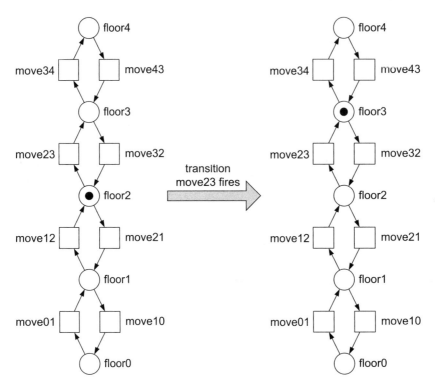

Figure 3.2
The marking before and after the firing of transition t23.

or a transition to a place. An arc between two places or between two transitions is not possible.

3.1.2 A More Interesting Example

The Petri net model of the elevator in figure 3.1 has five places and eight transitions, whereas the transition system of the elevator in figure 1.5 has five states. The Petri net model of the elevator does not represent the behavior of the system in a more implicit and compact way than a transition system. The reason is the simple structure of figure 3.1; each transition has one input and one output place. This restriction is not mandatory. Transitions may have arbitrarily many input and output places. Furthermore, places may contain more than one token, and more than one place may contain tokens at the same time, as shown in the following example.

A hospital has one X-ray department. An X-ray machine makes photographs of bones and organs of patients for detecting certain internal abnormalities—for example, a jaw fracture. The X-ray department has capacity problems; there is always a long queue of people waiting for an X-ray. Surveys among patients have indicated dissatisfaction with this wait time, and the management of the hospital is considering purchasing of a second X-ray machine. Because the purchase price of this machine is more than 250,000 euros, further investigation of the wait times is required. This problem is investigated by developing a process model of this business process.

From the perspective of the usage of the X-ray room, a patient can be in one of four possible states. First, the patient waits outside the room. Second, the patient is in the room before the photo is made. Third, the patient is in the room after the photo has been made. Fourth, the patient has left the room. We represent these four states of a patient in a Petri net by the four places wait, before, after, and gone.

There are three possible state transitions: when the patient enters, the state changes from wait to before; when the X-ray machine makes a photo, the state changes from before to after; and when the patient leaves the X-ray room, the state changes from after to gone. We represent these three state transitions in a Petri net by the transitions enter, make_photo, and leave.

Figure 3.3 depicts a first attempt at a Petri net modeling the business process of the X-ray machine. Each token in place wait represents a patient in the queue at the X-ray machine. A token in place before represents a patient in the X-ray room before the X-ray is made. After the X-ray has been made, there is a token in place after. Each token in place gone represents a patient who has left the X-ray room after a photo has been made.

Question 3.2   In which respect does the model fail?

To check whether this Petri net accurately models the business process of the X-ray machine (i.e., to validate the model in figure 3.3), we consider a number of successive markings. First, we assume the marking in figure 3.3; that is, there are three patients in the queue waiting for an X-ray. Figure 3.4 depicts the next marking, which occurs after the firing of transition enter.

This marking describes that a patient is in the X-ray room and two patients are still in the queue. There are two possibilities in this marking: either transition make_photo fires or transition enter fires again. Figure 3.5 depicts the marking, which is the result of the latter possibility.

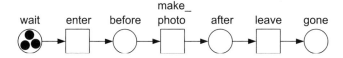

Figure 3.3
A first attempt at modeling the X-ray machine.

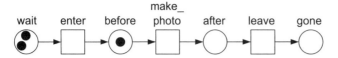

Figure 3.4
A Petri net model of a business process of an X-ray machine: The marking after transition enter has fired.

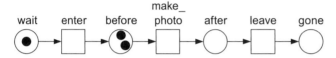

Figure 3.5
A Petri net model of a business process of an X-ray machine: The marking after transition enter has fired again.

In reality, this would mean that there are two or more patients at the same time in the X-ray room. This is not desirable! A patient may enter the X-ray room only after the previous patient has left the room. We must make sure that places before and after together do not contain more than one token. We do this by including the possible states of the X-ray room in the model. There are two possible states: the room can be free or occupied. We model this by adding two places to the model in figure 3.5. Figure 3.6 shows the resulting model.

A token in place free indicates that the room is free. If transition enter fires, the token from place free is removed, and one token is put in place occupied. This yields the marking in figure 3.7.

In the Petri net in figure 3.7, it is no longer possible that place before contains more than one token. As long as there is no token in place free, transition enter cannot fire again, because a transition can only fire if all its input places contain at least one token.

Question 3.3   When is a token put in place free?

A token is put in place free if transition leave fires. This is exactly what is intended: if a patient leaves the X-ray room, the next patient can enter the room.

To ensure this property, we do not need place occupied. We can model the property of the X-ray room of being free or not by the presence or absence of a token in place free.

The business process of the X-ray machine modeled in this section illustrates one of the advantages when modeling with Petri nets. Each token in figure 3.6 represents

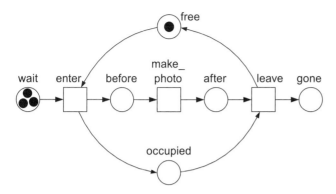

Figure 3.6
An improved Petri net for the business process of an X-ray machine.

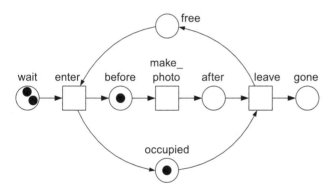

Figure 3.7
The marking of the improved Petri net for the business process of an X-ray machine after transition enter has fired.

a patient. If we increase the number of patients in the model, only the number of tokens increases. The structure of the model—that is, the number of places, transitions, and arcs—remains unchanged. In contrast, the size of the state-transition diagram of the transition system modeling the X-ray machine would increase if we increased the number of patients. This shows that Petri nets can compactly represent larger transition systems.

3.2 The Structure of Petri Nets

The structure of a Petri net is determined if we know the places, the transitions, and the ways in which they are connected with each other. In this section, we show that a Petri net can be described by a set of places, a set of transitions, and a set of arcs connecting places and transitions.

A Petri net contains zero or more places. Each place has a unique name, the *place label*. We can describe the places of a Petri net by the set P of place labels. For the Petri net in figure 3.7, the set is defined as:

$P = \{\text{wait, before, after, gone, free, occupied}\}$.

We can describe the transitions in a Petri net in the same way. Each transition has a unique name, the *transition label*. We describe the transitions of a Petri net by the set T of transition labels. The Petri net in figure 3.7 has three transitions:

$T = \{\text{enter, make\_photo, leave}\}$.

When we choose transition and place labels, we look for names that indicate what the place or the transition models. Transitions are the *active* nodes of a Petri net, because they can change the marking through firing. We therefore name transitions with verbs to express action. Places are the *passive* nodes of a Petri net because they cannot change the marking; we name places using nouns, adjectives, or adverbs. To avoid confusion, we use the symbol "_" ("underscore"), not a space, to separate words in labels.

In addition to the places and transitions, we must describe the arcs. There are two kinds of arcs—those that connect a transition and one of its input places and those that connect a transition and one of its output places. Like a transition in a transition system, we can represent an arc as an ordered pair (x, y). The set of arcs is a binary relation. As a Petri net has two kinds of arcs, we obtain two binary relations. The binary relation $R_I \subseteq P \times T$ contains all arcs connecting transitions and their input places. Likewise, the binary relation $R_O \subseteq T \times P$ contains all arcs connecting transitions and their output places. For the Petri net in figure 3.7, the two relations are defined as:

$R_I = \{\text{(wait, enter), (before, make\_photo), (after, leave),}$
$\quad\quad \text{(free, enter), (occupied, leave)}\}$
$R_O = \{\text{(enter, before), (make\_photo, after), (leave, gone),}$
$\quad\quad \text{(leave, free), (enter, occupied)}\}$.

The union $R_I \cup R_O$ of the relations R_I and R_O represents all arcs of a Petri net. This union is again a relation and denoted by F, the *flow relation*

$F = R_I \cup R_O \subseteq (P \times T) \cup (T \times P)$.

For the Petri net in figure 3.7, the flow relation F is defined as:

$F = \{\text{(wait, enter), (before, make\_photo), (after, leave), (free, enter),}$
$\quad\quad \text{(occupied, leave), (enter, before), (make\_photo, after), (leave, gone),}$
$\quad\quad \text{(leave, free), (enter, occupied)}\}$.

This set P of places, T of transitions, and flow relation F define the Petri net in figure 3.7. From a diagram showing the structure of a Petri net, we can derive the set P of places, the set T of transitions, and the flow relation F; in addition, for any given set P of places, set T of transitions, and flow relation F, we can draw the corresponding Petri net representation.

Definition 3.4 (Petri net)   A *Petri net* is a triple (P, T, F), where

1. P is a finite set of *places*.
2. T is a finite set of *transitions*.
3. $F \subseteq (P \times T) \cup (T \times P)$ is a *flow relation*.

Consequently, there is a one-to-one correspondence between the graphical representation of a Petri net and the triple (P, T, F).

Exercise 3.1   Draw the Petri net defined by $P = \{p1, p2\}$, $T = \{t1, t2\}$, and $F = \{(p1, t1),$ $(t1, p2), (p2, t1), (p2, t2), (t2, p2), (t2, p1)\}$.

We can now define the concepts of input place and output place in terms of flow relation F. A place p is an input place of a transition t if $(p, t) \in F$. The set ${}^\bullet t = \{p \mid (p, t) \in F\}$ defines all input places of a transition t. A place p is an output place of a transition t if $(t, p) \in F$. The set $t^\bullet = \{p \mid (t, p) \in F\}$ defines all output places of a transition t. We refer to ${}^\bullet t$ as the *preset of t* and to $t^\bullet$ as the *postset of t*.

In figure 3.7, transition enter has two input places (wait and free) and two output places (before and occupied). Hence, we have the preset ${}^\bullet$enter = {wait, free} and the postset enter${}^\bullet$ = {before, occupied}. In the same Petri net, transition leave has two input places (after and occupied) and two output places (gone and free) yielding the preset ${}^\bullet$leave = {after, occupied} and the postset leave${}^\bullet$ = {gone, free}.

Exercise 3.2   Consider the Petri net in figure 3.8.

1. Define the net formally as a triple (P, T, F).
2. List presets and postsets for each transition.

3.3   The Behavior of Petri Nets

In this section, we describe the behavior of a Petri net. The behavior is defined by the net structure, the distribution of tokens over the places, and the firing of transitions.

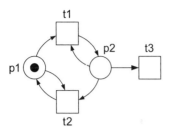

Figure 3.8
The Petri net of exercise 3.2.

3.3.1 An Informal Description of the Behavior of Petri Nets

Process models, such as Petri nets, describe the behavior of a system, which is determined by all possible state transitions. To formally describe the behavior of a Petri net, we first have to define the term *marking* (i.e., a system state).

The marking of a Petri net is determined by the distribution of tokens over the places of the net. A token is graphically rendered as a black dot. Places can contain tokens, transitions cannot. To describe the marking of the Petri net in figure 3.6, we must specify the number of tokens in each place. Table 3.1 shows this marking.

The Petri net in figure 3.8 has two places. Place p1 holds one token, place p2 does not hold a token.

Places in a Petri net hold tokens, whereas transitions can change the marking through firing. That is places are passive, and transitions are active. To fire a transition, it must be *enabled*. A transition is enabled if there is at least one token in each of its input places.

Example 3.5 Transition enter in figure 3.6 is enabled if there is at least one token in place wait and at least one token in place free. In the marking in figure 3.6, these conditions are fulfilled. Transition make_photo is enabled if place before holds at least one token. This condition is not fulfilled in figure 3.6.

Exercise 3.3 Consider the Petri net in figure 3.9.

1. Determine the marking of this net.
2. Are the transitions t1 and t2 enabled in figure 3.9?

Exercise 3.4 Under which conditions are the transitions in the Petri net in figure 3.8 enabled?

When a transition t fires, one token is removed from each of its input places, and one new token is added to each of its output places. We say that one token is *consumed from* an input place and one token is *produced in* an output place.

Table 3.1
The Marking of the Petri Net in Figure 3.6

Place	Number of tokens
wait	3
before	0
after	0
gone	0
free	1
occupied	0

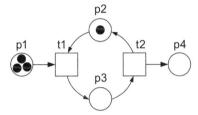

Figure 3.9
A Petri net showing transitions t1 and t2.

Example 3.6 In figure 3.6, transition enter is enabled. This transition can fire, thereby consuming from input place wait one token and from input place free one token. At the same moment, one token is produced in output place before and one token is produced in output place occupied. Figure 3.7 depicts the situation after the firing of transition enter.

When a transition t fires, the resulting number of tokens in any place p is equal to the initial number of tokens minus the number of consumed tokens plus the number of produced tokens. The total number of tokens in the net changes if the number of input places of transition t is not the same as the number of output places of transition t. Accordingly, the firing of a transition may increase or decrease the overall number of tokens.

When several transitions are enabled at the same moment, it is not determined which of them will fire. This situation is a *nondeterministic choice*. Even though we do not know in this case which transition will fire, we know that one of them will be fired. An example of a nondeterministic choice in a Petri net is shown in Figure 3.4. Transition enter and transition make_photo are both enabled at the given marking.

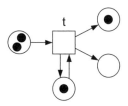

Figure 3.10
A Petri net for examining consecutive markings.

To gain insight into the dynamics of a Petri net, one can play the token game. Copy a Petri net and make sure that the places have a diameter of about 3 cm. Take several small coins, and put the coins in the places determined by the given initial marking. Reconstruct now the firing of the transitions by removing coins from the input places and adding coins to the output places for each firing. The Web page <http://www .workflowcourse.com> provides several interactive animations for playing the token game.

Exercise 3.5   Consider the Petri net in figure 3.10. Examine by means of the token game what the consecutive markings are, assuming the given initial marking.

The X-ray example illustrates that it is possible to go through several markings in a Petri net by a series of firings. The transitions keep firing until the net reaches a marking that does not enable any transition. Like the terminal state in transition systems, this marking is a *terminal marking*.

A marking m' is *reachable* from a marking m if there is a series of firings that lead to marking m'.

Exercise 3.6   Consider the Petri net in figure 3.8 and assume a marking m where every place contains exactly one token.

1. Which transitions are enabled at m?
2. What is the result of the firing of transition t1 in m?
3. What is the result of the firing of transition t2 in m?
4. What is the result of the firing of transition t3 in m?
5. What are the reachable markings from m, and which of these markings are terminal markings?

3.3.2   A Formal Description of the Behavior of Petri Nets
In section 3.3.1, we informally described the behavior of a Petri net by representing a marking of a Petri net as a table. In mathematical terms, we can represent such a

table as a function $m : P \to \mathbb{N}$, assigning a natural number to each place. Function m is a *multiset* or *bag*. A multiset is like a usual set (i.e., the order of the elements does not matter), but the same element may appear multiple times.

Example 3.7 Consider a set $\{a, b, c\}$ consisting of three elements. A possible multiset over these elements is, for example, $[a, b, b, c, c, c]$. In this multiset, element a appears once, element b twice, and element c appears three times. A more compact representation of this multiset is $[1 \cdot a, 2 \cdot b, 3 \cdot c]$ or just $[a, 2 \cdot b, 3 \cdot c]$. Another example is the multiset $[5 \cdot a, 3 \cdot b]$ where element a appears five times, element b three times, and element c does not appear.

The function m assigns to each place p a natural number that specifies the number of tokens in p. For the Petri net in figure 3.6, we can define m as:

$$m(\text{wait}) = 3, \quad m(\text{free}) = 1, \quad m(\text{before}) = 0,$$
$$m(\text{after}) = 0, \quad m(\text{gone}) = 0, \quad m(\text{occupied}) = 0.$$

A marking defines a multiset of the set P of places. We can, therefore, represent the marking m as the multiset $m = [\text{wait}, \text{wait}, \text{wait}, \text{free}]$ or more compact as $m = [3 \cdot \text{wait}, \text{free}]$.

If we model a system as a Petri net (P, T, F), then the set M of all possible markings of this net defines the state space of the system. The set M is described by the set of all functions m assigning to each place $p \in P$ a natural number. We can summarize the preceding discussion in the following definition.

Definition 3.8 (Marking)   A *marking* of a Petri net (P, T, F) is a function $m : P \to \mathbb{N}$, assigning to each place $p \in P$ the number $m(p)$ of tokens at this place. The set M of *all markings* of this net is the set of all such functions.

We can now define the concept *enabling*. A transition t is enabled at marking m if every input place of t contains at least one token.

Definition 3.9 (Enabledness)   In a Petri net (P, T, F), a transition $t \in T$ is *enabled at marking $m : P \to \mathbb{N}$ if and only if for all $p \in {}^{\bullet}t$, $m(p) > 0$.*

An enabled transition t can fire, thereby changing the marking m to a marking m'. If an enabled transition fires, it consumes one token from each of its input places and produces one token in each of its output places. We can calculate the successor marking m' from marking m as follows: the number $m'(p)$ of tokens in a place p is equal to the number $m(p)$ of tokens in p minus the consumed tokens plus the produced tokens. The number of consumed tokens is equal to one if p is an input place of t (i.e., $(p, t) \in F$)

and zero else. Likewise, the number of produced tokens is equal to one if p is an output place of t (i.e., $(t, p) \in F$) and zero else.

We can formalize the effect of the firing of a transition by a function w, assigning to each arc in flow relation F the value 1 and to each arc not contained in flow relation F the value 0. Formally, this function is defined by $w : (P \times T) \cup (T \times P) \to \{0, 1\}$ with $w((x, y)) = 1$ if $(x, y) \in F$ and $w((x, y)) = 0$ if $(x, y) \notin F$. Function w is the *weight function*.

Definition 3.10 (Transition firing)   For a Petri net (P, T, F), let w be the weight function and $m : P \to \mathbb{N}$ be the current marking. A transition $t \in T$ can *fire* if and only if it is enabled at m. The firing of t yields a new marking $m' : P \to \mathbb{N}$ where for all places $p \in P$, $m'(p) = m(p) - w((p, t)) + w((t, p))$.

Example 3.11   Consider the Petri net in figure 3.9. Transition t1 is enabled at marking m depicted in figure 3.9. The firing of t1 yields the marking m', defined as:

$$
\begin{aligned}
m'(\text{p1}) &= m(\text{p1}) - w((\text{p1}, \text{t1})) + w((\text{t1}, \text{p1})) &= 3 - 1 + 0 &= 2 \\
m'(\text{p2}) &= m(\text{p2}) - w((\text{p2}, \text{t1})) + w((\text{t1}, \text{p2})) &= 1 - 1 + 0 &= 0 \\
m'(\text{p3}) &= m(\text{p3}) - w((\text{p3}, \text{t1})) + w((\text{t1}, \text{p3})) &= 0 - 0 + 1 &= 1 \\
m'(\text{p4}) &= m(\text{p4}) - w((\text{p4}, \text{t1})) + w((\text{t1}, \text{p4})) &= 0 - 0 + 0 &= 0.
\end{aligned}
$$

To determine the behavior of a Petri net, we need to specify an initial marking. A Petri net with an initial marking is a Petri net *system*.

Definition 3.12 (Petri net system)   A *Petri net system* (P, T, F, m_0) consists of a Petri net (P, T, F) and a distinguished marking m_0, the *initial marking*.

3.4   Representing Petri Nets as Transition Systems

As described in section 1.4, the behavior of a system can be represented as a transition system (S, TR, s_0). Transition systems are the primal models of process modeling, because they are the most elementary formalism with which we can describe systems. We can also describe the behavior of a Petri net system (P, T, F, m_0) as a transition system (S, TR, s_0) by showing how to determine the state space S, the transition relation TR, and the initial state s_0 for the system (P, T, F, m_0).

The state space S of an arbitrary Petri net system (P, T, F, m_0) consists of all possible distributions of tokens over the places P; that is, state space S consists of all functions from places P to $\mathbb{N}$. We represent this set of functions by $M = P \to \mathbb{N}$. The initial state s_0 is defined by the initial marking m_0. The description of the transition relation TR for the Petri net system is more involved.

Let us consider two arbitrary states in state space S—that is, two markings m and m'. Transition (m, m') is an element of the transition relation TR if there is a transition t enabled at marking m, and the firing of transition t in marking m yields marking m'. In all other cases, transition (m, m') is not possible, and (m, m') is not an element of transition relation TR. We can formalize this by defining transition relation TR as the set of all pairs $(m, m') \in S \times S$ such that there is a transition $t \in T$ that is enabled at marking m and the firing of transition t in marking m yields marking m'.

Using the existential quantifier, we can express the condition "there is a transition $t \in T$" formally as "$\exists t \in T$." Section 3.3.2 described how to express the condition "transition t is enabled at marking m." Here, we use the universal quantifier:

$$\forall p \in {}^{\bullet}t : m(p) > 0.$$

We can also formalize the condition "the firing of transition t in marking m yields marking m'":

$$\forall p \in P : m'(p) = m(p) - w((p, t)) + w((t, p)).$$

The number $m'(p)$ of tokens in place p after firing of p is equal to the original number $m(p)$ of tokens minus the number $w((p, t))$ of consumed tokens plus the number $w((t, p))$ of produced tokens.

As a consequence, an arbitrary Petri net system (P, T, F, m_0) defines the following transition system (S, TR, s_0):

$$S = M = P \rightarrow \mathbb{N}$$
$$TR = \{(m, m') \in S \times S \mid \exists t \in T : (\forall p \in {}^{\bullet}t : m(p) > 0$$
$$\wedge (m'(p) = m(p) - w((p, t)) + w((t, p))))\}$$
$$s_0 = m_0.$$

This compact definition includes all concepts discussed in this chapter. Using a mathematical notation, we can describe a Petri net system precisely and succinctly. With just four lines of mathematics, we can formalize the semantics of concepts *state*, *state space*, *enabling*, *firing*, *production*, *consumption*, and *transition relation*.

3.5   Examples of Petri Net Models

In this section, we discuss two introductory examples of the relation between a Petri net and the business process or information system modeled by it.

3.5.1   Example: Consulting Specialists

In the outpatient clinic of a hospital, patients consult specialists. Each patient has an appointment with a certain specialist. We describe the course of business around a specialist as a process model. As a formalism, we use a Petri net.

The specialist receives patients. At each moment, the specialist is in one of the following three states: (1) the specialist is free and waits for the next patient (state free), (2) the specialist is busy treating a patient (state busy), or (3) the specialist is documenting the result of the treatment (state docu).

Every patient who visits a specialist is in one of the following three states: (1) the patient is waiting (state wait), the patient is treated by the specialist (state inside), or (3) the patient has been treated by the specialist (state done).

Figure 3.11 depicts the states of the specialist and the states of a patient. A patient goes through these states only once (per visit). The specialist goes through the three states in an iterative way.

For this business process, three events are important. First, the specialist starts with the treatment of a patient (event "start"). Second, the specialist finishes the treatment of a patient and starts documenting the results of the treatment (event "change"). Third, the specialist stops documenting (event "end").

We model the business process as a Petri net. If we look at the specialist separately, we see that there are three states (free, busy, and docu) and three transitions (start, change, and end). We can model each state of the specialist as a place and each transition as a Petri net transition. Figure 3.12 depicts the resulting Petri net. In the displayed marking, the specialist is in state free.

We model patients separately. Because a patient can be in one of three states, there are three places. A token represents a patient in the corresponding state. Figure 3.13 shows the resulting Petri net. In the displayed marking, there are three patients in state wait, and one patient is in state done.

Transition start in figure 3.12 represents the same event as transition start in figure 3.13. The same applies for transition change. If we want to map the whole course of business around the specialist, we can merge the two Petri nets by joining the equally labeled transitions. Figure 3.14 depicts the resulting net.

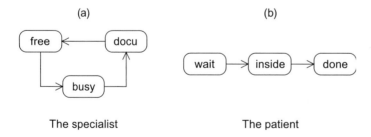

Figure 3.11
The possible states of a specialist and a patient.

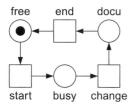

Figure 3.12
A Petri net modeling the state of the specialist.

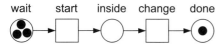

Figure 3.13
A Petri net modeling states of patients.

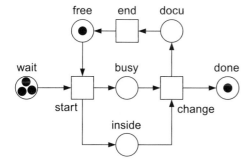

Figure 3.14
A Petri net model of a specialist treating patients.

Transitions start, change, and end represent the three possible events. The tokens in place wait represent the waiting patients. A token in place inside represents a patient who is being treated or examined by the specialist. Tokens in place done represent patients who have been treated or examined. The token in place free indicates that the specialist is in state free. If the specialist is busy treating a patient, a token is in place busy. A token in place docu indicates that the specialist is documenting certain results.

Exercise 3.7 We can describe marking m in figure 3.14 as $m = [3 \cdot$ wait, done, free].

1. Which markings are reachable from m by firing one transition once?
2. Which transitions are enabled at these new markings?
3. Which terminal markings are reachable from m?

Exercise 3.8 How must we adjust the structure or the marking of the Petri net in figure 3.14 if there are three specialists?

3.5.2 Example: Traffic Lights

A traffic light has three possible states: red, green, and orange. The light proceeds through these states in a fixed order. A traffic light is a system that can be modeled as a transition system (see exercise 1.14). Figure 3.15 shows that we can also model a traffic light as a Petri net.

A place of the Petri net in figure 3.15 corresponds to a state of the traffic light. Each transition represents a possible state transition. In the initial marking, which is depicted in figure 3.15, there is one token in place red, indicating that the traffic light is red. If each of the transitions rg, go, and or fires once, we are back in the initial marking.

Question 3.13 Figure 3.15 depicts one traffic light. How to model *k* traffic lights?

There are two obvious choices to model *k* traffic lights. First, one can distribute *k* tokens over the places in figure 3.15. Each token then represents the state of one traffic light. Second, one can copy the Petri net in figure 3.15 *k* times. Figure 3.16 shows two copies of the traffic light. The main difference between these solutions is shown when we consider the identity of each traffic light. Consider, for example, figure 3.15 with three tokens in place red, two tokens in place green, and one token in place orange. Although six traffic lights can be modeled this way, it is not clear which of the six traffic lights are red, green, or orange. By copying figure 3.15 six times and renaming

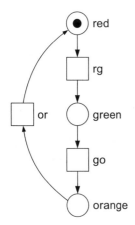

Figure 3.15
A Petri net modeling a traffic light.

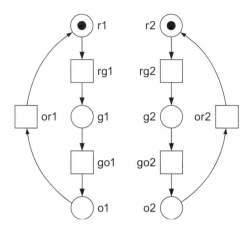

Figure 3.16
A Petri net model of two independent traffic lights.

the nodes, we also model six traffic lights. In this Petri net, however, there are $\frac{6!}{3!2!1!} = 60$ possible markings with three traffic lights in state red, two traffic lights in state green, and one traffic light in state orange. This shows that the second solution is more precise, because the different traffic lights can be distinguished.

Consider the situation in which there are two traffic lights at the crossing of two one-way roads. They have to work in such a way that there is always at least one red light; that is, at most one traffic light is green or orange. This situation cannot be modeled by copying figure 3.15, because the two traffic lights have to work in such a way that there is always at least one red light. To make sure that there is always at least one red traffic light, we add a special control place x to figure 3.16. Figure 3.17 depicts the resulting model.

When a traffic light turns green, the token in place x is removed. From that moment on, the other traffic light can no longer turn green. Place x holds a token only when both traffic lights are red.

Question 3.14   In which respect does the model in figure 3.17 fail?

If both traffic lights are red, it is not determined which of them will turn green. There is a nondeterministic choice in this case: either transition rg1 or transition rg2 fires.

Exercise 3.9   Repair the model in figure 3.17 such that, after the first traffic light turns red, only the second traffic light can turn green, and vice versa.

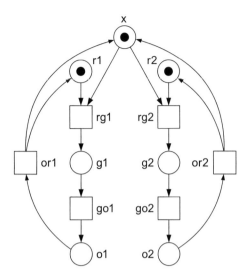

Figure 3.17
Two traffic lights with control place x.

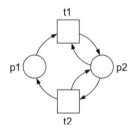

Figure 3.18
The Petri net of exercise 3.1.

3.6   Test Yourself

3.6.1   Solutions to Exercises

3.1   Figure 3.18 depicts the Petri net.

3.2

1. We obtain $P = \{p1, p2\}$, $T = \{t1, t2, t3\}$, and $F = \{(p1, t1), (t1, p2), (p2, t1), (p2, t3),$ $(p2, t2), (t2, p1), (p1, t2)\}$.

2. We obtain the following presets and postsets: ${}^{\bullet}t1 = \{p1, p2\}$, $t1^{\bullet} = \{p2\}$, ${}^{\bullet}t2 = \{p1, p2\}$, $t2^{\bullet} = \{p1\}$, ${}^{\bullet}t3 = \{p2\}$, and $t3^{\bullet} = \emptyset$.

Table 3.2
Marking of the Petri Net in Figure 3.9

Place	Number of tokens
p1	3
p2	1
p3	0
p4	0

3.3
1. We can represent the marking of the Petri net as shown in table 3.2.
2. Transition t1 is enabled, because each of the input places p1 and p2 holds at least one token. Transition t2, in contrast, is not enabled, because input place p3 is empty.

3.4   Transition t1 is enabled if there is at least one token in each of its input places p1 and p2. The same applies to transition t2. Transition t3 is enabled if there is at least one token in its input place p2.

3.5   In the initial marking depicted in figure 3.10, all input places of transition t contain at least one token. Transition t can fire, which leads to the marking depicted in figure 3.19.

In this marking, transition t is still enabled. It can fire again, yielding the marking in figure 3.20. In this marking, transition t is no longer enabled.

3.6
1. All three transitions are enabled. If more than one transition is enabled, it is not clear which of these transitions will fire. A nondeterministic choice needs to be made.
2. If transition t1 fires, then place p1 is empty and place p2 contains one token.
3. If transition t2 fires, then place p2 is empty and place p1 contains one token.
4. If transition t3 fires, then place p2 is empty and place p1 contains one token.
5. The following markings are reachable: [p1, p2] (i.e., the initial marking), [p2] (i.e., the marking after the firing of transition t1), [p1] (i.e., the marking after the firing of transition t2), [ ] (i.e., the marking after the firing of transition t3 in marking [p2]), and [p1] (i.e., the marking after the firing of transition t3 in the initial marking [p1, p2]). Markings [p1] and [ ] are the reachable terminal markings from initial marking m.

3.7
1. Only transition start is enabled at marking m: there is one token in place free (the specialist is free) and three tokens in place wait (there are waiting patients). Hence, transition start can fire, resulting in marking $m' = [2 \cdot \text{wait}, \text{inside}, \text{done}, \text{busy}]$.
2. After the firing of transition start, transition change is enabled, because there is a token in place busy and a token in place inside. Transition end is not enabled, because

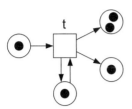

Figure 3.19
A Petri net showing that Transition t has fired but is still enabled.

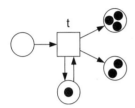

Figure 3.20
A Petri net showing that after transition t has fired again, it is no longer enabled.

place docu is empty. Transition start is also not enabled, because place free is empty. Transition change is, therefore, the only enabled transition.

3. Transitions start, change, and end will keep firing subsequently until all three patients are processed. At that moment, the specialist is in state free again, and all patients are in state done. Only one terminal marking $m' = [4 \cdot \text{done}, \text{free}]$ is, therefore, reachable.

3.8   If there are three specialists, we must take care that the three places free, busy, and docu together always contain exactly three tokens. Each of these tokens represents the state of one of the three specialists. As a consequence, the structure of the model does not have to be adjusted. In the initial marking, we must add two tokens to place free. However, in case there are two tokens in place busy and in place inside, there is no relation between these two sets of tokens. That means there is no explicit relation between a particular specialist and a particular patient, because in a Petri net tokens cannot be distinguished.

3.9   To ensure that the two traffic lights turn green in turn, we must add an additional place y. The idea is to model which traffic light must turn green next. There is a token in place x (place y) if the first (second) light has to turn green. Figure 3.21 depicts the adjusted model.

3.6.2   Further Exercises
Exercise 3.10   Explain the terms "enabled transition," "firing of a transition," "reachable marking," "terminal marking," and "nondeterministic choice" for Petri nets.

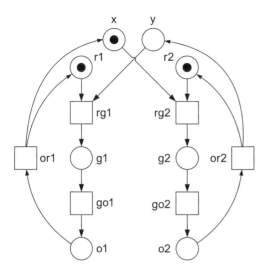

Figure 3.21
A Petri net model of two alternating traffic lights.

Exercise 3.11 Draw the Petri net system (P, T, F, m_0), which is defined as $P = \{p1, \dots, p7\}$, $T = \{t1, \dots, t6\}$, $F = \{(p1, t1), (p2, t2), (p3, t3), (p4, t1), (p4, t4), (p5, t5), (p6, t6),$ $(p7, t4)$, $(t1, p2), (t2, p3), (t3, p1), (t3, p4), (t4, p5), (t5, p6), (t6, p4),$ $(t6, p7)\}$, and $m_0 = [p1, p4, p7]$.

Exercise 3.12 Consider the Petri net system in figure 3.22.

1. Formalize this net as a quadruplet (P, T, F, m_0).
2. Give the preset and the postset of each transition.
3. Which transitions are enabled at m_0?
4. Give all reachable markings.
5. What are the reachable terminal markings?
6. Is there a reachable marking in which we have a nondeterministic choice?
7. Does the number of reachable markings increase or decrease if we remove (1) place p1 and its adjacent arcs and (2) place p3 and its adjacent arcs?

Exercise 3.13 Consider the Petri net system in figure 3.23.

1. Formalize this net as a quadruplet (P, T, F, m_0).
2. Give the preset and the postset of each transition.
3. Which transitions are enabled at m_0?
4. Give all reachable markings.
5. What are the reachable terminal markings?

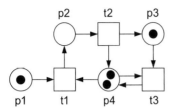

Figure 3.22
The Petri net system of exercise 3.12.

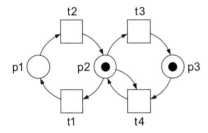

Figure 3.23
The Petri net system of exercise 3.13.

6. Is there a reachable marking in which we have a nondeterministic choice?

7. Does the number of reachable markings increase or decrease if we remove place p1 and its adjacent arcs?

Exercise 3.14   The firing of a transition t at marking m yields a successor marking m'. Function $m'(p)$ in definition 3.10 defines the effect of transition t on a place p. It is any one of $m(p) + 1$, $m(p) - 1$, or $m(p)$. Explain when each of the three effects occurs and formalize this by completing the following equation:

$$m'(p) = \begin{cases} m(p) - 1, & \text{if } \dots, \\ m(p) + 1, & \text{if } \dots, \\ m(p), & \text{if } \dots. \end{cases}$$

Exercise 3.15   Represent the Petri net system in figure 3.12 as a transition system assuming that

1. Each place cannot contain more than one token in any marking; and

2. Each place may contain any natural number of tokens in any marking.

Hint: Describe a marking of the net as a triple (x, y, z) with x specifying the number of tokens in place free, y in place busy, and z in place docu.

Exercise 3.16   A plant produces an item to order by a grinding step (event "g"), followed by a milling step (event "m"). After the milling step, the item is tested. If the test is positive (event "positive"), the item is sent to the customer (event "send") and the production of the next item can start; otherwise (event "negative"), the item is discarded and the production starts again with a grinding step. Items can be in any of the states wait, grinded, milled, to_be_sent, sent, and discarded. Suppose that there are initially two items in state wait. Model this business process as a Petri net system.

Exercise 3.17   Model the following treatment of a patient at a dentist as a Petri net system. If we look at the patient separately, there are five states: the patient is at home (state p_home), the patient is sitting in the waiting room (state p_wait), the patient is treated (state p_treat), the treatment is finished (state p_done), and the patient has left the practice (state p_left). There are four events: the patient enters the practice ("enter"); the treatment starts ("start"); the treatment is documented ("docu"); and the treatment ends ("end"). The dentist can be in three states: d_free, d_busy, and d_docu. There are three respective events: "start," "docu," and "end." The nurse can be either in state n_free or in state n_busy. There are two events in which the nurse is involved: "start" and "docu." Finally, the practice has a secretary. Either she sits at the reception (state s_reception), or she helps the dentist documenting the treatment and writing a prescription (state s_docu). For the documentation, there are two relevant events: "docu" and "end." Furthermore, when a patient enters the practice, the secretary takes care of the reception. Suppose that, initially, there are two patients at home, the dentist and the nurse are in state free, and the secretary is sitting at the reception desk. Hint: Model the patient first and then add the dentist, the secretary, and the nurse.

3.7   Summary

In this chapter, we introduced Petri nets as a formalism to specify process models. A Petri net has a graphlike structure, which is determined by the set of places, the set of transitions, and the flow relation. This structure can be graphically represented using circles, squares, and arcs. The behavior of a Petri net relies on the concept of a marking as a distribution of tokens over the places of the net. A marking corresponds to a state of the business process or information system modeled as the Petri net. Changing the marking of a Petri net is determined by the firing of transitions.

The exercises in this chapter are intended to provide an intuitive understanding of the Petri net basics. Although it is relatively easy to understand a Petri net, it is much more difficult to construct one. For this reason, we shall provide more challenging examples and exercises in later chapters.

After studying this chapter you should be able to:

- Explain the terms "place," "transition," "flow relation," "token," "input place," "output place," "preset," "postset," "enabled," "firing," "consumption," "production," "nondeterminism," "initial marking," "terminal marking," and "reachable marking."
- Model simple systems and business processes as Petri nets.
- Draw the accompanying Petri net system when place set P, transition set T, flow relation F, and m_0 are given and define for a given representation of a Petri net system the place set P, transition set T, flow relation F, and the initial marking m_0.
- Indicate for a given Petri net system which transitions are enabled, which transitions can fire, and which markings are reachable from a given marking.

3.8   Further Reading

In 1962, Carl Adam Petri introduced the central idea of the formalism of Petri nets in his PhD thesis (Petri 1962). This formalism was later named Petri nets. However, the original work of Petri differs from the concepts defined in chapter 3. In particular, the graphical representation of Petri nets was introduced later. For information about Carl Adam Petri, we refer to Brauer and Reisig (2009) who survey Petri's life and work.

Since the 1960s, there has been much research in the area of Petri nets. Once a year, there is an international conference on Petri nets at which researchers present their results. The Web page <http://www.informatik.uni-hamburg.de/TGI/PetriNets> provides material of the theory and application of Petri nets and related topics.

There are many textbooks and articles on Petri nets. Desel and Juhás (2001) provide a less technical introduction to Petri nets. Standard references are the textbooks by Reisig (1985, 2010), the book of Peterson (1981), the overview paper of Murata (1989), and the proceedings of earlier Advanced Courses on Petri Nets (Reisig and Rozenberg 1998; Desel, Reisig, and Rozenberg 2004). Furthermore, there is a well-written textbook about free choice Petri nets by Desel and Esparza (1995). Free choice Petri nets have some structural restrictions. The textbook of Girault and Valk (2002) presents much material about modeling with Petri nets. Recently, Diaz (2009) published a textbook on Petri nets, with a focus on analysis rather than modeling.

4 Application of Petri Nets

We can model the behavior of a system with Petri nets. While this is straightforward in the case of a single traffic light and an elevator with only three and five possible states, respectively, it is more difficult in the case of a complex information system. The goal of this chapter is, therefore, to introduce constructs needed for modeling larger systems with Petri nets. Sometimes such constructs are referred to as "patterns." We illustrate these patterns by constructing and analyzing several Petri nets.

We start with a discussion about the relationship between systems and their Petri net models (section 4.1). We next explain the basic modeling techniques needed for dealing with large systems. A Petri net consists of places, transitions, and tokens, and we show which aspect of a system can be mapped onto a place, a transition, and a token, respectively (section 4.2). We introduce the most common network structures of Petri nets (section 4.3), which cover most of the constructs that occur in systems. In addition to network structures, we present two extensions of Petri nets (place capacities and arc multiplicities) that facilitate the modeling of industrial systems (section 4.4). With the help of an example, we show how complex business processes can be modeled with Petri nets (section 4.5). Finally, we introduce the notion of a reachability graph that represents all reachable markings of a Petri net (section 4.6). This graph is a tool to verify a Petri net.

4.1 Two Claims about Modeling

We start the discussion about modeling by making two claims about the relationship between systems and their models. As discussed in section 2.1, information systems and the business processes they support are (discrete dynamic) systems. The first claim says that there are many Petri nets that can model a given system.

> Claim 1: *There are many ways to model the same system.*

We illustrate this claim with the elevator example of chapter 3. Figure 4.1 depicts the Petri net model of the elevator again. Each place corresponds to a state of the elevator,

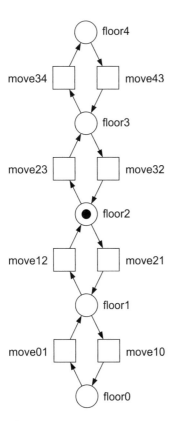

Figure 4.1
A Petri net modeling the elevator.

and each transition corresponds to an event. The state of the elevator is a number that determines the floor at which the elevator is.

The Petri net in figure 4.1 is not the only way to model the elevator. We can, for example, describe the state of the elevator by two numbers, showing how many floors the elevator can go up and how many floors it can go down. In figure 4.1, the elevator is at the second floor; hence, these numbers are 2 and 2, respectively. With a Petri net, we can describe the state of the elevator by the distribution of tokens over two places above and under. The number of tokens in place above and place under corresponds to the number of floors above and under the current floor of the elevator, respectively.

There are two events: the elevator can travel one floor up or one floor down. In the model, if the elevator travels one floor up, one token should be consumed from place above, and one token should be produced in place under. If the elevator travels one

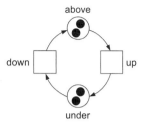

Figure 4.2
A different Petri net modeling the elevator.

floor down, the opposite should happen. We model this with two transitions, up and down, as shown in figure 4.2.

Question 4.1 Can the elevator go higher than the top floor?

If the elevator is at the top floor, place under contains four tokens and place above none. As a result, transition up cannot fire any more.

The Petri net in figure 4.2 behaves exactly like the Petri net in figure 4.1, illustrating that the same system can be modeled in more than one way.

In this book, we do not formalize notions of behavioral equivalence between process models but instead concentrate on interpretation. Different types of behavioral equivalence have been defined in the literature—for example, strong bisimulation (Park 1981), branching bisimulation (Glabbeek and Weijland 1996), and strong simulation (Milner 1989). These notions are based on the assumption that equivalent process models should be allowed to mimic each other's events. A detailed treatment of these notions is outside the scope of this book. Van Glabbeek (2001, 1993) provides a survey on behavioral equivalence.

In addition to being able to model the same system in different ways, there are several systems that correspond to a given Petri net. This is our second claim.

Claim 2: *Many systems can be modeled in exactly the same way.*

We illustrate this claim with the Petri net in figure 4.3 modeling the changing of the seasons. Its four places model the possible states—that is, the four seasons. The token in place spring shows the actual season. The transitions represent the state transitions; for example, transition t4 represents the transition from state winter to state spring.

The Petri net in figure 4.3 can also model other systems—for example, the activities of an office employee. The office employee is always in a certain state. Each place corresponds to one of the four states: looks_for_document, reads_document, performs_action,

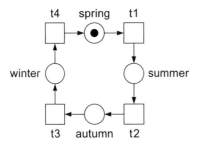

Figure 4.3
A Petri net modeling the four seasons.

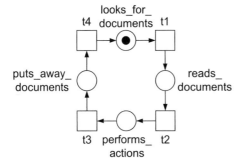

Figure 4.4
A Petri net modeling the activities of an office employee.

and puts_away_document. The office employee goes through these states in a fixed order. If we replace the place labels in figure 4.3 by the corresponding names of the office tasks, we describe the activities of an office employee with the same Petri net. Figure 4.4 depicts the resulting Petri net.

This example illustrates that one Petri net can model two different systems. Because we are not formalizing the notion of equivalence in this book, we focus instead on the interpretation associated with transitions and places. This interpretation can be formalized in terms of *ontologies*. The essential idea of an ontology is that there is a predefined list of terms extended with relations, such as "is a" (e.g., "a Porsche is a car"). Places and transitions can refer to this ontology so that different models can be compared using a common set of terms.

Exercise 4.1 Describe the event modeled by transition t1 in figure 4.3. Do the same for figure 4.4.

There are many other systems that fit with the Petri net in figure 4.3.

Question 4.2   How is this possible?

When we model a system, we represent it in an *abstract way*, thereby omitting those aspects of it that we do not consider *relevant*. The relevant aspects depend on the *task* the system model must perform. Models can be used as a specification of a system to be built and as an abstract system description that is intended to analyze a certain property of an existing system.

We can compare the modeling of a system with making a construction drawing of a house. Before the house is built, the architect first makes a construction drawing. On this construction drawing, many things are recorded—for example, the height, depth, and width of each room. The drawing also abstracts away from many aspects of the house. For example, a line on the construction drawing represents a wall, but the color, thickness, and texture of the wall are not described. Different houses could, therefore, comply with the same construction drawing. For instance, there could be two houses that are built according to the same construction drawing but that are on different sites and are made of different materials.

If we construct the process model of a system as a Petri net, we similarly omit certain aspects. In figure 4.3, for example, we omitted the day when a season changes and the weather. The model in figure 4.4 does not describe the time that the employee needs to perform an activity or what the document is about. A model is a simplification of the system that is being modeled; the model is an *abstraction* of the actual system. By abstracting away from irrelevant details, we obtain a model that describes the essential aspects of a system. Again, the details that are included depend on the purpose of the model.

To summarize claim 2, because we abstract away from certain aspects and details in a model, different systems like the four seasons and the activities of an office employee may be represented by the same Petri net.

Exercise 4.2   A city map is a model of a city that abstracts away from several aspects; for example, the map does not show the color of the buildings. Explain the kinds of abstractions used for representing a road.

While there are many ways to model the same system, and there are many systems that can be modeled in exactly the same way, there is often a clear distinction between models that are correct and models that are not correct. For example, the Petri net in figure 4.1 is not a correct model of a traffic light, and the Petri net in figure 4.3 is not a correct model of an elevator.

As there are many ways to model a given system, we often have to make choices. Do we model an elevator for a building with five floors as in figure 4.1 or as in figure 4.2? For example, we could say that the Petri net in figure 4.2 is more compact

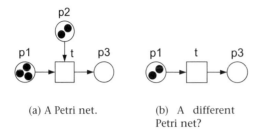

(a) A Petri net.   (b) A different
                            Petri net?

Figure 4.5
The Petri nets of exercise 4.3.

than the net in figure 4.1, because it does not represent every floor by a separate place. However, in figure 4.1, we can better recognize the five floors. Each modeling decision has advantages and disadvantages. The Petri net in figure 4.2 is more flexible, because we can change the number of floors without having to change the network structure of the Petri net; we just add or remove tokens such that their total number corresponds to the number of floors. Another advantage is that the model in figure 4.2 is more compact, but the relationship between the elevator system and its model is less obvious.

The quality of a model depends on, among other things, its simplicity, its size, and its comprehensibility; however, the quality of a model is hard to measure. As a matter of fact, the choice to model something in a particular way is often subjective and depends on the taste and the experience of the designer.

Exercise 4.3   A student wants to simplify the Petri net in figure 4.5(a) to the net in figure 4.5(b). Is this allowed?

To summarize claim 1, there are many ways to model a system correctly as a Petri net, and it is hard to judge which model is preferable. There are no strict rules that lead to the best modeling; instead, we provide modeling guidelines.

4.2   Modeling with Petri Nets

A Petri net consists of places, transitions, and tokens. When we model a system as a Petri net, we must decide whether a certain aspect or part of the system should be represented as a place, as a transition, or as a token. A certain aspect that we may want to model can be so complex that we cannot represent it as a place, a transition, or a token, but only as a combination of these modeling elements.

Example 4.3 To model a production system as a Petri net, we must represent products, machines, persons, and information flows. We must make certain choices; for example, do we model a machine as a token, a place, a transition, or a combination of these elements?

Example 4.4 Modeling the department of a hospital as a Petri net requires the representation of patients, doctors, operating rooms, drugs, and information flows. Do we represent a patient as a token, a place, a transition, or a combination of these elements?

To answer such questions, we discuss in this section the roles that tokens, places, and transitions can play.

4.2.1 The Role of a Token

A token can model various things. In the examples presented so far, a token represented a patient and a specialist but also a state of a traffic light. A token can play one or more of the following roles:

• A *physical object*—for example, a product, a part, a drug, or a person;
• An *information object*—for example, a message, a signal, or a report;
• A *collection of objects*—for example, a truck with products, a warehouse with parts, or an address file;
• An *indicator of a state*—for example, the indicator of the state in which a business process is or the state of an object, such as a traffic light; and
• An *indicator of a condition*: the presence of a token indicates whether a certain condition is fulfilled.

We can look at the role of a token in a Petri net in several ways. Consider, for example, the business process of a specialist treating patients from chapter 3, as presented in figure 4.6.

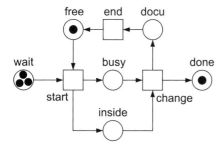

Figure 4.6
A Petri net modeling the business processes of a specialist.

We can view each token as a physical object. A token in places wait, inside, and done represents a patient. A token in places free, busy, and docu represents the specialist. We can also interpret the tokens as indicators of states. The token in place free shows the state of the specialist, and a token in place wait represents the state of a patient. Finally, we can view the token in place free as an indicator that the condition "specialist is free" is fulfilled.

4.2.2 The Role of a Place

Places may contain tokens. The role of a place in the network structure of a Petri net is, therefore, strongly connected with the tokens it can contain. A place can model:

- A *communication medium*—for example, a telephone line, a middleman, or a communication network;
- A *buffer*—for example, a depot, a queue, or a post bin;
- A *geographic location*—for example, a place in a warehouse, in an office, or in a hospital; and
- A *possible state or state condition*—for example, the floor where an elevator is or the condition that a specialist is available.

If a token represents a physical object or an information object (or a collection of one or both of them), the places of such tokens represent a medium, a buffer, or a geographic location. If the token is an indicator of a state, then the set of places where this token can be corresponds to its possible states. If a token indicates whether a condition is fulfilled, then the place of such a token represents a condition.

As a consequence, we can see the role of the places in figure 4.6 in different ways, depending on the way in which we interpret the role of the tokens. For example, if the tokens in places wait, inside, and done play the role of patients, then the places represent geographic locations; that is, they show where a patient is. We can also see place wait as a buffer, because the tokens in this place form a queue. Furthermore, we can see places wait, inside, and done as possible states of patients, whereas places free, busy, and docu represent the possible states of the specialist. The same places can represent conditions. An example of this is place busy, which can represent the condition "the specialist is busy."

Exercise 4.4 A place p can model (1) a medium, (2) a buffer, (3) a geographic location, (4) a state, or (5) a condition. What can we say in each of these five cases about the tokens in place p?

4.2.3 The Role of a Transition

Places are the passive elements of a Petri net. The tokens in a place represent a part of the state of the net, but a place cannot change the state. Transitions, in contrast, are the active elements of Petri nets. When a transition fires, the state of the net changes. The role of a transition is, therefore, to represent:

• An *event*—for example, starting an operation, the death of a patient, a season change, or the turning of a traffic light from red to green;
• A *transformation of an object*—for example, repairing a product, updating a database, or stamping a document; and
• A *transport of an object*—for example, transporting goods or sending a file.

In figure 4.6, the transitions represent events. We can also view transitions start and change as transformations: waiting patients are first transformed into patients who are inside the treatment room and then to patients who are done.

Exercise 4.5 Describe the role of the tokens, places, and transitions in figure 4.7.

4.2.4 Modeling Guideline
We can summarize the possible roles of tokens, places, and transitions with the following modeling guideline:

We represent events as transitions, and we represent states as places and tokens.

We represent the evolving states of a system by the distribution of tokens over the places. Each token in a place is part of the state. A token can model a physical object, information, or a combination of the two, but it can also model the state of an object

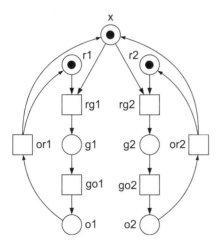

Figure 4.7
A Petri net modeling two traffic lights.

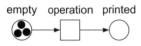

Figure 4.8
A model in which the making of a punch card happens instantaneously.

Figure 4.9
A model in which the making of a punch card does not happen instantaneously.

or a condition. We illustrate with an example how this guideline can help to design a Petri net.

A hospital has a machine to make punch cards. A punch card is a plastic card that contains the name, address, and date of birth of a patient. The information system of the hospital is connected to the punch card machine. This machine takes an empty punch card and prints the data of a patient on it. It can process only one punch card at a time, and the printing of a punch card takes time.

If we try to identify the states and events in this example, the first thought could be that every punch card can be in states empty (or unprocessed) and printed. The operation performed by the punch card machine is an event. This leads to the Petri net in figure 4.8.

However, making a punch card takes time. For this reason, we do not model it as an atomic event but instead distinguish a third state, in_operation. The events that we have to distinguish take care of the transition from state empty to in_operation and of the transition from state in_operation to printed. We call these events "start" and "stop." If we model the states as places and the events as transitions, we obtain the Petri net in figure 4.9.

Question 4.5 In which respect does the model in figure 4.9 fail?

According to the specification, the punch card machine can make only one punch card at a time, but, in figure 4.9, place in_operation can contain more than one token. We had the same problem with the X-ray machine example in section 3.1 and solved it by explicitly representing the state of the X-ray machine in the model. We can solve the punch card machine example in the same way. The machine can be in states free and busy. Event "start" takes care of the transition from free to busy, and event "stop" takes care of the transition from busy to free. In this way, we obtain the Petri net in figure 4.10.

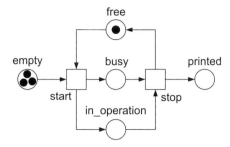

Figure 4.10
A Petri net modeling the punch card machine.

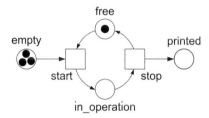

Figure 4.11
Places busy and in_operation can be merged.

Places free and busy represent the states of the machine, but we can also interpret these places as conditions. For example, a token in place free states that the condition "the machine is free" holds. Places empty, in_operation, and printed represent the states of the punch cards, but we can also see them as buffers or geographic locations.

If the machine is busy, a punch card is in operation, and vice versa. Consequently, the states busy and in_operation always occur together. Places busy and in_operation either contain one token each or are both empty. The number of tokens in these two places is always the same. For this reason, we can merge these two places into one place in_operation; see figure 4.11. A token in this place then states that the machine is in state busy, and the punch card is in state in_operation.

In the examples presented so far, we have described the states first and then tracked down the relevant events. One can also start by modeling the events, because states and events are closely related. In one system, the emphasis can be on the events, and, in another system, it can be on the states.

In example 4.3, we asked whether it is best to model a machine in a production system as a token, a place, a transition, or a combination thereof. In the case of the punch card machine, we cannot model the machine as a token, a place, or a transition. We must model it as a Petri net, as shown in figures 4.10 and 4.11.

Exercise 4.6   An elevator connects two floors. Each floor has a button to call the elevator if it is elsewhere. Pressing the call button at a floor has no effect if the elevator is already at this floor. The elevator contains a departure button. Pressing the departure button will cause the elevator to move to the other floor. Model this system as a Petri net system. Explain the choices you made.

4.3   Typical Network Structures

Places and transitions in a Petri net are connected by arcs. The way in which these nodes are connected determines the behavior of the network. It is, therefore, useful to take a closer look at several typical network structures.

In general, transitions represent events. The way in which transitions are connected determines the order in which they can fire. Let us assume that there are three events: x, y, and z. We discuss typical network structures to state that:

1. Event y happens after event x.
2. Event x and event y take place concurrently (at the same time or in any order).
3. Event x takes place before the concurrent events x and y happen.
4. Event z takes place after the concurrent events x and y have happened.
5. Event y or event z takes place after event x has happened.

4.3.1   Causality

Causality is a relationship between two events in a system that must take place in a certain order. In a Petri net, we may represent this relationship by two transitions connected through an intermediate place, as shown in figure 4.12.

4.3.2   Concurrency and Synchronization

Concurrency (i.e., parallelism) is an important feature of (information) systems. In a concurrent system, several events can occur simultaneously. For example, several users may access an information system like a database at the same time. If two transitions in a Petri net are not directly connected with each other, such as in figure 4.13, concurrency is possible.

In the model shown in figure 4.13, transitions x and y can fire independently of each other; that is, there is no causal relationship between the firing of x and of y. If

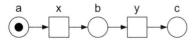

Figure 4.12
Causality: Transition y can fire only after transition x has fired.

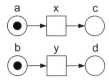

Figure 4.13
Concurrency: Transitions x and y occur simultaneously.

transitions x and y represent events, it is possible that these events happen in arbitrary order. This explicit modeling of concurrency is another advantage of using Petri nets as a process model. Transition systems, in contrast, cannot explicitly model concurrency.

Question 4.6 In figure 4.13, there are two concurrent transitions. Now assume that there are k concurrent transitions and that figure 4.13 denotes the case $k = 2$. How many markings are reachable for an arbitrary k? There is one initial marking and one terminal marking. How many different transition sequences lead from the initial marking to the terminal marking?

In figure 4.13, there are four possible markings, and there are two possible transition sequences (transition x followed by transition y and transition y followed by transition x). For an arbitrary k, there are 2^k reachable states and $k!$ possible transition sequences. For example, if $k = 10$, then there are $2^{10} = 1,024$ reachable states and $10! = 3,628,800$ possible transition sequences. If $k = 20$, then there are $2^{20} = 1,048,576$ reachable states and $20! = 2,432,902,008,176,640,000$ possible transition sequences. This hypothetical Petri net model shows how Petri nets can compactly represent concurrent systems without directly enumerating all possible combinations of transition sequences.

Exercise 4.7 A personal computer system consists of a tower and a screen. The screen and the tower can be turned on and off using a switch.

1. Model the process of switching the screen and the tower on and off as a Petri net.
2. Adjust this model in such a way that the screen can only be turned on after the tower has been turned on.

To model an event that occurs before two (or more) concurrent events, we must *split* the flow of tokens into two (or more) branches. This can be modeled as a Petri net using a transition with one input place and two (or more) output places. Figure 4.14 illustrates the construction.

With network structures, such as those shown in figures 4.13 and 4.14, we can model concurrency. In concurrent models, there is often a need for *synchronization*. We can

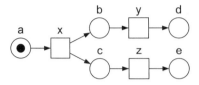

Figure 4.14
AND-split: Transition x occurs before the concurrent transitions y and z.

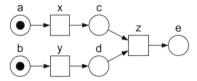

Figure 4.15
Synchronization: Transition z occurs after the concurrent transitions x and y.

model synchronization in a Petri net as a transition with at least two input places. In figure 4.15, transition z has two input places and can only fire after transitions x and y have fired. Assume that transitions x and y represent two concurrent production steps. Transition z can then represent an assembly step that can take place only after the results of the two previous production steps are available.

To illustrate the concepts of causality, concurrency, and synchronization, we model an IT project as a Petri net. A hospital has an outdated information system to support the financial administration. To replace the current information, the hospital starts a large automation project. At the start of the project, the functional requirements are collected. Next, the required equipment (hardware) and, at the same time, the required software is purchased. When the hardware and the software have been acquired, the information system can be integrated. After testing the information system, the project is finished.

We derive from the description that there are seven activities: (1) "start project," (2) "determine requirements," (3) "purchase hardware," (4) "purchase software," (5) "integration," (6) "test" and (7) "end project."

There are several causal relationships between these seven activities. As an example, there is a causal relationship between "start project" and "determine requirements": after the project has started, the requirements are determined. Furthermore, the purchase of hardware and software takes place concurrently. Finally, there is synchronization: the integration can start only after the hardware and the software have been deployed. We can model each of the seven activities as a transition. By using the structures in figures 4.12, 4.13, and 4.15, we obtain the Petri net in figure 4.16.

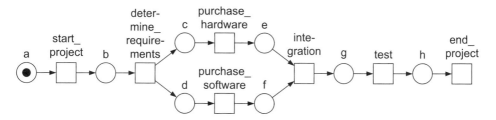

Figure 4.16
A Petri net of an automation project.

This example illustrates how we can apply Petri nets for modeling projects. Activities are represented as transitions, and places express the temporal dependencies between the various activities.

Exercise 4.8 We can consider the building of a house as a project. The main activities are "start project," "arrange building license," "make foundation," "make frames," "make roof," "build walls," "install roof," and "end of project." Model this building project as a Petri net.

Question 4.7 We showed how to model that transitions $x_1, x_2, \ldots, x_k$ can be executed in any order. How to model that these k transitions should all happen at the same time?

If transitions $x_1, x_2, \ldots, x_k$ should happen synchronously, we must merge them into a single transition.

4.3.3   Mutual Exclusion
In many systems, there are safety requirements of the following kind: after event x, either event y or event z happens. Events y and z, thus, exclude each other. This safety requirement is known as *mutual exclusion*. Figure 4.17 shows an example.

If transition x fires, then transitions y and z are enabled, but only one of them will fire. At that moment, a *choice* has to be made. Because this choice is not predetermined, it is an example of a nondeterministic choice—a concept we already introduced in section 3.3.

Exercise 4.9 In which markings do transitions x and y in figure 4.18 require a non-deterministic choice to be made?

Mutual exclusion can be used to model the situation of two traffic lights on a crossing. When both traffic lights are red, the next step is for only one of them to turn green.

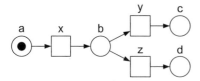

Figure 4.17
Mutual exclusion of transitions y and z.

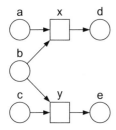

Figure 4.18
Transitions x and y exclude each other.

Figure 4.7 depicts this situation. If both traffic lights are red; that is, if each of the places r1, r2, and x contains a token, transition rg1 and transition rg2 are enabled, and a nondeterministic choice must be made. In this model, it is possible that the first traffic light turns green over and over again, and the second traffic light always remains red. The converse is also possible. By allowing one traffic light to turn green over and over again, the other traffic light is not treated "fairly." In figure 3.21, we adjusted the model in figure 4.7 such that the two traffic lights turn green in turn.

4.4   Additional Model Constructs

In section 4.3, we introduced typical network structures for Petri nets. These structures cover the most frequently used structures of business processes and information systems. The aim of this section is to present two additional modeling concepts. First, we show how we can ensure that a place of a Petri net does not contain more than a specified number of tokens. Afterward, we introduce a concept that allows a transition to consume multiple tokens from an input place and to produce multiple tokens in an output place.

4.4.1   Place Capacities
When modeling a system, we often must deal with capacities. For example, only one patient may be in an X-ray room at a time, and a desk employee can only serve one

patient at a time. To represent these capacities in the Petri net model of the system, we need to guarantee that a place p cannot contain more than a number n of tokens in any reachable marking. That means, if place p already contains n tokens at a certain marking m, then no transition having place p in its postset must be enabled at m. If this condition holds, we say that place p has a *capacity* of n tokens. We have encountered the concept of a place capacity several times—for example, the X-ray machine in figure 3.6 and the punch card machine in figure 4.10.

Consider again the Petri net of a punch card machine in figure 4.10. To ensure that this model can make only one punch card at a time, we had to explicitly model the two states the punch card machine can be in as places free and busy. We explained that only one of these places is necessary; see figure 4.11. Through this construction, we can impose an upper limit on the number of tokens that a certain place may contain. In figure 4.11, place in_operation holds at most one token for the given initial marking; that is, this place has a capacity of one. In the example of the X-ray machine in section 3.1, the sum of the tokens in places before and after is limited to one.

The following example illustrates how to ensure a place capacity. A car manufacturer buys fuel injection pumps from a supplier. To reduce the warehouse space, at most three pumps are in stock. From the viewpoint of the pumps, two events are important: a pump is either delivered or built in a car. This leads to three states: not_delivered, in_stock, and built_in. Figure 4.19 depicts the accompanying Petri net.

The number of tokens in place in_stock corresponds to the number of pumps in stock. In figure 4.19, it is possible that the supplier delivers too many pumps, thus resulting in more than three tokens in place in_stock. To prevent such overaccumulation of pumps, we add an additional place, free. The construction works as follows. Every transition that consumes one token from place in_stock has to produce one token in place free. Likewise, every transition that produces one token in place in_stock has to consume one token from place free. If, in the initial marking, the sum of tokens in places in_stock and free is equal to the capacity of place in_stock (i.e., three tokens), this construction guarantees that place in_stock will never hold more than three tokens. Figure 4.20 illustrates this construction.

We can verify that the warehouse cannot contain more than three pumps according to this construction. The sum of the tokens in places in_stock and free is always equal to three. If transition deliver fires, a token is consumed from place free and a token is

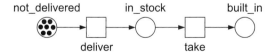

Figure 4.19
A Petri net without place capacity: The supplier may deliver too many pumps.

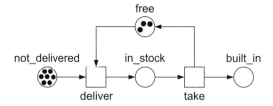

Figure 4.20
A Petri net with place capacity: Place in_stock has a capacity of three tokens.

produced in place in_stock, but the sum of tokens in these two places is not changed. As the sum is also not changed if transition take fires, we conclude that the maximum number of tokens in place in_stock is equal to three.

Exercise 4.10 A hospital employs four cardiologists who can be either in state active or in state stand-by. A cardiologist who is stand-by can be called at any moment and then becomes active. After some time, this cardiologist returns to the state stand-by. In the start state, there are two cardiologists active and two stand-by.

1. Model the business process around these four cardiologists as a Petri net.
2. How should the model be adjusted if at most two cardiologists can be active?

Exercise 4.11 The Brisbane CityCat system is an urban transportation system using catamarans to quickly move people along the Brisbane River. Let us assume that there are four stops named *A*, *B*, *C*, and *D*. CityCats move from one stop to the other, first upstream (*A,B,C,D*) and then downstream (*D,C,B,A*). There are 10 CityCats. Initially, all CityCats are in a dedicated harbor denoted by *X*. Depending on the workload, CityCats are put into service (moved from harbor *X* to stop *A*) or taken out of service (moved from stop *A* to harbor *X*). The number of CityCats in service may, therefore, vary between 0 and 10. Possible moves of a CityCat are *X,A,B,C,D,C,B,A,B,C,D,C,B,A,X*; *X,A,B,C,D,C,B,A,B,C,D,C,B,A,B,C,D,C,B,A,X*; or *X,A,B,C,D,C,B,A,X*. A CityCat can only turn at stop *D*; that is, a move *X,A,B,A,X* or *X,A,B,C,B,A,X* is not possible. The stops have a capacity of one; that is, only one CityCat can dock at a particular stop at a time. The capacity of the river is large enough to fit all CityCats in between any two stops. Model the Brisbane CityCat system as a Petri net (including its initial marking). There is no need to distinguish individual CityCats.

4.4.2 Arc Multiplicities

In the Petri nets we have seen so far, at most one arc connected a place to a transition, and vice versa. From now on, we may have more than one arc from a place to a transition or from a transition to a place. For this reason, we speak about the *multiplicity*

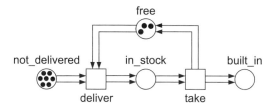

Figure 4.21
A Petri net with arc multiplicities.

of an arc. If there are five arcs from a place to a transition, we consider this as an arc whose multiplicity is five. We illustrate this with the car manufacturer example from section 4.4.1; see figure 4.20.

The car manufacturer improves its production process and now always takes two pumps from stock. To avoid disrupting the production process, the supplier must deliver two pumps at once. The warehouse capacity is, however, still restricted to three pumps. We model the adjusted business process as a Petri net using arc multiplicities, as illustrated in figure 4.21.

As in figure 4.20, each token in places not_delivered, in_stock, and built_in represents a pump. What has changed from figure 4.20 is that all arcs now have a multiplicity of two. The multiplicity of an arc indicates how many tokens are consumed or how many tokens are produced when the associated transition fires; for example, if transition deliver in figure 4.21 fires, two tokens are consumed from each of the input places not_delivered and free. Accordingly, transition deliver is only enabled if there are at least two tokens in each of its input places. Furthermore, transition deliver produces two tokens in output place in_stock.

We formalize arc multiplicities by extending the weight function w that was introduced in definition 3.10. This function assigns to each arc a natural number greater than zero, its *multiplicity*. Formally, we can define the weight function w of a Petri net (P, T, F) by

$$w : F \to \mathbb{N} \setminus \{0\}.$$

In the example in figure 4.21, we have $w((\text{not\_delivered}, \text{deliver})) = 2$ and $w((\text{deliver}, \text{in\_stock})) = 2$. In the examples considered so far, the weight function assigns by default the value 1 to each arc.

The weight function w maps each arc of the flow relation F to a natural number greater than zero. Function w can be extended in a straightforward manner such that pairs that do not exist in F are mapped to zero (as described in definition 3.10). Formally, this extended function w is defined by

$$w : (P \times T) \cup (T \times P) \to \mathbb{N}$$

where $w((x,y)) > 0$ if $(x,y) \in F$ and $w((x,y)) = 0$ if $(x,y) \notin F$, for all $(x,y) \in (P \times T) \cup (T \times P)$.

With this extended weight function, we can define the behavior of a Petri net with arc multiplicities. A transition t is enabled at marking m if every input place p of t contains at least as many tokens as the multiplicity $w((p,t))$ of the arc from p to t is. An enabled transition t consumes from each input place p as many tokens as indicated by the multiplicity $w((p,t))$, and it produces in each output place p' as many tokens as indicated by the multiplicity $w((t,p'))$.

Definition 4.8 (Petri net with arc multiplicities)   A *Petri net with arc multiplicities* (P, T, F, w) consists of a Petri net (P,T,F) and a weight function $w : (P \times T) \cup (T \times P) \to \mathbb{N}$. A transition $t \in T$ is *enabled at marking* $m : P \to \mathbb{N}$ if and only if for all $p \in {}^{\bullet}t, m(p) \geq w((p,t))$. An enabled transition t can *fire* yielding a new marking $m' : P \to \mathbb{N}$, where for all $p \in P$, $m'(p) = m(p) - w((p,t)) + w((t,p))$.

Graphically, we represent an arc multiplicity by either drawing the respective number of arcs between two nodes or by annotating an arc with a natural number representing the multiplicity.

Example 4.9 Consider the Petri net in figure 4.21. Transition deliver is enabled at marking m depicted in figure 4.21. The firing of transition deliver yields a marking m' defined as:

$$m'(\text{not\_delivered}) = m(\text{not\_delivered}) - w((\text{not\_delivered}, \text{deliver}))$$
$$+ w((\text{deliver}, \text{not\_delivered}))$$
$$= 7 - 2 + 0 = 5$$
$$m'(\text{in\_stock}) = m(\text{in\_stock}) - w((\text{in\_stock}, \text{deliver})) + w((\text{deliver}, \text{in\_stock}))$$
$$= 0 - 0 + 2 = 2$$
$$m'(\text{built\_in}) = m(\text{built\_in}) - w((\text{built\_in}, \text{deliver})) + w((\text{deliver}, \text{built\_in}))$$
$$= 0 - 0 + 0 = 0$$
$$m'(\text{free}) = m(\text{free}) - w((\text{free}, \text{deliver})) + w((\text{deliver}, \text{free}))$$
$$= 3 - 2 + 0 = 1.$$

Exercise 4.12 Consider the Petri net system in figure 4.22 with the given initial marking m_0.

1. Which transitions are enabled at m_0?
2. What are the reachable markings from m_0, and which of these markings are terminal markings?

In the case of arc multiplicities, we must adjust the concept of place capacities. For example, in figure 4.21, the arcs from and to place free also have the multiplicity two.

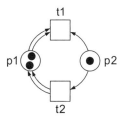

Figure 4.22
The Petri net of exercise 4.12.

To ensure that the sum of tokens in places free and in_stock equals three, transition take must produce as many tokens in place free as it consumes from place in_stock. Likewise, transition deliver must produce as many tokens in place in_stock as it consumes from place free. This way, the sum of tokens in places in_stock and free remains three.

Exercise 4.13 What happens if there is initially an odd number of tokens in place not_delivered as in figure 4.21?

4.5 Example: Language Institute

The goal of this section is to describe how to model a more complex business process as a Petri net.

Consider the business process of a language institute that offers three language courses: English, German, and French. Students need to register before they can join a course. Registered students can choose one of the three courses. Every course has a specific duration, and the number of participating students is limited. At most, 20 students can join the English course; the other courses have a capacity of 10 persons each. If a course is open, students may choose the course. After a course has been started, students who have not yet chosen this course cannot take part any more. Students are not allowed to drop a course once they start. After the course has been finished, a student can decide either to follow another course (without registering again and with the possibility to do the same course again) or to deregister and to leave. To give other students a chance to take part in a language course, students are not allowed to remain in a course. Consequently, if in the new semester a course is opened, the number of participants is zero initially.

Question 4.10 How can we model this business process as a Petri net?

From the description, we identify two objects that we need to model: the life cycle of a student in the language institute and the state of a course. Let us first consider the life cycle of a student in the language institute. Students can be in any of the following states: (1) not yet registered at the language institute (state free); (2) registered (state registered); (3) participant of any of the three courses English, German, and French (states E_student, G_student, and F_student); (4) left a course (state left); and (5) deregistered (state deregistered). A student can register at the language institute (event "register"), choose one of the three courses (events "choose_E", "choose_G", and "choose_F"), leave the respective course (events "leave_E", "leave_G", and "leave_F"), choose a new course (event "new_choice"), and deregister (event "deregister"). We model each state as a place and each event as a transition. A token models the student's state. Figure 4.23 depicts the resulting Petri net. As students can choose between the three courses, we model this by a nondeterministic choice between transitions choose_E, choose_G, and choose_F. Place left collects all students who left a course.

Each course has a maximum number of participants. For the English course, for example, we have to ensure that place E_student in figure 4.23 holds at most 20 tokens; that is, at most 20 students may choose the English course. We achieve this by adding a place maxE, which is initially marked with 20 tokens. Each transition that produces a token in place E_student (i.e., transition choose_E) consumes a token from place maxE. Likewise, each transition that consumes a token from place E_student (i.e., transition leave_E) produces a token in place maxE. That way, the sum of tokens in the two places E_student and maxE is equal to 20 at any marking. We use the same construction for the two other courses.

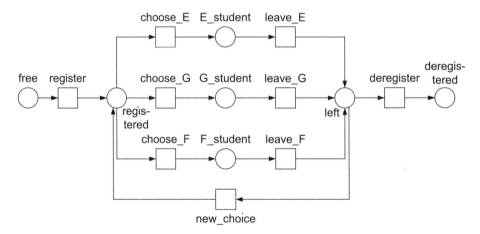

Figure 4.23
The Petri net modeling the states of a student.

Next, we model the states of a course. A course can be in three states: it is open (state open), it is started (state lesson), and it is finished (state holiday). To switch between these three states, we need three events: the course starts (event "start"), it finishes (event "finish"), and it opens again (event "empty"). With three places and three transitions, we can model the life cycle of a course. Figure 4.24 depicts the complete model of the language institute.

According to the specification of the business process, students may only choose a course if the course has not started. For this reason, transition choose_E checks whether the course is still in state E_open (i.e., there must be a token in place E_open). The same construction is used for the German and the French courses. Another requirement is that students who participate in a course cannot remain in that course after it has finished. In figure 4.24, we guarantee that transition empty_E is not enabled until all students have left the course. This is the case if place E_student does not contain any token and consequently place maxE contains 20 tokens. Adding place E_holiday to the input and output places of transition leave_E guarantees that students cannot drop a chosen course before it ends. Again, the same construction has been used for the German and French courses.

Question 4.11   How can we remodel the Petri net in figure 4.24 such that at most 25 students are registered at the same time?

In our model, this means that the sum of tokens in places registered, E_student, G_student, F_student, and left must be less than or equal to 25. We can achieve this easily by adding a place maxR (maximum registrations) that contains initially 25 tokens. Place maxR must be an input place of transition register and an output place of transition deregister. That way, for each newly registered student, we consume a token from place maxR; and for each deregistered student, we produce a token in place maxR. This construction guarantees the required capacity.

Question 4.12   The language institute wants for efficiency reasons to rotate the German and the French course. How must we adjust the Petri net in figure 4.24? (Suppose that initially the German course is offered.)

Because of this requirement, we must make sure that the institute offers the German course first and, after this course has finished, it offers the French course, and so on. To this end, we have to remove arc (empty_G, G_open), because, after the German course is finished and all students have left, the French course must be opened. In addition, we add an arc (empty_G, F_open). Likewise, we remove arc (empty_F, F_open) and add an arc (empty_F, G_open). Finally, we need to remove the token from place F_open.

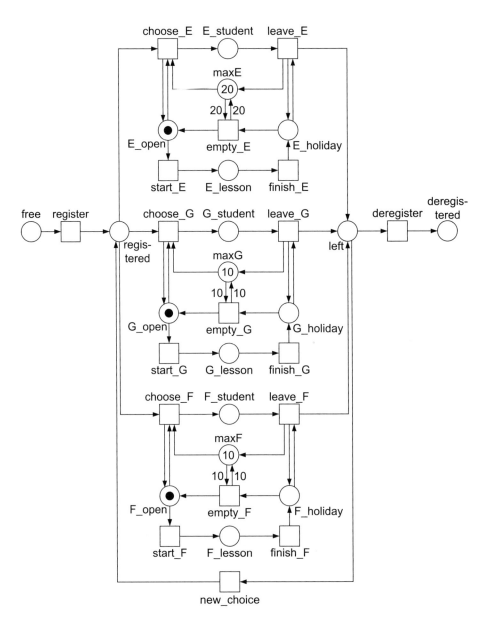

Figure 4.24
The Petri net modeling the whole language institute.

Figure 4.25 shows the two extensions just discussed. The newly added nodes and arcs are highlighted using bold font.

4.6   Reachability Graphs

When we have modeled a system as a Petri net system (P, T, F, m_0), we often want to know more about the behavior of that net. Questions we could ask ourselves include:

- How many markings are reachable?
- Which markings are reachable?
- Are there any reachable terminal markings?

As we know the initial marking m_0 for the given Petri net system, we answer such questions by calculating the set of markings reachable from m_0. We represent this set as a graph—the *reachability graph* of the net. Its nodes correspond to the reachable markings and its edges to the transitions moving the net from one marking to another.

As an illustration, consider again the Petri net system in figure 4.26(a) modeling the four seasons. Figure 4.26(b) depicts the accompanying reachability graph that represents the set of markings that are reachable from the initial marking shown in figure 4.26(a).

Each of the reachable markings is represented as a multiset; that is, a set where the same element may appear multiple times. Multiset [spring] thus represents the marking in figure 4.26(a). The incoming edge without source pointing to this node denotes that this marking is the initial marking. We used the same notation in section 1.4 to highlight the initial state in a state-transition diagram. In addition, we labeled each edge of the reachability graph with the transition that fired in the corresponding marking.

From the reachability graph in figure 4.26(b), we can conclude that the net in figure 4.26(a) has four reachable markings. If a marking m is reachable from the initial marking m_0, then the reachability graph has a path from the start node to the node representing marking m. This path represents a sequence of transitions that have to be fired to reach marking m from m_0. We refer to this transition sequence as a *run*. A run is *finite* if the path and hence the transition sequence is finite. Otherwise, the run is *infinite*. For example, the path from marking [spring] to marking [winter] is a run of the net in figure 4.26(a). We represent this run as $\langle t1, t2, t3 \rangle$. The net in figure 4.26(a) has one infinite run: $\langle t1, t2, t3, t4, t1, \ldots \rangle$.

Figure 4.26(b) does not have terminal markings; that is, at each of the reachable markings, a transition is enabled. The reachability graph for this simple example does not provide new insights, however, for industrial systems with billions of states, reachability graphs are helpful.

For the example of the two traffic lights shown in figure 4.27(a), it is important to know whether a marking in which both traffic lights are green is reachable. We

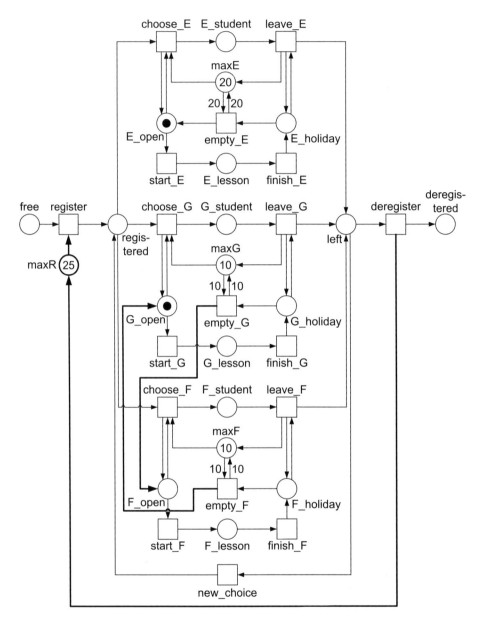

Figure 4.25
The Petri net modeling the extended language institute.

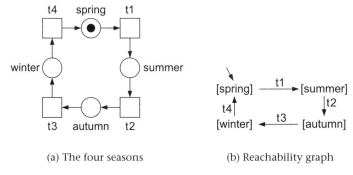

(a) The four seasons   (b) Reachability graph

Figure 4.26
The reachability graph of the four seasons.

can verify this by constructing the accompanying reachability graph, as shown in figure 4.27(b).

We can see from this reachability graph that there is no reachable marking in which both traffic lights are green. Nodes like [g1, g2, x] and [g1, g2] do not occur in figure 4.27(b). We can also see from figure 4.27(b) that the two traffic lights do not have any terminal markings. This reflects the fact that the traffic lights form (like the four seasons) an ongoing (i.e., perpetual) system. Every finite run of figure 4.27(a) can be extended to an infinite run.

Exercise 4.14   Construct the reachability graph of the Petri net system in figure 4.11.

Our discussion shows that we can verify certain properties of a Petri net system by inspecting its reachability graph. For a simple Petri net system, it is easy to construct the accompanying reachability graph, but for more complex nets, reachability graphs can become huge, and it is possible to forget markings. For example, a Petri net system with 100 places in which each place contains at most one token can have 2^{100} reachable markings! Nets of such a size often occur when we model industrial systems. Accordingly, it is good to know that there is an algorithm to construct the reachability graph of a given Petri net system automatically. We can implement this algorithm as a computer program and investigate whether certain markings are reachable and whether there are any terminal markings.

Question 4.13   Consider a Petri net (P, T, F, w) with $P = \{p\}$, $T = \{t\}$, $F = \{(t, p)\}$, and $w((t, p)) = 2$. Assume the initial marking m_0 is empty—that is, $m_0(p) = 0$. Give the reachability graph.

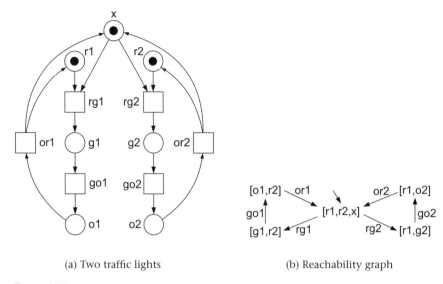

(a) Two traffic lights   (b) Reachability graph

Figure 4.27
The reachability graph of the two traffic lights.

The reachability graph of this simple Petri net has infinitely many nodes. This shows again that Petri nets can represent a complex state space in a compact manner. The nodes are of the form $[2 \cdot k \cdot p]$ where $2 \cdot k$ is some even natural number indicating the number of tokens in p.

As the number of nodes is infinite, we cannot calculate the complete reachability graph of this net. As a consequence, we cannot verify properties of this net by inspecting its reachability graph. Fortunately, it is possible to construct the *coverability graph* (Karp and Miller 1969). This graph is a finite representation of the reachability graph and can also be used for analysis. In chapter 8, we investigate reachability graphs and coverability graphs of Petri nets in more detail. We also show which properties we can verify by inspecting these graphs.

Finally, we want to clarify the relation between the reachability graph of a given Petri net system and the accompanying transition system. The transition system represents the state space of the modeled system, thus representing all possible markings M of the net. The set M contains markings that are reachable from the given initial marking but also markings that are not. As a result, the reachability graph is a *subgraph* of the transition system. By removing all states (together with adjacent transitions) from the transition system that are not reachable from the initial state, we obtain the reachability graph of the net.

4.7   Test Yourself

4.7.1   Solutions to Exercises

4.1   In figure 4.3, transition t1 represents a state transition of the four seasons. The firing of transition t1 corresponds to the season change from spring to summer.

In figure 4.4, transition t1 represents a state transition of the office employee. The firing of transition t1 corresponds to the start of reading a document.

4.2   The roads on the map are drawn much wider than they are in reality. They also have a different color than in reality. Furthermore, the map does not show the materials a road is made of, the condition of a road, and so on.

4.3   If transition t fires, then the effect is in both nets the same: one token is consumed from place p1 and one token is produced in place p3. After transition t has fired twice, it is not enabled in both nets, but there is an important difference: place p1 in figure 4.5(a) contains one token and place p1 in figure 4.5(b) does not. As a token models an object and it is present in only one of these two nets, we cannot replace the net in figure 4.5(a) by the net in figure 4.5(b).

4.4   If place p represents a medium, a buffer, or a geographic location (case 1, 2, or 3), then there can be several tokens in p. We may model a limited capacity of such a place by assigning a maximum number of tokens to it.

If place p models the state of an object, a process, or a system (case 4), then the maximum number of tokens in place p is equal to one; however, if place p represents the states of multiple objects, processes, or systems, then it can hold more than one token.

If place p represents a condition (case 5), then it contains at any moment at most one token. Presence of a token indicates whether or not the condition is fulfilled.

4.5   The token in place r1 shows that the condition "the first traffic light is red" is fulfilled. We can say something similar about the token in place r2. The token in place x shows that the condition "both traffic lights are red" is fulfilled.

We can also interpret the tokens in places r1 and r2 as indicators of the state of the traffic lights. Places r1, g1, and o1 represent the possible states of the first traffic light, whereas places r2, g2, and o2 represent the possible states of the second traffic light. The transitions in figure 4.7 represent switching events.

4.6   The elevator moves between two floors. Hence, it is natural to model each floor as a place (floor1 and floor2) and the elevator as a token in these places. The elevator moves if someone presses the departure button or if someone calls it at a different floor. Transitions dep12 (move from the first to the second floor), dep21 (move from the second to the first floor), call12 (the elevator is at the first floor and called at the second floor), and call21 (the elevator is at the second floor and called at the first

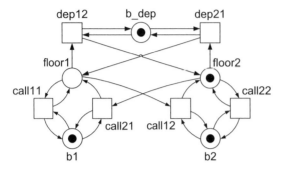

Figure 4.28
The elevator of exercise 4.6.

floor) model these four events. In addition, we need two transitions call11 and call22. They model that someone calls the elevator from its current floor. Places b_dep, b1, and b2 model the three buttons. Each of these places initially contains a token. Figure 4.28 depicts the corresponding Petri net system.

In the initial marking of figure 4.28, the elevator is at the second floor. From the model, we can see that at any marking someone can call the elevator or press the departure button and move to another floor. The role of the three button places is a bit odd in figure 4.28. They always contain one token and do not restrict the firing of transitions at any point in time, because we assume all actions to be atomic. If this was not the case, we would need to model the state of each button as, for example, pressed and not_pressed.

4.7
1. There are four possible events: "the display is turned on," "the display is turned off," "the PC tower is turned on," and "the PC tower is turned off." The state of the whole system is determined by the state of the display and the PC tower; both can be on and off.

Transitions turn_d_on (turn display on), turn_d_off (turn display off), turn_t_on (turn PC tower on), and turn_t_off (turn PC tower off) model the events. Places d_on (display on) and turn_d_off (display off) model the two states of the display, and places t_on (PC tower on) and t_off (PC tower off) model the two states of the PC tower. We thus obtain the model in figure 4.29.

Figure 4.29 consists of two unconnected nets: one for the display and one for the PC tower. As a result, transitions in one net can occur concurrently to transitions in the other net.
2. The events and the states are the same as in (1), but event "the display is turned on" may only happen if the PC tower has been turned on. Figure 4.30 depicts the resulting model.

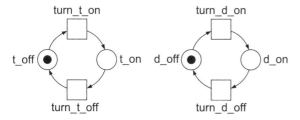

Figure 4.29
A Petri net model showing turning on a display and a PC tower independently of one another.

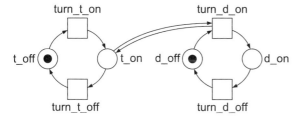

Figure 4.30
A Petri net model showing that turning on the display requires that the PC tower has been turned on first.

The arc from place t_on to transition turn_d_on makes sure that transition turn_d_on is only enabled when there is a token in place t_on and in place d_off. The return arc from transition turn_d_on to place t_on ensures that the firing of transition turn_d_on only reads the token in place t_on (one token is consumed from place t_on and one token is produced in place t_on). Turning on the display does not influence the state of the PC tower.

4.8   From the description, we derive that there are eight activities: "start project," "arrange building license," "make foundation," "make frames," "make roof," "build walls," "install roof," and "end of project." We represent each activity with a transition. Places model the coordination of these activities. There are many dependency relationships between the activities—for example, between "start project" and "arrange building license." We have concurrency, because the roof can be made while the foundation and the frames are made and the walls are built. The frames can be made while the foundation is made. There is also synchronization; for example, the roof can only be installed after the roof of the house has been finished and the walls have been built. With the constructs already illustrated in figures 4.12, 4.13, and 4.15, we can model causality, concurrency, and synchronization. Figure 4.31 depicts the resulting Petri net. As soon as the building license has arrived, three activities can take place

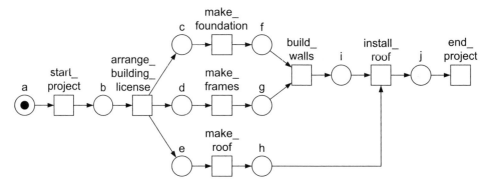

Figure 4.31
The Petri net of exercise 4.8.

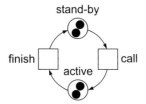

Figure 4.32
A Petri net modeling the states of four cardiologists.

simultaneously: "make foundation," "make frames," and "make roof." The rest of the network is straightforward.

4.9   If there is one token present in each of the places a, b, and c, both transitions are enabled, and there is a nondeterministic choice. If there is only a token in place b, no transition will fire; and if there is a token in place a and a token in place b, but no token in place c, then transition x will fire.

4.10
1. We model the two states active and stand-by of a cardiologist as places active and stand-by. There are two possible events: (1) a cardiologist becomes active, and (2) a cardiologist finishes his job and is again standing by. We model these two events as transitions call and finish. Figure 4.32 depicts the Petri net system modeling the four cardiologists.
2. We can model that at most two cardiologists are active by adding an additional place x. This place ensures that the capacity of place active is at most two; see figure 4.33.

4.11   Figure 4.34 depicts the Petri net. A CityCat can be in the harbor X; in one of the four stops A, B, C, or D; or between stops A and B, B and C, or C and D. We model each

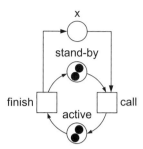

Figure 4.33
A Petri net model: At most two cardiologists can be active at the same time.

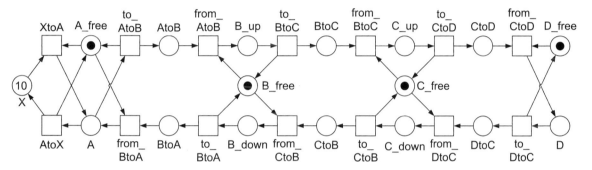

Figure 4.34
A Petri net modeling the Brisbane CityCat system.

state as a place. To distinguish whether a CityCat is moving upstream or downstream, each state between two stops is either upstream or downstream (e.g., AtoB or BtoA). The same distinction holds for stop B and stop C where a CityCat cannot turn (e.g., we have states B_up and B_down). The transitions model the flow of the CityCats. With places A_free, B_free, C_free, and D_free, we guarantee that only one CityCat can dock at a stop at a time. Initially, these places hold a token each; place X initially contains 10 tokens, each representing a CityCat.

4.12
1. The arc multiplicities of (p1, t1), (t2, p1), (p2, t1), and (p2, t2) are two, two, one, and one, respectively. Because place p1 contains two tokens and place p2 one token, we conclude that both transitions are enabled at the initial marking.
2. The initial marking is [2 · p1, p2]. In this marking, transition t1 can fire, yielding the marking [ ]. The firing of transition t2 in the initial marking [2 · p1, p2] leads to a marking [4 · p1]. Markings [ ] and [4 · p1] are terminal markings.

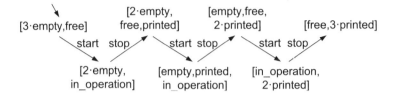

Figure 4.35
The reachability graph of the Petri net system in figure 4.11.

4.13 In this case, we have a terminal marking that contains one token in place not_delivered; that is, the supplier does not deliver one pump.

4.14 Figure 4.35 depicts the reachability graph.

4.7.2 Further Exercises

Exercise 4.15 Explain the terms "causality," "concurrency," "synchronization," "mutual exclusion," "place capacity," "arc multiplicity," and "reachability graph."

Exercise 4.16 When we model a hospital as a Petri net, we must represent patients, doctors, operation rooms, and information flows as places, transitions, and tokens. Accordingly, we must make many choices—for example, the way in which we model a patient. Why is it not sensible to represent a patient as a place or transition?

Exercise 4.17 Consider the following game. A bowl is filled with red and black balls. A move of the game consists of taking two balls out of the bowl without looking at their color. If it turns out that the two balls are of the same color, a black ball should be put back, otherwise a red one. (We assume that players can have extra black balls at their disposal if necessary.) We want to make a model that describes how the content of the bowl changes. The state of the bowl is determined at a certain moment by the number of red and black balls in the bowl.

1. Which events can we distinguish?
2. Model this game as a Petri net system (i.e., give the initial marking).

Exercise 4.18 From a bridge, frogs jump into a stream, nondeterministically choose one of the two banks to swim to, and then hop to the bridge to start over again. A lovely girl picks up every third frog from the stream, kisses the frog, and puts the frog back on the bridge. Model this fairy tale as a Petri net. Suppose that three frogs are initially on the bridge.

Exercise 4.19 Every Petri net with place capacities can be transformed into a Petri net in which each place contains at most one token. The idea of the transformation is to model each place p with capacity $k > 1$ by $k + 1$ places $p_0, \ldots, p_k$. A token in each of these places simulates a marking where place p in the original net contains the number of tokens according to the subscript. As an example, a token in place p_3 simulates three tokens in place p. This transformation is known as unfolding. In addition to unfolding places with capacities, a transition having place p in its preset or postset must be unfolded. Unfold the Petri net system with place capacities depicted in figure 4.20. To simplify the construction, assume that $m_0(\text{not\_delivered}) = 1$ and that the capacity of place in_stock is two (and not three).

Exercise 4.20   Consider the handling of insurance claims at Sunny Side Corp., Australia. Sunny Side distinguishes simple claims and complex claims. The type of the claim is determined in the first step.

For simple claims, Sunny Side carries out two steps independently: it checks the insurance policy of the insured party for validity and retrieves the statement of a local authority. When both results are available, in a next step Sunny Side checks the statement against the policy. If the result is positive, Sunny Side makes a payment to the insured party; if the result is negative, Sunny Side sends a rejection letter.

For complex claims, Sunny Side carries out three steps independently: it checks the insurance policy of the insured party for validity, retrieves the statement of a local authority, and asks for two witness statements. The business process can only proceed if both witness statements are available. Again, when both results are available, in a next step Sunny Side checks the statements of the local authority and witnesses against the policy. If the result is positive, Sunny Side makes a payment to the insured party; if the result is negative, Sunny Side sends a rejection letter.

1. Model this business process as a Petri net.
2. From time to time, Australia has to cope with large fires. As a result, Sunny Side is flooded with claims concerning the fires and the water damage from extinguishing the fires. If more than 150 claims are in the system of Sunny Side (i.e., claims that have been classified but not yet fully processed), the throughput decreases dramatically. Therefore, the management of Sunny Side decided, in such cases, to skip the extended procedure. Instead, only the check against validity of the insurance policy is made for new cases.

Draw a Petri net in which you clearly model the described situation; that is, in the case of more than 150 claims, the short procedure is followed and, in case of fewer cases, the initial procedure is followed. State the initial marking explicitly in your model. Show how the original model needs to be changed.
3. Suppose we want to change the business process of (1) as follows: If there are more than 150 claims in the system, then every new claim is determined to be simple; and if there are less than or equal to 150 claims in the system, a new claim is determined

to be complex. This choice and hence the whole business process *cannot* be modeled as a Petri net. Explain why it is not possible to model this choice by means of place capacities and arc multiplicities.

Exercise 4.21 Consider the following business process for handling traffic offenses. Every offense is registered after arrival. After registration, procedures "judge the traffic offense" and "investigate the history" are started concurrently. In procedure "judge the traffic offense," the traffic offense is classified as either "severe" or "normal." Severe traffic offenses are then temporary judged, and, in a second step, a final judgment is delivered. Normal traffic offenses are judged in one step. Procedure "investigate the history" contains two steps that can be completed in arbitrary order: collect information about earlier traffic offenses and collect information about other offenses committed by the offender. The fine is determined after both procedures are finalized. If the traffic offense is not fined, it will be archived right away; otherwise, a transfer form is sent to the offender and subsequently the traffic offense will be archived.

1. Model this business process as a Petri net.
2. To avoid long processing times, the business process is changed as follows: If more than 100 traffic offenses are processed at the same time (i.e., registered offenses that are not archived yet), every new traffic offense will be processed by an alternative procedure. This procedure contains only one step: the offense is registered and archived. If fewer than 100 offenses are processed at the same time, the original procedure will be followed. Show how the original model needs to be changed.

Exercise 4.22 A factory produces one type of bicycles. The parts (frame, pedal, wheel, and brake) are purchased from various suppliers. The factory needs three assemblies steps to make a bicycle. First, a machine of type B assembles a frame and two pedals into semi-product_1. In the second assembly step, a machine of type A assembles semi-product_1 and two wheels into semi-product_2. In assembly step three, a machine of type B mounts two brakes (front and back) to semi-product_2. After this third assembly step, the bicycle is ready. Currently, the factory has three type-A machines and seven type-B machines. Every machine has a capacity of one.

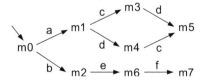

Figure 4.36
The reachability graph of exercise 4.23.

1. Model this business process as a Petri net system. Distinguish between the two types of machines and whether the machines are available or not. Assume that the company has initially four copies of each part.
2. Give a run from the initial marking to a marking where a bicycle has been produced.

Exercise 4.23   Construct a Petri net system that has the reachability graph in figure 4.36.

4.8   Summary

In this chapter, we investigated the relations between systems and business processes and between systems and process models. A process model does not represent all aspects of a system and omits certain aspects that are deemed irrelevant. Consequently, a process model is an abstraction of the system. A process model is always constructed for a particular goal—for example, to serve as a specification of a system to be built or to represent some aspects of an existing system. Before modeling a system, its purpose should be clear, because the purpose of the model determines which aspects of the system are relevant.

We also introduced how a system can be modeled as a Petri net and explained the role of places, transitions, and tokens in a process model. As a guideline, we represent events as transitions and states as places and tokens. The behavior of many systems follows some basic patterns: events are causally ordered, they can be executed concurrently, and so on. To model large systems, we showed how basic constructs can be mapped onto Petri nets. To express more complicated aspects of a system, we extended Petri nets with place capacities and arc multiplicities. As models can become very complex, they should be analyzed. The notion of a reachability graph as a representation of all reachable markings of a net can be used for this purpose.

In chapter 3, we described some advantages of using Petri nets as a modeling formalism. We mentioned the graphical representations, the mathematical foundation, and the more compact and implicit way of modeling. In this chapter, we described another advantage: Petri nets can explicitly model concurrency. In other formalisms, such as transition systems, this is either not possible or added as an afterthought.

After studying this chapter you should be able to:

• Explain the terms "causality," "concurrency," "synchronization," "mutual exclusion," "place capacity," "arc multiplicities," "run," and "reachability graph."
• Verify whether a given Petri net system models a description of a system or business process.
• Apply the network structures for causality, concurrency, synchronization, and mutual exclusion.
• Model simple systems as Petri nets.
• Construct the corresponding reachability graph for a given Petri net.

5 Extending Petri Nets by Adding Color and Time

In chapters 3 and 4, we investigated Petri nets as a process modeling technique with several advantages. Petri nets have a strong mathematical foundation and unambiguous semantics. This enables us to apply various analysis techniques to Petri net models. In addition, Petri nets allow for an intuitive graphical representation and are, therefore, accessible and usable for nonexperts. Modeling with Petri nets also has a serious disadvantage: Petri nets fall short if they are used to precisely model complex systems.

In this chapter, we show that it is impossible to model complex enterprise information systems and complex business processes as Petri nets (section 5.1), and we discuss two extensions of Petri nets that overcome this disadvantage.

The first extension entails the explicit modeling of *data*. To this end, a token carries a color (i.e., a data value) and is *distinguishable* from other tokens. The resulting modeling technique is a colored Petri net. Instead of introducing a concrete language to define data types of colored Petri nets, we investigate only the concepts and define data types in terms of multisets (section 5.2). We further show that we can determine data types and data values of tokens in a colored Petri net from the corresponding data model of the system (section 5.3).

The second extension involves the explicit modeling of *time* in a Petri net. A token can carry a time stamp. The time stamp specifies the point in time at which this token is available (section 5.4). With a delayed availability of consumed tokens, we can model that activities take time.

Finally, we extend Petri nets with data *and* time and obtain a Petri net–based process modeling technique that is powerful enough to model industrial systems (section 5.5). In chapter 6, we make these concepts operational by providing a concrete language and a tool for modeling and analyzing Petri nets extended with color and time.

5.1 Why Petri Nets Are Not Sufficient

Petri nets can model the behavior of a system, but they have three serious weaknesses and, hence, fall short as a modeling technique for complex industrial systems. In the following sections, we describe these weaknesses.

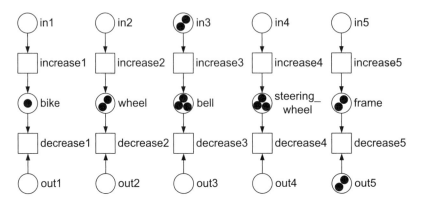

Figure 5.1
A Petri net modeling a part of an inventory management system.

5.1.1   Problem 1: Large Network Size

The first problem associated with Petri nets is their tendency to become *very large* for industrial applications. Because of the tremendous size of the resulting nets, they are hard to understand, and modeling becomes time consuming.

We illustrate this problem with an example. An inventory management system is an information system for keeping up to date with the stock quantity of each product. Suppose that we want to model an inventory management system. For each product, we must maintain the number of items in stock. We model each type of product as a place. If there are five products, we need at least five places. There are two kinds of events: the stock of a certain product may be either increased or decreased. We model these events as transitions. For each product, there is one transition for increasing the stock and one for decreasing the stock. Consequently, we need at least $5 \cdot 2 = 10$ transitions.

Figure 5.1 depicts a Petri net that models a part of the inventory management system in a simple way. Places bike, wheel, bell, steering_wheel, and frame serve as a store of the quantity of the stock of each product; for example, a token in place bike represents a bike that is still in stock. For each product, there are two transitions: one to increase the stock and one to decrease the stock. These transitions are governed by places in1, in2, in3, in4, in5 and out1, out2, out3, out4, out5, respectively. We leave out consideration of how tokens are produced in these places. The model is self-explanatory; for example, the stock of bikes increases by one through the firing of transition increase1 if place in1 contains a token.

For only five products, the corresponding Petri net is manageable; the net consists of 15 places and 10 transitions. However, large producers—for example, truck manufacturers—have over 100,000 products in stock. The corresponding Petri net would have to contain more than $100,000 \cdot 3 = 300,000$ places and $100,000 \cdot 2 = 200,000$ transitions! It is clear that we cannot easily model such situations as a Petri net, because the resulting nets are too large to handle.

What figure 5.1 shows is that the net structure modeling the increase and decrease of stock is the same for each product. As a result, for every additional product, we need to duplicate the structure consisting of three places and two transitions. This duplication is caused by using *indistinguishable* tokens in a Petri net. To distinguish two tokens representing different products, we must put them in two places. In other words, a token's place determines the object represented by a token.

5.1.2   Problem 2: Limited Expressive Power

The second problem associated with Petri nets is that they fall short in adequately modeling industrial systems. In exercise 4.20(3), we modeled the handling of insurance claims. In particular, we wanted to model that an activity is executed only if there are not more than 150 running instances in the system. As a further restriction, the maximum number of instances was unknown. In a Petri net, this activity is modeled as a transition. To adequately model this situation, we must ensure that this transition is only enabled if the condition is satisfied. We reasoned that it is not possible to model a condition $x \leq y$ using a Petri net if the upper bound of x—that is, the maximum number of running instances—is not known at design time. Conditions such as $x \leq y$ often occur in industrial systems. To model such systems, we therefore need a way to express conditions like $x \leq y$ in the model.

We cannot express this condition with a Petri net. As in the case of the problem of large network size, the use of indistinguishable tokens causes this problem. The value represented by a token can only be determined by the token's place. In this example, a token represents a natural number of running instances. The token's place then determines the concrete value of the token. As the maximum number of running instances in this example is not given, we need an infinite number of places to model this system, which is impossible.

5.1.3   Problem 3: No Explicit Modeling of Time

The third problem associated with Petri nets is that they cannot explicitly model time. It is easy to express causality between events in a Petri net, but it is hard to indicate *when* an event takes place and *how long* it takes. The traffic light modeled in figure 5.2 illustrates this issue. The Petri net model makes sure that the three states of the traffic light occur in a fixed order, but it does not include information about the temporal aspects of the traffic light. It is not known, for example, how long the traffic light is red, green, or orange.

Because Petri nets cannot describe the temporal aspects of a system, it is not possible to assess the performance of the modeled system. If we want to model a crossing, we would be interested in how many cars this crossing can handle in each hour. On the

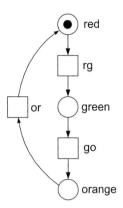

Figure 5.2
A Petri net of a traffic light without explicit modeling of time.

basis of a model of a production system of a car factory, we would want to determine how many cars the factory can produce each week. The performance of a system is often expressed in terms of flow time, waiting time, utilization, and costs and items for each time unit.

When implementing a new information system, it is wise to analyze a temporal model of the information system beforehand. The analysis can investigate whether the information system can satisfy the performance demands.

Example 5.1 In a hospital, a central database records the medical data of patients. Sometimes members of the medical staff have to wait too long for certain bits of data. The reason for this delay is that the central computer has to handle too many transactions at peak times. The hospital wants to replace this central computer with a faster one. Before purchasing a new central computer, hospital administrators want insight into the performance improvements that can be expected. The performance of the central computer may be expressed in terms of the number of transactions for each minute and the average response time.

Information systems typically contain time-dependent components; for example, the information system of a bank may perform certain transactions only at night. The information system may also schedule tasks at particular times. There are systems that bring situations to the user's attention at certain times; for example, an order processing system should create an alert if the processing of an order takes too much time. Time also plays an important role in the communication between the information system and its users. The messages of the information system should be visible on the screen— for example, for a certain amount of time.

To summarize, Petri nets can model causal relationships between different events, but they cannot explicitly model time because the firing of transitions in a Petri net is *timeless*.

5.1.4 Running Example

We identified three weaknesses of Petri nets: they may become too large in size, they are not expressive enough, and they do not explicitly model time. The first two weaknesses are caused by the use of indistinguishable black tokens, and the third weakness is caused by the fact that the firing of transitions is timeless. To overcome these problems, we propose *two extensions* of Petri nets. The first extension from indistinguishable black tokens to colored tokens (i.e., data objects) allows for a more compact model. For example, we can replace the Petri net modeling the inventory management system in figure 5.1 by a colored Petri net that consists of three places and two transitions. In addition, we can use token colors to assign a condition to each transition. This allows us to define additional conditions, such as $x \leq y$, that need to be satisfied to enable a transition. As a second extension, we *add time* to Petri nets. This extension allows us to adequately describe temporal aspects of a system.

We clarify these extensions with the example of making a punch card in a hospital, described in sections 2.4 and 4.2. In a hospital, there is a service desk where patients can have a punch card made. This punch card contains information about the name, address, date of birth, and gender of the patient. In addition, every patient receives an identifier. There is one employee working at the service desk. At any moment, the employee can help at most one patient. If the employee serves a patient, then the desk is occupied; otherwise, it is free. We assume that the time it takes to make a punch card depends on the experience (expressed in years) of the employee. For this reason, the employee number and the number of years experience of the service desk employee are recorded.

We make a first attempt to model this business process as a Petri net. Patients wait for their turn, then they are helped, and finally they leave in possession of their punch card. The corresponding states are wait, in_handling, and done. The service desk employee is either in state free or in state busy. There are two events: the employee starts making a punch card, and the employee is done and hands over the punch card to the patient.

In figure 5.3, the states are represented as places and the events as transitions. Place wait represents the queue in front of the desk. A token in place wait represents a patient waiting to be helped, whereas a token in place done represents a patient who has received a punch card. As states busy and in_handling coincide, we combine them and represent them as place busy. Accordingly, a token in place busy represents an employee who is busy making a punch card, and a patient who is being helped. Although

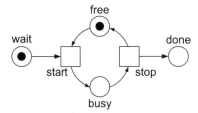

Figure 5.3
A Petri net model of the patient punch card service desk.

figure 5.3 is identical to figure 4.11 in section 4.2, a token in place free in figure 4.11 models the state of the punch card machine and of an employee in figure 5.3, for instance.

In this first model of the punch card desk, several aspects are not yet considered. First, we cannot retrieve *information* about patients and employees. If we want to include this information in a Petri net, then we need a large number of places and transitions. Furthermore, the *time* that is necessary for making a punch card is not modeled.

In the remainder of this chapter, we address these aspects in a natural way by extending Petri nets with color and time.

5.2   Extending Petri Nets by Adding Color

In this section, we address the first extension of Petri nets, the step from indistinguishable to distinguishable tokens by assigning to each token in a Petri net a certain value, referred to as *color*. Petri nets extended with color are *colored Petri nets*. We first give an informal description of colored Petri nets, and then we formalize colored Petri nets. Finally, we illustrate that Petri nets are just a special case of colored Petri nets.

5.2.1   An Informal Description of Colored Petri Nets

When modeling a system as a Petri net, we must represent elements of this system as tokens, places, and transitions. As indicated in chapter 4, tokens can model physical objects, information objects, collections of objects, states, and conditions. In the business process of the punch card desk (see figure 5.3), a token models a patient, for instance. In this example, we want to distinguish between different patients. To this end, we include information about the identifier, name, address, date of birth, and gender of the patient. However, in a Petri net, it is not possible to describe the attributes of a token. It is, therefore, natural to extend Petri nets in such a way that every token carries a value. A token that represents a certain patient then has a value from which we can derive the five attributes.

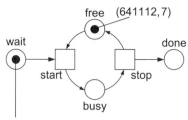

(12345, Peter, "Kerkstraat 10, Amsterdam", 13-Dec-1962, male)

Figure 5.4
A colored Petri net modeling the patient punch card service desk.

Figure 5.4 provides an example of such a value. Place wait contains a single token. This token has the value

(12345, Peter, "Kerkstraat 10, Amsterdam", 13-Dec-1962, male).

A token with this value represents the request of patient Peter for a punch card. Peter is male. He lives at Kerkstraat 10 in Amsterdam and was born on December 13, 1962. His identifier is 12345.

Likewise, a token in place free models an employee characterized by an employee number and a number of years of experience. The token in figure 5.4 has the value

(641112, 7).

It represents the employee with number 641112 and seven years of experience.

A Petri net like the one shown in figure 5.4 in which every token has a certain value is a *colored Petri net*. In a colored Petri net, a place contains similar tokens—that is, tokens that represent the same kind of object. We compare this with an object model in which objects of the same kind belong to the same object class—for example, instances of a class in a UML class diagram. Place wait in figure 5.4 contains, for example, only tokens that represent patients. Place free, in contrast, contains only tokens that represent employees. Each place is, therefore, associated with a certain type. This *place type* indicates which kind of tokens a place can carry. The value of a token has to comply with the token's place type.

According to the specification, we can describe a patient with the five attributes identifier, name, address, date of birth, and gender. Without introducing a specific syntax to denote place types, an obvious place type for place wait is the Cartesian product

Patient = Id × Name × Address × DateOfBirth × Gender.

An employee is described by an employee number and a number of years of experience. We can describe the place type of place free by

Employee = EmpNo × Experience.

Question 5.2 What do the tokens in places busy and done represent?

A token in place busy represents an employee who is busy with processing the data of a patient. Because the value of a token in place busy should contain information about the employee and the patient, the place is of type (Employee, Patient). A possible value is

((641112, 7), (12345, Peter, "Kerkstraat 10, Amsterdam", 13-Dec-1962, male)).

A token in place done represents a patient with a punch card; hence, the type of this place is Patient.

Exercise 5.1 When can we not distinguish between two tokens in a colored Petri net?

We can describe the marking of a Petri net by giving the number of tokens for each place. To describe the marking of a colored Petri net, we also need to describe the values of these tokens. Table 5.1 represents the marking that is displayed in figure 5.4.

The behavior of a Petri net is defined by the initial marking and the firing of transitions. A transition is enabled and can fire if there are enough tokens in its input places. Lifting the concept of enabledness from Petri nets to colored Petri nets, transition start is enabled if there is a patient in place wait and an employee in place free. The firing of transition start should consume one patient from place start and one employee from place free and produce one token in place busy. The value of this token contains information about the employee and the patient for whom the punch card is made. For the colored Petri net in figure 5.4, the token produced in place busy has the value

((641112, 7), (12345, Peter, "Kerkstraat 10, Amsterdam", 13-Dec-1962, male)).

Figure 5.5 depicts this marking.

The effect of firing transition start is annotated; see figure 5.5. In the marking depicted in figure 5.5, only transition stop is enabled, and the firing of transition stop leads to the marking in figure 5.6. The information contained in the consumed token is distributed over the values of the two produced tokens. Figure 5.5 depicts the effect of firing transition stop, too.

Table 5.1
The Marking of the Colored Petri Net in Figure 5.4

Place	Value
wait	(12345, Peter, "Kerkstraat 10, Amsterdam", 13-Dec-1962, male)
free	(641112, 7)
busy	
done	

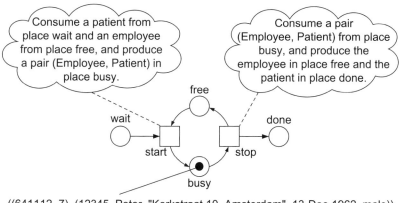

((641112, 7), (12345, Peter, "Kerkstraat 10, Amsterdam", 13-Dec-1962, male))

Figure 5.5
A colored Petri net: The marking after the firing of transition start.

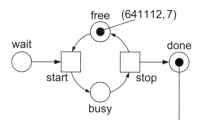

(12345, Peter, "Kerkstraat 10, Amsterdam",.13-Dec-1962, male)

Figure 5.6
A colored Petri net: The marking after the firing of transition stop.

This example shows that the rules of the token game that apply to a colored Petri net look similar to those for a Petri net. In a colored Petri net, a transition t is enabled if each input place of t contains enough tokens; however, there is an additional rule. We illustrate it with another example.

Consider a product quality check within a manufacturing line. Suppose that three products A, B, and C are manufactured. A machine scans each product. With this scan, the machine recognizes whether the product quality is low or high. Low-quality products are put into one container, and high-quality products are put into another one.

We model this quality check as the Petri net in figure 5.7. Places unchecked, low, and high model the states of a product. Transitions check_low (i.e., the product is of low quality) and check_high (i.e., the product is of high quality) model the scan.

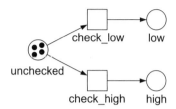

Figure 5.7
A Petri net modeling a product quality check.

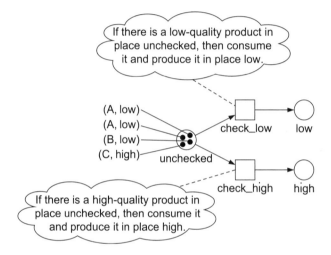

Figure 5.8
A colored Petri net modeling the quality check.

The current model does not specify the type of a product—that is, whether it is product A, B, or C. It further abstracts from the quality of products and models the decision into which container a product is put by a nondeterministic choice.

We extend the Petri net in figure 5.7 by adding color. Figure 5.8 depicts the resulting colored Petri net. Each place is of type Product, and a product can be specified as

Product = ProdType × Quality.

For example, a token in place unchecked can have the value (A, low), (B, low), or (C, high). We can also represent the marking in figure 5.8 as a table; see table 5.2. For each place, table 5.2 lists the value of each token.

According to the specification, transition check_low should only be enabled if there is a low-quality product in place unchecked. Firing this transition consumes this product

Table 5.2
The Marking of the Colored Petri Net in Figure 5.8

Place	Value
unchecked	(A, low)
	(A, low)
	(B, low)
	(C, high)
low	
high	

from place unchecked and produces it in place low. Accordingly, transition check_high should only be enabled if there is a high-quality product in place unchecked. If transition check_high fires, the high quality product is consumed from place unchecked and produced in place high. The effect of these transitions is annotated in figure 5.8.

As an example, the token with value (B, low) enables transition check_low but not transition check_high. Likewise, the token with value (C, high) enables transition check_high but not transition check_low. A transition in a colored Petri net, unlike in a Petri net, is not necessarily enabled if all input places contain enough tokens; enabledness of a transition may also depend on the value of a token.

Exercise 5.2 Section 3.1 described how to model an elevator as a Petri net. Model this elevator in a simple way as a colored Petri net. How do you define the place types and the transitions?

An enabled transition t in a colored Petri net can fire. If transition t fires, then a token from each input place of t is consumed, and a token is produced in each output place of t. We can calculate the value of this produced token from the values of the consumed tokens; for example, if transition start in figure 5.4 fires, the token that is produced in place busy contains the values of the two consumed tokens.

5.2.2   A Formal Description of Colored Petri Nets
In this chapter, we have informally described the network structure and the behavior of colored Petri nets, introduced place types and values for tokens, and described the effect of the firing of a transition. In the following section, we introduce the formal semantics of a colored Petri net.

Each place in a colored Petri net has a certain type, such as Patient or Employee. A token in this place is of this type and has a value. As in a Petri net, a place in a colored Petri net may contain tokens with the same value but also tokens with different values.

For example, place unchecked in figure 5.8 contains two tokens with value (A, low) and a token with value (B, low). As a consequence, we must refer to multiple tokens in one expression. For this purpose, we need *multisets*, as introduced in section 3.3. Recall that in a multiset, the same element can appear multiple times. The three multisets

$$m(\text{unchanged}) = [(A, \text{low}), (A, \text{low}), (B, \text{low}), (C, \text{high})]$$
$$m(\text{low}) = [\,]$$
$$m(\text{high}) = [\,]$$

describe marking m shown in figure 5.8 (where [ ] denotes the empty multiset). Marking $m(\text{unchanged})$ is a multiset containing the three elements (i.e., products) (A, low), (B, low), and (C, high). Element (A, low) appears twice and the two other elements appear once.

Formally, we have for each place type, such as Patient, Employee, and Product, a set U, the *universe*, containing all possible values of that place type. A multiset over U is then a mapping $f : U \to \mathbb{N}$ that assigns to each element $u \in U$ a natural number $f(u)$. Each element $u \in U$ specifies a value of the place type represented by U. Let $\mathcal{M}(U)$ denote the set of all possible multisets over universe U. If $\mathcal{M}$ denotes the union of the sets $\mathcal{M}(U)$, for all universes U, then we can define a marking m of a colored Petri net as the mapping

$$m : P \to \mathcal{M}$$

where P denotes the set of places of the colored Petri net, and m assigns a multiset $\mathcal{M}(U)$ to any place $p \in P$, with U representing the place type of p.

Example 5.3 For a place type lowercase characters, the universe is the set $U = \{a, b, \ldots, z\}$. Possible multisets over U are $[2 \cdot a, 2 \cdot b, 2 \cdot c, 4 \cdot d, 5 \cdot e]$, $[a, 2 \cdot b, 3 \cdot c, 4 \cdot d, 5 \cdot e]$, and $[2 \cdot a, 2 \cdot b, 2 \cdot c, 2 \cdot d, 3 \cdot e]$. For the second multiset, we have $f(a) = 1$, $f(b) = 2$, $f(c) = 3$, $f(d) = 4$, $f(e) = 5$, and f assigns zero to all other characters. As another example, the set $U = \{(A, low), (A, high), (B, low), (B, high), (C, low), (C, high)\}$ is the universe of place type Product. Possible multisets over U are $[2 \cdot (A, low), (B, low), (C, high)]$ and $[(B, low), (B, high), (C, high)]$.

Exercise 5.3 Describe the marking in figure 5.4 as a multiset.

Having formalized place types, token values, and markings, we can now consider the behavior of a colored Petri net. The firing of transitions not only changes the distribution of tokens over the places, but it may also change the colors (i.e., the values) of the tokens flowing through the network. This requires a specification of enabledness and firing of transitions. For this purpose, we introduce *arc inscriptions*.

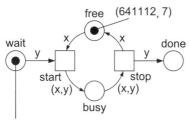

(12345, Peter, "Kerkstraat 10, Amsterdam", 13-Dec-1962, male)

Figure 5.9
The colored Petri net of figure 5.4 with arc inscriptions.

Figure 5.9 depicts a colored Petri net of the patient punch card service desk extended with arc inscriptions. Consider the three arcs connecting transition start with its input and output places. The arc inscriptions contain two variables x and y. Variable x is of type Employee and variable y of type Patient. Transition start is enabled if there exists one token in place free whose value can be assigned to variable x, and there exists one token in place wait whose value can be assigned to variable y. If transition start fires, the token from place free assigned to variable x and the token from place wait assigned to variable y are consumed, and a token with value (x,y) is produced in place busy. Because a place may contain tokens of different values, we can assign different values to a variable. A concrete assignment is a *binding*. In figure 5.9, each input place of transition start contains only one token. Accordingly, there is only one binding of transition start:

(start, ⟨x = (641112, 7),

   y = (12345, Peter, "Kerkstraat 10, Amsterdam", 13-Dec-1962, male) ⟩).

Figure 5.10 depicts the marking obtained after firing transition start. As with Petri nets, we can also calculate for colored Petri nets how the marking changes if a transition fires. Given a marking m and a binding of a transition t, we can calculate the marking m' that results from firing transition t in marking m in this binding. Multiset $m'(p)$ in any place p is equal to multiset $m(p)$ in marking m minus the values of the consumed tokens plus the values of the produced tokens. As a marking maps each place to a multiset, *we treat the value of each arc inscription as a multiset*; that is, x is shorthand for $[x]$. To keep the arc inscriptions simple, we do not show the squared brackets in the graphics. The two operations, addition and subtraction, are defined for multisets in a straightforward manner.

Example 5.4 Consider two multisets $\alpha = [2 \cdot a, 3 \cdot b, 5 \cdot c]$ and $\beta = [a, 3 \cdot b]$. The sum of these multisets is defined as $\alpha + \beta = [3 \cdot a, 6 \cdot b, 5 \cdot c]$ and the difference as $\alpha - \beta = [a, 5 \cdot$

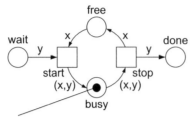

((641112, 7), (12345, Peter, "Kerkstraat 10, Amsterdam", 13-Dec-1962, male))

Figure 5.10
A colored Petri net with arc inscriptions: The marking after the firing of transition start.

c]. The difference $\beta - \alpha$ is undefined, because multiset β has no element c, but multiset α does. Furthermore, multiset β contains only one element a, whereas multiset α contains two elements a. In other words, subtraction $\beta - \alpha$ of two multisets is only defined if the number of each element in multiset β is greater than or equal to the number of the respective elements in multiset α.

As an example, marking m' in figure 5.10 can be calculated from marking m in figure 5.9 as follows:

$m'(\text{free}) = m(\text{free}) - [(641112, 7)] + [\,]$
$\qquad = [(641112, 7)] - [(641112, 7)] + [\,] = [\,]$
$m'(\text{wait}) = m(\text{wait}) - [(12345, \text{Peter, "Kerkstraat 10, Amsterdam"},$
$\qquad\qquad 13\text{-Dec-}1962, \text{male})] + [\,]$
$\qquad = [(12345, \text{Peter, "Kerkstraat 10, Amsterdam", 13-Dec-1962, male})] -$
$\qquad\quad [(12345, \text{Peter, "Kerkstraat 10, Amsterdam", 13-Dec-1962, male})] + [\,]$
$\qquad = [\,]$
$m'(\text{busy}) = m(\text{busy}) - [\,] + [((641112, 7), (12345, \text{Peter},$
$\qquad\qquad \text{"Kerkstraat 10, Amsterdam", 13-Dec-1962, male})]$
$\qquad = [\,] - [\,] + [((641112, 7),(12345, \text{Peter, "Kerkstraat 10, Amsterdam"},$
$\qquad\quad 13\text{-Dec-}1962, \text{male})]$
$\qquad = [((641112, 7), (12345, \text{Peter, "Kerkstraat 10, Amsterdam"},$
$\qquad\quad 13\text{-Dec-}1962, \text{male})]$
$m'(\text{done}) = m(\text{done}) - [\,] + [\,]$
$\qquad = [\,] - [\,] + [\,] = [\,].$

Note that a binding of a transition t assigns values only to variables that occur in arc inscriptions surrounding t. Moreover, if there is no arc, the empty multiset [ ] is assumed to be produced or consumed. As an example, in the previously described binding, the value of variable y on the arc connecting place free and transition start evaluates to the multiset [(641112, 7)], whereas transition start does not influence the multiset corresponding to place done. This also shows that the namespace of a variable is restricted to the arc inscriptions surrounding a transition.

Consider transition stop. The arcs connecting transition stop with its input and output places contain variables x and y as arc inscriptions. There is a binding assigning the same values to variables x and y as mentioned earlier. This binding enables transition stop. If transition stop fires, then a token of value (x,y) is consumed from place busy. In addition, a token with value x is produced in place done, and a token with value y is produced in place free.

Exercise 5.4   Calculate the successor marking m' from the marking m in figure 5.10.

With arc inscriptions, we can formally specify the behavior of the colored Petri net in figure 5.10; however, arc inscriptions are not sufficient to formalize the behavior of colored Petri nets in general. Sometimes it is necessary that a transition is only enabled at a certain binding; for example, in the model of the product quality check in Figure 5.8, transition check_low is enabled only in the case of a low-quality product and transition check_high only in the case of a high-quality product. To model such conditions, we can use a transition *guard*. A guard defines an additional constraint that must be fulfilled before a transition is enabled. We illustrate the concept of a guard with the product quality check example.

Figure 5.11 depicts a colored Petri net with arc inscriptions and two simple guards. Variable x is of type Product. The guard of transition check_low is defined as [x.Quality=low] and specifies that the value of attribute Quality in variable x must be low. Likewise, the guard of transition check_high is defined as [x.Quality=high] and specifies that the value of attribute Quality in variable x must be high. The behavior of this net is defined as follows. There are three potentially enabled bindings of transition check_low in figure 5.11:

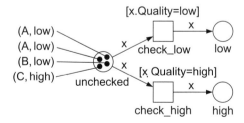

Figure 5.11
The colored Petri net of figure 5.8 with guards.

(check_low, ⟨x = (A, low)⟩)
(check_low, ⟨x = (B, low)⟩)
(check_low, ⟨x = (C, high)⟩).

Transition check_low is only enabled at the first and at the second binding, because then the product quality is low and the guard of transition check_low evaluates to true. In contrast, in the third binding, the guard evaluates to false, because the product quality is high.

Similarly, we have the following three potential bindings for transition check_high:

(check_high, ⟨x = (A, low)⟩)
(check_high, ⟨x = (B, low)⟩)
(check_high, ⟨x = (C, high)⟩).

Transition check_high is not enabled at the first two bindings, because its guard evaluates to false; however, at the third binding, transition check_high is enabled.

Formally, arc inscriptions and guards are *expressions*. An expression may contain constants and variables. By assigning to each variable of an expression a value, we can calculate the value of this expression. The difference between an arc inscription and a guard is that the value of an arc inscription is always a *multiset*, whereas the value of a guard is a *Boolean* (i.e., true or false).

The following two definitions summarize our observations regarding the network structure and the behavior of colored Petri nets.

Definition 5.5 (Colored Petri net)   A *colored Petri net* is a Petri net in which every place has a *type*, and every token has a *value* (i.e., a color) that complies to the place type. An arc in a colored Petri net may have an *arc inscription*. An arc inscription is an expression with some variables that evaluate to a multiset. A transition can have a *guard*. A guard is a Boolean expression, and it may have variables in exactly the same way than arc inscriptions (of arcs surrounding that transition) have.

Definition 5.6 (Binding)   Let t be a transition of a colored Petri net. A *binding of transition t* allocates a concrete value to the variables that occur in the arc inscriptions of arcs surrounding t. These values should be of the corresponding type. Transition t is *enabled at a binding* if there are tokens matching the values of the arc inscriptions and the guard of t evaluates to true. An enabled transition *fires* while consuming and producing the corresponding tokens.

Exercise 5.5   Show that the business process of exercise 4.20(3) can be modeled as a colored Petri net. Draw only the relevant places and transitions and define the place types.

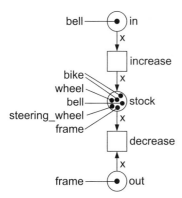

Figure 5.12
A colored Petri net modeling a part of an inventory management system.

Exercise 5.6   Model the informally described colored Petri net of exercise 5.2 as a colored
Petri net.

   We started this chapter describing that a Petri net modeling a simplified inventory
management system can consist of more than 300,000 places and more than 200,000
transitions if the system keeps more than 100,000 product types in stock. When we use
a colored Petri net instead of a Petri net, we only need three places and two transitions
to model this system; see figure 5.12.
   Each place in figure 5.12 is of type StockItem. Place stock contains all stock items.
Transition increase increases the stock, and transition decrease decreases the stock. Transition increase is enabled if there is a token in place in whose value can be assigned to
variable x. This variable is of type StockItem. If transition increase fires, then the token
from place in is consumed, and a token of the same value is produced in place stock.
Transition decrease is only enabled if there is a token in place out that has the same
value as a token in place stock. The firing of transition decrease consumes the respective
tokens from places stock and out.

Exercise 5.7   Extend the model in figure 5.12 such that each stock item is a pair consisting of a product and the product's quantity in stock. Furthermore, it should be possible
to increase and decrease the quantity of a stock item by a number *n* while firing each of
these transitions once. Use the marking displayed in figure 5.1 as the initial marking.

5.2.3   Petri Nets Are a Special Case of Colored Petri Nets
Colored Petri nets extend Petri nets by adding data. In this section, we investigate the
relation between colored Petri nets and Petri nets. We show that Petri nets are a special
case of colored Petri nets by defining Petri nets as colored Petri nets.

A marking of a (classical or colored) Petri net is a distribution of tokens over the places of the net. In a Petri net, tokens are indistinguishable and graphically represented as black dots. In this sense, each place of a Petri net has the same place type, BlackDot. Accordingly, a Petri net has only the universe $U =$ {BlackDot} containing a single value. A colored Petri net, in contrast, may have several place types and hence several universes. As each place type may be arbitrarily complex, the universe representing this place type is a set that may contain an infinite number of values.

Technically, a marking of a colored Petri net is a function m that maps each place to a multiset. Applying this mapping to a Petri net, we obtain a function $m : P \rightarrow \mathcal{M}$ with $\mathcal{M}$ as the set of all multisets over universe {BlackDot}. As universe {BlackDot} is just a singleton set, we do not have to explicitly mention that a place contains, for example, three tokens of type BlackDot. It suffices to specify the *number of tokens* in each place (as we did in definition 3.8 with $m : P \rightarrow \mathbb{N}$).

Petri nets do not have arc inscriptions, because only tokens of the same value flow through the network. If we define a Petri net as a colored Petri net, then we need to assign an arc inscription to each arc. An arc inscription is an expression with variables of type BlackDot. Arc inscriptions can, for example, specify arc multiplicities of a Petri net. In figure 5.13, we specify by an expression [x,y] that every arc has a multiplicity of two. Variables x and y are of type BlackDot; thus, we consume two tokens from each input place and produce two tokens in each output place.

These considerations illustrate that we can describe any Petri net by a colored Petri net that has only places of type BlackDot. The opposite does not hold in general (unless one allows Petri nets with an infinite number of places and transitions). This shows that colored Petri nets have a higher expressiveness than Petri nets; that is, there are systems, such as the one in exercise 4.20(3), that cannot be modeled as a Petri net but can be modeled as a colored Petri net.

We conclude this section by briefly comparing classical and colored Petri nets. A colored Petri net is a Petri net extended by adding data. Modeling with colored Petri nets results in more compact process models as the examples in this section have

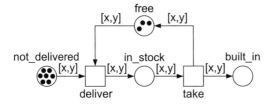

Figure 5.13
Modeling the arc multiplicities of figure 4.21 with arc inscriptions.

shown. Whereas the complexity of a Petri net is encoded in the network structure, the complexity of a colored Petri net is encoded in the place types and expressions.

The increased expressiveness of colored Petri nets compared to Petri nets allows us to model systems as colored Petri nets that cannot be modeled as Petri nets. Moreover, we did not put any restrictions on expressions in a colored Petri net. As a result, colored Petri nets are *Turing complete*; that is, every system that can be modeled as a Turing machine can also be modeled as a colored Petri net. In contrast, Petri nets are not Turing complete. The increased expressiveness of colored Petri nets is advantageous if we want to model industrial systems, but the analysis of colored Petri nets is much more complicated, because certain questions, such as "Can a marking m be reached from the initial marking m_0?," cannot be decided in general.

5.3   Determining Place Types

In section 5.2, we introduced colored Petri nets. We determined the type of a place without using a systematic method; however, for complex systems, a more systematic approach is preferable. The approach of this section is to derive the data information that is needed for determining the place types of the colored Petri net from the data model of a system.

To cope with the complexity of industrial systems, a system model is split into a data model and a process model (see section 1.5). The data model (e.g., a UML class diagram) describes the state space of a system, and the process model (e.g., the colored Petri net) describes the transition relation of the system. Given a system specification, we can develop a data model. In section 2.4, we discussed the construction of UML class diagrams. A data model represents the basic entities of the system together with their interrelationships, thereby structuring the state space of the system. The places and the tokens of a colored Petri net are related to the data model. Accordingly, we can use the data model to derive the place types of a colored Petri net. We illustrate this with some examples.

As a first example, we revisit the process of making patient punch cards, as introduced in section 5.1. Figure 5.14 depicts the UML class diagram of this example as introduced in section 2.4 and a process model described as a Petri net. We now want to determine the place types of the Petri net by inspecting the class diagram.

A token in place wait represents a waiting patient, and a token in place done represents a patient who has received a punch card. Tokens in both places represent values of a certain data entity, and both places have the same place type—class Patient in the class diagram in figure 5.14. A token in place free represents an employee who is free to serve the next waiting patient. So, place free is assigned to class Employee in figure 5.14. Finally, a token in place busy represents an isBusyWith-link between an employee and

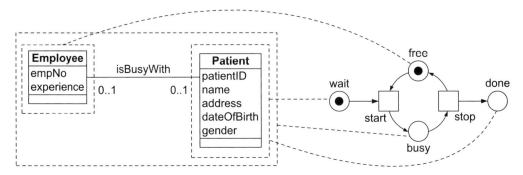

Figure 5.14
Data and process model of the patient punch card service desk.

a patient. So, the place type of busy may be constructed by combining the values of classes Employee and Patient.

This example illustrates that a place type may directly correspond to either a class or an interrelationship between two or more classes. This typically applies in the case of stores as shown in the example. A token in such a place represents an object (or link) of the corresponding class. As a class diagram defines the attributes of each class, we can derive from the classes the data structure of each place type. A token in a place is an instance of the respective class in the class diagram. For example, a token in place free is a value of place type Employee and corresponds to an instance of class Employee. We can represent a token and a class instance as a table. For tokens, we described this in section 5.2.1 and for class instances in section 2.4.

Unfortunately, not every place type directly corresponds to a class or an interrelationship between several classes. Sometimes, a place type only partially corresponds to a class or several classes; that is, it does not contain all attributes. Moreover, there are also places whose tokens represent certain auxiliary variables having plain values that are not at all related with the class diagram (e.g., variables temporarily used in computation). Typically, the value of such a token corresponds to some basic data type, such as a number or a string. We illustrate this with another example.

Recall the business process of a transportation company introduced in exercise 2.8. Figure 5.15 depicts again the UML class diagram of this business process, and figure 5.16 depicts a part of the process model. Initially, an order is sent to the transportation company specifying a product and a weight or volume. As a first step, an identifier is assigned to this order (transition getId). Next, the company chooses an appropriate trailer that can load the ordered product. In case of a solid product, a cargo trailer must be chosen (transition chooseCargo) and for liquids a tanker trailer must be chosen (transition chooseTanker).

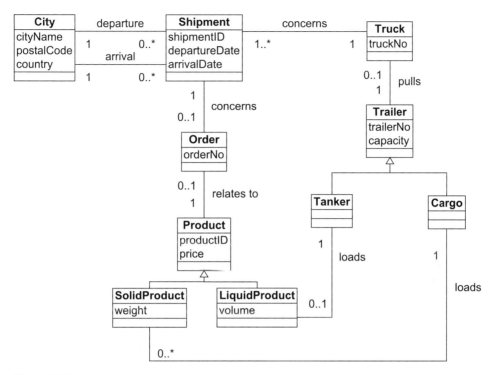

Figure 5.15
The UML class diagram of the transportation company.

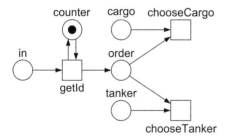

Figure 5.16
A Petri net modeling a part of the transportation process.

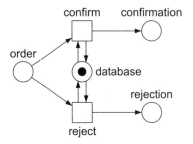

Figure 5.17
A Petri net modeling a train reservation system.

Question 5.7 What are the place types in figure 5.16?

As a token in place in models an ordered product, place in is of type Product. A token in place counter contains the current order number. Firing transition getId generates an order number for an ordered product. Place counter is an example of a place whose type is not related to any of the classes in figure 5.15. For example, its type may be Number, and every firing of transition getId increments then the token in place counter by one. A token in place order is of type Order × Product. Place cargo and place tanker correspond to the UML classes of the same name.

Exercise 5.8 Figure 5.17 depicts a Petri net modeling a simplified train reservation process. A token in place order models the details of a train trip. If a seat for the requested train ride is available, transition confirm sends the reservation details. If no seat can be reserved, transition reject rejects the request. Determine the place types of the net from the UML class diagram in figure 2.11.

To summarize, systems are often designed by first developing a data model. As this model facilitates the structuring and the organizing of data entities, we can derive the necessary information from it to determine the place types of a colored Petri net that serves as a process model of the system.

5.4 Extending Petri Nets by Adding Time

In this section, we address the second extension of Petri nets and take the step from timeless firing of transitions to timed firing of transitions. Extending Petri nets with time allows us to adequately describe temporal aspects of a system in the model. An obvious approach to introduce time is to assign to each transition a certain delay specifying how long the firing of this transition takes. The firing of a transition would then consume the tokens from its input places, and, after the specified delay, it would produce tokens in its output places. However, this approach has a drawback. We may not see the complete marking at any point in time, because some tokens may be hidden inside a transition. Moreover, several analysis techniques are no longer applicable if firing is no longer atomic. For this reason, we introduce another approach: we extend Petri nets by adding time to tokens and transitions. A token may carry a *time stamp*, and a transitions may produce tokens with a *delay*. We first discuss the concept of time stamps for tokens.

5.4.1 Time Stamps

We return to the example of the patient punch card service desk; in the specification given in section 5.1, we stated that making a punch card takes time. Figure 5.3 depicts a Petri net modeling the patient punch card service desk. In this model, we cannot represent how long it takes to make a punch card. In the following section, we illustrate how we can extend the model in figure 5.3 with time.

When we consider time, we assume a *global clock* representing the model time. Time passes in *time units*. The concrete value of a time unit—that is, whether it represents one second, two minutes, or five hours—depends on the system specification. To each token we assign a *time stamp*. The time stamp indicates from which moment with respect to the global clock the token can be consumed by a transition.

In figure 5.18, we have associated a time stamp with each token of figure 5.3. The tokens in place wait represent patients who want to have a punch card made. The token with time stamp 2 represents a patient who arrives at time 2 at the desk. At time 4, two more patients arrive. The token in place free with time stamp 0 specifies that the desk employee is available from time 0. At time 0, only the employee is available; at time 2, the employee and one patient are available; and at time 4, the employee and all three patients are available.

We can describe the marking of a Petri net extended with time by presenting the number and time stamps of tokens in each place. Table 5.3 shows the marking of figure 5.18.

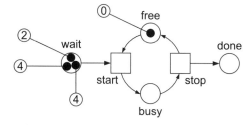

Figure 5.18
The patient punch card service desk model extended with time stamps.

Table 5.3
The Marking of Figure 5.18

Place	Token with time stamp
wait	2
	4
	4
free	0
busy	
done	

A token is available for consumption only from the moment when its time stamp is less than or equal to the present time. A transition can fire only if all tokens to be consumed are available.

Definition 5.8 (Enabling time)   The *enabling time* of a transition t is the time point at which its input places contain enough available tokens such that t is enabled.

As an example, transition start in figure 5.18 has an enabling time of 2, because this is the earliest time at which in place wait and in place free a token is available.

For determining the enabling time of a transition, we first collect from each input place a token with a minimal time stamp (i.e., the next token to be consumed from this place). Likewise, if two tokens need to be consumed from a single place, we consider the two tokens having minimal time stamps, and so on. The enabling time is then equal to the maximum of the time stamps of the tokens to be consumed. When determining the enabling time for transition start, we thus do not consider the two tokens with time stamp 4, but only the token with time stamp 2 in place wait and the token with time stamp 0 in place free.

If multiple transitions are enabled at a certain moment, it is not determined which of these transitions will fire first; that is, there is a nondeterministic choice. Moreover, all tokens with a time stamp less than or equal to the current time can be consumed. In the marking displayed in figure 5.18, only transition start is enabled and will fire at time 2. In contrast, the marking of the Petri net in figure 5.19 gives rise to a nondeterministic choice. Transition t1 and transition t2 are enabled at time 4. Which of these transitions fires first is decided nondeterministically.

Assume now that we have a situation as in figure 5.20 in which various transitions are enabled, with different enabling times. In figure 5.20, transition t2 is enabled at time 1, and transition t1 is enabled at time 2. As transition t2 has the smallest enabling time, it may fire then. We also call the moment at which transition t2 fires the *firing time* of t2. This firing time is *equal* to the enabling time of transition t2. The firing time of

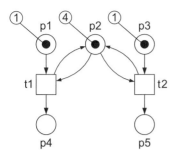

Figure 5.19
The marking of a Petri net with a nondeterministic choice.

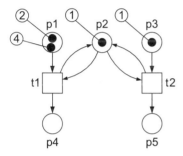

Figure 5.20
A Petri net showing two enabled transitions with different enabling times.

transition t2 is, furthermore, equal to the minimum of the enabling times of all enabled transitions. In other words, as soon as a transition is enabled, it *must* fire. Accordingly, transition t2 fires at time 1, and transition t1 fires at time 2.

When a transition fires, it consumes tokens from its input places and produces tokens in its output places. Only available tokens can be consumed; that is, the time stamps of the tokens must be less than or equal to the firing time. Furthermore, the tokens must be consumed in the order of their time stamps. For example, if transition t1 in figure 5.20 fires, the token with time stamp 2 is consumed first from place p1.

Exercise 5.9   Which markings are reachable from the given marking in figure 5.20? What are the enabling and firing times? Assume tokens are produced without any delay.

The behavior of a Petri net is defined by the markings being reachable from the initial marking. Adding time to Petri nets incorporates another dimension to the behavior of the net: the passing of time. To illustrate this additional dimension, consider again figure 5.18. This figure depicts the marking of the net at time 0 but also at time 1. This

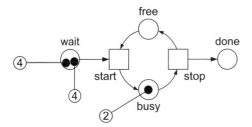

Figure 5.21
A Petri net showing the marking of the punch card service desk after firing of transition start.

example illustrates that the passing of time does not necessarily change the marking of the net. Figure 5.21 depicts the marking at time 2 (after firing transition start). The time spent in this marking is 0, because transition stop will also fire at time 2.

5.4.2 Delays

We have seen the role that time stamps play, but we have not yet discussed how the time stamp of a produced token is determined. The time stamp of a produced token is equal to the firing time increased by a possible *delay*. So far, we have assumed this delay to be zero. This delay is determined by the transition that fires. The firing itself is timeless and hence an atomic action. The delay, however, ensures that produced tokens cannot be consumed before the delay has passed. Hence, this delay has the same effect as specifying that firing of a transition takes time.

Assume that making a punch card takes three time units. The marking displayed in figure 5.22 determines that transition start will fire at time 2. In this figure, the delays for produced tokens are attached to the arcs connecting transition start with its output place busy. We represent a delay by @+ followed by the delay. As an example, tokens that transition start produces in place busy obtain a delay of three time units, denoted by @+3. It thus takes three time units before transition stop can fire. In this way, we model that making a punch card takes three time units. Tokens that transition stop produces in places free and done do not obtain a delay (i.e., their delay is equal to zero). That way, we model that the employee can immediately start helping the next patient. Figure 5.23 depicts the marking after firing transition start. The token in place busy has a time stamp equal to $2 + 3 = 5$, because transition start fires at time 2 and the delay of the produced token is equal to 3.

At the marking of figure 5.23, only transition stop is enabled. The enabling time of stop is equal to 5. Transition stop, thus, will fire at time 5. Table 5.4 describes the resulting marking.

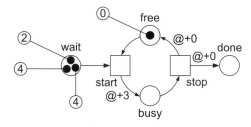

Figure 5.22
A Petri net extended with time.

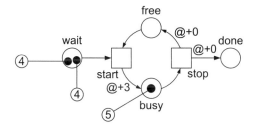

Figure 5.23
A Petri net extended with time: The marking after the firing of transition start.

Exercise 5.10 Transitions start and stop in figure 5.23 keep firing until a final marking is reached. Describe the sequence of evolving markings in tabular form, starting from the marking described in table 5.4.

The Petri net in figure 5.22 models that making a punch card takes exactly three time units and that one patient request comes in at time 2 and two other requests at time 4. A question that we can ask is:

Question 5.9 How long do the patients have to wait?

We obtain the answer from the terminal marking of this net; see table 5.5. The time stamps of the tokens in place done show when the punch card of each patient is made. The token with time stamp 11 states that the last patient had to wait $11 - 4 = 7$ time units.

This example shows how we can use Petri nets extended with time to analyze temporal aspects of a system. By modeling an information system as a Petri net, we can investigate the expected performance of the system. In this example, we assume fixed delays. In chapter 8, we show that we can sample delays from probability distributions and that we can use delays as input for simulation experiments.

Table 5.4
The Marking of the Net in Figure 5.23 after Transition stop Has Fired

Place	Time stamp
wait	4
	4
free	5
busy	
done	5

Table 5.5
The Terminal Marking of the Net in Figure 5.23

Place	Time stamp
wait	
free	11
busy	
done	5
	8
	11

We conclude this section by comparing Petri nets and Petri nets extended with time. Extending Petri nets with time increases the expressiveness of the formalism, because time can be explicitly expressed in the model. As in the case of adding data, the increased expressiveness helps to adequately model industrial systems, but it makes the analysis of such nets harder. Interestingly, every run of a Petri net with time is also a run of the corresponding Petri net. However, the opposite does not hold in general. As an example, transition t1 cannot fire before transition t2 in figure 5.20, but, after removing the time stamps, transition t1 can fire before transition t2.

5.5   Petri Nets with Color and Time

Petri nets can be extended with time as described in section 5.4. As Petri nets are a special case of colored Petri nets, colored Petri nets can also be extended with time. We illustrate a colored Petri net with time using an extension of the patient punch card service desk example.

Our starting point is the colored Petri net in figure 5.9. We want to extend this net with time, because making punch cards takes time. This time, however, the time needed for making a punch card depends on the experience of the employee. If the employee has been employed for more than five years, then making a punch card takes three time units; otherwise, it takes four time units. Figure 5.24 depicts the modified Petri net.

To describe the marking of a Petri net with color and time, we must specify for each place the value and the time stamp of each token. The token in place wait in figure 5.24 represents a patient. This token has a value and carries a time stamp. Table 5.6 displays the marking of figure 5.24.

In section 5.2, we defined the behavior of a colored Petri net by adding arc inscriptions and guards to the network structure and by defining the notion of a binding. When we consider a Petri net with color and time, we must further take into account that tokens in the input places carry a time stamp and tokens in the output places may have a delay. We describe the effect of firing transition start in figure 5.24 as follows:

- Exactly one token is produced in place busy.
- The value of this token is the record that we get by combining the values of the two consumed tokens.
- The delay of this token depends on attribute Experience. If this attribute value is greater than five, then the delay is equal to three time units; otherwise, the delay is equal to four time units.

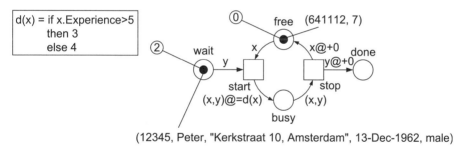

(12345, Peter, "Kerkstraat 10, Amsterdam", 13-Dec-1962, male)

Figure 5.24
The patient punch card service desk modeled as a Petri net with color and time.

Table 5.6
The Marking of the Petri Net in Figure 5.24

Place	Time stamp	Value
wait	2	(12345, Peter, "Kerkstraat 10, Amsterdam", 13-Dec-1962, male)
free	0	(641112, 7)
busy		
done		

In section 5.4, the delay of the token produced by transition start was equal to three time units. In a Petri net extended with color and time, we can make the delay dependent on the values of the consumed tokens. The delay for making a punch card can now depend on the experience of the employee who makes the card. Because delays depend on the values of the consumed tokens, we can no longer attach them in the form of simple numbers to the outgoing arcs of a transition. Instead, we must specify an expression that is evaluated. In figure 5.24, we defined a function d that takes variable x as its argument. This function calculates the delay, given the value of attribute x.Experience. Because we do not want to introduce a certain syntax for expressions, figure 5.24 depicts only an informal specification of function d. Arc inscription (x,y)@+d(x) defines that a delay of d(x) time units is added to token (x,y) produced in place busy.

Based on these considerations, we define a transition t in a Petri net with color and time to be enabled if there exists a binding that enables t and there is no other transition for which a binding exists with a smaller enabling time. The presence of data requires that we consider bindings of transition t, and the presence of time forces the firing of a transition as soon as it is enabled (i.e., transitions are eager).

Definition 5.10 (Enabledness at a binding)   A transition t in a Petri net with color and time is *enabled at a binding* if no other binding (of t or of any other transition) exists with a smaller enabling time.

In the marking displayed in figure 5.24, there is only one binding

(start, ⟨x = (641112, 7),
        y = (12345, Peter, "Kerkstraat 10, Amsterdam", 13-Dec-1962, male) ⟩).

This binding enables transition start. The enabling time of start is equal to 2. At time 2, transition start may fire. Table 5.7 shows the resulting marking. As the employee has seven years of experience, delay function d(x) returns three time units. Therefore, the resulting time stamp is equal to $2 + 3 = 5$.

Table 5.7
Firing Transition start

Place	Time stamp	Value
wait		
free		
busy	5	((641112, 7), (12345, Peter, "Kerkstraat 10, Amsterdam", 13-Dec-1962, male))
done		

Exercise 5.11   This exercise is a continuation of exercise 5.6. Suppose the elevator takes three time units to travel up one floor and two time units to travel down one floor. Add this temporal information to the model of exercise 5.6.

5.6   Test Yourself

5.6.1   Solutions to Exercises

5.1   We cannot distinguish between two tokens in a colored Petri net if they are in the same place and have the same value (color).

5.2   Using a colored Petri net, we do not need to introduce a place for every floor. Instead, we need one place that always contains a token. The value of this token represents the location of the elevator. There are two possible events: First, the elevator travels up one floor, and, second, the elevator travels down one floor. We model each event as a transition; see figure 5.25.

Place floor is of type (natural) Number. The token in this place has, as a value, the floor number of the elevator. Transition down is enabled if the elevator is not at the ground floor. If transition down fires, then a token from place floor is consumed, and a token is produced in place floor. The value of this token is equal to the old value decreased by one. Transition up is enabled if the elevator is not at the fourth floor (i.e., the top floor). If transition up fires, then the token from place floor is consumed, and a token is produced in place floor. The value of this token is equal to the old value increased by one.

5.3   We can describe this marking as

m(free) = [(641112, 7)]
m(wait) = [(12345, Peter, "Kerkstraat 10, Amsterdam", 13-Dec-1962, male)]
m(busy) = [ ]
m(done) = [ ].

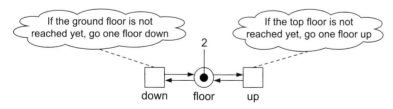

Figure 5.25
The colored Petri net model of exercise 5.2.

5.4   We can calculate marking m' as follows:

$$m'(\text{free}) = m(\text{free}) - [\,] + [(641112, 7)]$$
$$= [(641112, 7)]$$
$$m'(\text{wait}) = m(\text{wait}) - [\,] + [\,]$$
$$= [\,]$$
$$m'(\text{busy}) = m(\text{busy}) - [((641112, 7),(12345, \text{Peter},$$
$$\text{"Kerkstraat 10, Amsterdam", 13-Dec-1962, male)}] + [\,]$$
$$= [\,]$$
$$m'(\text{done}) = m(\text{done}) - [\,] + [(12345, \text{Peter, "Kerkstraat 10, Amsterdam"},$$
$$\text{13-Dec-1962, male)}]$$
$$= [(12345, \text{Peter, "Kerkstraat 10, Amsterdam", 13-Dec-1962, male)}].$$

5.5   Figure 5.26 depicts the colored Petri net fragment. Place claims is of type Number; all other places are of type Claim. Accordingly, variable x is of type Number, and variable y is of type Claim. Recall that if there are more than 150 claims in the system, then a claim is determined to be simple; otherwise, the claim is determined to be complex. We can express this condition with two guards. Note that only the firing of transition complex increases the number of claims. If transition simple fires, then the system executes the respective claim in a single step.

5.6   Figure 5.27 depicts the colored Petri net. We use a variable of type Number. To avoid the elevator traveling down while being at the ground floor and traveling up while being at the top floor, we add a guard to each transition. The guard at transition down evaluates to true if the elevator is not at the ground floor, and the guard of transition up evaluates to true if the elevator is not at the fourth floor. The firing of transition down decreases the floor number, and the firing of transition up increases it.

5.7   Figure 5.28 depicts the colored Petri net. Each place is of type StockItem = Product × Number. Variable x is of type Product, and variables y and z are of type Number. To increase the quantity of a product of the stock, we consume the respective stock

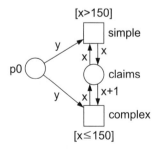

Figure 5.26
The colored Petri net model of exercise 5.5.

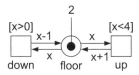

Figure 5.27
The colored Petri net model of exercise 5.6.

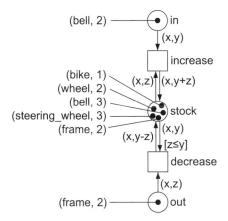

Figure 5.28
The colored Petri net model of exercise 5.7.

item from place stock and the products that should be added to the stock from place in and produce the sum of the numbers y and z in place stock. Likewise, we can decrease the quantity of a product of the stock. The guard of transition decrease makes sure that we remove only available products from the stock.

5.8   A token in place order should specify a train trip. According to the data model, we can derive the departing and the arrival station from the attributes of class TrainTrip. Therefore, it is sufficient that place order is of type TrainTrip. A token in place database must contain information about the train trip, the train, its coaches, and which seats are reserved. The place type is the Cartesian product TrainTrip × Train × Coach × Reservation. A token in place confirmation provides the reservation details. So place confirmation is of type Reservation. The type of place rejection is not determined by the data model. We can, for example, model a rejection message as an indistinguishable (black) token and also as an empty reservation.

5.9   At time 1, transition t2 is enabled. This transition fires at time 1, yielding the marking in table 5.8.

At time 2, transition t1 is enabled. This transition fires at time 2, yielding the marking in table 5.9.

Finally, at time 4, transition t1 is enabled again. It fires at time 4, yielding the marking in table 5.10.

5.10   The starting point is the marking of table 5.4. Transition start is enabled, with enabling time 5. Firing transition start produces a token in place busy. This token has a delay of three time units. Table 5.11 shows the resulting marking.

Transition stop is now enabled, with enabling time 8. Firing this transition produces a token in place free and in place done without delay. Table 5.12 shows the resulting marking.

Now transition start fires again. Table 5.13 shows the resulting marking.

Finally, transition stop fires. Table 5.5 shows the resulting terminal marking.

5.11   Figure 5.29 depicts the colored Petri net of figure 5.27 extended with delays. We added to the token produced by transition down a delay of two time units and to the token produced by transition up a delay of three time units.

Table 5.8
The Marking of the Net in Figure 5.20 after Transition t2 Has Fired at Time 1

Place	Time stamp
p1	2
	4
p2	1
p3	
p4	
p5	1

Table 5.9
The Marking of the Net in Figure 5.20 after Transition t1 Has Fired at Time 2

Place	Time stamp
p1	4
p2	2
p3	
p4	2
p5	1

Table 5.10
The Marking of the Net in Figure 5.20 after Transition t1 Has Fired at Time 4

Place	Time stamp
p1	
p2	4
p3	
p4	2
	4
p5	1

Table 5.11
The Marking after Firing Transition start

Place	Time stamp
wait	4
free	
busy	8
done	5

Table 5.12
The Marking after Firing Transition stop

Place	Time stamp
wait	4
free	8
busy	
done	5
	8

Table 5.13
The Marking after Firing Transition start Again

Place	Time stamp
wait	
free	
busy	11
done	5
	8

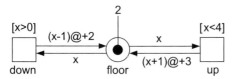

Figure 5.29
The Petri net of exercise 5.11 with color and time.

5.6.2 Further Exercises

Exercise 5.12 Explain the terms "place type," "token value," "arc inscription," "guard," "binding," "time stamp," "delay," and "enabling time."

Exercise 5.13 Consider a simple banking system. The system manages accounts. Each account has an account number, an account holder, and a balance. Account holders may deposit or withdraw money. Only amounts less than 5,000 euros can be withdrawn. In addition, the system does not accept transactions that lead to a negative balance.

1. Model this system as a colored Petri net.
2. Determine the place types for the model in (1) assuming that the UML class diagram in figure 2.10 is the corresponding data model.

Exercise 5.14 The production process of a car toy consists of four steps: assembly, painting, drying, and packaging. In the assembly step, a production worker assembles four wheels and a chassis. This step takes five minutes. Next, a painter paints the product. This takes eight minutes. After painting, the product dries for at least twenty minutes before it can be packed. The room in which the products can dry is limited in size: at most ten products can dry there at the same time. Finally, a production worker packages of the toy car. This takes ten minutes. The company employs three production workers and two painters. The capacity of every employee is one.

1. Model the production process as a Petri net extended with time. Show the initial marking and how time is modeled.
2. Cars can be painted in two colors (blue and red). Red cars take seven minutes to be painted and twenty-five minutes to dry, and blue cars take nine minutes to be painted and eighteen minutes to dry. Change the solution in (1) in such a way that this is possible.

Exercise 5.15 A catering company employs two waiters and five cooks. If the company handles the catering for a party with n guests ($n > 10$), then the following (simplified) process is followed. First, a cook prepares the meal. This takes $n/2$ man-hours. Second, a waiter garnishes the food. This takes $n/10$ man-hours. Finally, the meal is served. This step can be done by a cook or a waiter, and it takes $n/5$ man-hours for a cook and $n/10$ man-hours for a waiter. All activities are executed by persons having the right qualifications; for example, a waiter cannot act as a cook.

1. Model this business process as a Petri net with color and time. The unit of time is one man-hour.
2. Change the model in (1) in such a way that there are two waiters and one cook occupied for each serving of a meal.

Exercise 5.16   The Sieve of Eratosthenes is a simple algorithm to find all prime numbers $\{2, 3, 5, 7, \dots\}$ of a given set of numbers $\{2, 3, 4, 5, 6, 7, 8, \dots, n\}$. Model the following variant of this algorithm as a colored Petri net. The model should first generate the set $\{2, 3, 4, 5, 6, 7, 8, \dots, n\}$. On the created numbers, we apply the algorithm of Eratosthenes. The algorithm takes in each step two numbers of the set $\{2, 3, 4, 5, 6, 7, 8, \dots, n\}$ such that one number is an integer factor of the other number. The smaller number is returned to the set, and the other number is removed.

Exercise 5.17   In this example, we consider the problem of the dining philosophers as introduced by Dijkstra (1971): "Five philosophers, numbered from 1 through 5 are living in a house where the table laid for them, each philosopher having his own place at the table: Their only problem—besides those of philosophy—is that the dish served is a very difficult kind of spaghetti, that has to be eaten with two forks. There are two forks next to each plate, so that presents no difficulty: as a consequence, however, no two neighbours may be eating simultaneously." Figure 5.30 illustrates this example.

1. Model the philosopher system as a Petri net. It is assumed that each philosopher simultaneously (and indivisibly) picks up his pair of forks. Analogously, he puts them down in a single indivisible action. Each philosopher may be represented by two

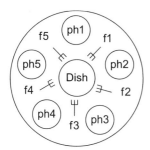

Figure 5.30
Five philosophers *ph1, ..., ph5* eating with forks *f1, ..., f5*.

places (think and eat) and two transitions (take and putdown forks). Each fork may be represented by a single place that holds a token when the fork is not used.

2. Model the same system as a colored Petri net that contains the two color sets *Phils* = {*ph1*, . . . , *ph5*} and *Forks* = {*f1*, . . . , *f5*}, representing the philosophers and the forks, respectively. (Hint: Let both color sets be of type Number; that is, represent each philosopher and each fork by an integer.)

3. Modify the model created in (2) such that each philosopher first takes his right fork and next the left one. Analogously, the philosopher first puts down his left fork and then his right one. Does this modification change the overall behavior of the model?

5.7   Summary

In this chapter, we presented two extensions of Petri nets: the extension adding color (i.e., values) to tokens and the extension adding time to tokens. Both extensions have proven to be important for modeling industrial systems.

In a colored Petri net, tokens are—in contrast to those of Petri nets—distinguishable. A token represents a concrete object and has a value. Every place in a colored Petri net has a type that determines which kind of tokens it may contain. We can use the value of a token to keep up to date with information about the object represented by the token. To this end, the firing of a transition not only changes the distribution of tokens in the net, but it may also change the value of tokens. To formalize the behavior of colored Petri nets, we introduced arc inscriptions and transition guards. An arc inscription is an expression that specifies which values flow through the network structure if a transition fires. Arc inscriptions typically have variables that are bound to concrete values during execution. Variables have a type. To restrict the binding of these variables, transitions may have a guard. A guard is an additional condition that needs to be satisfied to enable the transition. The combination of tokens in a given marking, arc inscriptions, and guards results in a set of bindings. A binding corresponds to an enabled transition with a fixed allocation of values to variables that occur in the arc inscriptions surrounding this transition.

Colored Petri nets have formal semantics, like Petri nets do. A marking in a colored Petri net maps each place to a multiset. If a transition fires with a particular binding at a marking m, then the successor marking of m can be calculated from m and from the arc inscriptions surrounding the respective transition by applying addition and subtraction on multisets.

Colored Petri nets allow for a more compact and precise model of a system than Petri nets do. They are more expressive than Petri nets and can, therefore, model systems that cannot be modeled as a Petri net. We illustrated that information about the colors can be derived from the data model of the system to be modeled.

We can describe the temporal aspects of a system by extending Petri nets with time. The time stamps of tokens and the delayed availability of produced tokens allow us to model when an event happens and how long it takes. In contrast to Petri nets, a transition in a Petri net with time fires as soon as it is enabled; that is, a transition is eager and can be disabled by other transitions taking tokens from its input places. As a further difference, the marking of the model not only depends on the current marking but also on the time. As for colored Petri nets, the extension of Petri nets with time increases the expressiveness of the model.

Petri nets with data and time combine the concepts of color and time. They provide a modeling technique that allows us to model complex business processes and information systems in detail. As a guideline, one should first design a process model as a colored Petri net and then extend the model by adding time.

After studying this chapter you should be able to:

• Explain why Petri nets are not suitable for modeling complex information systems.
• Explain the concepts: "place type," "token value," "arc inscription," "guard," "binding," "time stamp," "delay," and "enabling time."
• Determine the reachable markings of a given Petri net extended with color and time for a given initial marking.
• Design a simple Petri net with color and time given a textual description.

5.8 Further Reading

Extending Petri nets by adding data has been studied since the 1970s. Many variants of colored Petri nets have been developed. Most of these variants use variations of concepts introduced in this chapter. The standard reference for colored Petri nets is the textbook of Jensen and Kristensen (2009). Jensen and Kristensen defined the semantics of colored Petri nets by means of the functional programming language Standard ML (Milner et al. 1997). As a consequence, place types can be specified as standard constructs from programming languages, and expressions can be defined by functions. CPNs are supported by software tools, such as CPN Tools. Reisig (1998) introduced with algebraic high-level Petri nets another variant of colored Petri nets. The semantics of such nets are defined in terms of the mathematical concept of an algebra. Place types are elements, and expressions are operations of this algebra. Algebraic high-level Petri nets are particularly used to model distributed (network) algorithms. In his recent introduction to Petri nets, Reisig (2010) uses a similar formalization of colored Petri nets as presented in this chapter. From a historical point of view, predicate/transition nets of Genrich and Lautenbach (1981) are relevant. However, unlike colored Petri nets, these nets are not supported by mature software tools, such as CPN tools.

To model temporal aspects of systems, Petri nets must be extended by time. In this chapter, we introduced time stamps for tokens and delays to model temporal behavior.

Jensen and Kristensen (2009) use the same concept and consider Petri nets with color and time. Further variants to specify time constraints in Petri nets exist in the literature. The notion of a time stamp can be generalized to time intervals, for instance. A time interval specifies a period rather than a certain point in time at which a token is available. Furthermore, time stamps or time intervals do not necessarily need to be added to tokens. There are variants of Petri nets with time where time is attached to transitions or arcs. Textbooks on Petri nets with time have been published by Wang (1998), Cheng (2002), and Diaz (2009). The lecture notes of the Advanced Course on Petri Nets edited by Reisig and Rozenberg (1998) provide further material on this topic.

6 Colored Petri Nets: The Language

In chapter 5, we extended Petri nets with color and time. We used multisets to formalize the behavior of such Petri nets with color and time (CPNs). Whereas a Petri net is defined by the diagram of its network structure, a Petri net with color and time requires additional descriptions to result in a complete specification.

In this chapter, we provide a concrete syntax for Petri nets with color and time. To this end, we present a concrete language for Petri nets with color and time with the *Colored Petri Net* (CPN) *language*, as introduced by Kurt Jensen and supported by CPN Tools. We choose the CPN language for three reasons. First, it is a graphical language that allows us to express the network structure and the additional descriptions of a Petri net model with color and time in terms of a diagram. Second, the CPN language has formal semantics; that is, the meaning of every concept is defined in a complete and unambiguous manner. Third, an abundance of analysis methods is available for CPNs in addition to software products like CPN Tools that support the modeling and analysis of CPN models.

The CPN language is based on the functional language Standard ML. It inherits, therefore, the basic types, type constructors, basic functions, operators, and expressions from Standard ML, but it also provides additional constructs. We start with an introduction to types and values supported by the CPN language (section 6.1). Then we show how color sets for places can be specified (section 6.2), and we present the definition of markings as multisets (section 6.3). We introduce the syntax of arc inscriptions and guards to define the behavior of CPNs (section 6.4). Furthermore, we show how time can be added to CPNs (section 6.5). Because the CPN language is based on Standard ML, functions play an important role in this language. We introduce the concept of recursive functions and of pattern matching. In addition, we give an overview of statistical functions that can be used to create simulation models (section 6.6). Finally, we show the application of CPNs with two examples (section 6.7).

6.1 Types and Values

The CPN language is based on the functional language Standard ML. In this section, we review the basic types and the type constructors offered by Standard ML.

Table 6.1 presents the five *basic types* of Standard ML. Integers and reals (i.e., real numbers) have a unary operator ~ for specifying negative values; that is, ~5 denotes −5. Reals can have a dot to specify decimal places and an exponential notation e. Strings are written between double quotes. Type bool is used for logical expressions, and with type unit we can define indistinguishable "black" tokens; that is, type unit has only one value: the empty value is often denoted by ().

Standard ML also defines several basic operators for these basic types. Table 6.2 lists these operators.

The result type of the basic comparison operators is bool. The second operand in a logical AND is only evaluated if the first operand evaluates to true. Similarly, the

Table 6.1

The Basic Types of Standard ML

Basic type	Description
int	Represents integers, e.g., 100 and ~100 (i.e., −100).
real	Represents reals, e.g., ~10.5, 17e2 (i.e., 1,700), and 17e~2 (i.e., 0.17).
string	Represents strings, e.g., "Hello World" and "13-Dec-1962".
bool	Represents the Booleans true and false.
unit	Has only one value: ().

Table 6.2

The Basic Operators of Standard ML

Basic operators	Description
~	The unary negation operator for int and real
+, -	Addition and subtraction operator for int and real
*	Multiplication operator for int and real
div, mod	Division and modulo operator for int
^	Concatenation operator for string
=, <>, <, >, <=, >=	The basic comparison operators applicable to most types
not	The logical negation
andalso	The logical AND
orelse	The logical OR
if then else	A ternary condition operator

second operand in a logical OR is only evaluated if the first operand evaluates to false. The `if then else` operator is a ternary operator that uses three arguments. The first argument is a Boolean expression to decide whether the "then" part or the "else" part should be taken. The second and third argument should be of the same type. This is the result type one obtains when applying the `if then else` operator. All other operators are standard for most programming languages and therefore self-explanatory.

Example 6.1 The expression `(5+10) div 5` is of type `int` (i.e., 3), the expression `(5+10) mod 5` is of type `int` (i.e., 0), the expression `"Kerkstraat 10" ^ ", " ^ "Amsterdam"` is of type `string` (i.e., "Kerkstraat 10, Amsterdam"), the expression `1=1 orelse 2=2` is of type `bool` (i.e., true), and the expression `if 1=1 then "OK" else "NOK"` is of type string (i.e., "OK"). Finally, the expression `if 2=3 then "YES" else 6+2` is incorrect, because the second and third operand are not of the same type. Likewise, the expression `not "Amsterdam"` is incorrect, because the negation requires an operand of type `bool`.

Exercise 6.1 Determine the type and the result of the following expressions:

1. `1<2 orelse 3>4`
2. `"Hello" ^ " " ^ "World" = "Bye"`
3. `not(true andalso (1=0)).`

6.2 Defining Color Sets

Places in a colored Petri net are typed, meaning all tokens in a place have a value of a common type. In CPN terms, this means that all tokens in a given place should belong to the same *color set* (i.e., type). This implies that each place has a color set. The CPN language distinguishes between simple and compound color sets. Simple color sets are the basic types inherited from Standard ML. Using color set constructors, we can combine simple color sets into compound color sets.

6.2.1 Simple Color Sets

Simple color sets are defined in a straightforward manner. Using the basic types of Standard ML, which we introduced in section 6.1, the color sets `INT`, `STR`, `B`, and `U` are defined as follows:

```
color INT = int;
color STR = string;
color B = bool;
color U = unit;
```

We did not define a color set for reals. The reason is that, in CPN Tools, reals cannot be used as a color set, because equality is undefined for reals. However, in functions, expressions, etc., reals can be used. Moreover, reals can be converted to integers (rounding) or strings.

Using the basic types, we can construct *subsets* of these simple color sets:

```
color Age = int with 0..130;
color Temp = int with ~30..40;
color Alphabet = string with "a".."z";
```

Color set `Age` is a subset of `int`. Only the values $0, 1, 2, \ldots, 130$ are allowed. Color set `Temp` is the set of integers between -30 and 40. `Alphabet` is a color set that corresponds to all strings that use only lowercase letters of the alphabet.

Using the `with` construct, we can construct subsets of one of the basic types but also define simple *enumerations*.

```
color YN = with Y|N;
color Gender = with male|female;
color Beer = with Corona|Heineken|Miller|Tuborg;
```

Color set `YN` has two values, `Y` and `N`, that represent yes and no. Color set `Gender` also has two values, whereas color set `Beer` has four values. Note that the enumerated values become reserved words; for example, after defining color set `YN`, value `Y` can no longer be used freely in expressions.

It is also possible to redefine the basic types `bool` and `unit`:

```
color MyBool = bool with (no,yes);
color BlackToken = unit with null;
```

Color set `MyBool` has two possible values: `no` corresponds to false and `yes` corresponds to true. Color set `BlackToken` renames its only value `()` to `null`.

6.2.2 Compound Color Sets

Beside the simple color sets, the CPN language also supports the definition of new and more complex color sets from simpler ones. Such a *compound color set* can be defined using the type constructors `product`, `record`, and `list`.

Using the type constructor `product`, we can define the Cartesian product of at least two color sets:

```
color Coordinates = product INT * INT * INT;
color HumanAge = product Gender * Age;
```

Possible values of these color sets are `(1,2,3)` and `(~4,66,0)` for `Coordinates` and `(male,50)` and `(female,3)` for `HumanAge`.

The type constructor record is similar to product:

```
color CoordinatesR = record x:INT * y:INT * z:INT;
color CD = record artist:STR * title:STR * noftracks:INT;
```

Possible values of these color sets are {x=1,y=2,z=3} and {x=~4,y=66,z=0} for CoordinatesR and {artist="Rammstein",title="Reise, Reise",noftracks= 11} and {artist="Nightwish",title="Wishmaster",noftracks=12} for CD.

The main difference between type constructors product and record is the way attributes are represented. In a product, the position matters; in a record, the label matters. That is, {x=1,y=2,z=3} and {y=2,x=1,z=3} refer to the same value, but (1,2,3) and (2,1,3) are different. However, a record can express every color set that can be expressed as a product, and vice versa.

The third type constructor, list, allows us to sequentially order values of a color set:

```
color Names = list STR;
color ListOfBeer = list Beer;
```

Possible values of these constructors are ["John","Liza","Paul"] and [] for Names and [Tuborg] and [Miller,Corona] for ListOfBeer.

The product and record constructs are used to structure values with a fixed content. The list construct, in contrast, is more dynamic, because a list may have an *arbitrary* number of elements; for example, ListOfBeer may have no elements (i.e., value []) or many, as in [Miller,Corona,Heineken,Heineken,Miller,Tuborg].

The three type constructors are highly relevant for practical applications. We can also build color sets by combining several type constructors. For example, we can define a list [{artist="Rammstein",title="Reise, Reise",noftracks=11}, {artist="Nightwish",title="Wishmaster","noftracks=12}] of CDs:

```
color ListOfCD = list CD;
```

Table 6.3 shows operators and constants that further support the use of these type constructors.

Table 6.3
Operators/Constants for the Type Constructors

Construct	Description
[]	The empty list
list1^^list2	Concatenate two lists list1 and list2
e::list	Add an element e to the head of list list
#x rec	Extract element x from record rec
#i prod	Extract the ith element from product prod

Example 6.2 The expression `[1,2]^^[3,4]` evaluates to the list `[1,2,3,4]`. An example for adding an element to a list is `"a"::["b","c"]`, which yields the list `["a","b","c"]`. The expression `#x(x=1,y=2,z=3)` evaluates to the integer 1 and the expression `#2(10,20,30)` to the integer 20.

Finally, the CPN language also makes it possible to define *constants*:

```
val name = "Peter":string;
val coord = (10,20,30):Coordinates;
val cd = {artist="Rammstein",title="Reise, Reise",noftracks=11}:CD;
```

Exercise 6.2 What is wrong with each of the following expressions?

1. `#4(4,5,6)`
2. `#1(1)`
3. `[Tuborg]::[Corona,Miller]`

6.3 Defining Markings

In section 6.2, we described how the color set of a place in a colored Petri net can be defined using basic types and type constructors. Places should only contain tokens of the corresponding color set. As a place can hold multiple tokens, and tokens may also have the same value, a marking maps each place to a *multiset*. In the CPN language, a multiset is denoted by:

```
x1'v1 ++ x2'v2 ++ ... ++ xn'vn
```

where `v1` denotes an element (i.e., a value) of the multiset, and `x1` denotes the multiplicity of element `v1` in the multiset, and so on.

Each place in a CPN has an *initialization expression*. If the initialization expression is not present, the place is assumed to be empty—that is, contains the empty multiset. By convention, we omit the empty multiset in the graphical representation and show a place that is empty in the initial marking. If the initialization expression matches the color set of the place, the place contains one initial token. If the initialization expression yields a multiset, then the place may contain multiple tokens.

Figure 6.1 illustrates the three possible situations. Place p1 is of color set INT and place p2 of color set STR. In figure 6.1(a), both places are empty in the initial marking; that is, they contain the empty multiset and therefore no token. In figure 6.1(b), both places contain one token whose value is stated by the color set of the place. In figure 6.1(c), place p1 holds six tokens (one token of value 2 and five of value 4), and place p2 also holds six tokens (one token of value "John" and five of value "Sara").

The places in figure 6.1 are depicted as ellipses rather than circles, because this is the typical representation of CPNs. There is no semantic difference between ellipses and

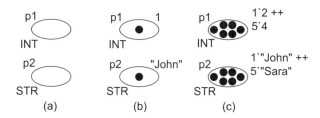

Figure 6.1
Three types of initialization expressions.

circles; but, in this chapter, we follow the conventions of CPNs and tools like CPN Tools.

6.4   Arc Inscriptions and Guards

The firing of a transition in a colored Petri net not only changes the distribution of tokens over the places, but it also changes the values of the tokens flowing through the network structure. In chapter 5, we explained the need for adding expressions to formalize the behavior of colored Petri nets. Expressions appear as arc inscriptions and as transition guards. In this section, we show how expressions can be defined using the CPN language.

6.4.1   Arc Inscriptions
An arc inscription is an expression that evaluates to a multiset. The simplest arc inscriptions are constants—for example, the value () of type `unit`, the integer 2, and the string `"Peter"`—and variables. We define variables as follows:

```
var x:INT;
var s:STR;
var c1,c2:CD;
```

The first line defines a variable x of type `int`, the second line a variable s of type `string`, and the third line defines two variables c1 and c2 of type CD.

Using constants, variables, the basic operators of Standard ML (see table 6.2), or operators and constants for the type constructors (see table 6.3), we can define arc inscriptions, such as x+5 and s^^#artist(c1).

We illustrate the definition of arc inscriptions with the patient punch card service desk example of figure 5.9. Figure 6.2 depicts the corresponding CPN model. The color set definitions are shown in the diagram (as is customary in CPN Tools). Note that we introduced the two constants, Peter and Ann, only to simplify the diagram.

```
color Name = string;
color Address = string;
color DateOfBirth = string;
color PatientID = int;
color EmpNo = int;
color Experience = int;
color Gender = with male|female;
color Pat = product PatientID * Name * Address * DateOfBirth * Gender;
color Emp = product EmpNo * Experience;
color EP = product Emp * Pat;
var p:Pat;
var emp:Emp;
val Peter = (12345, "Peter", "Kerkstraat 10, Amsterdam", "13-Dec-1962", male);
val Ann = (641112, 7);
```

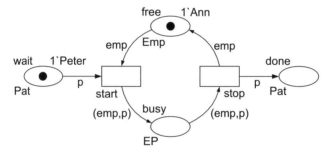

Figure 6.2
A colored Petri net model of the patient punch card service desk.

6.4.2 Guards

A guard is a Boolean expression that is associated with a transition. It is an additional condition that needs to be satisfied to enable the transition. That way, a guard puts an additional condition on enabling of a binding of a transition. We use the same graphical notation for guards as in chapter 5; that is, a guard is enclosed by square brackets. Examples of guards are [x=y+z], [x<>y], and [x<z] for variables x, y, and z of type int.

We illustrate guards in the CPN language by recapitulating the business process modeling the product quality check (see figure 5.11). Figure 6.3 depicts the corresponding CPN model. We define the color sets ProdType and Quality as enumerations. With the extraction operator #, we can access the quality element of a product and compare it to the values low and high.

Exercise 6.3 Show the corresponding CPN model of the inventory management system specified in figure 5.28.

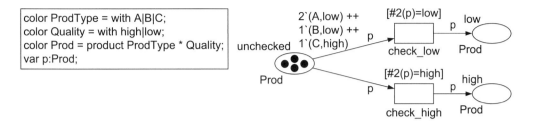

Figure 6.3
A colored Petri net model of the product quality check.

6.4.3 Functions

For the simple examples we have seen so far, we can put all the logic into arc inscriptions and guards. For more complex problems, this is typically impossible. In such situations, it is often convenient to use *functions*. A function can make an arbitrary complex calculation to be used in guards, arc inscriptions, and initialization expressions.

To illustrate the role of functions, consider figure 6.4. Transition max consumes from each of the places p1, p2, and p3 one token and produces the maximum of the values of the three tokens in place p4. To do this, the arc inscription on the arc connecting transition max to place p4 has a nested if-then-else statement:

```
if (y>z) andalso (y>x) then y else if x>z then x else z
```

To allow for more compact arc inscriptions, we can replace this expression by a function call as shown in figure 6.5. Function maximum3 is defined as:

```
fun maximum3(a:INT,b:INT,c:INT) =
   if (b>c) andalso (b>a) then b
   else if a>c then a else c;
```

We see the same two if-then-else statements in this definition. They are both needed, because function maximum3 takes the maximum of three integers rather than two. However, it is also possible to decompose function maximum3 into two calls of function maximum2:

```
fun maximum2(a:INT,b:INT) = if a>b then a else b;
fun maximum3(a:INT,b:INT,c:INT) = maximum2(a,maximum2(b,c));
```

In the redefined function maximum3, function maximum2 is applied to variable a and the maximum of variables b and c. The latter value is an integer, which is obtained by applying function maximum2 to variables b and c.

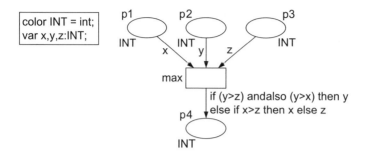

Figure 6.4
An example of a colored Petri net not using functions.

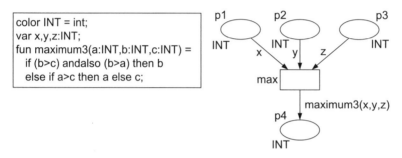

Figure 6.5
An example of a colored Petri net using the dedicated function maximum3.

6.4.4 Further Information on Arc Inscriptions and Guards

In a colored Petri net, expressions can in principle be arbitrary. The only restrictions are that (1) an arc inscription must be evaluated to a multiset of the proper type and (2) a guard needs to evaluate to a Boolean. The CPN language provides a concrete syntax to describe expressions. Although not explicitly shown in the examples so far, it is possible

- To have arc multiplicities;
- To have multisets as arc inscriptions on the ingoing arcs of a transition;
- To use constants or expressions without variables as arc inscriptions; and
- To produce and consume tokens of any type as long as the type matches the type of the corresponding place.

The only requirement is that expressions in guards and in arc inscriptions on the outgoing arcs of a transition can be bound to a concrete value; that is, typically it is not allowed to have a variable that does not appear in the arc inscription of one of the incoming arcs of this transition but that appears in the guard or in an arc inscription of an outgoing arc of this transition. Otherwise, it is impossible to bind this variable given a specific marking, because the number of possible bindings is unrestricted.

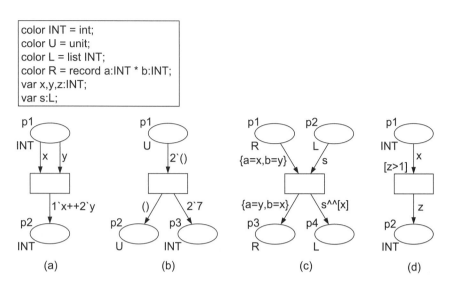

Figure 6.6
Constructs that are allowed (a, b, c) and a constructs that is not allowed (d).

Figure 6.6 depicts examples that show the situations described previously. The CPN in figure 6.6(a) has an arc inscription that evaluates to a multiset. The transition binds an integer to variables x and y and produces one token with value x and two tokens with value y in place p2. In figure 6.6(b), the transition consumes two tokens of type `unit` and produces one token of type `unit` in place p2 and two tokens with value 7 in place p3. The CPN in figure 6.6(c) consumes a record and a list and produces the record with swapped values in place p3 and a list (where the value of x has been added to s) in place p4. Finally, figure 6.6(d) shows a situation that is not allowed, as variable z is unbound (i.e., not bound to any value).

Figure 6.7 shows four situations illustrating possible arc inscriptions and the binding concept. The CPN in figure 6.7(a) consumes an integer x and a Boolean b. Depending on the value of variable b, a token is produced in the output place. Note that the expression [b]%x is shorthand for "if b then 1`x else empty." In figure 6.7(b), a similar construct is used; that is, a token is produced if variable b is bound to true. In this case, however, variable b does not need to appear on any ingoing arc. This is possible, because color set B is a small color set. As a result, all possible bindings can be computed. When simulating such a net with an unbound variable, one binding is selected randomly (all bindings have equal probability). Figure 6.7(c) shows another example of an unbound variable having a small color set. In this case, a quantity of x beers of the same brand are produced. There is one binding for each brand. Finally, the CPN in figure 6.7(d) produces one token in one of the output places.

```
color INT = int;
color L = list INT;
color B = bool;
color Beer = with Corona|Heineken|Miller|Tuborg;
var x:INT;
var s:L;
var b:B;
var a:Beer;
```

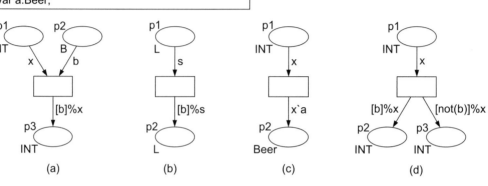

Figure 6.7
Examples illustrating arc inscriptions and binding.

Figure 6.8 shows another example with more advanced arc inscriptions. Tokens in places p1 and p2 represent players, whereas tokens in places t1 and t2 represent teams. A team consists of zero or more players. Transitions move1 and move2 relocate players and teams. Transition unpack takes one "team token" and produces a multiset of "player tokens." Note that the arc inscription on the ingoing arc represents a single token, whereas the arc inscription on the outgoing arc represents a multiset of tokens. If variable t is bound to ["Mike","Pete","John"], then transition unpack produces three tokens, each representing one player, in place p1.

6.5 Time

To investigate the performance of systems or to model temporal aspects of systems, the CPN language allows for adding time stamps to tokens as introduced in section 5.4. A token has a concrete value and may, in addition, carry a time stamp. This time stamp indicates the earliest time at which this token can be consumed. To model tokens carrying a time stamp, the corresponding color set must be made a *timed color set* by adding the term `timed`. As an example, the declarations

```
color TimedINT = int timed;
color TimedList = list timed;
```

define timed color sets for integers and for lists.

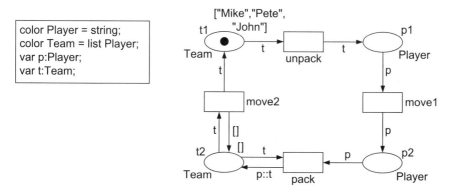

color Player = string;
color Team = list Player;
var p:Player;
var t:Team;

Figure 6.8
An example in which a list is mapped to a multiset of produced tokens.

Tokens in a place of type timed color set carry a time stamp. All other tokens do not carry a time stamp and are, therefore, always available for consumption. Delays can be put in the arc inscription of an outgoing arc of a transition. As in section 5.4, we represent such a delay as @; for example, expression x@+44 denotes that a token with value x is produced with a delay of 44 time units.

To illustrate the time concept of the CPN language, figure 6.9 depicts the patient punch card service desk example of figure 5.24 where we added time to the model.

Time in CPN Tools is by default represented as an infinite integer (IntInf); that is, time is not restricted by bounds on the int type. Section 6.6.3 provides more information on this. As of Version 3.0 of CPN Tools, time can be of type real. The expression x@++3.14 on an output arc denotes that a token with value x and a delay of 3.14 time units is produced.

This completes our introduction to the CPN language. Recall that a CPN model consists of two parts: declarations and network structure. Figure 6.10 summarizes the main ingredients of a CPN model.

6.6   More on Functions

The CPN language is based on the functional programming language Standard ML. Functional programming emphasizes the definition and application of *functions*. In functional programming, computation proceeds by *evaluating expressions* in contrast to (traditional) imperative programming, in which computation proceeds by the sequential execution of statements and is based on the concept of a *state*. Functions in Standard ML are a powerful construct supporting features such as recursion and polymorphism.

```
color Name = string;
color Address = string;
color DateOfBirth = string;
color PatientID = int;
color EmpNo = int;
color Experience = int;
color Gender = with male|female;
color Pat = product PatientID * Name * Address * DateOfBirth * Gender timed;
color Emp = product EmpNo * Experience timed;
color EP = product Emp * Pat timed;
var p:Pat;
var emp:Emp;
val Peter = (12345, "Peter", "Kerkstraat 10, Amsterdam", "13-Dec-1962", male);
val Ann = (641112, 7);
fun d(emp:Emp) = if #1(emp)>5 then 3 else 4;
```

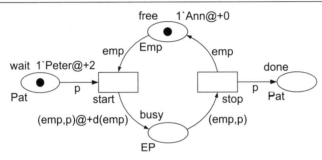

Figure 6.9

A colored Petri net model of the patient punch card service desk extended with time.

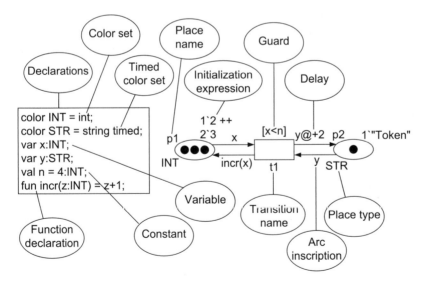

Figure 6.10

The elements of a colored Petri net model.

In this section, we introduce these concepts. We also discuss the probabilistic functions (i.e., random distribution functions) provided by the CPN language. These functions are often used in combination with time—for example, in simulation models.

6.6.1 Recursive Functions

Recursion is the method of defining functions in which a function calls itself. In this way, a form of iteration is created without using iterative constructs, such as loops. To illustrate the concept of recursion, we consider the factorial of a given integer n:

$$n! = \prod_{i=1}^{n} i.$$

For example, $10! = 10 \cdot 9 \cdot 8 \cdot 7 \cdot 6 \cdot 5 \cdot 4 \cdot 3 \cdot 2 \cdot 1 = 3{,}628{,}800$. Let us define a recursive function *fac* to calculate this. Recursion always has (1) a *base* of the induction and (2) the inductive *step*. The base is a trivial value for which we know the answer; for example, for the function *fac* we know that $fac(1) = 1$. The inductive step describes the relation between results of the function of higher parameter values and results of the function of lower parameter values. For the function *fac*, there is a clear relation between two subsequent parameter values i and $i - 1$. For parameter values i that are greater than 1 holds: $fac(i) = i \cdot fac(i - 1)$. Observe that the result for the higher parameter value i is expressed in terms of the result for the lower parameter value $i - 1$. By repeatedly applying the general inductive step until the base is reached, the factorial of any positive integer can be derived. In the example, we have $fac(10) = 10 \cdot fac(9)$, $fac(9) = 9 \cdot fac(8)$, ..., $fac(2) = 2 \cdot fac(1)$, and finally $fac(1) = 1$ (base). In the CPN language, we may use an if-then-else statement to distinguish between the general inductive step and the base:

```
color INT = int;
fun fac(i:INT) = if i>1 then i*fac(i-1) else 1;
```

Another example for a recursive function is the sequence of the Fibonacci numbers $0, 1, 1, 2, 3, 5, 8, 13, \ldots$. The function *fib* calculating the Fibonacci numbers is defined as $fib(0) = 0$, $fib(1) = 1$, and $fib(n) = fib(n - 1) + fib(n - 2)$, for $n \geq 2$. We can define this function as follows:

```
fun fib(x:INT) = if x<2 then x else fib(x-1) + fib(x-2);
```

For $n = 3$, we get $fib(3) = fib(2) + fib(1)$. By $fib(2) = fib(1) + fib(0) = 1$ and $fib(1) = 1$, we conclude $fib(3) = 2$.

The CPN language inherits from Standard ML several standard functions for the type constructor `list`. Most of these functions are recursive functions. Table 6.4 shows the standard functions for lists.

Table 6.4

List Functions

Function	Description
hd list	Head (i.e., the first element) of list
tl list	Tail (i.e., list without the first element) of list
length list	Length of list
rev list	Reverse list
map f list	Uses function f on each element in list and returns a list with all the results
foldr f z list	Returns $f(e_1, f(e_2, \ldots, f(e_n, z) \ldots))$, where list $= [e_1, e_2, \ldots, e_n]$
foldl f z list	Returns $f(e_n, \ldots, f(e_2, f(e_1, z)) \ldots)$, where list $= [e_1, e_2, \ldots, e_n]$
List.nth(list,n)	nth element in list, where $0 \leq n <$ length list
List.take(list,n)	Returns first n elements of list
List.drop(list,n)	Returns what is left after dropping the first n elements of list
List.exists p list	Returns true if predicate p is true for some element in list
List.null list	Returns true if list is empty

Example 6.3 Let $L = [1, 2, 3, 4, 5]$ be a list of integers. The head of list L is $hd(L) = 1$ and the tail $tl(L) = [2, 3, 4, 5]$. The length of list L is $length(L) = 5$, and the reverse is $rev(L) = [5, 4, 3, 2, 1]$. We further obtain List.take$(L, 3) = [1, 2, 3]$ and List.drop$(L, 3) = [4, 5]$.

With these standard functions, we can define other functions. We illustrate this using the inventory management system specified in figure 5.12. Instead of representing the stock by a set of tokens, each specifying a single product, we model the stock by a single token of value list. Figure 6.11 depicts the resulting CPN model.

This CPN model uses three recursive functions. Function check obtains a list of stock items, each represented by a Product and a Number attribute. It analyzes whether each stock item has a nonnegative Number attribute. The base is the situation that the list is empty. In this case, function check returns true. In the inductive step, we check the head of the list. If the value of the Number attribute of the head is less than zero, the function returns false; otherwise, the function is applied to the tail of the list.

When a product is added to the stock, function incrs updates the list of stock items. It obtains as parameters a stock item x to be added and a list s. In the base, the list is empty, and we add item x to the list. In the inductive step, we first check whether the head of the list and item x have the same Product attribute. If this is the case, we

```
color Product = string;
color Number = int;
color StockItem = product Product * Number;
color Stock = list StockItem;
var x:StockItem;
var s:Stock;
fun incrs(x:StockItem,s:Stock) = if s=[] then [x]
                        else if #1(hd(s)) = #1(x) then (#1(hd(s)),#2(hd(s)) + #2(x))::tl(s)
                        else hd(s)::incrs(x,tl(s));
fun decrs(x:StockItem,s:Stock) = incrs((#1(x),~(#2(x))),s);
fun check(s:Stock) = if s=[] then true
                    else if #2(hd(s))<0 then false
                    else check(tl(s));
val initstock = [("bike",1), ("wheel",2), ("bell",3), ("steering_wheel",3), ("frame",2)]:Stock;
```

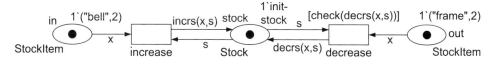

Figure 6.11

A colored Petri net model of the inventory management system.

calculate the sum of their Number values. If the products are different, we try to add item x to the next element of list s by applying function incrs to item x and the tail of list s.

Finally, function decrs updates the list of stock items when some items of a single product are taken from stock. This function calls function incrs by negating the Number value of item x. In the guard of transition decrease, we call function check with argument decrs(x,s); that is, list s after removing stock item x.

The following function calculates the total number of products in stock:

```
fun totalstock(s:Stock) =
   if s=[] then 0
   else #2(hd(s))+totalstock(tl(s));
```

Function totalstock works on parameters of type Stock—that is, a list of stock items, each represented by a Product and a Number attribute. Function totalstock takes the sum of all products. The base is the situation that the list is empty; that is, there are no products left in the list, and, therefore, function totalstock returns 0. In the inductive step, we take the head hd(s) of the list and build the sum of the Number attribute of this stock item and function totalstock applied to the tail tl(s) of the list.

Exercise 6.4   Construct a function `maxstock` that calculates the maximal stock of a single product. Define a function `maxstockname` that returns the product that has a maximum number of items using function `maxstock`.

Functions can have more than one argument. Function `enoughstock` is an example:

```
fun enoughstock(s:Stock,n:Number) =
   if s=[] then []
   else if #2(hd(s))>=n then hd(s)::enoughstock(tl(s),n)
        else enoughstock(tl(s),n);
```

This function returns a list with just the products for which at least the given number of items is available; for example, `enoughstock(s,8)` returns a list of all stock items of list s with at least eight items in stock.

Question 6.4   How can we construct a function `enoughstockn(s,n)` that calculates the number of products having at least n items in stock?

The answer to this question is not difficult:

```
fun enoughstockn(s:Stock,n:Number) =
   if s=[] then 0
   else if #2(hd(s))>=n then 1+enoughstockn(tl(s),n)
        else enoughstockn(tl(s),n);
```

An alternative answer to the question would be to use function `enoughstock` and a function to calculate the length of a list. For this purpose, we can use the built-in function `length`, which calculates the length of any list; see table 6.4. Using these two functions, we can define function `enoughstockn` as:

```
fun enoughstockn(s:Stock,n:Number) = length(enoughstock(s,n));
```

Beside standard functions, such as `hd` and `tl`, table 6.4 also lists functions that have functions as arguments. Such a function is a *higher-order function*. The functions `map`, `foldr`, and `foldl` are higher-order functions.

Function `map` applies a function to all elements of a given list. That way, it is possible to increase the values of each element of a list of integers, for instance.

```
color IntList = list INT;
val myIntList = [1,2,3,4]:IntList;
fun incr(i:int) = i+1;
```

We can now apply function incr to each element of `myIntList` just by applying the `map` function. The function call

```
map incr myList
```

evaluates to the list [2, 3, 4, 5]. Function `foldr` can, for example, be used to add up all elements of a list. The function call

```
foldr op+ 0 myIntList
```

evaluates to $1 + 2 + 3 + 4 = 10$. As shown in table 6.4, this function works as follows: $op + (1, op + (2, op + (3, op + (4, 0))))$, where $op+$ is the normal addition function—that is, $op + (a, b) = a + b$. First, the function calculates the sum of the last element of the list and zero. In the next step, it calculates the sum of the last but one element of the list and the result of the previous step, and so on.

Exercise 6.5 Show that we can use function `foldr` to define the concatenation of two lists without any need for recursion. Define a function `conc` such that $conc([a, b, c], [d, e, f])$ evaluates to $[a, b, c, d, e, f]$.

Exercise 6.6 Define a function `odd` that returns the odd elements of a given list. (Hint: Define a function even such that function `odd` treats the odd elements of the list and function `even` treats the even elements.)

6.6.2 Pattern Matching

The CPN language supports the concept of *pattern matching*. Pattern matching does not extend the expressive power of the language but allows for a more compact notation. For example, instead of using the built-in head and tail functions `hd` and `tl` and explicit if-then-else statements, the notation `[]` can be used for the empty list and `x::y` for lists containing at least one element, where x is the head and y is the tail. Consider, for example, the following function definition without pattern matching:

```
fun lenlist1(s:Stock) =
   if s=[] then 0
   else 1+lenlist1(tl(s));
```

This function calculates the number of different products in stock. This corresponds to calculating the length of list s. Using pattern matching, we can redefine this function to:

```
fun lenlist2([]) = 0 |
    lenlist2(si::s) = 1+lenlist2(s);
```

Now there are two patterns, `[]` and `si::s`. The first one considers the empty list and the second one a list containing at least one element. If we compare the definitions of functions `lenlist1` and `lenlist2`, there are several differences. First, the if-then-else statement is replaced by a horizontal bar |. Second, there is no need to use the tail function, because pattern `si::s` can be used to refer to the tail. Finally, function `lenlist1` is explicitly defined for lists of type `Stock`, whereas function `lenlist2` can be applied to *any* list. The pattern matching mechanism makes it clear that function `lenlist2` only accepts lists. In the definition of function `lenlist2`, the type of elements in the list is not important. Therefore, the definition applies to any list. In this way, the CPN language allows for *polymorphism*; that is, one function is defined independent of the exact type (in this case any list).

Pattern matching allows for more compact definitions. We illustrate this with some examples. First, we redefine function `totalstock`.

```
fun totalstock([]:Stock) = 0 |
    totalstock(si::s) = #2(si)+totalstock(s);
```

Another example for using pattern matching is an alternative definition of function `maxstock`.

```
fun maxstock([]:Stock) = [] |
    maxstock(si::s) = if #2(si)>maxstock(s) then #2(si)
                      else maxstock(s);
```

In a similar way, we can translate the other functions already given. As an example, consider function incrs used in the CPN model in figure 6.11. This function can be redefined as follows:

```
fun incrs(x:StockItem,[]:Stock) = [x] |
    incrs (x,(si::s)) = if #1(si) = #1(x)
                        then (#1(si),#2(si)+#2(x))::s
                        else si::incrs(x,s);
```

To conclude this section on pattern matching, we show three example definitions of polymorphic functions.

```
fun reverse([]) = [] |
    reverse(x::y) = reverse(y)^^[x];
fun odd([]) = [] |
    odd(x::y) = x::even(y);
fun even([]) = [] |
    even(x::y) = odd(y);
```

Function `reverse` reverses any list—for example, `reverse([1, 2, 3])` = [3, 2, 1]. Functions odd and even were introduced in exercise 6.6 and are now defined using pattern matching. Consequently, they can now be applied to any list.

Exercise 6.7

1. Write a polymorphic function `exists` that checks whether an arbitrary list contains an element that satisfies a predicate p. The return value of this function is true if such an element exists and false otherwise.

2. Write a polymorphic function `filter` that collects from an arbitrary list all elements that satisfy a predicate *p*. The return value of this function is the empty list `[]` if no such element exists and a list with all elements satisfying *p* otherwise.

6.6.3   Random Distribution Functions

We can model systems and business processes as CPNs. CPNs can be analyzed to check the correctness of a system or to estimate its performance. One of the most widely used analysis techniques is simulation. It allows us to analyze the performance of a system and to validate the model. To use a CPN model as a simulation model, the CPN language offers time-related functions and statistical functions. In the following section, we highlight several functions that are useful for simulation purposes.

When simulating a process model, we often need to know the current time in the model. This may be useful for measuring cycle times, for instance. To this end, the CPN language provides a function `time()` that returns the current model time. This function cannot be used on ingoing arcs of a transition and in guards, because this would lead to semantical problems. The return type of the function `time()` is an infinite integer (`IntInf`) and needs to be cast to a proper type, such as `int` or `string`. Table 6.5 lists four of the cast functions provided by the CPN language.

Version 3.0 of CPN Tools also supports time stamps of type `real`. This way, conversion can be avoided. For example, the expression `x@++exponential(3.14)` assigns a delay to a token sampled from a negative exponential distribution with expected value $\frac{1}{3.14}$.

When using a CPN model as a simulation model, it is necessary to attach probabilities to certain events. For example, the duration of a production step may be sampled from a probability distribution, or a path in the process model is taken with a certain probability. There are two ways to achieve this: (1) using the function `ran()` on a *finite* color set or (2) using one of the predefined random distribution functions.

A finite color set has only a finite number of possible values. Examples of finite color sets are

Table 6.5
Time-Related functions

Function	Description
`IntInf.toInt(time())`	Converts `time()` to an `int`.
`IntInf.fromInt(i)`	Converts `int i` to a time value of type `IntInf`.
`IntInf.toString(time())`	Converts `time()` to a `string`.
`IntInf.fromString(s)`	Converts `string s` to a time value of type `IntInf`.

```
color B = bool;
color Age = int with 0..99;
color Gender = with male|female;
```

It is possible to apply function `ran()` to these color sets to obtain a random value from these sets; for example, `B.ran()` yields a Boolean, `Age.ran()` yields an integer between 0 and 99, and `Gender.ran()` yields `male` or `female`. Every value of a color set has an equal probability. The function `ran()` can be used in other functions or on outgoing arcs of a transition. An outgoing arc of a transition with an arc inscription `Age.ran()` produces a token with a value between 0 and 99. An outgoing arc of a transition with an arc inscription `if B.ran() then 1'Age.ran() else empty` produces a token with a value between 0 and 99 but only in 50 percent of the cases. An outgoing arc of a transition with an arc inscription `Gender.ran()@+Age.ran()` produces a token with a delay between 0 and 99 time units and value `male` or `female`, for instance.

As shown in figures 6.7(b), 6.7(c), and 6.7(d), it is also possible to use variables on outgoing arcs. For small color sets, one binding is sampled from all possible bindings. Alternatively, it is possible to use predefined random distribution functions. Table 6.6 lists these functions. For example, the function `uniform(a:real, b:real):real` yields a random number between parameters a and b. The probability distribution is uniform; that is, any value between parameters a and b has the same probability. The two parameters a and b and the result are reals. As tokens and delays cannot be of type `real`, the result of `uniform(a,b)` needs to be cast to another type, typically `int`. For this purpose, one can use the functions `floor`, `ceil`, and `round`. The function `floor(r)` produces the greatest integer not greater than parameter r. The function `ceil(r)` produces the least integer not less than parameter r. The function `round(r)` yields the integer nearest to parameter r.

Example 6.5 Given a variable $x = 5.2$, we have `floor(x)=5`, `ceil(x)=6`, and `round(x)=5`. The function `floor(uniform(1.0,5.0))` returns 1, 2, 3, or 4 (each with equal probability); the function `ceil(uniform(1.0,5.0))` returns 2, 3, 4, or 5 (each with equal probability); and the function `round(uniform(1.0,5.0))` returns 1, 2, 3, 4, or 5. In the final example, the probability of value 1 or value 5 is equal to the probability of value 2.

The function `bernoulli(p:real):int` returns an integer taken from a Bernoulli distribution with probability p of success—that is, `bernoulli(p)` $= 1$ with probability p, where p is a real with $0 \leq p \leq 1$.

The function `binomial(n:int,p:real):int` returns a sample from a binomial distribution with n experiments and probability p for success. Parameter n is an integer,

Table 6.6
Random Distribution Functions

Function	Description
bernoulli(p:real):int	For $0 \leq p \leq 1$, bernoulli(p) samples a value from a Bernoulli distribution: with probability p, the result is 1, otherwise 0.
binomial(n:int,p:real):int	For $n \geq 1$ and $0 \leq p \leq 1$, binomial(n,p) samples a value from a binomial distribution. The result is an integer $0, 1, \ldots, n$. The expected value is $n \cdot p$.
chisq(n:int):real	For $n \geq 1$, chisq(n) samples a value from a chi-square distribution. The expected value is n.
discrete(a:int,b:int):int	For $a < b$, discrete(a,b) samples a value from a discrete distribution where all values $\{a, a+1, \ldots, b-1, b\}$ have an equal probability.
erlang(n:int,r:real):real	For $n \geq 1$ and $r > 0$, erlang(n,r) samples a value from an Erlang distribution; that is, the sum of n independent exponentially distributed values with parameter r. The expected value is n/r.
exponential(r:real):real	For $r > 0$, exponential(r) samples a value from an exponential distribution with mean $1/r$.
normal(n:real,v:real):real	For $v \geq 0$, normal(n,v) samples a value from a normal distribution with mean n and variance v.
poisson(m:real):int	For $m > 0$, poisson(m) samples a value from a Poisson distribution with intensity m. The mean is m.
student(n:int):real	For $n \geq 1$, student(n) samples a value from a student's t distribution with n degrees of freedom.
uniform(a:real,b:real):real	For $b > a$, uniform(a,b) samples a value from a uniform distribution with mean $(a+b)/2$.

and parameter p a real with $0 \leq p \leq 1$. For example, throwing a dice 50 times and observe how many times a six was thrown corresponds to a binomial distribution with parameters $n = 50$ and $p = 1/6$—that is, binomial(50,0.166666).

The sum of the squares of n independent normally distributed random variables with mean 0.0 and standard deviation 1.0 is a chi-square distribution with n degrees of freedom. The corresponding function is chisq(n:int):real. This distribution is mainly used for statistical tests.

The function discrete(a:int,b:int):int is the discrete version of the function uniform(a,b); for example, the function discrete(1,5) generates numbers 1, 2, 3, 4, or 5 with equal probability. The function discrete(a,b) corresponds to the function floor(uniform(real(a),real(b+1))), where the functions real() and floor() cast a value to the proper type.

The function `erlang(n:int,r:real):real` can be used to obtain values from an Erlang distribution with parameters n and r, where n is a positive integer and r a positive real. An Erlang distribution with parameters n and r can be generated by adding n random numbers from an exponential distribution with parameter r.

One of the most widely used random distribution functions for simulating interarrival times in a simulation is the function `exponential(r:real):real`, where r is a positive real. This function can be used to generate a Poisson arrival process.

Three other random distribution functions are `normal(n:real,v:real):real`, `poisson(m:real):int`, and `student(n:int):real`. The function `normal(n,v)` returns a sample from a normal distribution with mean n and variance v. The function `poisson(m)` returns an integer taken from a Poisson distribution with intensity m. The function `student(n)` returns a sample from a student's t distribution with n degrees of freedom.

Recall that by default time in CPN models is represented as an infinite integer rather than a real. Therefore, one needs to choose an appropriate timescale and cast reals to integers when assigning a value or a time stamp to a token. One should choose a timescale of milliseconds rather than seconds, seconds rather than minutes, or minutes rather than hours. For example, if the sending of a message takes between 1 and 2 seconds, one should not choose the timescale of seconds, because the function `discrete(1,2)` and the function `floor(uniform(1.0,3.0))` generate value 1 or 2; that is, it is not possible to have a real in between these two integers. If, instead, a timescale of milliseconds is used, we can use the function `discrete(1000,2000)` or the function `floor(uniform(1000.0,2001.0))` to get a more continuous view of time.

In the latest version of CPN Tools, version 3.0, it is also possible to use real time stamps. Expression `x@++uniform(1.0,3.0)` assigns a real-valued delay to a token with value x. When using real-valued time stamps, conversions to integers are not needed.

6.7   Examples of Colored Petri Net Models

We conclude this chapter by describing two additional CPN models and introduce design choices.

6.7.1   Example: Signing Documents

The first example is a business process modeling the signing of documents. The business process involves two entities: documents to be signed and persons that sign those documents. Each document needs to be signed by precisely three persons. It is not allowed that the same person signs the same document multiple times. Moreover, not more than five documents can be in the signing phase at the same time. Figure 6.12 depicts the resulting CPN model.

```
color Doc = string;
color Person = string;
color Signatures = list Person;
color SignedDoc = product Doc * Signatures;
color BlackToken = unit;
var d:Doc;
var p:Person;
var s:Signatures;
fun notin(p:Person,[]:Signatures) = true |
    notin(p,h::s) = if p=h then false else notin(p,s);
fun count([]) = 0 |
    count(h::s) = 1+count(s);
```

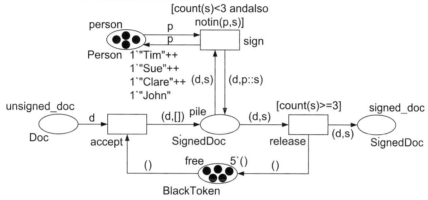

Figure 6.12
A colored Petri net model for signing documents.

The network structure represents that a document can be in any one of the three states unsigned, partially signed, and fully signed. Accordingly, the net contains three places unsigned_doc, pile, and signed_doc. Transitions accept and release control the work in progress. Firing transition accept produces an unsigned document in place pile. If a document has been signed by three persons, it is moved to place signed_doc by firing transition release. Transition sign models signing a document. All persons are in place person.

For purposes of simplicity, persons and documents are represented as strings in figure 6.12. To keep track of the signatures, color set SignedDoc includes a list of signatures. Each signature is represented by the name of the corresponding person. Transition sign adds signatures to this list by matching a person and a document. The guard of transition sign specifies the condition for such a match: there should be less than three signatures on the document, and only persons who did not sign yet are allowed to put their signature on the document. The guard of transition sign uses the recursive function notin that returns true if person p does not appear in the signature list s. Transition release has a guard to make sure that only documents with three signatures are released.

As the specification requires that at most five documents can be in the signing phase at the same time, we must ensure that place pile cannot contain more than five tokens. To this end, place free has been added that initially contains five tokens. As the value of these tokens is not relevant, we used type unit. Each token in place free represents a free slot. The way place free is connected to transitions accept and release guarantees that place pile has a capacity of five.

Exercise 6.8 Replace place free in figure 6.12 with a place holding always one token with a value to show the number of documents being processed.

6.7.2 Example: Thermostat

The second example is a simple thermostat system illustrating the use of time in CPNs. Consider a room with some temperature at any point in time. There is a heater to warm up the room, and there is a door that opens every hour such that part of the warmth escapes. When the door is opened, the room temperature suddenly drops by 3°C. The heater has a capacity of heating the room 1°C every fifteen minutes. If the heater is on, the room temperature rises by $4 - 3 = 1$°C each hour. Therefore, there is a control system, the thermostat, that switches off the heater. The thermostat follows the following rules. If the room temperature drops below 18°C, the heater is switched on. If the temperature rises above 22°C, the heater is switched off. Figure 6.13 depicts the corresponding CPN model.

Place temp records the temperature. Initially, it is 15°C. Places on and off represent the two states of the thermostat. These places hold uncolored tokens (i.e., tokens of type unit). We added place heater for timing purposes. This place has a timed color

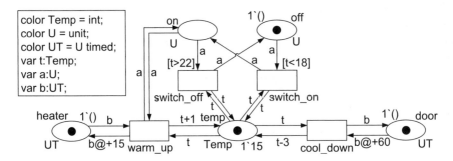

Figure 6.13
A colored Petri net model for a thermostat.

set (UT), and the delay of its token makes sure that the room temperature can rise only 1°C every fifteen minutes. Similarly, we added place door, also of type UT, to make sure that once every hour the door opens. Variables a and b are introduced for the arc inscriptions relating to uncolored tokens. We can also replace these variables by constants of value ().

Exercise 6.9   Describe the room temperature starting in the initial marking shown; that is, play a timed, colored "token game."

Note that playing the timed, colored token game is exactly what happens in a simulation tool.

Exercise 6.10   Extend the model in figure 6.13 such that there is a day program and a night program. From midnight to 8 a.m., the thermostat keeps the temperature between 14°C and 18°C. (If the room temperature drops below 14°C, the heater is switched on. If the room temperature rises above 18°C, the heater is switched off.) During the day— that is, from 8 a.m. to midnight—the thermostat keeps the room temperature between 18°C and 22°C as shown in figure 6.13.

6.8   Test Yourself

6.8.1   Solutions to Exercises
6.1
1. The type is bool, and the value is true.
2. The type is bool, and the value is false.
3. The type is bool, and the value is true.

6.2
1. Operator #4 aims at obtaining the fourth element of tuple (4,5,6) that consists only of three elements.
2. A product is defined of at least two color sets; here, the tuple (1) has, however, only a single element.
3. Operator :: adds an element to a list; [Tuborg] is, however, a list and not an element. The correct expression is Tuborg::[Corona,Miller] or [Tuborg]^^ [Corona,Miller].

6.3   Figure 6.14 depicts the CPN model.

6.4   The base of the induction is the empty list, and the inductive step is the nonempty list. If the list is empty, the function should return zero; otherwise, the number of items of the first product in the list should be compared with function maxstock applied to the tail of the list. Using recursion, the result can be obtained. We define:

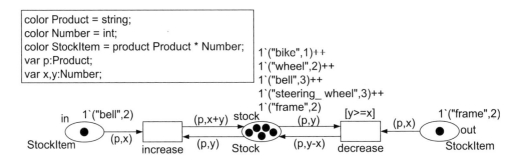

Figure 6.14
A colored Petri net model of the inventory management system.

```
fun maxstock(s:Stock) =
    if s=[] then 0
    else if #2(hd(s))>=maxstock(tl(s)) then #2(hd(s))
        else maxstock(tl(s));
```

To obtain a product that has a maximum number of items, we define the function `maxstockname` as follows:

```
fun maxstockname(s:Stock) =
    if s=[] then "no product found"
    else if #2(hd(s))=maxstock(tl(s)) then #1(hd(s))
        else maxstockname(tl(s));
```

The function `maxstockname` calls the function `maxstock`. The base returns the string `"no product found"`. This string is only returned if the list is actually empty; that is, if there are no products in stock. If there are multiple products having the same quantity, the first product in the list is selected.

6.5   The function `conc` can be defined as:

```
fun conc(xs,ys) = foldr op:: ys xs;
```

Let $xs = [a, b, c]$. According to the definition of function `foldr` (see table 6.4), function `conc(xs,ys)` evaluates to $op :: (a, (op :: (b, (op :: (c, ys))))) = a :: (b :: (c :: ys)))$. That means, list xs is unfolded, and its elements are consecutively in reverse order concatenated with ys.

6.6   The function `odd` can be defined as:

```
color L = list INT;
fun odd(x:L) = if x=[] then []
                else hd(x)::even(tl(x));
fun even(x:L) = if x=[] then []
                else odd(tl(x));
```

The function odd takes the head of a list L and calls then the function even with the tail of list L. The function even skips the head of the list and calls the function odd with the tail.

6.7

1. The function can be defined as follows:

```
fun exists(p,[]) = false |
    exists(p,(x::xs)) = p(x) orelse exists(p,xs);
```

The base is the empty list, and the inductive step is the nonempty list. For an empty list, predicate p evaluates to false, hence the function returns false. In the inductive step, the function returns true if the head of the list satisfies predicate p; otherwise, the function exists is applied to the tail of the list.

2. The function is defined as:

```
fun filter(p,[]) = [] |
    filter(p,(x::xs)) = if p(x) then x::filter(p,xs)
                        else filter(p,xs);
```

Again, the base is the empty list, and the inductive step is the nonempty list. For an empty list, the function returns the empty list, because there is no element that satisfies predicate p. In the inductive step, the head of the list is checked. If it satisfies predicate p, then it is concatenated to a list of elements collected from the tail; otherwise, the function filter is applied to the tail of the list.

6.8   Figure 6.15 depicts the CPN model. Place count contains one token representing the number of documents in progress. Note that a guard has been added to transition accept.

6.9   At time 0, the room temperature is 15°C (0:15). The thermostat switches on at the same time, and the temperature instantly raises to 16°C (0:16). At the same time, the door opens, and the room temperature drops to 13°C (0:13). Note that the two events take place at the same time, but their order could be reversed and still result in 13°C at time 0. There is a delay of fifteen minutes after the room temperature rises to 14°C (15:14), and so on. A possible run is thus $\langle(0:15), (0:16), (0:13), (15:14), (30:15), (45:16), (60:17), (60:14), (75:15), (90:16), (105:17), \dots\rangle$.

6.10   Figure 6.16 depicts the CPN model. We use two places to distinguish between day and night and two additional places to fix the minimum and the maximum room temperature of the respective program. Transitions switch_to_night and switch_to_day model the switch between the two programs. Transition switch_to_night sets the minimum and maximum temperature to 14°C and 18°C, and switch_to_day sets the values to 18°C and 22°C. A timed token in places night and day precisely models the respective time intervals.

```
color Doc = string;
color Person = string;
color Signatures = list Person;
color SignedDoc = product Doc * Person;
var d:Doc;
var p:Person;
var s:Signatures;
fun notin(p:Person,[]:Signatures) = true |
    notin(p,h::s) = if p=h then false else notin(p,s);
fun count([]) = 0 |
    count(h::s) = 1+count(s);
color INT = int;
var x:INT;
```

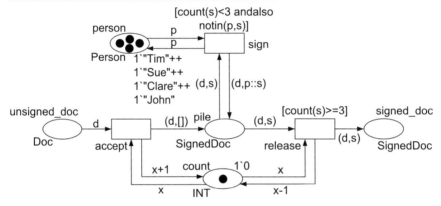

Figure 6.15
The colored Petri net model of exercise 6.8.

6.8.2 Further Exercises

Exercise 6.11 The following example is taken from Jensen (1997a). A small model railway has a circular track with two trains, A and B, that move in the same direction. The track is, for safety reasons, divided into seven sectors $S = \{S_1, S_2, \ldots, S_7\}$ (see figure 6.17). At the start of each sector, a signal post shows whether a train may proceed or not. By a set of sensors situated at the signal posts, it can be automatically determined whether a given sector is empty or not. To allow a train to enter a sector S_i, the sector must be empty. Moreover, the next sector S_{i+1} also must be empty, because a train could be situated at the beginning of sector S_{i+1}. As a result, it may be impossible for the incoming train to stop before colliding with the train ahead.

1. Model the train system as a Petri net. Each sector S_i may be represented by three places o_{iA}, o_{iB}, and e_i (where o_{iA} is shorthand for "sector S_i is occupied by train A", o_{iB} is shorthand for "sector S_i is occupied by train B", and e_i is shorthand for "sector S_i is empty." Play the token game for the constructed model.

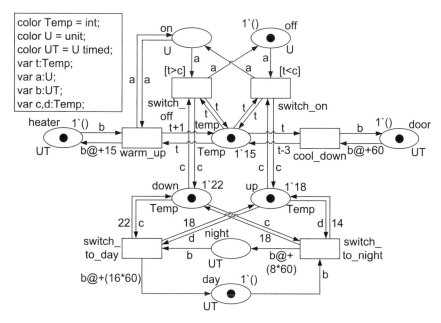

Figure 6.16
A colored Petri net model of the thermostat with day and night program.

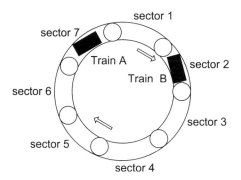

Figure 6.17
A railway system with seven sectors and two trains.

2. Model the same system as a CPN model in which each sector is described by two places o_i (i.e., sector S_i is occupied by a train) and e_i. Place o_i has the set $\{A, B\}$ as possible token colors, whereas place e_i is just a placeholder. Play the token game of the constructed CPN model. Compare the CPN model with the Petri net in (1).

3. Model the same system as a CPN model that has only two places o and e and a single transition move.

Exercise 6.12   Consider a database system in which authors can submit articles. The articles are stored in such a way that it is possible to get a sequential list of articles for each author. In the list, the oldest articles appear first. The system should support three actions: "submit an article" (with the name of the author and the article), "query articles of an author," and "add an author" to the database. Each article can have multiple authors; that is, the article is stored once for each author, and only authors already registered in the database can submit articles. Model this system as a CPN model.

Exercise 6.13   Consider the CPN model in figure 6.18.

1. Define function f(a,X) in such a way that element a is appended as the head of the list X.

2. Define function f(a,X) in such a way that the result is a sorted list that contains the elements from X and element a.

3. Define function f(a,X) in such a way that the result is a sorted list that contains the elements from X and element a, but each number may not be in the list more than once.

Exercise 6.14   Model the following business process of an auction. A list of objects is sold in the order of that list. Every object is from a client and has a minimum price. A bid should exceed the minimum price and the previous bid if any. If there was no bid during the last ten time units, then the object is sold to the highest bidder. Whenever all objects are sold, a list with the sold objects, their price, and the new owner is produced. As a simplification, one can assume that there is always at least one bid.

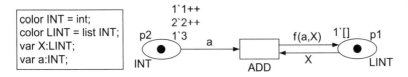

Figure 6.18
The colored Petri net model of exercise 6.13.

Exercise 6.15 Consider the following concert reservation system. In this system, we give attention to the booking of seats for particular events. The system offers an interface to the user modeled by four places create_event, request, reject, and confirm. A token in place create_event creates an event—for example, "Rammstein at Gelredome on 6 December 2009." Once the event is created, people can request tickets by producing a token in place request. Such a request is identified by the person's name and the event ID (i.e., a string uniquely identifying the event—for example, "Rammstein at Gelredome on 6 December 2009"). We assume that for each event a fixed number of seats is available, say, $1,000$. These seats are numbered $1, 2, \ldots, 1000$. A request is rejected if no more seats are available. A request is confirmed if there is still a seat available. In this case, the seat number is returned. An example token passed back by place confirm is ("Peter Jansen","Rammstein at Gelredome on 6 December 2009",542), indicating that Peter successfully obtained a reservation for the Rammstein concert and that his allocated seat number is 542.

The following color sets, functions, and variables are given:

```
color Name = string;
color Event = string;
color Seat = int with 1..1000;
color NxE = product Name * Event;
color NxExS = product Name * Event * Seat;
fun seats() = Seat.all();
var n:Name;
var e:Event;
var s:Seat;
```

Note that the function `seats()` returns the list $[1, 2, 3, \ldots, 1000]$.

1. Model the reservation system based on the previous description. The internal database of the office should keep track of free seats and reserved seats (with corresponding name information) for each event. Clearly identify any additional declarations, arc inscriptions, color sets, and other extensions that are needed.

2. Extend the CPN model with payments and the printing of tickets. All tickets for a particular event are printed at the same time, and only tickets that have been paid for are printed. It is not possible to pay twice for the same seat or for a seat that has not been reserved. Such an invalid payment is declined by the reservation system, and a rejection message is sent back to the environment. Valid payments, on the other hand, are confirmed by sending a confirmation message. The printing of the tickets is triggered by the environment (a single message triggers the printing of all paid tickets for an event), and the printed tickets are sent from the reservation system to the environment. Each ticket has a name, an event ID, and a seat number. After the tickets for an event are printed, all subsequent reservations or payments for this event are rejected. Clearly

identify the new interface places, additional declarations, arc inscriptions, color sets, and other extensions that are needed.

Exercise 6.16 Consider the following business process of a take-away restaurant. The restaurant receives an order through a place order_in. Color set Order is one of the declarations given:

```
color Customer = string timed;
color Product = with coffee | tea | beer | fish | chips timed;
color Order = product Customer * Product timed;
var c:Customer;
var p:Product;
```

An example of an order is ("John",beer); that is, one serving of beer for customer John. Customers can order only one item at a time. Each incoming order gets an order number to uniquely identify a request. It takes one minute to accept an order and to attach a number to it. The acceptance of an order triggers the production of food and drinks. Things are produced in parallel whenever possible, and each item is linked to a particular customer order (i.e., given an order ("John",beer), the beer is produced specifically for John). It takes two minutes to prepare a drink (i.e., coffee, tea, or beer) and three minutes to prepare food (i.e., one serving of fish or chips). When the item is produced, the customer is called, and the items are delivered. The delivery takes one minute. There are five employees working in the take-away restaurant. There is one employee accepting orders and delivering items to the customers. There are two employees preparing drinks and two employees preparing food, but employees preparing the food can also prepare drinks. An employee can do only one task at a time.

Model the restaurant based on the previous description. You will need to introduce additional declarations (e.g., for the order number). Customer orders do not need to be handled in a fixed order (i.e., one customer order can overtake another one), but there should not be unnecessary waiting (i.e., resources are eager to help customers and work in parallel when possible).

Exercise 6.17 This exercise is a continuation of the Brisbane CityCat system from exercise 4.11. Model the Brisbane CityCat system as described in exercise 4.11 as a colored Petri net, including its initial state. Moreover, take the following five aspects into account:

1. Distinguish individual CityCats (1, 2, ..., 10).
2. There are two types of CityCats: slow and fast ones. CityCats 7, 8, 9, and 10 are of a newer generation; they only need five minutes to move from one stop to another. The older CityCats (1, 2, ..., 6) need ten minutes.

3. CityCats are not allowed to overtake one another. Therefore, a slower CityCat may slow down a faster one. Moreover, there can be a queue of CityCats in front of a stop. In this case, a first-come, first-served (FCFS) queuing discipline is used.

4. Upstream CityCats have priority over downstream CityCats. For example, if there are CityCats queuing for stop B, then the CityCats originating from A (upstream) have priority over CityCats originating from C (downstream).

5. Each stop at A, B, C, or D takes five minutes to allow passenger to embark or disembark.

6.9   Summary

In this chapter, we presented a precise syntax for Petri nets extended with color and time (CPNs) as introduced in chapter 5. For this purpose, we introduced the CPN language. The CPN language provides the basic types int, real, string, bool, and unit. With these basic types and the type constructors product, record, and list, one can define arbitrarily complex place types.

Arc inscriptions and guards define the behavior of transitions in a colored Petri net. The CPN language offers constants, variables, and operators on the basic types and type constructors to define arc inscriptions and guards. More complex expressions can be conveniently defined as functions. To this end, the CPN language provides standard functions for the basic types and type constructors. It further supports more advanced concepts for functions, such as recursion and polymorphism.

The CPN language also supports the extension of Petri nets with time. It provides a syntax to describe time stamps of tokens and delays, and it allows color sets to be extended to timed color sets. In addition to designing CPN models, the CPN language also offers the possibility of simulating CPN models. To allow for realistic simulation experiments, it provides a number of statistical functions.

A CPN model consists of a graphical description of the network structure and of declarations. The network structure consists of—as in the case of Petri nets—places, transitions, and arcs. Declarations are defined using the CPN language. There are four types of declarations: (timed) color sets to define place types, constants, variables, and functions.

After studying this chapter you should to be able to:

- Use the basic types `int`, `real`, `string`, `bool`, and `unit` and the type constructors `product`, `record`, and `list` of the CPN language;
- Use the basic operators for these types;
- Formulate arc inscriptions, guards, and initialization expressions;
- Define more complex expressions using functions; and
- Formulate Petri nets with color and time using the CPN language.

6.10   Further Reading

The CPN language is based on Standard ML. Standard ML is a popular functional programming language developed in the 1980s. In 1987, Robin Milner and his team won the British Computer Society Technical Award for Technical Excellence for their work on Standard ML. The language was standardized in 1990 and is one of a very few programming languages with a fully formal definition, giving it significant appeal for research purposes and for industrial-strength applications. One of the important features of the language is that it is safe: all errors that could crash an ML program are detected at compile time or handled neatly at runtime. This property makes program development and debugging much easier than in most other programming languages. For an overview of Standard ML, we refer to textbooks of Milner et al. (1997), Ullman (1998), and Paulson (2010).

CPNs allow for the modeling of systems in which communication, synchronization, and resource sharing play an important role. The CPN language combines the strengths of Petri nets with the strengths of high-level programming languages. Petri nets provide the primitives for process interaction, whereas the CPN language provides the primitives for the definition of data types and the manipulation of data values. There have been several proposals to extend Petri nets with color or time—for example, the ExSpect language (Hee 2009) and CPN-Ami (Hamez et al. 2006). However, the proposal by Kurt Jensen (1997a, 1997b, 1997c) has been most successful. One of the main advantages of CPNs is their strong theoretical basis and the existence of tools to support the modeling and analysis of CPN models. CPN Tools has been successfully applied in many industrial applications. An excellent overview of CPNs and their application is given in the textbook of Jensen and Kristensen (2009). For more information about CPN Tools, we refer to the Web page; see <http://www.cpntools.org>.

7   Hierarchical Petri Nets

Petri nets extended with color and time (CPNs) are suitable to model the behavior of complex systems. However, despite their expressiveness, CPNs still do not provide the modeling power needed for modeling industrial systems. The weakness of CPNs is that they try to capture all behavior in one comprehensive net and do not represent the hierarchical structure of a system. As a consequence, the CPN model is typically not manageable.

For that reason, we present a third extension of Petri nets in this chapter: *hierarchy*. Extending Petri nets with hierarchy makes it possible to reflect the hierarchical structure of a system in a Petri net model. Hierarchical CPNs can model a wide variety of systems ranging from the controller of a washing machine to the claims handling process in a large insurance company. We can model any system using this technique. Although the extension with hierarchy does not add expressive power in a formal sense, it facilitates the modeling of large and complex systems, such as information systems and business processes from practice.

We introduce hierarchical modeling and illustrate two approaches, top-down and bottom-up modeling, to obtain a hierarchical system description (section 7.1). There are many ways to extend Petri nets with hierarchy. We present the hierarchy concept supported by the CPN language and tools like CPN Tools. The idea is to decompose a CPN into modules. A module has an interface and is replaced by a substitution transition. First, we give an informal introduction to Petri nets extended with hierarchy (section 7.2) and then show a concrete syntax, which is based on the CPN language (section 7.3). Hierarchical CPNs facilitate the modeling of large and complicated systems. We illustrate this by modeling a production system (section 7.4) and a logistic network (section 7.5).

7.1   Hierarchical Modeling: Top-Down versus Bottom-Up Modeling

The task of a designer of an information system is to model the system to be built or to model an existing system. A designer must take into account many conditions when modeling a system. The model must represent all relevant aspects of the system. For a designer, it is a challenge to fulfill this condition, because, as described in this book, models can become complex.

Example 7.1 Suppose we want to model the information system of a car manufacturer. The information system should support the business processes of all departments of the car manufacturer. Departments include manufacturing, purchasing of materials and components, delivery of manufactured cars, research and development, and human resources. The business process of each individual department is already complex and results in a large process model. The process model of the overall information system aggregates the process models of the individual departments. The individual business processes are intertwined, which is another source of complexity for the model of the overall information system.

Despite its enormous size and complexity, we can model the information system of the car manufacturer as a CPN. The formalism of CPNs provides designers with a modeling technique that is powerful enough to construct a process model of any information system. However, CPNs only support the design of flat and unstructured models. This makes the design of complex models almost impossible.

Designers usually concentrate on a single aspect of a system and extend the model step by step. The CPN model describing the information system of the car manufacturer would have thousands of places and transitions, assuming that we are interested in a detailed model. In a CPN, we must represent the elements of the system as places, transitions, and tokens. These elements do not allow us to structure the model. Moreover, it is almost impossible to lay out the network structure of large models to allow the individual business processes in the overall model to be recognized. In addition, it is impossible for people to oversee models of this size; even if we could generate the model, it would be useless. It is impossible to discuss design decisions or implementation details of a system with users or with programmers on the basis of an unstructured model. Concepts to abstract from parts of the model are needed.

To accomplish the design of complex systems, models are usually designed following a *hierarchical approach*. The idea is to have several levels of abstraction of the system and to refine elements at the higher level into more detailed elements.

There are two ways to obtain a hierarchical description. In the *top-down approach*, we start at the highest level. The system to be designed is viewed as a *black box*, and only its interactions with its environment, such as its inputs and outputs, are considered. In the next step, we look into the black box to identify its essential parts. We *decompose* the system into *modules*. We can then again view each of these modules as a black box and decompose them into smaller modules. We repeat this process until we have reached the desired degree of detail, based on the purpose of the model. By following the top-down approach, we obtain a hierarchical description of a complex system.

Example 7.2 On the highest level of abstraction, we see the car manufacturer as a black box having raw materials and car components as its input and cars as its output. If we look into the black box, we identify the departments of the car manufacturer and how these departments are connected. For example, the manufacturing and purchasing processes are connected. In addition, research and development may affect manufacturing and purchasing. Delivery and research and development are, in contrast, not connected. We can further examine the business processes of the individual departments. In the case of the manufacturing process, we may see the individual steps, such as installing the engine and mounting the tires, which are necessary to produce a single car. We can examine these steps further. To mount the tires, each tire needs to be placed on the hub, and then the nuts are tightened.

If we refine the system in this way, we obtain a hierarchical description. The resulting model is structured and hence more manageable despite of its tremendous size. A designer can use this model as a communication medium for users and programmers, because all aspects that are not relevant can be abstracted away at higher levels.

The *bottom-up approach* starts at the lowest level and works in the opposite direction as the top-down approach. First, the elementary modules are described in detail. These modules are then aggregated to form larger modules, which is known as the *composition* of modules into larger modules. We can repeat this process until we reach the highest level of abstraction.

Example 7.3 In the bottom-up approach, we start with the elementary business processes describing, for example, mounting the tires or installing the engine. In the next step, we consider the complete manufacturing process by aggregating the elementary business processes. We continue this approach until we reach the highest level, in which we can see the car manufacturer as a black box.

For modeling industrial systems, it is essential to describe them hierarchically. Multiple levels of abstraction and refinement help to cope with the complexity of large systems. In the literature, this design paradigm is known as *divide-and-conquer* strategy.

Exercise 7.1 Answer the following two questions:

1. The divide-and-conquer strategy is useful when developing a complicated computer program. Which facilities are being offered by modern programming languages to support this strategy?

2. What is the preferred strategy in software development: a top-down approach or a bottom-up approach?

Petri nets and CPNs, as described in chapter 6, do not have any mechanism to support hierarchical modeling. A Petri net has a flat structure without any substructures. In the remainder of this chapter, we extend Petri nets with hierarchy.

The extension with hierarchy allows us to represent the compositional structure of a system in its Petri net model and *reuse* subnets (i.e., models of existing modules). In practice, we often must deal with modules that recur across various systems or even in the same system. If we can reuse an already defined module, we do not need to redefine it for each new occurrence. Reuse greatly increases efficiency by avoiding duplication.

7.2   Informal Introduction to the Extension with Hierarchy

We use a two-step approach to introduce hierarchy. In this section, we informally discuss the extension with hierarchy. In section 7.3, we give a concrete syntax for hierarchical CPNs based on the CPN language.

7.2.1   A First Example of a Hierarchical Petri Net

The main reason to extend Petri nets with hierarchy is to develop more compact models with a compositional network structure. We illustrate this with the help of the model of the patient punch card service desk in figure 7.1.

The model in figure 7.1 gives a detailed description of the desk showing the way in which the desk operates, but we want to start modeling at a higher level without addressing any details. In this case, we do not want to bother with the exact working of a service desk. Instead, we want to consider the desk as a whole.

Figure 7.2 depicts the model of the patient punch card service desk at a very high level. In this figure, there is a desk that is connected to places wait and done. The desk is represented by a square having the HS symbol next to it. This symbol stands for "hierarchical substitution" and states that the square has been decomposed. In other

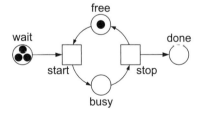

Figure 7.1
A model of the patient punch card service desk.

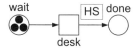

Figure 7.2
A high-level description of the patient punch card service desk.

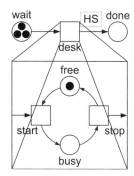

Figure 7.3
A module corresponds to a subnet.

words, such a square represents a *module*. A module corresponds to a subnet. As an example, figure 7.3 illustrates that module desk in figure 7.2 corresponds to a subnet with two transitions and two places.

By viewing certain subnets of a complex Petri net as modules and condensing them into a square symbol, we can define the *compositional structure* of the net under consideration. In this way, we obtain a hierarchical description that consists of two or more layers. In figure 7.3, for instance, we find two layers.

A subnet itself is composed of places, transitions, arcs, and possibly other modules. It is possible that a module contains modules; that is, the hierarchical structure can have any number of levels.

The extension with hierarchy requires the decomposition of a system into *modules*, also referred to as subprocesses and subsystems. A module is a CPN and can, hence, consume and produce tokens just like a transition. The module in figure 7.2 can, for example, consume tokens from place wait and produce tokens in place done. Modules are described in detail in this section.

Question 7.4 Can the desk module in figure 7.2 be modeled as a *transition*?

In this book, we have seen that transitions are the active components of a Petri net. The firing of a transition changes the marking of a Petri net. The firing of a transition is an *atomic* (i.e., indivisible) action. This means that, at the same moment when the transition consumes tokens from its input places, it also produces tokens in its output places. The values and the time stamps of the produced tokens may depend only on the values and time stamps of the consumed tokens. This implies that a transition has *no internal state* and cannot do something spontaneously because of internal processes. After all, a transition can only fire because of the presence of certain tokens in its input places.

There are three reasons why we cannot replace the desk module in figure 7.2 with a single transition:

• The events at a service desk cannot be modeled as an *atomic* action. The making of a punch card is characterized by the start and the end of serving a patient. Making a punch card does not happen instantaneously! The firing of a transition is, in contrast, an atomic action and cannot model two successive events.

• The desk has an *internal state*: either place free or place busy contains a token. Depending on this state, the desk will react differently to tokens present in place wait. In contrast, a transition has no internal state and cannot model whether the desk employee is free or busy.

• If the desk employee is busy, the desk will produce a token in place done without direct control from outside. This is again a property, which a transition does not have. The firing of a transition is always triggered by the presence of tokens in its input places.

Consequently, there are modules that we cannot represent by a single transition. If we decompose a complex information system into parts, we cannot model these parts without using modules. It is for this reason that we have introduced a module as a new modeling element.

The essential difference between a module and a transition is that a transition does not have an internal state. A transition cannot contain tokens; that is, a transition does not have *memory*. The result of the firing of a transition does not depend on possible previous firings of this transition but only on the values of the consumed tokens. In contrast, a module can have memory. Because a module is a subnet that can contain places, it can have an internal state. This internal state corresponds to a certain distribution of tokens over its places.

It is not a coincidence that the symbol that we use for a module looks similar to a transition. We consider a transition as an *elementary module*. For this reason, the symbol of a transition is equal to the symbol of a module, except for the *HS* symbol.

Sometimes we need to use the same subnet more than once. In this case, we want to reuse the same module several times if necessary. The use of modules clearly simplifies the reuse of subnets.

7.2.2 A More Interesting Example of Hierarchy

We further exemplify the idea of hierarchical Petri nets by revisiting the ticket reservation office, which was introduced in chapter 6 (see exercise 6.15). Figure 7.4 depicts the CPN model again. The model provides a detailed specification of the ticket reservation.

On a higher level of abstraction, we are not interested in the network structure of the reservation office; only the reservation service interface is important. Figure 7.5 depicts the corresponding CPN model. This model represents the reservation office as a black box. It abstracts from all details and shows only the four interface places create_event, request, reject, and confirm that the reservation module offers to its environment. Interface places have a type specifying the type of connection to the environment. The type can be input place, output place, or input and output place. Aspects other than the type of connection and the color set are not relevant at the higher level.

```
color Name = string;
color Event = string;
color Seat = int with 1..1000;
color NxE = product Name * Event;
color NxExS = product Name * Event * Seat;
color FreeSeats = list Seat;
color TakenSeat = product Seat * Name;
color TakenSeats = list TakenSeat;
color EventData = product Event * FreeSeats * TakenSeats;
fun seats() = Seat.all();
var n:Name;
var e:Event;
var s:Seat;
var fs:FreeSeats;
var ts:TakenSeats;
```

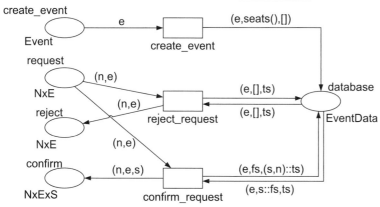

Figure 7.4
A colored Petri net model of the reservation office.

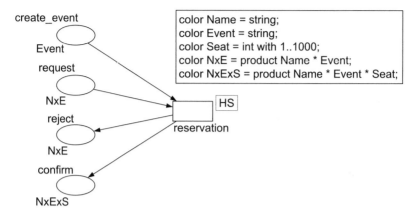

Figure 7.5
A module of the reservation office.

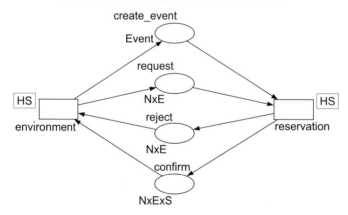

Figure 7.6
A module of the reservation office and its environment.

Using the CPN in figure 7.5, we can show on an abstract level how the reservation module interacts with its environment. Figure 7.6 shows the module interacting with some environment.

7.3 Hierarchical Colored Petri Net Models

In this section, we provide a concrete notation for hierarchical CPNs on the basis of the CPN language and illustrate these concepts by decomposing a more complex CPN model into a hierarchical CPN.

7.3.1 Notation

We use CPN language terminology and refer to a module as a *page*. A page is a CPN model consisting of places, transitions, arcs, and tokens. There are two types of transitions: *elementary transitions* and *substitution transitions*. An elementary transition is an ordinary transition, as introduced in the previous chapters. A substitution transition refers to a *subpage*. A subpage corresponds to a module that is contained in another module. If there is a module *A* containing another module *B*, then we refer to *A* and *B* as pages. If we want to emphasize the relation between these pages, we say that *A* is the *superpage* of *B*, and *B* is a subpage of *A*.

The semantics of a substitution transition are defined by replacing the substitution transition by a copy of the page it refers to. A substitution transition refers to precisely *one* subpage, but multiple substitution transitions may refer to the *same* subpage definition. When multiple substitution transitions refer to the same page, they share a common definition, but each substitution transition has a private copy of the page.

A substitution transition has no guard, and the arcs connecting a substitution transition to input and output places have no inscriptions. For a substitution transition, it does not make sense to add guards or arc inscriptions, because its semantics are specified by the corresponding subpages. Although there are no arc inscriptions, places at the higher level (i.e., input and output places of a substitution transition) need to be linked to elements at the lower level. For this purpose, the CPN language defines *sockets* and *ports*. A socket corresponds to a place at the higher level, whereas a port corresponds to a place at the lower level. By relating a socket and a port, the two places are semantically merged into one place.

Figure 7.7 illustrates the idea of using ports and sockets. The model has two pages: (1) superpage main containing two places wait and done and one substitution transition desk and (2) subpage desk_module containing four places input_pat, free, busy, and output_pat and two elementary transitions start and stop. The HS notation states that transition desk is a substitution transition. The hierarchy inscriptions next to the substitution transition show to which page desk refers, and it maps ports onto sockets. As mentioned, substitution transition desk is linked to page desk_module. Port input_pat is mapped onto socket wait, and port output_pat is mapped onto socket done. Only

```
color Name = string;
color Address = string;
color DateOfBirth = string;
color PatientID = int;
color EmpNo = int;
color Experience = int;
color Gender = with male|female;
color Pat = product PatientID * Name * Address * DateOfBirth * Gender timed;
color Emp = product EmpNo * Experience timed;
color EP = product Emp * Pat timed;
var p:Pat;
var emp:Emp;
val Peter = (12345, "Peter", "Kerkstraat 10, Amsterdam", "13-Dec-1962", male);
val Ann = (641112, 7);
fun d(emp:Emp) = if #1(emp)>5 then 3 else 4;
```

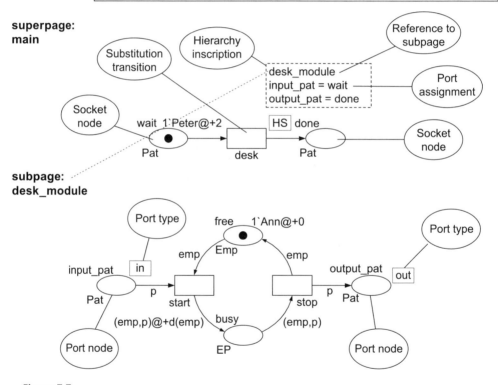

Figure 7.7

A hierarchical colored Petri net model of the patient punch card service desk process.

input and output places of a substitution transition can serve as sockets, but any place on a subpage can serve as a port. The presence of a port type shows that a place is a port. There are three types of ports: *In*, *Out*, and *In/Out*. Ports of type *In* can only be assigned to input places of the corresponding substitution transition. Ports of type *Out* can only be assigned to output places of the corresponding substitution transition. Ports of type *In/Out* can serve as input and output place.

Figure 7.7 names all relevant concepts and shows the notations used, but it does not show the semantics of this model. The semantics of a hierarchical CPN model correspond to the flat CPN model in which each substitution transition is replaced by a copy of the corresponding subpage. To this end, sockets and ports are merged. In the example, places wait and input_pat and places done and output_pat are merged. As a result, we obtain the flat model that we described in the previous chapter (see figure 6.9).

In figure 7.7, we assumed a one-to-one correspondence between substitution transition desk and subpage desk_module, but multiple substitution transitions may refer to the same page. As the same subpage may be used in multiple contexts, we distinguish between a *page definition* and a *page instance*. Figure 7.7 shows two page definitions: main and desk_module. For substitution transition desk, subpage desk_module is instantiated once.

We clarify the difference between page definition and page instance with figures 7.8 and 7.9. Figure 7.8 depicts a page definition main, which has two substitution transitions, desk1 and desk2. Both substitution transitions refer to page definition desk_module in figure 7.9. Although there is only one page definition desk_module, there are two page instances: one for substitution transition desk1 and one for substitution transition desk2. The presence of two page instances becomes visible if we remove the hierarchy by replacing each substitution transition by an instance of the corresponding page definition. Figure 7.10 shows the flattened page definition main. The duplication of places free and busy and transitions start and stop in figure 7.10 illustrates the importance of hierarchy inscriptions. Without the port assignments in figure 7.8, it would be unclear how sockets and ports should be merged.

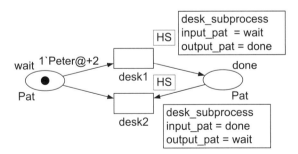

Figure 7.8
Page definition main.

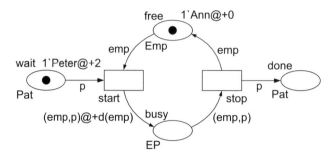

Figure 7.9
Page definition desk_module.

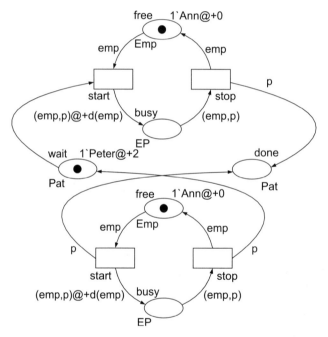

Figure 7.10
Semantics of page definition main as a flat colored Petri net model.

7.3.2 Example: Thermostat

To further illustrate hierarchal CPNs, consider the CPN model of a thermostat with a day and night program given as an exercise in section 6.7. Figure 7.11 depicts the flat CPN model. This CPN model has no structure and represents the complete specification in a single diagram. Suppose we want to make a *hierarchical* model of the thermostat with a day and night program. At the highest level, we only want to see that the entire system controls the temperature. At the intermediate level, we decompose the system into two main parts: one for the heating process (the top part of figure 7.11) and one for the day and night program (the bottom part of figure 7.11). At the lowest level, we specify these two parts in more detail.

Figure 7.12 depicts the top-level page main consisting of a place and a substitution transition. We use the same name for the substitution transition and the corresponding subpage.

Figure 7.13 depicts subpage complete_system. The socket in figure 7.12 and the *In/Out* port in figure 7.13 are named temp. We could have used different names for them, but if a page is instantiated only once, there is no need to use context-independent names for ports. If there is reuse, the port typically has a name different from the socket. Page complete_system has two substitution transitions, heating_process and

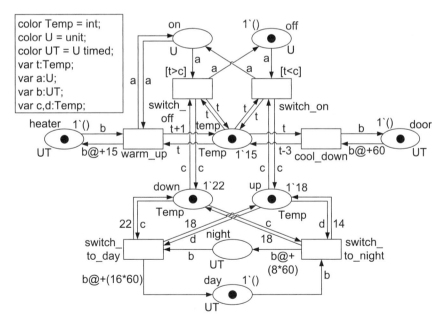

Figure 7.11
A flat colored Petri net model of a thermostat with a day and night program.

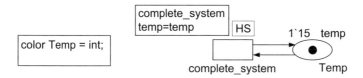

Figure 7.12
Definition of page main.

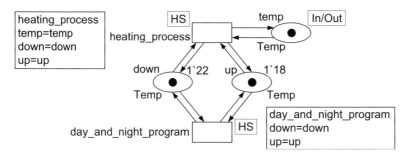

Figure 7.13
Definition of page complete_system.

day_and_night_program, referring to the two main modules of the system. Place temp is a port, and places down and up serve as sockets. The latter two places represent the interface of the two main parts of the system.

Figure 7.14 depicts the definition of page heating_process. This page has three ports of type *In/Out*.

Finally, figure 7.15 depicts the definition of page day_and_night_program. This page has two ports of type *In/Out*. In contrast to page heating_process, no port of figure 7.15 is merged with place temp at one of the higher levels.

Figures 7.12, 7.13, 7.14, and 7.15 present a hierarchical CPN model consisting of four pages. The design of this model makes a divide-and-conquer strategy possible. If we want to modify the day and night program, only page day_and_night_program needs to be modified or replaced by another page. Each of the four pages could also be reused in another model. We achieved this by defining the initial marking of places down and up on the level of page complete_system. That way, the corresponding ports in pages heating_process and day_and_night_program are independent of the superpage that may use these pages.

Flattening the hierarchical CPN model specified by figures 7.12, 7.13, 7.14, and 7.15 yields the CPN model in figure 7.11. If we design such a system from scratch, we could either use a top-down approach or a bottom-up approach; that is, we could either start with pages day_and_night_program and heating_process and compose

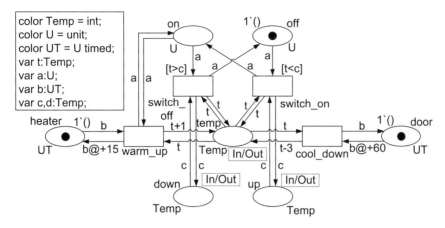

Figure 7.14
Definition of page heating_process.

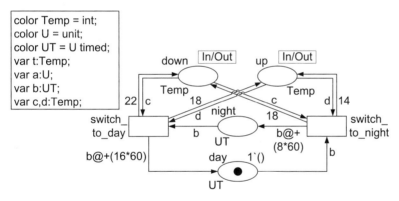

Figure 7.15
Definition of page day_and_night_program.

them into page complete_system (bottom-up approach), or we could start with page complete_system and decompose the system into two parts and then specify pages day_and_night_program and heating_process (top-down approach). This shows that the proposed modeling technique is neutral with respect to the two design approaches. Tools like CPN Tools support both design approaches.

Figure 7.16 depicts a screenshot of the thermostat example modeled in CPN Tools. There are minor differences between the notation used in this chapter and CPN Tools. CPN Tools shows the name of the corresponding subpage rather than the HS symbol. In addition, CPN Tools represents each substitution transition as a rectangle with double-line borders (see figure 7.16).

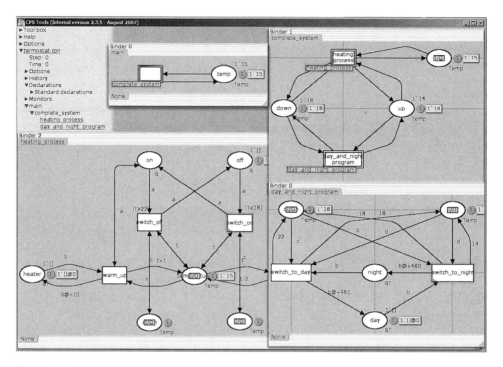

Figure 7.16
Hierarchical colored Petri net model of the thermostat using CPN Tools.

Exercise 7.2   Consider again Dijkstra's dining philosophers (1971) as introduced in exercise 5.17. Assume that both forks need to be taken at the same time.

1. Model this using a hierarchical CPN model. Make sure that you model the behavior of a philosopher only once, and use the color set BlackToken of type `unit`.
2. Change the model such that philosophers can take one fork at a time, but avoid a fixed ordering of philosophers. Do not allow the system to deadlock.

7.4   Example: Production System

In this section and section 7.5, we present two examples to further illustrate the design of process models using hierarchical CPNs. The first example is a process model of a production system.

7.4.1   Specification
A factory manufactures three types of products: A, B, and C. The production of each product requires three production steps. To manufacture any of the products, the

Table 7.1

The Processing Times of Products A, B, and C for Work Centers WC1, WC2, and WC3

Products	Work centers		
	WC1	WC2	WC3
A	2	5	8
B	3	6	9
C	4	7	1

Table 7.2

The Number of Resources for Each Work Center

Work center	Resources
WC1	4
WC2	5
WC3	6

factory needs an initial product, which is obtained from a supplier. This initial product is then processed by three work centers—WC1, WC2, and WC3—in a fixed order. The production process for products A, B, and C is identical, but the processing time in each work center depends on the type of product (A, B, or C). Table 7.1 lists the processing times. For example, the first production step at WC1 takes two time units for product A and three time units for product B.

Each work center has a fixed number of resources. Each resource can process all types of products. The capacity of a resource is equal to one; that is, at any point in time, a resource can only process one product. We assume that there are no setup times. Table 7.2 lists the number of resources for each work center.

The production system is *kanban* controlled, which means that the number of products in between each production step is limited. In our example, there can be no more than two products of type A, one of type B, and one of type C. The final production step is only executed if there is demand (i.e., there is no stock of end products). As a consequence, the customer order decoupling point is in between work centers WC3 and WC2; that is, work center WC3 produces to order, whereas work center WC2 produces to stock. For the initial products, there cannot be more than two products of type A, one of type B, and one of type C in stock. Initial products are ordered one by one. Table 7.3 shows the replenishment lead times.

Table 7.4 specifies the demand for end products. For simplicity we assume all times to be fixed. Recall that the CPN language provides a library of stochastic functions, which allow for the specification of any distribution (see table 6.6).

Table 7.3
Replenishment Lead Times of the Initial Products

Product	Lead time
A	2
B	1
C	2

Table 7.4
Time between Two Subsequent Customer Orders

Product	Time between orders
A	7
B	9
C	8

Given this specification, the challenge is to adequately model the production system.

7.4.2 Modeling

Figure 7.17 shows an initial attempt to model the production system. We decomposed the system into five modules: the supplier, the customer, and the three work centers. Each of these modules is modeled as a substitution transition. The substitution transitions are connected by two types of places, product places and kanban places. The product places represent the flow of products from the supplier, via the three work centers, to the customer. The kanban places represent the flow of information to trigger production or replenishment.

Each of the three substitution transitions wc1, wc2, and wc3 represents a work center. The behavior of each work center is similar, but the number of resources and the processing times vary from work center to work center. The top-level page in figure 7.17 does not allow for reuse, because mapping substitution transitions wc1, wc2, and wc3 to the same subpage would result in three identical page instances, violating the specification. For this reason, we need to parameterize the work centers with the number of resources and the processing time for each type of product. To do this, we refine the top-level page in figure 7.17 to the one in figure 7.18.

In figure 7.18, each substitution transition corresponding to a work center is connected to two additional places. One place indicates the number of resources and the other place the processing times of each product. For example, transition wc1 is

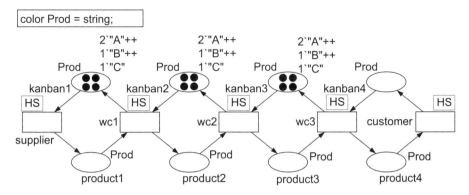

Figure 7.17
Initial design of top-level page.

connected to place resources_wc1. In the initial marking, place resources_wc1 holds one token with value four, indicating that WC1 has four resources. Transition wc1 is also connected to place processing_times_wc1. Initially, this place holds one token for each product type. The value of each token is the Cartesian product of the corresponding product type and the processing time. For instance, the processing time of product A is two time units.

Similar to the work centers, substitution transitions supplier and customer have an additional place. These places show the lead time of the initial order (i.e., place c_lead_time) and the time between two subsequent customer orders (i.e., place c_ia_time). In the initial marking, place c_lead_time holds for each product type one token specifying the lead time of the corresponding product type. Likewise, place c_ia_time contains one token for each product type specifying the time in between two subsequent orders of the same type. Figure 7.18 also represents the hierarchy inscriptions. These inscriptions specify the mapping of the substitution transitions onto pages and the merging of sockets and ports.

Figure 7.19 depicts page supplier. Orders arrive at port kanban_in. Firing transition accept_order produces a token in place oip (order in progress) with a delay t equal to the order lead time obtained from port io_lead_time. Because the token for place oip carries a time stamp, the place has a timed color set PTimed (for the declaration, see figure 7.18). After the specified delay, transition deliver_order delivers the order in port product_out.

Page main in figure 7.18 declares the connection between page supplier and the places surrounding the substitution transition bearing the same name. Ports kanban_in, product_out, and io_lead_time in figure 7.19 merge with sockets kanban1, product1, and io_lead_time in figure 7.18, respectively. Transition accept_order in figure 7.19 uses this information to add the proper delay to tokens that are produced in place oip.

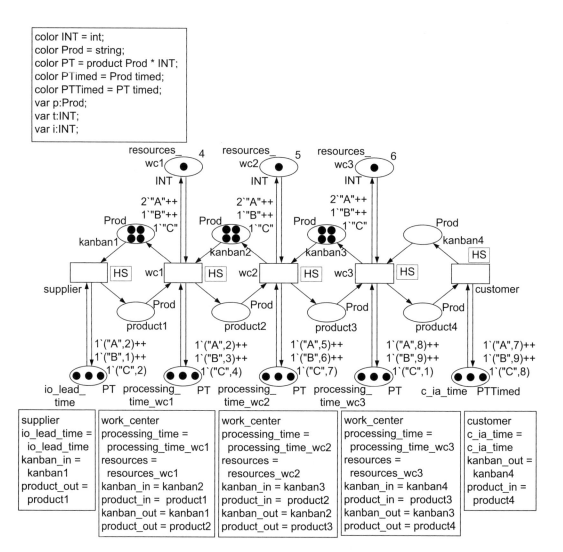

Figure 7.18
Improved design of top-level page main.

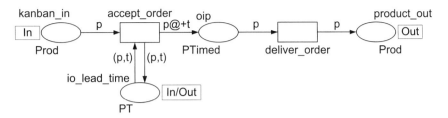

Figure 7.19
Page supplier.

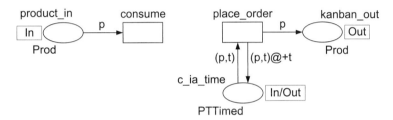

Figure 7.20
Page customer.

Figure 7.20 depicts page customer. Transition consume models the consumption of delivered products by removing delivered products from port product_in. Transition place_order models the ordering of products. This transition places for each product every t time units an order in port kanban_out. Tokens consumed from place c_ia_time are, hence, returned with the specified delay t. The initial marking of c_ia_time in figure 7.18 encodes the concrete value of t. Because of the delay, port and socket c_ia_time have a timed color set PTTimed.

Page work_center in figure 7.21 is the most complex page of this example. It models a production step. Transition start_proc starts this production step. After a delay of t time units—production takes time—transition end_proc completes this production step. The production can only start if at least one resource is available (modeled by guard [i>=1]). Furthermore, an initial product p in port product_in and a kanban token, which indicates that there is a need to produce a product p, must be available. The firing of transition start_proc decreases the number of free resources by one, whereas the firing of transition end_proc increases this number by one. The latter firing indicates the completion of the production step. Place wip has a timed color set PTimed, and a delay of t time units (representing the processing time for product p in the work center) is assigned to tokens produced in this place.

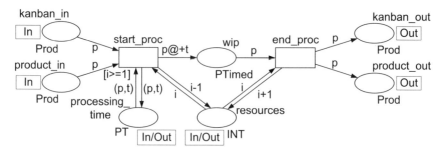

Figure 7.21
Page work_center.

Table 7.5
The Setup Times for Switching from One Product Type to Another One

	To		
From	A	B	C
A	0	1	2
B	1	0	1
C	2	1	0

Figure 7.18 shows the connections between sockets and ports and the initial marking of places connected to the *In/Out* ports processing_time and resources. The initial marking determines the delays and the number of resources for work centers WC1, WC2, and WC3.

Exercise 7.3 Flatten the hierarchical CPN model in figures 7.18, 7.19, 7.20, and 7.21. How many places and transitions does the flattened CPN model have?

Exercise 7.4 In the hierarchical CPN model in figures 7.18, 7.19, 7.20, and 7.21, production in a work center starts after the required product *and* the kanban are present. The kanban is only returned after completion of the production step. Modify the model such that kanbans are only used to control inventory *in between* work centers and not *within* work centers.

Exercise 7.5 Modify the hierarchical CPN model to take into account the setup times in table 7.5 for example, switching from product A to product C takes 2 time units. The setup times are identical for all work centers but vary from product to product.

7.5   Example: Logistic Networks

In this section, we model various procurement systems using hierarchical CPNs. First, we model a procurement system for a single organization using several inventory policies described in the literature. Afterward, we extend the model to a complete supply chain involving several organizations.

7.5.1   Introduction

A procurement system is an information system that helps an organization automate the purchasing processes. Organizations usually have a stock, which may be distributed over several stocking points. On an abstract level, goods can arrive at a stocking point in the case of replenishment and can leave a stocking point if they are delivered to a customer or a supplier.

Figure 7.22 depicts the interface between a stocking point and its environment. A substitution transition models the stocking point. Customer orders arrive at place customer_order and are delivered (if possible) to place customer_delivery. To replenish inventory of specific products, the procurement system can send replenishment orders to place repl_order. A replenishment arrives at place repl_delivery. The four places are of type PQ. For example, a token with color (A,15) in customer_order represents a request for 15 products of type A. The place type used in figure 7.22 suggests that an order refers to only one product type.

The CPN in figure 7.22 models one stocking point. To model an entire supply chain, we could connect places repl_order and repl_delivery to the model of another stocking point or to the model of a supplier. Likewise, we could connect places customer_order and customer_delivery to the model of another stocking point or to the model of a customer.

Figure 7.22 shows the essence of a procurement system. It must balance supply and demand by keeping inventory. In the remainder of this section, we model various

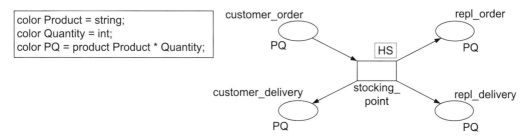

Figure 7.22
A substitution transition modeling a stocking point.

inventory policies rather than complex supply chains. An inventory policy should answer the following questions:

- How often should the inventory status be determined?
- When should a replenishment order be placed?
- How large should the replenishment order be?
- What do we do with a customer order in an out-of-stock situation?

There could be many other issues, such as shipment consolidation, but we do not address these issues. There may be many product types in stock. We assume that the same inventory policy is applied to all product types and that there are no dependencies between product types. However, there may be parameters, such as reorder points, that depend on the product type.

Let us first address the question, "What do we do with a customer order in an out-of-stock situation?" There are many ways to answer this question; for example, if the expected replenishment time is less than one week, the organization could ask the customer to wait or otherwise not accept the order. There are two extreme cases: *complete backordering* and *complete lost sales*. Complete backordering means that any demand, when out of stock, is backordered and delivered as soon as the stocking point is replenished. Complete lost sales means that any customer order, when out of stock, is lost.

Example 7.5 When ordering an ice cream in an out-of-stock situation, the customer is likely to either go to another place or not eat ice cream. In this case, it is unlikely that the customer will wait for replenishment, thus creating a backorder. In contrast, when ordering a new car, it is unlikely that the car dealer has a car with the equipment required by the customer. In this case, a backorder is placed, and the car will be produced according to the customer's requirements.

With or without backorders, the procurement system must replenish the stocking point. For this purpose, it must review its current inventory level. This review can be done continuously or periodically. If the inventory level is subject to *periodic review*, one needs to specify the length R of the review period. If the inventory level is subject to *continuous review*, there is no need to specify this (i.e., $R = 0$). In both cases, one needs to specify a *reorder point s*; that is, if the inventory level falls below s, then the procurement system generates a replenishment order.

To avoid a procurement system repeatedly ordering products without new demands, the inventory policy measures the inventory level on the basis of the *inventory position* rather than the *stock on hand*. The stock on hand is the stock that is physically on the shelf and hence can never be negative. The inventory position is the stock on hand plus the sum of pending replenishment orders minus the backorders. If the inventory position is less than or equal to s, the procurement system places an order.

If the inventory position is greater than s, the procurement system postpones the replenishment until the inventory position is less than s (continuous review) or until a new evaluation is made at the end of the next review period (periodic review). The size of the replenishment may be fixed or variable. If the size is fixed, we use Q to denote the *order quantity*. If the size is variable, we use S to denote the *maximum order level*. In the latter case, $S - x$ is the order quantity, where x is the inventory position at the time of ordering.

If we abstract from backorders, there are four possible inventory policies: (s, Q), (s, S), (R, s, S), and (R, S). A procurement system following the (s, Q) inventory policy orders a fixed quantity whenever the inventory position falls below reorder point s. If the procurement system follows the (s, S) inventory policy, it orders a variable quantity (maximum order level S minus the inventory position) whenever the inventory position falls below reorder point s. Inventory policy (R, s, S) uses periodic review (R is the review period), a reorder point s, and a maximum order level S. If, at the time of review, the inventory position is less than or equal to the reorder point s, the procurement system orders enough to raise the inventory position to S. The (R, S) inventory policy also uses periodic review R and a maximum order level S but does not use a reorder point; that is, at the end of every review period, the procurement system orders enough to raise the inventory position to S.

In the remainder of this chapter, we model possible subpages for the substitution transition in figure 7.22. We investigate complete backordering and complete lost sales—that is, the two most extreme cases.

7.5.2   Complete Lost Sales Policies

In the following section, we abstract from backorders and model four complete lost sales policies—that is, policies in which customer orders are served immediately or never. To keep the models small, we decompose substitution transition stocking_point in figure 7.22 into two substitution transitions customer-b and replenishment-b, yielding the page shown in figure 7.23. The former substitution transition models the connection of the stocking point to the customer, and the latter models the replenishing of the stocking point. Place stock represents the stock on hand (i.e., the physically present stock). For purposes of simplification, we consider only two products, A and B. However, the model is generic; that is, by changing the initial marking, the stock may contain any set of products.

First, we consider page customer-b in figure 7.24. This CPN receives customer orders from port customer_order. A customer order (p,a) consists of a product type p and a quantity a. Transition t1 models a customer order that cannot be delivered from stock, because the required quantity a exceeds the quantity b in stock. Because we assume complete lost sales, the order is removed from port customer_order. Transition t2 models a customer order that can be delivered from stock. The guard ([b>=a]) ensures that

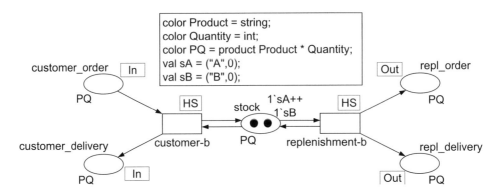

Figure 7.23
Decomposing figure 7.22 for complete lost sales policies.

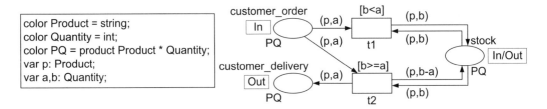

Figure 7.24
Page customer-b.

the required quantity is available. Transition t2 consumes the customer order from port customer_order, delivers the order to port customer_delivery, and updates the stock.

In the remainder of this section, we model page replenishment-b. This page varies depending on the complete lost sales policy chosen, whereas page customer-b remains unchanged.

Figure 7.25 depicts page replenishment_(s,Q)-b modeling the (s, Q) policy (i.e., continuous review and fixed order quantity) without backorders. The procurement system places orders in port repl_order. Ordered products arrive at port repl_delivery. Place ordered stores replenishment orders, which still need to arrive. Recall that replenishment orders are needed to determine the inventory position. Places order_point and order_quantity model parameter s and Q of the (s, Q) policy, respectively.

As place stock in figure 7.23 has an initial marking for products A and B, each of the internal places in page replenishment_(s,Q)-b in figure 7.25 contains two tokens, one for product A and one for product B. The constants in the declarations part of figure 7.25 specify the orders, order quantities, and reorder points. For example, product A has a fixed order quantity $Q = 150$ and a reorder point $s = 50$, and no orders are placed.

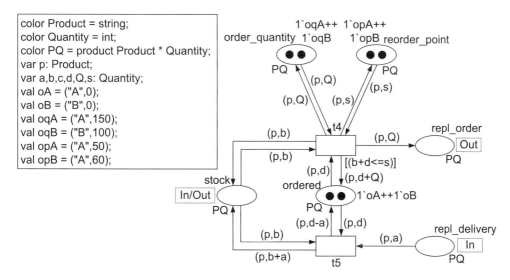

Figure 7.25
Page replenishment_(s,Q)-b.

Transition t4 models the ordering of a fixed quantity at the moment the inventory position falls to reorder point *s* or below. Variables b, d, Q, and s are bound to the stock quantity, the number of ordered products, the order quantity *Q*, and the reorder point *s*, respectively. The inventory position is, hence, the sum b+d of the stock on hand and the already ordered quantity. Guard [b+d<=s] ensures that the inventory position is less than or equal to the reorder point and, hence that a replenishment is needed. Transition t4 places a replenishment order and updates the sum of pending replenishment orders in place ordered. Transition t5 models the actual replenishment. Ordered products arrive at port repl_delivery and update the corresponding tokens in places ordered and stock.

Next, we model the (*s*, *S*) inventory policy. According to this policy, the procurement system orders a variable quantity whenever the inventory position falls below reorder point *s*. This variable quantity is equal to the maximum order level *S* minus the inventory position. Page replenishment_(s,S)-b in figure 7.26 models this inventory policy.

Figure 7.26 is similar to page replenishment_(s,Q)-b in figure 7.25. The only differences are in the arcs and places surrounding transition t4. Place order_quantity modeling the order quantity *Q* in figure 7.25 has been replaced by place max_order_level representing the maximum order level *S*. Again, an initial marking is given for the two products *A* and *B*. Variables b, d, S, and s are bound to the stock quantity, the number of ordered products, the maximum order level *S*, and the reorder point *s*, respectively. Firing of

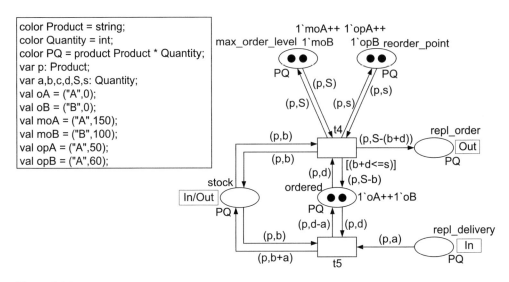

Figure 7.26
Page replenishment_(s,S)-b.

transition t4 results in a new replenishment order of quantity S-(b+d), which is equal to the maximum order level S minus the inventory level b+d. The quantity of ordered products in place ordered is, hence, set to d+(S-(b+d))=S-b. Again, guard [b+d<=s] of transition t4 ensures that this transition fires only if the inventory position is less than or equal to reorder point s.

Figure 7.27 depicts page replenishment_(R,s,S)-b. This page models the (R, s, S) inventory policy. In contrast to page replenishment_(s,S)-b, the procurement system evaluates the inventory position every R time units; that is, there is a periodic review. For this purpose, transition t6 fires every R time units for each product. Place check, therefore, periodically triggers transitions t4 and t4' to evaluate a specific product. As transition t4 has two firing modi, we added a transition t4'. Transition t4 models that the procurement system places a replenishment order of S-(b+d) products and updates the number of ordered products. This transitions is enabled if the inventory position is less than or equal to the reorder point s. Transition t4' models that the procurement system places no replenishment order and is enabled if the inventory position is greater than the reorder point s.

Page replenishment_(R,S)-b in figure 7.28 models the final inventory policy without backordering. This page is similar to the previous page, replenishment_(R,s,S)-b. The main difference is that, at the end of every review period, the procurement system places an order, independent of the inventory position. For this purpose, transition t4 places a replenishment order of quantity S-(b+d) without checking the size of the

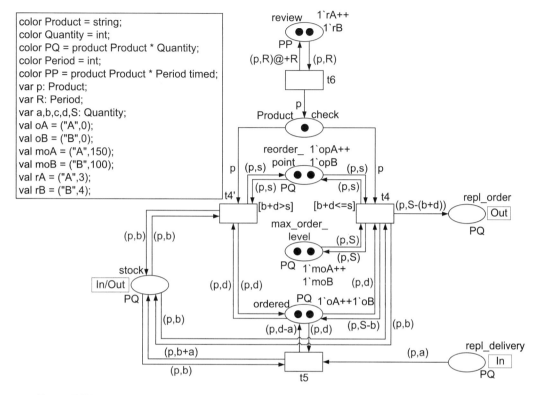

Figure 7.27
Page replenishment_(R,s,S)-b.

inventory position. As this policy does not use a reorder point, place reorder_point has been removed from page replenishment_(R,S)-b.

This concludes the presentation of inventory policies with complete lost sales. Next, we consider the situation with complete backordering; that is, a customer order that cannot be served immediately is turned into a backorder and delivered later when the product is available.

7.5.3   Complete Backordering Policies

In this section, we assume that whenever an organization cannot deliver a customer request because of an out-of-stock situation, the procurement system will backorder this request. We consider four complete backordering policies.

As we deal with backorders, we need to store them. To do this, we need to decompose the substitution transition in figure 7.22 differently than in the case of complete lost sales (see figure 7.23). The decomposition yields again two substitution transitions that

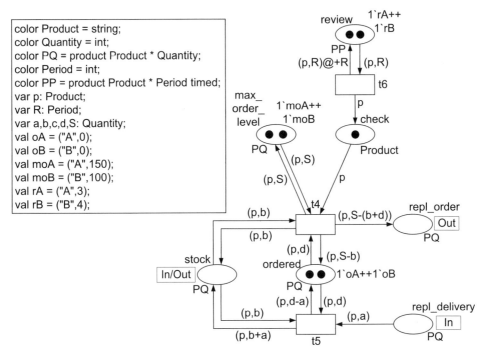

Figure 7.28
Page replenishment_(R,S)-b.

model the connection of the stock to the customer and the replenishment of the stock. But this time, we have in addition to place stock also a place backordered storing the backorders. Figure 7.29 depicts the corresponding CPN model.

Figure 7.30 depicts page customer+b. Transition t1 models the situation in which the customer's order can be delivered from stock. In contrast to transition t2 in figure 7.24, the guard of transition t1 is strengthened to make sure that it fires only if there are no backorders; that is, backorders have priority over usual orders. Transition t2 models the situation in which there is not enough stock on hand to fulfill the customer order. Instead of just consuming the token from place customer_order without further action (as transition t1 in figure 7.24), the customer order becomes a backorder. Each token in place backorder represents a backorder. If the stock is replenished, transition t3 delivers backordered products to the customer and decreases the number of backorders. The guard of transition t3 checks whether there are enough products (of the right type) in stock. Each token in place backordered keeps track of the total number of items backordered for each product.

Next, we model four replenishment policies. Again, we start with the (s, Q) inventory policy. Page replenishment_(s,Q)+b in figure 7.31 models this policy with complete

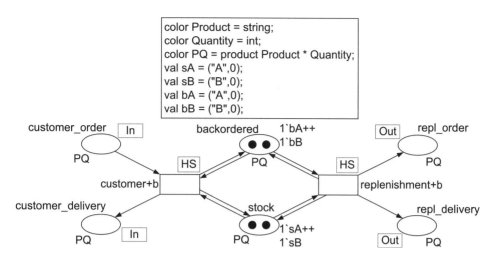

Figure 7.29
Decomposing figure 7.22 for complete backordering policies.

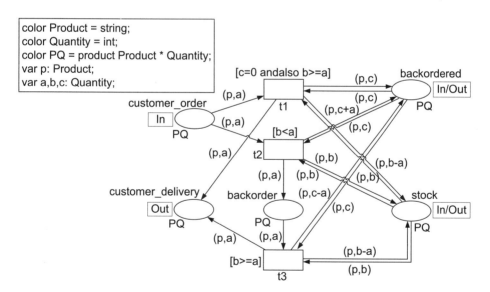

Figure 7.30
Page customer+b.

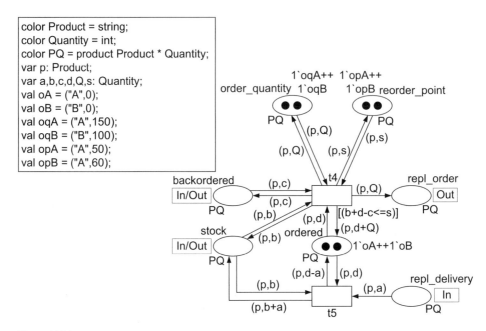

```
color Product = string;
color Quantity = int;
color PQ = product Product * Quantity;
var p: Product;
var a,b,c,d,Q,s: Quantity;
val oA = ("A",0);
val oB = ("B",0);
val oqA = ("A",150);
val oqB = ("B",100);
val opA = ("A",50);
val opB = ("A",60);
```

Figure 7.31
Page replenishment_(s,Q)+b.

backordering. There is only one difference between this page and the page in figure 7.25: as the inventory position is no longer b+d but b+d-c (i.e., stock on hand plus ordered products minus backorders), the guard of transition t4 is modified.

Exercise 7.6 Give page replenishment_(s,S)+b, which models an (s, S) inventory policy with complete backordering.

Page replenishment_(R,s,S)+b in figure 7.32 models the (R, s, S) inventory policy with complete backordering. We construct this page by combining page replenishment_ (R,s,S)-b with the constructs for backordering given for page replenishment_(s,Q)+b in figure 7.31.

Exercise 7.7 Give the page replenishment_(R,S)+b that models an (R, S) inventory policy with complete backordering.

7.5.4 Modeling Supply Chains
In this section, we modeled eight standard inventory policies described in the literature. Figure 7.22 shows a substitution transition modeling a single stocking point. We can combine stocking points into supply chains. As an example, figure 7.33 depicts a supply chain consisting of four stocking points, each using a different inventory policy. The

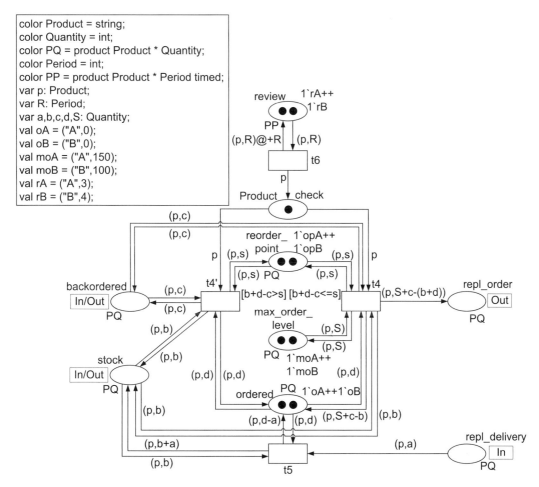

Figure 7.32
Page replenishment_(R,s,S)+b.

stock is circular; that is, products circulate without ever being consumed. Figure 7.33 is counterintuitive, because products flow from right to left rather than from left to right. This has no deeper meaning; the semantics of a CPN model are independent of its layout.

Exercise 7.8 Consider the supply chain in figure 7.33.

1. The initial marking of each subpage is given in the corresponding figures in this section. What happens, given these initial markings?
2. What would happen if stocking points without complete backordering are connected?

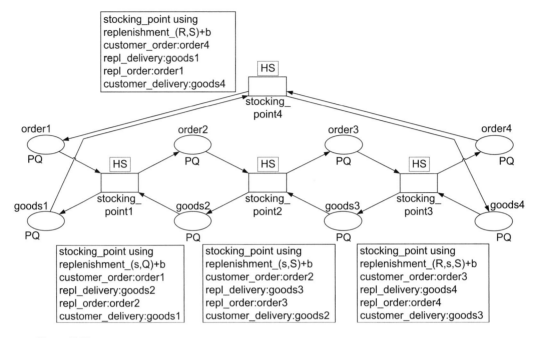

Figure 7.33
A supply chain.

The page definitions in figure 7.33 assume two products, *A* and *B*. In a more realistic scenario, one would like to allow for parameterized subpages; that is, internal places are promoted to ports such that the initial marking of these places can be configured at the superpage level. Consider, for example, page replenishment_(R,s,S)+b in figure 7.32. Places order_up_to_level, order_point, and review could be transformed into ports. This would allow for an initialization by the corresponding sockets at the superpage level. That way, it is possible to specify the values of *S*, *s*, and *R* for each product at the superpage level. Hence, without changing the initial marking of a subpage, it is possible to configure the stocking point.

We presented a similar solution in section 7.4 in which page work_center has six port nodes (see also figure 7.21). Of these six ports, ports processing_time and resources parameterize page work_center. Figure 7.18 depicts the connections between sockets and ports, and the initial marking of places connected to *In/Out* ports processing_time and resources. That way, the delays and the number of resources depend on work center WC1, WC2, or WC3. Such an approach could also have been used for the stocking point specified in this section.

7.6   Test Yourself

7.6.1   Solutions to Exercises
7.1
1) Using the divide-and-conquer strategy, a programming problem is divided into smaller subprograms. Modern programming languages, such as C++ and Java, offer the option of defining *functions* and *procedures*. Because functions and procedures can, in turn, be composed of other functions and procedures, it is possible to decompose the program into small simple functions and procedures. In object-oriented programming, the divide-and-conquer strategy is used as well: a system is decomposed into a collection of interacting objects.

2) When implementing a computer program, we usually adopt a mixed approach. The programming problem is divided into smaller problems (i.e., the top-down approach), at the same time that several basic functions and basic procedures are defined in the beginning and are being used at many places (bottom-up approach). As a consequence, we have a mixture of top-down and bottom-up approaches.

7.2
1) Figures 7.34 and 7.35 specify the two pages required to model the process using a hierarchical CPN model. The behavior of a philosopher is modeled only once, and no colored tokens (other than tokens of type `unit`) are used. The only possible value of variable b is (). On every arc, we can, hence, replace variable b by the constant ().

2) Changing the model such that philosophers can take one fork at a time does not influence the top-level page in figure 7.34. We only need to adapt page philosopher. Figure 7.36 depicts the modified page. It is essential that it is possible to return a fork without eating. Otherwise, the system can deadlock; for example, assume that all five philosophers take the right fork.

7.3   We can construct the flat CPN model by recursively replacing substitution transitions by subpages until there are no substitution transitions. We do not represent the resulting flat model, but it is easy to derive that the flat model has twenty places and ten transitions.

7.4   The only page that we need to modify is page work_center (see figure 7.21). Figure 7.37 depicts the modified page. It is designed such that kanbans are used only to control inventory *in between* work centers and not *within* work centers.

7.5   Because all work centers have the same setup time, it suffices to modify page work_center (see figure 7.21). Figure 7.38 depicts the extended model. We add two places: last to remember the last product type and setup to store the setup times. The latter place could also have been replaced by a function.

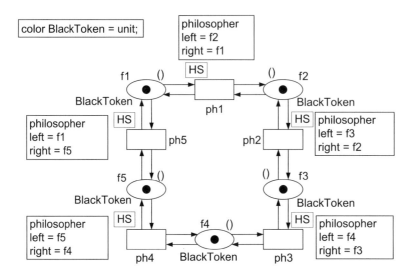

Figure 7.34
Definition of top-level page for philosopher example.

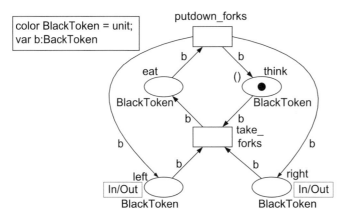

Figure 7.35
Definition of page philosopher.

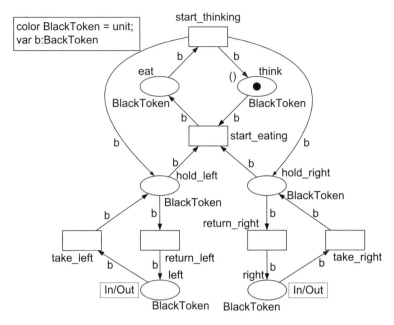

Figure 7.36
Alternative definition of page philosopher.

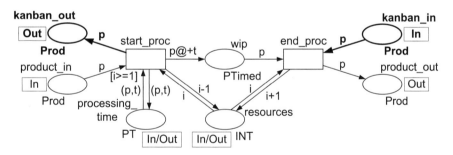

Figure 7.37
Alternative definition of page work_center to limit kanban control to inventory in between work centers.

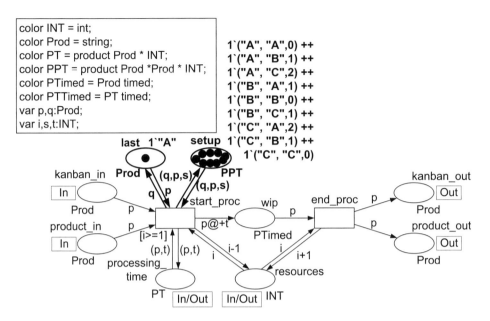

Figure 7.38
Alternative definition of page work_center with setup times.

7.6   Figure 7.39 depicts page replenishment_(s,S)+b.

7.7   Figure 7.40 depicts page replenishment_(R,S)+b.

7.8
1. The supply chain is empty; that is, there is not a single product in the entire chain. For that reason, only backorders are generated.
2. Each of the stocking points assumes that ordered products will eventually be delivered. This is not the case if stocking points without complete backordering are connected, because those stocking points remove orders without delivery.

7.6.2   Further Exercises

Exercise 7.9   Explain the concepts "elementary transition," "substitution transition," "hierarchy inscriptions," "page," "subpage," "superpage," "page definition," "page instance," "socket," "port," "port type," and "port assignment."

Exercise 7.10   Flatten the supply chain in figure 7.33. How many places and transitions does the resulting CPN have?

Exercise 7.11   Page customer-b in figure 7.23 models the situation in which we assume complete lost sales. Modify customer-b such that partial shipments are allowed; that is,

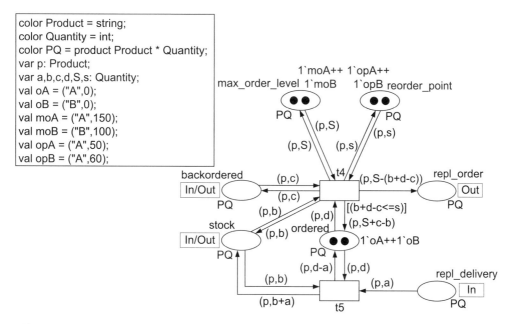

Figure 7.39
Page replenishment_(s,S)+b.

if ten products are ordered and only six products are on hand, then six products are delivered, and only the remaining demand is lost.

Exercise 7.12 Page customer+b in figure 7.30 models the situation in which we assume complete backordering. Modify customer+b such that partial shipments are allowed; that is, if ten products are ordered and only six products are on hand, then six products are delivered, and four are backordered.

Exercise 7.13 Consider the top-level CPN model in figure 7.41. This model depicts a transport system consisting of an environment placing requests, a routing system generating commands, and the actual trucks driving from one location to another to load and offload goods. In addition, the following variables are given:

```
var t:Truck;
var a:Action;
var c:Capacity;
var v,v0,v1,v2:Volume;
var l,l0,l1,l2:Location;
var rid:ReqID;
```

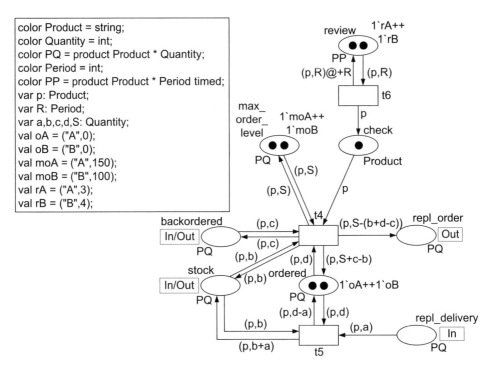

Figure 7.40
Page replenishment_(R,S)+b.

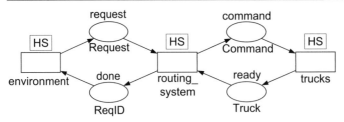

Figure 7.41
Page main of the transport system.

We assume that there are ten trucks $(1, \ldots, 10)$. Each of these trucks has a capacity of 100 cubic meters. The environment sends requests of type Request to the routing system. Each request has an identifier of type ReqID, the location from which the goods need to be shipped, the location to which the goods need to be shipped, and the volume of the shipment in cubic meters. A value $(\texttt{rid}, \texttt{l1}, \texttt{l2}, \texttt{v})$ of type Request corresponds to the request for a shipment from $\texttt{l1}$ to $\texttt{l2}$ that has a volume $\texttt{v}$ and is identified by $\texttt{rid}$. Once the request has been executed; that is, the shipment is completed, an acknowledgment is sent through place done.

The routing system collects these requests and issues real-time instructions to the truck drivers via place command; that is, a continuous stream of commands is sent to the trucks, and these are processed one by one. A value $(\texttt{t}, \texttt{l}, \texttt{rid}, \texttt{a})$ of type Command states that truck $\texttt{t}$ should move to location $\texttt{l}$ to do action $\texttt{a}$. There are two types of actions: "load" and "offload." Both are parameterized by $\texttt{rid}$. For example, command $(\texttt{5}, \texttt{"Rotterdam"}, \texttt{45646}, \texttt{load})$ means that truck 5 should move to Rotterdam to load shipment 45646. Any request results in two commands: one to load the goods at the start location and one to offload the goods at the destination. Commands are executed one by one; that is, for a truck, there cannot be multiple active commands. There may be times when a truck contains goods corresponding to different requests. Multiple subsequent actions can be performed at the same location (e.g., offloading three shipments and loading two new ones). This can be achieved by sending subsequent commands referring to the same location. The execution of each command is acknowledged via place ready of type Truck.

As indicated before, each truck has a capacity, and each shipment requires a volume. The control system should avoid exceeding the maximum capacity, but it should allow for combined shipments; that is, there are times when a truck contains goods corresponding to multiple requests. There is no need to split shipments over multiple trucks, because each request results in precisely two commands for a truck ("load" and "offload"). There is a continuous flow of requests coming from the environment according to the stochastic interarrival distribution $\texttt{discrete(10,15)}$. The time required to execute a command is given by function *delay*. Given two locations $\texttt{l1}$ and $\texttt{l2}$, *delay*$(\texttt{l1}, \texttt{l2})$ is the time required to move from $\texttt{l1}$ to $\texttt{l2}$ and to (off)load one shipment.

Model the three subpages environment, routing_system, and trucks according to the preceding specification. There is no need to think of a sophisticated planning and routing strategy as long as the solution meets the specification (e.g., things should fit in a truck, and it should be possible to combine shipments).

7.7   Summary

Most industrial systems, in particular information systems, are large and complicated. A hierarchical description is typically required to manage and to understand such systems. From a theoretical point of view, CPNs are expressive enough to model any system, but the resulting model is a potentially large, flat CPN that lacks representation of the hierarchical system structure. Such models are difficult to understand.

In this chapter, we presented an approach to extend CPNs with hierarchy. The idea is to model each part of a system as a module. A module is a CPN with a set of interface places. Two modules can be aggregated to a compound module by merging related interface places. That way, it is possible to design a system from modules. Organizing a system as a set of modules allows us to introduce hierarchy to CPNs. We abstract from the inner structure of a module and replace the module by a substitution transition, which is connected to the same interface places as the module. Another advantage of using modules is that they can be reused in the same and in other system models.

We demonstrated with two more involved examples that hierarchical design simplifies the modeling, although it does not increase modeling power. Hierarchical CPNs can be used to design a system model in a top-down and bottom-up manner. The syntax introduced is based on the CPN language and is supported by CPN Tools.

After studying this chapter you should be able to:

- Explain why a hierarchical system design is necessary.
- Apply the hierarchy modeling technique to a given complex CPN.
- Explain the concepts: "elementary transition," "substitution transition," "hierarchy inscriptions," "page," "subpage," "superpage," "page definition," "page instance," "socket," "port," "port type," and "port assignment."
- Formulate hierarchical CPNs.
- Determine whether a given (part of a) system can be modeled as a transition.
- Flatten a given hierarchical CPN model.

7.8   Further Reading

There are several ways to add hierarchy to Petri nets, and there are differences between Petri net–based languages and tools. The hierarchy concept that we introduced in this chapter composes a system from modules. A module is a Petri net in which certain places serve as an interface. Two modules are composed by merging related places of these modules. By replacing each module with a substitution transition, we can express hierarchy in a Petri net. Jensen and Kristensen (2009) formalize hierarchical CPNs.

Another approach for defining modules is to specify the module interface as a set of transitions rather than as a set of places. Whereas merging places models asynchronous communication—that is, sending a token by one module is not synchronized with the receiving of this token by the other module—merging transitions models synchronous communication. Synchronous communication plays a dominant role in process algebra (Fokkink 2010; Baeten, Basten, and Reniers 2009; Bergstra, Ponse, and Smolka 2001).

A token in a CPN can model the value of an object. According to the object-oriented computing paradigm, an object may be not only a data object that can change its value but may also have behavior. For example, an object of type worker may have a certain value (e.g., name, date of birth, and address) and may be in several states, such as idle and busy. To model such objects, Valk (2004) proposed the *nets-in-nets* or *nested nets* paradigm. A nested net is a Petri net in which a token may represent a Petri net modeling the behavior of the respective object. Nested nets can be arbitrarily nested. That way, nested nets support the modeling of hierarchy. The Renew tool (Kummer et al. 2004) (see <http://www.renew.de>) supports the modeling, execution, and analysis of nested nets.

8 Analyzing Petri Net Models

We introduced Petri nets as a formalism to specify the behavior of enterprise information systems and business processes. The resulting process models can be used for different purposes. In section 1.5, we discussed the relation of business processes, information systems, and models. Process models can be design oriented or analysis oriented. In this chapter, we concentrate on the latter and introduce a wide range of Petri net analysis techniques.

There are two kinds of analysis: *design-time analysis* and *runtime analysis*. The purpose of design-time analysis is to analyze the process model, whereas runtime analysis analyzes running business processes and enterprise information systems. The analyses require different types of analysis techniques.

In this chapter, we first investigate which properties of a model are worth analyzing (section 8.1). Then we introduce reachability analysis using techniques such as the reachability graph and the coverability graph (section 8.2). These techniques explore the state space of the model and can be used to check various properties of the model. Some properties of a Petri net can also be verified by analyzing its network structure. As this is often more efficient than exploring the state space, we present several structural analysis techniques (section 8.3). Reachability analysis and structural analysis are only applicable at design time or when (re)configuring a system. In addition to verification, we can also simulate Petri nets. Simulation is particularly useful in analyzing the performance of Petri nets and in validating the model (section 8.4). Process mining and data mining are examples of runtime analysis techniques. In the last part of this chapter, we introduce process mining techniques and relate them to Petri nets (section 8.5). Process mining techniques can reveal process models and can be combined with other techniques such as simulation. All analysis techniques mentioned in this chapter are supported by open source tools that are readily available. Finally, we provide pointers to these tools (section 8.6).

get the detailed book

8.1   What Do We Want to Analyze?

In chapter 1, we introduced the life cycle model of an enterprise information system. Figure 8.1 depicts this model again. Thus far, we have mainly concentrated on the design of (information) systems and business processes and on building executable models using CPN Tools; in this chapter, we explore the analysis of such models. Figure 8.1 shows that analysis is performed at design time (design analysis phase) and at runtime (runtime analysis phase). In this section, we discuss typical questions that can (and sometimes also need to) be answered in these two phases.

8.1.1   Design-Time Analysis

In the design analysis phase, our goal is to gain insight into the behavior of the information system that we want to design. To do this, we *analyze the process model* that models the behavior of this information system. In the requirements phase, we specified the properties that the information system must satisfy. Analysis is the process by which we investigate whether the information system satisfies these properties and, hence, conforms to its specification. During the analysis process, we ask questions about the information system, some questions correspond to a property of the information system, but because specifications are not complete, we also ask questions that are not determined by the specification.

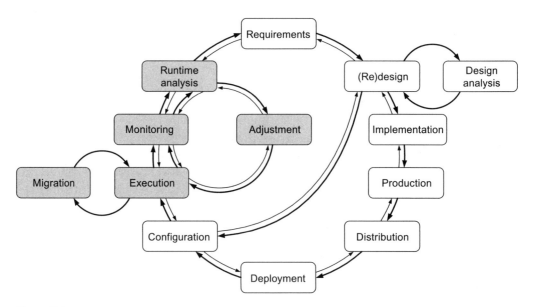

Figure 8.1
The life cycle model of an enterprise information system.

Suppose we want to design an ATM. We may ask:

- Is the pin always checked before the account balance is displayed?
- How long does it take for the ATM to check the pin?
- Can the intended functionality of the ATM in principle be used?
- Can a user crash the ATM?

We can have several models representing various alternative design decisions. The goal of the analysis is to compare these models. If we have to develop a new information system for the management of the drug inventory of a pharmacy, we ask the following questions:

- How long do customers have to wait in front of the desk?
- How often is a drug not in stock?
- What is the average stock of a certain drug?
- What is the turnover speed of a certain drug?
- Are the ordered drugs delivered on time?

We distinguish between *qualitative* and *quantitative* properties. If a question corresponds to a qualitative property, then the answer is always yes or no. The question, are the ordered drugs delivered on time? can be answered with yes or no. It is an example of a question corresponding to a qualitative property. The first, third, and fourth question that we asked about the ATM process also correspond to qualitative properties. All other questions correspond to *quantitative* properties, because the answer is a number.

We can answer all of these questions by applying the right *analysis technique*. The choice of technique depends on the type of property that we are interested in analyzing. There are, for example, analysis techniques that are only suitable for analyzing qualitative properties. The success of an analysis technique depends on the quality of the model used. The model must be suited for the chosen analysis technique, and it should represent all relevant aspects about the system so an assessment can be made of whether the property holds. In other words, the property determines which aspects of the information system a designer must model (and at what level of detail). For example, we cannot answer the question, what is the turnover speed of a certain drug? if our model does not represent time.

In this chapter, we distinguish three types of design-time analysis: *validation, verification*, and *performance analysis*. As introduced in section 1.3, validation checks whether the model correctly reflects what it intends to represent. For example, the designer may have misinterpreted important requirements. For this reason, end users and domain experts must validate the model to avoid implementing a flawed system. Verification looks at the internal consistency of the model and the relation between the model and its specification. For example, verification techniques can detect problems, such as deadlocks and the inability to reach terminal state. The results help to correct such problems. Note that verification does not replace validation. A model must work as intended by the stakeholders. Performance analysis aims at making predictions about key performance indicators, such as response times, flow times, service levels, and utilization. For example, it is important to identify possible bottlenecks of a system at design time. Quantitative questions are typically answered through performance analysis.

One of the advantages of using Petri nets as a process model is the existence of various analysis techniques. Like most formalisms, we can analyze the state space of a Petri net by applying *reachability analysis* (e.g., reachability graphs and coverability graphs). In addition, there are several techniques investigating properties of a Petri net (e.g., invariants, traps, and siphons) by using techniques that directly analyze the *structure of the net*. Reachability analysis and structural techniques are verification techniques. In contrast, Markov chain analysis, queuing networks, and simulation are techniques to analyze the performance of a Petri net model. Simulation can also support validation. However, when validating a model using simulation, the emphasis is not on predicting key performance indicators but on animating the behavior so that users can check the model. Validation can also be supported by gaming; that is, users interact with the simulated model. In this chapter, we introduce verification techniques and simulation for Petri net models.

Exercise 8.1 A branch office of a bank has two cash dispensers. Customers of the branch office can withdraw money from their account through these dispensers. To do so end, the customer must input a check card and the correct pin. The two cash dispensers are connected with the central database of the branch office. In this database, data about check cards and accounts are stored.

In the present situation, there are regularly long waiting times for customers who want to withdraw money. Therefore, the management of the branch office wants to replace the old cash dispensers with new ones. In addition, they would like to improve the connection with the central database. By modeling the new situation with a CPN, the management wants to investigate the new solution.

Name at least three qualitative and three quantitative properties that need to be analyzed.

8.1.2   Runtime Analysis

Although design-time analysis is important, it can be misleading. Even though the model may suggest that no problems are possible—that is, on paper the enterprise information system has good performance and provides safety guarantees—there may be substantial problems at runtime. Moreover, organizations need to continuously improve their performance to successfully compete with other organizations. *Therefore, analysis does not stop once a new business process or information system is implemented.* As figure 8.1 shows, business processes need to be monitored and analyzed at runtime. Such analysis may lead to minor adjustments but also to rigorous redesigns.

Information systems are becoming more and more intertwined with the operational business processes in most organizations. As a result, today's information systems record a multitude of events. ERP systems such as SAP record various transactions, making it possible to extract information about operational processes. The volume of event data is growing rapidly. The use of Radio Frequency Identification (RFID) tags will enable us to monitor supply chains at a detailed level; access cards used in public transport make it possible to monitor movements of people; and services provided via the Internet allow for a unified and systematic recording of business events. More and more devices, such as medical equipment, will be connected to the Internet and provide information about their usage. *Given these data streams, it is not wise to restrict analysis to handmade models.* For this reason, we investigate runtime analysis using event logs.

The most widely used collection of runtime analysis techniques is referred to as *data mining*. Data mining aims at extracting patterns from examples. Originally, data mining had a negative connotation and was sometimes referred to as data dredging, data snooping, or data fishing, but nowadays it is an established research domain with a huge practical impact. Data mining techniques are widely used to analyze operational business processes. Examples of classical data mining tasks are *classification*, *clustering*, *regression*, and *association rule learning*. Classification arranges the data into predefined groups—for example, to identify typical characteristics of customers who do not pay their bills on time. Clustering is like classification, but the groups are not predefined; for example, the typical groups of patients following more or less the same treatment process. Regression attempts to find a function that models the data with the least error. Regression analysis can show that the amount of money spent can be derived from someone's age and income, for instance. Association rule learning searches for relationships between variables. For example, for a supermarket it may be deduced that people who buy diapers typically also buy beer.

Data mining techniques are versatile and can help answer a wide range of questions. However, classical data mining techniques do not focus on the business process, and their output is typically a set of rules, a decision tree, or a simple characterization, rather than a process model. Notions such as causality, concurrency, and synchronization typically do not play a role. In contrast, the goal of *process mining* is to extract process-related information from these event data to, for example, automatically discover a process model by observing events recorded by an enterprise information system. Process mining includes the automated discovery of Petri nets from event logs. Based on observed events (e.g., activities being executed or messages being exchanged), a process model is constructed. As most business processes are highly concurrent, and activities may have complex dependencies, simple data mining techniques cannot adequately capture the underlying business process. Fortunately, there are dedicated process-mining techniques that can discover Petri nets and other process models.

8.2 Reachability Analysis

A common verification technique is to explore the state space of a model and to analyze whether the desired property holds in every state. If the model is a Petri net, the state space is the reachability graph of the net. We investigate the reachability graph as a tool to verify an abundance of properties.

8.2.1 Reachability Graph

We introduced reachability graphs for Petri net systems in section 4.6. A reachability graph consists of nodes and edges. Each node corresponds to a reachable marking of the net, and each edge to a transition moving the net from one marking to another one. Figure 8.2(a) depicts again the Petri net system modeling the patient punch card service desk process and figure 8.2(b) the corresponding reachability graph.

The reachability graph in figure 8.2(b) shows all markings that are reachable from the initial marking [2 · wait, free] in figure 8.2(a). For example, marking [wait, busy] is reachable from the initial marking but also marking [free, 2 · done]. In section 4.6, we introduced the notion of a run as a sequence of transitions that have fired. We can see from the reachability graph in figure 8.2(b) that every run of figure 8.2(a) is finite.

Question 8.1 Consider Petri net systems extended with color. How can we calculate the reachability graph of a colored Petri net system?

We can calculate the reachability graph of a colored Petri net system in the same way as the reachability graph of a Petri net system. There is only one difference: the edges of the reachability graph of a colored Petri net system represent *bindings* rather than transitions. We can treat time stamps in the same way. Moreover, hierarchy can easily be removed by flattening the net.

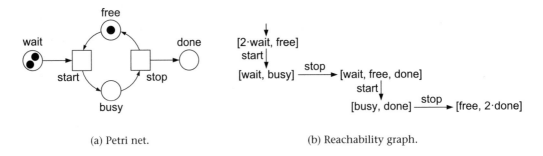

(a) Petri net.   (b) Reachability graph.

Figure 8.2
The patient punch card service desk process and its reachability graph.

```
color Name = string;
color Address = string;
color DateOfBirth = string;
color PatientID = int;
color EmpNo = int;
color Experience = int;
color Gender = with male|female;
color Pat = product PatientID * Name * Address * DateOfBirth * Gender;
color Emp = product EmpNo * Experience;
color EP = product Emp * Pat;
var p:Pat;
var emp:Emp;
val Peter = (12345, "Peter", "Kerkstraat 10, Amsterdam", "13-Dec-1962", male);
val Sara = (23456, "Sara", "Rozenstraat 2, Amsterdam", "1-May-1974", female);
val Ann = (641112, 7);
```

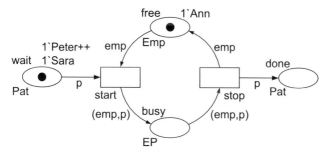

Figure 8.3
Colored Petri net of the patient punch card service desk process.

Figure 8.3 depicts a colored Petri net system of the patient punch card service desk process. In the initial marking of figure 8.3, employee Ann is at the desk, and two customers, Peter and Sara, wait to get served.

Figure 8.4 shows the reachability graph of figure 8.3. Every node depicts the marking of each place as a multiset. Every edge is annotated with the respective binding. The reachability graph in figure 8.4 has eight nodes. In contrast, the reachability graph of the uncolored Petri net system has only five nodes (see figure 8.2(b)). The distinction between the two customers in the colored Petri net system almost doubles the number of nodes.

The Petri nets shown so far have a small and acyclic reachability graph. This is, unfortunately, not always the case. The model in figure 8.5(a) is a small Petri net, but it has infinitely many reachable markings and, therefore, no finite reachability graph. The reason is that there is an infinite run if we alternately fire transitions t1 and t2 infinitely often and in every cycle, transition t2 produces a token in place p3, as shown in figure 8.5(b).

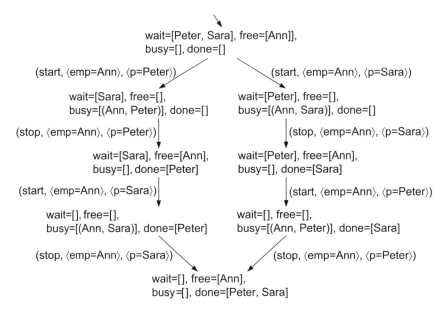

Figure 8.4
Reachability graph of figure 8.3.

Reachability Graphs for Different Types of Petri Nets   We mentioned in section 5.2 that the extension of Petri nets with color considerably increases the expressive power of Petri nets. Even though adding color usually results in more compact models, reachability analysis of colored Petri nets is typically more complex and, from a computational point of view, tends to be intractable for most applications. We can automatically transform any colored Petri net with finite color sets into a Petri net. As the net in figure 8.3 contains places having infinite color sets, we cannot transform it into a Petri net, unless we fix a concrete initial marking or allow for a Petri net with infinitely many places and transitions.

Extending classical or colored Petri nets with time further increases the expressive power of Petri nets. Reachability analysis becomes more complex, because the time dimension must be added to the states in the reachability graph. Hence, the state-space grows, and analysis becomes more difficult. We do not provide an example of a reachability graph of a timed net, but it can be constructed easily using a similar approach as for colored Petri nets. Each token has a color and carries a time stamp, and the nodes in the reachability graph correspond to multisets of such timed colored tokens.

Unlike color and time, the extension with hierarchy does not complicate reachability analysis. Every Petri net with hierarchy can be transformed into a Petri net without hierarchy. For this reason, we do not distinguish between hierarchical Petri nets and flat Petri nets.

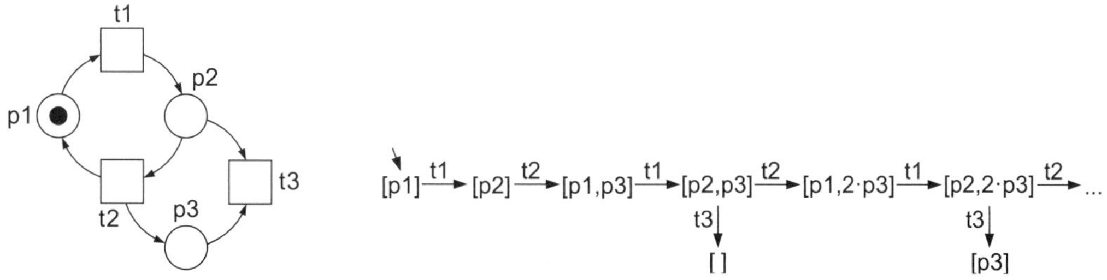

(a) Petri net.   (b) Reachability graph.

Figure 8.5
A Petri net system with infinitely many reachable markings.

8.2.2 Standard Petri Net Properties

The reachability graph of a Petri net system serves as a tool for verifying various properties. In this section, we define seven Petri net–specific properties that can be verified by inspecting the reachability graph of the Petri net system. We illustrate these properties using the Petri net system shown in figure 8.5(a).

Boundedness   Sometimes we must ensure that a place p in a Petri net can have a limited capacity k; that is, at any stage of the execution, it does not contain more than $k \in \mathbb{N}$ tokens. To this end, we must inspect every reachable marking. Even if not specified, the absence of an upper bound for the number of tokens in a place is usually a hint that the model (or the system) is incorrect.

A Petri net system is *k-bounded* (or bounded for short) if and only if no place $p \in P$ contains more than k tokens in any reachable marking. Otherwise, the net is *unbounded*. If k is equal to one, the Petri net system is *safe*.

An important property holds for bounded Petri net systems: they always have a finite number of reachable markings.

In figure 8.5(a), places p1 and p2 are safe, and place p3 is unbounded.

Terminating   Another property is whether a Petri net system is terminating; that is, it always reaches a terminal marking for which no transition is enabled.

A Petri net system is *terminating* if and only if every run is finite.

Accordingly, a Petri net system with a finite and acyclic reachability graph is terminating. Furthermore, a terminating Petri net system has only finitely many runs.

Figure 8.5(a) is not terminating, because it has an infinite run. In contrast, the Petri net systems in figures 8.2(a) and 8.3 are terminating.

Deadlock freedom   A highly relevant question is whether a Petri net can reach a terminal marking. A terminal marking is referred to as a *deadlock*. For example, a Petri net modeling an operating system should never reach a terminal marking.

A Petri net system is *deadlock free* if and only if at least one transition is enabled at every reachable marking.

Figure 8.5(a) is not deadlock free, because [ ], [p3], and [2 · p3] are examples of reachable terminal markings. If we removed transition t3 and its adjacent arcs from figure 8.5(a), the resulting Petri net system would be deadlock free.

Dead transition We are interested in knowing whether the functionality of a system can in principle be used. The functionality of a Petri net system can be used if every transition occurs in at least one run. Otherwise, the Petri net system has dead transitions.

A transition t of a Petri net system is *dead* if and only if t is not enabled at any reachable marking.

Figure 8.5(a) does not have dead transitions.

Liveness A property stronger than the absence of dead transitions is liveness. The liveness property ensures that a transition can always become enabled again.

A transition t is *live* if and only if from every reachable marking m there is a marking m' reachable such that t is enabled at m'. A Petri net system is live if and only if every transition $t \in T$ is live.

Clearly, liveness and terminating exclude each other: if a Petri net system has a terminal marking or is terminating, then it is not live. Moreover, a live Petri net system cannot be terminating. Furthermore, if a Petri net system is live, then it does not have dead transitions.

The Petri net system in figure 8.5(a) is not live, because it has reachable terminal markings; for example, no transition is enabled at marking [p3].

Home-marking Liveness ensures that a transition can be enabled from any marking. Similar, the home-marking property guarantees that a marking can always be reached again.

A marking m is *home-marking* if and only if from any reachable marking we can reach m. A Petri net system is *reversible* if and only if its initial marking is a home-marking.

A Petri net is reversible if its reachability graph is strongly connected.

The Petri net in figure 8.5(a) does not have a home-marking. Consequently, the net is not reversible.

Example 8.2 Figure 8.7 depicts a Petri net system and its reachability graph. Each place is safe. As a consequence, the net is safe, and the reachability graph has only finitely many nodes. The net is not terminating, because there is an infinite run $\langle t1, t3, t2, t3, t2, \dots \rangle$. The net is deadlock free, because every node in figure 8.7(b) has at least one outgoing edge. Furthermore, the net is live and, hence, does not have dead transitions. Finally, each reachable marking is a home-marking, and therefore the net is reversible.

```
CPN Tools state space report:

 Statistics
 ------------------------------------------------------------------
  State Space
     Nodes:  5
     Arcs:   10

 Boundedness Properties
 ------------------------------------------------------------------
  Best Integer Bounds
                          Upper       Lower
        Net'p1 1          1           0
        Net'p2 1          1           0
        Net'p3 1          1           0
        Net'p4 1          1           0
        Net'p5 1          1           0

 Home Properties
 ------------------------------------------------------------------
  Home Markings
     All

 Liveness Properties
 ------------------------------------------------------------------
  Dead Markings
     None
  Dead Transition Instances
     None
  Live Transition Instances
     All
```

Figure 8.6
Part of analysis report generated by CPN Tools for the Petri net system shown in figure 8.7(a).

There are tools to automatically analyze Petri nets. For example, CPN Tools provides the report shown in figure 8.6 for the Petri net shown in figure 8.7(a).

Exercise 8.2   Analyze whether the Petri net system in figure 8.8 is bounded, terminating, live, deadlock free, reversible, or has dead transitions or home-markings.

8.2.3   Fairness
When modeling a system or a business process, we typically must deal with decisions made by the system. Depending on the level of abstraction, such a decision can be modeled as a nondeterministic choice between two transitions or as a complicated

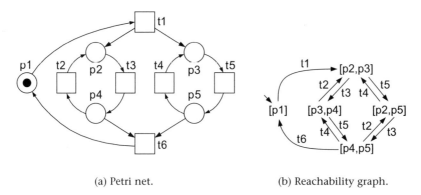

(a) Petri net.   (b) Reachability graph.

Figure 8.7
A Petri net system and its reachability graph.

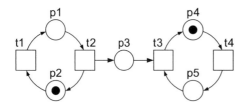

Figure 8.8
The Petri net system of exercise 8.2.

decision procedure involving transition guards, arc inscriptions, or both. We illustrate this concept with an example. Consider the customer service of a bank. Customer mail arrives and is distributed among the employees. There are several ways to realize this distribution—for example, the distribution can be uniform or employees get new mail as soon as they have completed the previous batch.

We are often not interested in explicitly modeling how the decision is made, but an abstract model can allow behavior where one employee answers all mail, while all other employees do nothing. Another example is the model involving two traffic lights that need to operate in a safe manner and where a nondeterministic choice is made to determine which right turns green after each cycle. The first traffic light might always turn green, because the model allows for this behavior. Dijkstra's dining philosophers (1971) (see exercise 17) serve as another example in which a nondeterministic choice may lead to undesirable behavior. The dining philosophers share forks with their neighbors, and there are many runs where one philosopher never eats. This is the *starvation problem*. To identify such situations, we introduce *fairness*. The motivation behind fairness is to detect those transitions in a Petri net that cannot fire infinitely often while being enabled infinitely often. For this reason, fairness is defined only on *infinite runs* of a Petri net. We consider four fairness notions. Let t be a transition of a Petri net.

Impartial   Transition t is *impartial* if and only if t occurs infinitely often in every infinite run of the net.

Fair   Transition t is *fair* if and only if t occurs infinitely often in every infinite run of the net where t is enabled infinitely often.

Just   Transition t is *just* if and only if t occurs infinitely often in every infinite run of the net where t is continuously enabled from a marking onward.

Not fair   Transition t is *not fair* if and only if t is not just; that is, there is an infinite run of the net where t is continuously enabled from a marking onward and does not fire any more.

Impartial considers *all* infinite runs, whereas fair and just only consider *some* infinite runs. Hence, impartial is the strongest fairness notion, meaning that if a transition is impartial, then it is fair and just. If a transition is fair, then it is just. The reason is that fair considers all infinite runs where t has to be enabled infinitely often, but only a subset of these infinite runs enable t continuously. Hence, the notion of fair is stronger than the notion of just and we conclude:

impartial   implies   *fair*   implies   *just*.

Example 8.3   Consider the Petri net system in figure 8.7(a). There is an infinite run $\langle t1, t3, t2, t3, t2, \ldots \rangle$ where transitions t1, t4, t5, and t6 do not occur infinitely often. We conclude that transitions t1, t4, t5, and t6 are not impartial. Similarly, existence of the infinite run $\langle t1, t5, t4, t5, t4, \ldots \rangle$ proves that transitions t2 and t3 are not impartial. If transition t1 is enabled, it always fires. Consequently, if transition t1 is infinitely often enabled, then it fires infinitely often. Transition t1 is fair. Transition t6 is not fair, because in the infinite run $\langle t1, t5, t3, t2, t3, t2, \ldots \rangle$, it is infinitely often enabled but does not fire. However, it is just; that is, in every infinite run where transition t6 is continuously enabled from a marking onward, it fires infinitely often. The infinite run $\langle t1, t3, t5, t4, t5, t4, \ldots \rangle$ shows that transition t2 is neither fair nor just. Consequently, it is not fair. The same holds for transitions t3, t4, and t5.

The four notions of fairness are implemented in CPN Tools. Figure 8.9 shows the fairness diagnostics generated by CPN Tools for the model in figure 8.7(a).

Example 8.4   Consider figure 8.5(a). There is a single infinite run $\langle t1, t2, t1, t2, \ldots \rangle$. Transitions t1 and t2 are impartial, because they occur infinitely often. In contrast, transition t3 is trivially just, because there is no infinite run where this transition is

```
CPN Tools state space report:
  ...
 Fairness Properties
 -------------------------------------------------------------------
        Net't1  1             Fair
        Net't2  1             No Fairness
        Net't3  1             No Fairness
        Net't4  1             No Fairness
        Net't5  1             No Fairness
        Net't6  1             Just
```

Figure 8.9
Fairness-related diagnostics generated by CPN Tools for the Petri net system shown in figure 8.7(a).

```
CPN Tools state space report:
  ...
 Fairness Properties
 -------------------------------------------------------------------
        Net't1  1             Impartial
        Net't2  1             Impartial
        Net't3  1             Just
```

Figure 8.10
Part of analysis report generated by CPN Tools for the Petri net system shown in figure 8.5(a).

continuously enabled from some marking onward. Figure 8.10 depicts a fragment of the report generated by CPN Tools.

Originally, Lehmann, Pnueli, and Stavi (1981) introduced the notion of fairness. Most important are fair and just, which are also referred to as *strong fairness* and *weak fairness* in the literature (Clarke, Grumberg, and Peled 2000). Jensen and Kristensen (2009) formalize impartial for CPNs. The examples in this section are restricted to Petri nets, but the extension to CPNs is straightforward. The only caveat is that the state space has to be finite to compute these properties using CPN Tools.

Exercise 8.3   Determine which of the transitions in figure 8.8 are impartial, fair, just, and unfair.

8.2.4   Verifying Unbounded Petri Nets Using the Coverability Graph
The reachability graph represents all reachable markings of a Petri net. This graph allows for various analysis. Unfortunately, we can only calculate the reachability graph of a

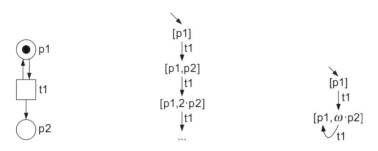

(a) Petri net system.   (b) Reachability graph.   (c) Coverability graph.

Figure 8.11
Motivation for using a coverability graph.

Petri net with *finitely* many reachable markings. A Petri net only has finitely many reachable markings if it is bounded. As a consequence, if a Petri net has at least one unbounded place, its reachability graph has infinitely many nodes and cannot be calculated. Figure 8.5(a) and figure 8.11(a) depict two unbounded Petri nets. In the former net, place p3 is unbounded and, in the latter net, place p2. For both nets, we cannot calculate the complete reachability graph.

For unbounded Petri nets, there is a technique to represent the reachability graph in an *abstract* manner. This abstract representation is the *coverability graph* (Karp and Miller 1969). For any Petri net, the coverability graph has only finitely many nodes. The core idea of the coverability graph is to represent those infinite parts of a reachability graph, where some places become unbounded, in a finite manner.

We illustrate the idea of a coverability graph using the Petri net system in figure 8.11(a). The reachability graph of this net lists all markings [p1], [p1, p2], [p1, 2·p2], ..., as illustrated in figure 8.11(b). In contrast, the coverability graph in figure 8.11(c) represents this path [p1, p2], [p1, 2·p2], ... by a single *abstract marking* [p1, ω·p2] where the ω symbol denotes that place p2 is unbounded. The abstraction is based on the observation that [p1, p2] $\geq$ [p1]. That means marking [p1,p2] is greater than or equal to marking [p1]. In both markings, there is one token in place p1, and, in addition, marking [p1,p2] has one token in place p2. The definition of enabledness and firing of a transition are *monotonous* and, hence, guarantee that if transition t1 is enabled at marking [p1], it is enabled at marking [p1,p2] as well. As this also holds for the successor marking [p1, 2·p2] of [p1,p2], we can continuously fire transition t1 and exceed any bound of place p2. Instead of explicitly showing each reachable marking of sequence [p1], [p1, p2], [p1, 2·p2], ..., we indicate that place p2 eventually becomes unbounded by representing marking [p1,p2] by [p1, ω·p2]. Calculating the successor marking of marking [p1, ω·p2] yields this marking again, because place p2 is already unbounded. This explains the self-loop in figure 8.11(c).

Before we present the concrete algorithm for calculating a coverability graph, we must formalize the notion of an ω-*marking*. We perceive ω as the limit of reachable markings. If a place $p \in P$ contains ω at a marking m—that is, $m(p) = \omega$—then p is unbounded. That is, ω denotes infinity. We extend the notion of a marking m for a Petri net (P, T, F) as introduced in definition 3.8 by defining

$$m : P \rightarrow \mathbb{N} \cup \{\omega\}$$

with

$$\omega + n = \omega \quad \text{and} \quad \omega - n = \omega, \quad n \in \mathbb{N}.$$

To calculate a coverability graph of a Petri net, we construct the reachability graph of this net while applying the following modification:

> For every calculated marking m' and for every marking $m \neq m'$ on a path from the initial marking m_0 to m', if $m' \geq m$, then set $m'(p) = \omega$, for all $p \in P$ with $m'(p) > m(p)$.

The algorithm works as follows: we calculate the reachability graph of the net. For each newly calculated marking m', we check all markings m on a path from the initial marking m_0 to marking m', such that marking m' is greater than or equal to m. As markings m and m' are required to be different, there is at least one place p that has more tokens in marking m' than in marking m. This situation causes an infinite path in the reachability graph, because the path σ from m to m' can be repeated in m', yielding a marking m'' with $m'' \geq m'$, and so on. We conclude that place p is unbounded, and we assign $m'(p) = \omega$.

Example 8.5 Consider the Petri net system in figure 8.5(a) and the beginning of its reachability graph in figure 8.5(b). We construct the coverability graph as follows: we start with the initial marking [p1], fire t1, and reach marking [p2]. As [p2] $\not\geq$ [p1], we continue. Firing transition t2 yields marking [p1, p3]. Because [p1, p3] $\geq$ [p1] and place p3 contains more tokens in marking [p1, p3] than in marking [p1], we replace marking [p1, p3] with [p1, $\omega \cdot$ p3]. Firing transition t1 yields marking [p2, $\omega \cdot$ p3]. We have [p2, $\omega \cdot$ p3] $\geq$ [p2], but because place p3 already has an ω-marking, we do not need to change this marking. Next, we fire transition t3, yielding marking [$\omega \cdot$ p3] (recall that $\omega - 1 = \omega$). Firing of transition t2 yields marking [p1, $\omega \cdot$ p3], which is already present. Figure 8.12 depicts the coverability graph of the net in figure 8.5(a).

The construction of the coverability graph is *not unique*, because more than one transition can be enabled at a certain marking. Depending on the transition that we fire first, we may calculate intermediate markings in a different order, which may result in different coverability graphs. The example in figure 8.13, by Reisig (2010), illustrates this.

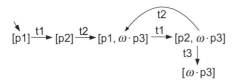

Figure 8.12
The coverability graph of figure 8.5(a).

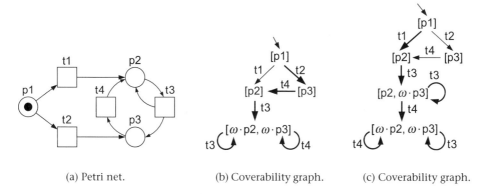

(a) Petri net. (b) Coverability graph. (c) Coverability graph.

Figure 8.13
Coverability graph construction is not unique.

Example 8.6 The Petri net in figure 8.13(a) has two unbounded places, p2 and p3. In figure 8.13(b), we calculate the coverability graph by firing transition sequence ⟨t2, t4, t3⟩, yielding markings [p3], [p2], and [p2, p3]. As [p2, p3] ≥ [p3], we replace marking [p2, p3] with [ω · p2, p3]. Additionally, we have [ω · p2, p3] ≥ [p2], and hence we replace marking [ω · p2, p3] with [ω · p2, ω · p3]. In contrast, if we calculate the coverability graph by firing transitions t1 and t3, yielding markings [p2] and [p2, p3] (see figure 8.13(c)), we only cover place p3. More precisely, we have [p2, p3] ≥ [p2] and, hence, replace marking [p2, p3] with [p2, ω · p3]. Only after firing transition t4 do we cover place p2 ([2 · p2, ω · p3] ≥ [p2, ω · p3]), thus yielding marking [ω · p2, ω · p3].

The coverability graph is an abstract representation of the reachability graph of a Petri net. It can be used to analyze the net. The following five properties hold for coverability graphs:

• The reachability graph and the coverability graph of a bounded Petri net are equivalent.

• The coverability graph of a Petri net is always finite.

- A transition t of a Petri net is dead if and only if it does not appear in the coverability graph.
- A place p of a Petri net is k-bounded if and only if p does not contain more than k tokens in any marking of the coverability graph.
- Every run of a Petri net can be mimicked in the coverability graph.

A bounded Petri net does not have any unbounded places. Because we assign an ω-marking only to an unbounded place, we can conclude the first property. The second property is a consequence of the abstraction. The coverability graph represents every infinite part of the reachability graph in a finite manner and is, hence, an overapproximation of the reachable markings of a Petri net. For this reason, two Petri nets with different reachability graphs may have the same coverability graph. Figure 8.14 shows an example. This explains the fifth property. Properties three and four are straightforward.

Example 8.7 From the coverability graph in figure 8.12, we derive the following properties of the Petri net in figure 8.5(a): first, the net does not have dead transitions, because all three transitions appear in the coverability graph. Second, places p1 and p2 are safe, and place p3 is unbounded.

Exercise 8.4 Construct the coverability graph of the Petri net system in figure 8.8. Which properties of the net can you derive from the coverability graph?

As for Petri nets, we can calculate a coverability graph for colored Petri nets. The construction algorithm is the same as for Petri nets, but if a colored Petri net has a color set representing an infinite data domain, the coverability graph is not necessarily finite. The next exercise highlights this situation.

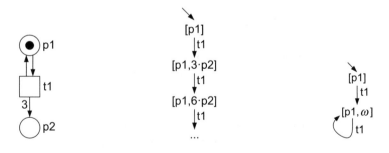

(a) Petri net system.   (b) Reachability graph.   (c) Coverability graph.

Figure 8.14
A Petri net system (a) with the same coverability graph (c) as figure 8.11(a) but a different reachability graph (b).

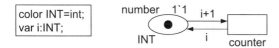

Figure 8.15
The colored Petri net system of exercise 8.5.

Exercise 8.5 Construct the coverability graph for the colored Petri net system in figure 8.15. Why does the resulting graph have infinitely many nodes?

8.2.5 Advanced Reachability Analysis

The reachability graph of a Petri net allows a wide range of analyses. Most of the example reachability graphs presented in this section and in section 4.6 consist of only few nodes. For this reason, we can calculate them all by hand. In section 4.6, we noted that this is not possible for Petri nets modeling industrial systems. For example, a safe Petri net with just 100 places may have 2^{100} reachable markings (in worst case). Hence, brute force implementations to automatically calculate the reachability graph are not applicable. Reachability analysis suffers because even small systems have far more reachable states than a computer can handle. This phenomenon is known as the *state explosion problem* (Valmari 1998).

There are several reasons why a Petri net can have a large reachability graph. One reason is *unboundedness*. To deal with unbounded Petri nets, we introduced the coverability graph. Other reasons are places with *infinite or huge color sets*, the model *size*, and time. In the following section, we consider another reason in more detail: *concurrency*. If several transitions can fire concurrently, then the reachability graph contains all permutations of these firings. Figure 8.16(a) depicts a simple Petri net system. This net has three concurrent branches containing two transitions each. Figure 8.16(b) depicts the resulting reachability graph. The reachability graph consists of twenty-nine nodes. In general, if we have n concurrent branches with k reachable markings each, then the number of reachable markings is equal to k^n. In our example, we have $3^3 = 27$ markings. For ten branches we have already $3^{10} = 59{,}049$ markings!

In most cases, it is not necessary to calculate the complete reachability graph. Instead, it is possible to analyze the property in question by inspecting a significantly smaller number of reachable markings. We illustrate this using figure 8.16.

Suppose we are interested in whether the net in figure 8.16(a) is deadlock free. The brute-force approach to verify deadlock freedom is to check whether every node in the reachability graph has at least one successor node. As all paths from marking [2,3,4] to marking [8,9,10] are only permutations of the six transitions t2, . . . , t8, it is sufficient to consider only the states of a single path. Accordingly, figure 8.16(b) highlights one possible path, which is sufficient to prove deadlock freedom. A verification technique

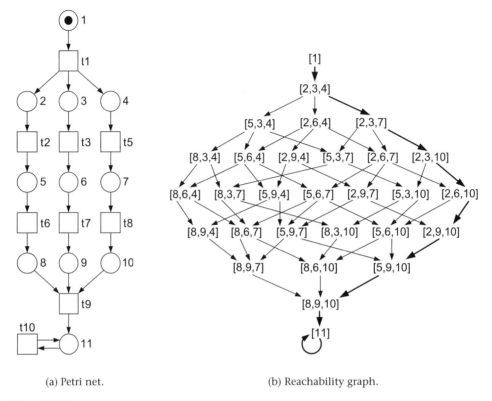

(a) Petri net.   (b) Reachability graph.

Figure 8.16
The path shown in boldface is sufficient to decide deadlock freedom.

that exploits the fact that concurrency leads to different orderings of transitions is *partial order reduction* (Valmari 1991; Godefroid 1991; Peled 1993). This method aims at reducing the number of transition orderings ideally to one while guaranteeing that the reduced reachability graph conforms to the specification if and only if the complete reachability graph does.

8.3   Structural Analysis

Reachability analysis of Petri nets, as introduced in the previous section, allows for the verification of a wide range of properties. At the same time, reachability analysis is an expensive analysis technique because of the state explosion problem. In addition, state-of-the-art state space analysis tools are not designed for laymen and require much experience and knowledge in the verification techniques used. Fortunately, the theory of Petri nets allows for another kind of analysis, which exploits the network structure of the net. The advantage of this structural analysis is that the network structure is typically much smaller than the number of reachable markings. Structural analysis of Petri nets exploits the fact that the effect of firing a transition can be represented as a *vector*. Properties of Petri nets can, consequently, be proven by applying linear algebraic techniques. The weakness of structural analysis techniques is that they are limited to few properties and provide only sufficient or necessary conditions (unless restricted to a particular subclass of Petri nets).

In this section, we introduce two kinds of invariants of Petri nets: *place invariants* and *transition invariants*. A place invariant assigns to each marking an integer value that remains invariant to any transition firing. A transition invariant characterizes potential sequences of transitions that correspond to cycles in the reachability graph. In addition, we show how invariants can be automatically calculated.

We can define place and transition invariants for Petri nets and for CPNs. As CPNs require more technicalities, we restrict ourselves to Petri nets in this section.

8.3.1 Place Invariants

The Petri net in figure 8.17 models the process of marrying and divorcing. Tokens in place man represent unmarried men, and tokens in place woman represent unmarried women. Each token in place couple represents a married couple.

A property of this model is that marrying and divorcing cannot change the total number of persons involved. This means that the number of tokens in place man plus the number of tokens in place woman plus twice the number of tokens in place couple is constant—namely, seven in figure 8.17. We can prove this property by establishing a place invariant. To obtain a more formal notion of place invariants, we introduce the two concepts *weight* and *weighted token sum*.

In a Petri net, we can assign a *weight* to each place in the net. In the Petri net of figure 8.17, we can associate weight one to place man, weight one to place woman, and weight two to place couple.

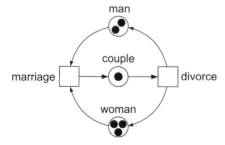

Figure 8.17
A Petri net modeling marriage and divorce.

If we assign a weight z to a place p, we can calculate the product $z \cdot m(p)$ of the weight z of place p and the number $m(p)$ of tokens in p at a marking m. If we do so for all places $p_1, \ldots, p_k$, we obtain the following equation:

$$z_1 \cdot m(p_1) + \cdots + z_k \cdot m(p_k) = z_0.$$

The constant z_0 is the *weighted token sum* of marking m. The marking in figure 8.17 has a weighted token sum of

$$(2 \cdot 1) + (3 \cdot 1) + (1 \cdot 2) = 7.$$

The two tokens in place man have together a weight of $2 \cdot 1 = 2$, the three tokens in place woman have together a weight of $3 \cdot 1 = 3$, and the token in place couple has a weight of $1 \cdot 2 = 2$. The weighted token sum is, thus, 7.

With the concepts of weight and weighted token sum, we can define place invariants. A *place invariant* assigns to each place $p \in P$ of a Petri net (P, T, F) a weight z such that the weighted token sum remains constant in every reachable marking. Formally, a place invariant can be written as:

$$z_1 \cdot p_1 + \cdots + z_k \cdot p_k = z_0.$$

The value of each place p is defined by the number $m(p)$ of tokens in any reachable marking m. A place invariant represents a kind of preservation law.

Place invariants are derived from the network structure only. Hence, the initial marking of a Petri net is irrelevant. When we write $z_1 \cdot p_1 + \cdots + z_k \cdot p_k = z_0$, we mean that the weighted token sum remains constant. The addition of the actual weight in a particular marking (i.e., z_0) is optional and just added for interpretation purposes. The weighted token sum $z_1 \cdot p_1 + \cdots + z_k \cdot p_k$ should be constant for *any* initial marking. Any Petri net has a trivial place invariant: $0 \cdot p_1 + \cdots + 0 \cdot p_k$. This is the invariant that assigns weight zero to all places. In the remainder of this chapter, we only consider nontrivial place invariants.

For the Petri net in figure 8.17, we obtain a place invariant

$1 \cdot \text{man} + 1 \cdot \text{woman} + 2 \cdot \text{couple}.$

To check whether this is a place invariant, we must investigate whether any transitions can change the corresponding weighted token sum. If transition marriage fires, two tokens of weight one are consumed and one token of weight two is produced. Transition marriage, thus, cannot change the weighted token sum. If transition divorce fires, a token of weight two is consumed, and two tokens of weight one are produced. So, transition divorce cannot change the weighted token sum, either. For the initial marking shown in figure 8.17, the weighted token sum is 7. This indicates the total number of persons in the model. However, if initially there are 513 persons involved, the weighted token sum remains 513. This illustrates that place invariants hold for any initial marking.

The Petri net in figure 8.17 has more invariant properties. In addition to the total number of persons, the number of men remains constant. The total number of tokens in places man and couple is always equal to three for the given initial marking. This is the case, because $1 \cdot$ man $+ 0 \cdot$ woman $+ 1 \cdot$ couple $= 3$ is a place invariant. We can omit all places of weight zero and simply write man $+$ couple $= 3$. Let us check whether this equation is an invariant. If transition marriage fires, a token of weight one is consumed from place man, and a token of weight one is produced in place couple. Transition marriage, thus, cannot change the number of tokens in places man and couple. If transition divorce fires, the opposite happens. Transition divorce, thus, cannot change the weighted token sum, either. What applies to place man, also applies to place woman. That means, woman $+$ couple $= 4$ is a place invariant as well.

So far, the weights have been positive numbers. However, weights can also be negative.

Exercise 8.6   Another invariant property of the model in figure 8.17 is that the *difference* between the number of women and the number of men is always equal to one. Prove this using a place invariant.

As a further example, we consider the Petri net in figure 8.18 modeling two traffic lights. This model has already been introduced in section 3.5. Figure 8.18 has the following place invariants:

$$r1 + g1 + o1 = 1$$
$$r2 + g2 + o2 = 1$$
$$x + g1 + o1 + g2 + o2 = 1.$$

The first and second invariant state that each traffic light is always in one of the three states. From the third invariant we can derive that at most one token is in places g1, o1, g2, and o2. We can interpret from this invariant that at most one traffic light is green or orange.

Adding or subtracting two place invariants yields a new place invariant. By adding the first two place invariants of figure 8.18, we obtain the place invariant $r1 + g1 + o1 + r2 + g2 + o2 = 2$. We can subtract the third place invariant from this place invariant and obtain the place invariant $r1 + r2 - x = 1$. This can be verified easily by checking the effect of each transition on this weighted token sum. Any linear combination of invariants is actually an invariant. The invariant $r1 + r2 - x = 1$ can be rewritten as follows: $r1 + r2 = 1 + x$. Because $x \geq 0$, we deduce $r1 + r2 \geq 1$; that is, the total number of tokens in places r1 and r2 is greater than or equal to one. From this, we can derive that always at least one traffic light is red.

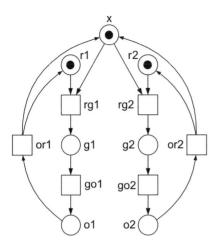

Figure 8.18
A Petri net modeling two traffic lights.

Exercise 8.7 Consider the Petri net modeling a specialist in figure 4.6. Verify whether the following equations are place invariants and, if so, interpret them:

1. free + busy + docu = 1;
2. wait + inside + done = 4;
3. free + 2 · busy + docu = 1;
4. free + 2 · busy + docu + wait + done = 5; and
5. busy − inside = 0.

8.3.2 Transition Invariants

Transition invariants are the counterparts of place invariants. We use transition invariants to prove that a Petri net returns to a marking after a certain series of transition firings. These transition firings correspond to a cycle in the reachability graph. For systems with cyclic behavior, it is often a requirement that the system can return to a state. For example, for an elevator that starts at a certain floor, it is natural to expect that it eventually returns to that floor. If we look at the Petri net in figure 8.17, we see that firing transition marriage twice, followed by firing transition divorce twice, returns the net to its initial marking.

A transition invariant assigns a weight to each *transition*. We represent a transition invariant in the same way as a place invariant. A transition invariant for the Petri net in figure 8.17 is

2 · marriage + 2 · divorce.

This invariant indicates that firing both transitions twice in an arbitrary order results in the initial marking again. Note that marriage + divorce is a transition variant as well.

A *transition invariant* assigns to each transition a *nonnegative* weight z such that firing each transition z times does not change the marking. Let $t_1, \ldots, t_n$ be the transitions of the Petri net. A transition invariant is defined as

$$z_1 \cdot t_1 + \cdots + z_n \cdot t_n.$$

As with place invariants, there is always a trivial transition invariant that assigns weight zero to all transitions. An interpretation of this invariant is that not firing any transitions will keep the net in the same marking.

Question 8.8 What are the transition invariants for the traffic lights in figure 8.18?

If each of the three transitions rg1, go1, and or1 in figure 8.18 fires exactly once, the net returns to its initial marking. Consequently, there is a transition invariant that assigns weight one to transitions rg1, go1, and or1. We write this transition invariant as rg1 + go1 + or1. This invariant corresponds to one cycle of the left traffic light. Also, $2 \cdot$ rg1 + $2 \cdot$ go1 + $2 \cdot$ or1 is a transition invariant. This transition invariant indicates that firing each transition twice results again in the initial marking. Given the symmetry in the model, we also find the transition invariant rg2 + go2 + or2 for the right traffic light.

A transition invariant does not state in which order the transitions should fire. Only the number of firings for each transition is fixed. It is possible that the transitions in the transition invariant cannot fire at all. Suppose that we remove from figure 8.18 the token in places r1, r2, and x. Then no transition can fire. Nevertheless, rg1 + go1 + or1 and rg2 + go2 + or2 are still transition invariants. They show that *if* the respective transitions fire exactly once, *then* the Petri net is in the initial marking again. The reason is that invariants are *structural* properties of the net that do not depend on the initial marking.

The Petri net in figure 8.2(a) has no nontrivial transition invariant; that is, no series of transition firings in any marking m results in m again. The reason is that the firing of any transition cannot be undone by one or more other firings. The firing of transition start has, for example, the effect that a token is removed from place wait without having the possibility to reproduce a token in this place.

Exercise 8.8 Is start_production + end_production a transition invariant of the Petri net system in figure 8.19? If not, give another transition invariant.

8.3.3 The Incidence Matrix

We can describe the behavior of a Petri net with linear algebraic equations. The idea is to represent markings m and m' as column vectors $\underline{m}$ and $\underline{m}'$. If marking m' can be reached from marking m by firing a transition t, then we can represent the effect of firing t as a column vector $\underline{t} = \underline{m}' - \underline{m}$.

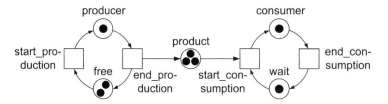

Figure 8.19
Petri net system modeling a producer and a consumer.

Consider the Petri net in figure 8.17. The firing of transition marriage in the initial marking m_0 depicted yields a marking $m = [\text{man}, 2 \cdot \text{couple}, 2 \cdot \text{woman}]$. We can write this as the addition of the following vectors:

$$\underline{m} \quad = \quad \underline{m_0} \quad + \quad \underline{t}$$

$$\begin{pmatrix} 1 \\ 2 \\ 2 \end{pmatrix} = \begin{pmatrix} 2 \\ 1 \\ 3 \end{pmatrix} + \begin{pmatrix} -1 \\ 1 \\ -1 \end{pmatrix}.$$

The column vectors refer to place man (top), place couple (middle), and place woman (bottom), respectively. This example explains why Petri nets were called *vector addition systems* in the past.

Let (P, T, F) be a Petri net with places $p_1, \ldots, p_k \in P$. We can represent a marking m as the column vector

$$\underline{m} = \begin{pmatrix} u_1 \\ \vdots \\ u_k \end{pmatrix} \quad \text{with } m(p_i) = u_i, \quad 1 \leq i \leq k$$

where u_i represents the number of tokens in place p_i at marking m. In the previous example, we had

$$\underline{m_0} = \begin{pmatrix} 2 \\ 1 \\ 3 \end{pmatrix} \quad \text{with } m_0(\text{man}) = 2, m_0(\text{couple}) = 1, \text{ and } m_0(\text{woman}) = 3.$$

Likewise, we can represent the effect of a transition $t \in T$ as a column vector

$$\underline{t} = \begin{pmatrix} v_1 \\ \vdots \\ v_k \end{pmatrix} \quad \text{with } v_i = w((t, p_i)) - w((p_i, t)), \quad 1 \leq i \leq k.$$

Recall that we can calculate the effect that the firing of t has on a place $p \in P$ as the number $w((t, p))$ of tokens produced in p minus the number $w((p, t))$ of tokens consumed from p. In the previous example, the effect of transition marriage on place man, place couple, and place woman is $0 - 1 = -1$, $1 - 0 = 1$, and $0 - 1 = -1$, respectively. This results in vector

$$\underline{\text{marriage}} = \begin{pmatrix} -1 \\ 1 \\ -1 \end{pmatrix}.$$

So far, we have illustrated that we can represent markings and the effect of transitions as column vectors. We can combine the vectors $\underline{t}_1, \ldots, \underline{t}_n$ of all transitions $t_1, \ldots, t_n \in T$ and define a matrix C, the *incidence matrix*:

$$C = \begin{pmatrix} \underline{t}_1 & \cdots & \underline{t}_n \end{pmatrix} = \begin{pmatrix} v_{11} & \cdots & v_{n1} \\ \vdots & & \vdots \\ v_{1k} & \cdots & v_{nk} \end{pmatrix}.$$

The incidence matrix has a row for each place $p \in P$ and a column for each transition $t \in T$. An element v_{ij} represents the effect of transition t_i on place p_j. The Petri net in figure 8.17 has the following incidence matrix:

$$C = \begin{pmatrix} \underline{\text{marriage}} & \underline{\text{divorce}} \end{pmatrix} = \begin{pmatrix} -1 & 1 \\ 1 & -1 \\ -1 & 1 \end{pmatrix}.$$

Exercise 8.9 Give the incidence matrix of the Petri net in figure 8.19.

The incidence matrix of a Petri net can be applied for analysis. One application is reachability analysis. Consider the marking $m_0 = [2 \cdot \text{man}, \text{couple}, 3 \cdot \text{woman}]$ in figure 8.17. Firing of transitions marriage, divorce, and again marriage yields marking $m = [\text{man}, 2 \cdot \text{couple}, 2 \cdot \text{woman}]$. We can represent this in vector notation as

$$\begin{array}{ccccccccc} \underline{m} & = & \underline{m}_0 & + & \underline{\text{marriage}} & + & \underline{\text{divorce}} & + & \underline{\text{marriage}} \end{array}$$

$$\begin{pmatrix} 1 \\ 2 \\ 2 \end{pmatrix} = \begin{pmatrix} 2 \\ 1 \\ 3 \end{pmatrix} + \begin{pmatrix} -1 \\ 1 \\ -1 \end{pmatrix} + \begin{pmatrix} 1 \\ -1 \\ 1 \end{pmatrix} + \begin{pmatrix} -1 \\ 1 \\ -1 \end{pmatrix}.$$

If we replace the sum of equal vectors by the scalar multiplication, we can simplify this equation to

$$\underline{m} \quad = \quad \underline{m}_0 \quad + \quad 2 \cdot \text{marriage} \quad + \quad \text{divorce}$$

$$\begin{pmatrix} 1 \\ 2 \\ 2 \end{pmatrix} = \begin{pmatrix} 2 \\ 1 \\ 3 \end{pmatrix} + 2 \cdot \begin{pmatrix} -1 \\ 1 \\ -1 \end{pmatrix} + \begin{pmatrix} 1 \\ -1 \\ 1 \end{pmatrix}.$$

The incidence matrix of a Petri net represents the effects of all transitions. We can, therefore, replace the addition of the transition vectors by the product of the incidence matrix and a column vector $\underline{x}$ specifying, for each transition, how often we need to add the respective vector to the initial marking m_0:

$$\underline{m} \quad = \quad \underline{m}_0 \quad + \quad \mathbf{C} = \left(\text{marriage} \quad \text{divorce} \right) \cdot \quad \underline{x}$$

$$\begin{pmatrix} 1 \\ 2 \\ 2 \end{pmatrix} = \begin{pmatrix} 2 \\ 1 \\ 3 \end{pmatrix} + \begin{pmatrix} -1 & 1 \\ 1 & -1 \\ -1 & 1 \end{pmatrix} \cdot \begin{pmatrix} 2 \\ 1 \end{pmatrix} -$$

$$= \begin{pmatrix} 2 \\ 1 \\ 3 \end{pmatrix} + \begin{pmatrix} -2 + 1 \\ 2 - 1 \\ -2 + 1 \end{pmatrix}$$

$$= \begin{pmatrix} 1 \\ 2 \\ 2 \end{pmatrix}.$$

The column vector $\underline{x}$ is the *Parikh vector* and maps each transition $t \in T$ to the number of occurrences of t in the run, changing the initial marking m_0 to m. In the example, vector $\underline{x}$ is such that transition marriage fires twice and transition divorce fires once.

If there is a run from the initial marking m_0 to a marking m in a Petri net, then the number of transitions that must be fired (specified by the Parikh vector $\underline{x}$) is determined by the equation

$$\underline{m} = \underline{m}_0 + \mathbf{C} \cdot \underline{x}.$$

This equation is the *state equation* of a Petri net. Using the state equation, we can prove a sufficient criterion for *nonreachability of a marking m*. If the equation system

$$\mathbf{C} \cdot \underline{x} = \underline{m} - \underline{m}_0$$

does not have any integer solution for vector $\underline{x}$, then marking m is not reachable from the initial marking m_0.

Unfortunately, we cannot prove reachability of marking m using the incidence matrix, because, even for an unreachable marking m, the state equation can have an integer solution. The next exercise illustrates this.

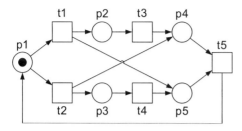

Figure 8.20
The Petri net of exercise 8.10.

Exercise 8.10 Show for the Petri net system in figure 8.20 that the unreachable marking $m = [p2, p3]$ has an integer solution for $\underline{x}$ in $\mathbf{C} \cdot \underline{x} = \underline{m} - \underline{m}_0$.

8.3.4 Applications of the Incidence Matrix

We can apply the incidence matrix $\mathbf{C}$ of a Petri net to analyze nonreachability of a marking m. The state equation provides a necessary (but not sufficient) criterion for reachability. There are even more applications of the incidence matrix including the calculation of place and transition invariants. In the remainder of this chapter, we formalize place and transition invariants in terms of the incidence matrix $\mathbf{C}$.

Calculating Place Invariants A *place invariant* assigns to each place a weight such that the weighted token sum remains constant in every reachable marking. As already introduced, we can represent a place invariant for a Petri net with k places $p_1, \ldots, p_k$ as an equation

$$z_1 \cdot p_1 + \cdots + z_k \cdot p_k = z_0.$$

In this equation, z_i denotes the weight that is assigned to place p_i, and p_i denotes the value of place p_i that is defined by the number $m(p_i)$ of tokens in any reachable marking m. The constant z_0 is the weighted token sum given a particular marking. A place invariant ensures that the firing of any transition does not change z_0. This is the case if, for every transition t, the sum of the effects of t on all places is zero. We can express this using the incidence matrix $\mathbf{C}$ as follows:

$$(z_1 \cdots z_k) \cdot \mathbf{C} = \underline{0}.$$

In this equation, $(z_1 \cdots z_k)$ is a $1 \times k$ matrix, and $\mathbf{C}$ is a $k \times n$ matrix (i.e., the Petri net has k places and n transitions). Hence, the product is a $1 \times n$ matrix (i.e., a row vector) where every element is equal to zero. Every integer solution $(z_1 \cdots z_k)$ of this equation is a place invariant. We can determine the constant z_0 by calculating the weighted token sum of the initial marking:

$z_0 = (z_1 \quad \cdots \quad z_k) \cdot \underline{m}_0.$

We illustrate the interpretation of the previous equation by using an example. For the Petri net system in figure 8.17, the equation has the form

$$(z_1 \quad z_2 \quad z_3) \cdot \begin{pmatrix} -1 & 1 \\ 1 & -1 \\ -1 & 1 \end{pmatrix} = (0 \quad 0)$$

$$(-z_1 + z_2 - z_3 \quad z_1 - z_2 + z_3) = (0 \quad 0).$$

This example illustrates that, for each transition t, we calculate the sum over the product of the weighted effect of t on each place p. For transition marriage, we calculate the weighted effects $-z_1$, z_2, and $-z_3$ for places man, couple, and woman, respectively. The sum of these three values is $-z_1 + z_2 - z_3$; that is, if $-z_1 + z_2 - z_3 = 0$, then the firing of transition marriage does not change the weighted token sum. Likewise, the sum of the weighted effects of transition divorce is equal to $z_1 - z_2 + z_3$. If $z_1 - z_2 + z_3 = 0$, then the firing of transition divorce does not change the weighted token sum either. This yields an equation system with two equations:

I: $-z_1 + z_2 - z_3 = 0$

II: $z_1 - z_2 + z_3 = 0.$

Any integer solution for z_1, z_2, z_3 satisfying both equations is a place invariant. Examples of possible integer solutions for $(z_1 \quad z_2 \quad z_3)$ are: $(0 \quad 0 \quad 0)$, $(1 \quad 1 \quad 0)$, $(0 \quad 1 \quad 1)$, $(1 \quad 2 \quad 1)$, and $(1 \quad 0 \quad -1)$. The first solution is the *trivial solution*, meaning vector $\underline{0}$ is a place invariant for *any* Petri net. The second and third solutions say that the number of men and women does not change. If we calculate the weighted token sum for each solution and the initial marking, we obtain the following five place invariants:

$0 \cdot$ man $+ \quad 0 \cdot$ couple $+ \quad\quad 0 \cdot$ woman $= \quad\quad 0$

$1 \cdot$ man $+ \quad 1 \cdot$ couple $+ \quad\quad 0 \cdot$ woman $= \quad\quad 3$

$0 \cdot$ man $+ \quad 1 \cdot$ couple $+ \quad\quad 1 \cdot$ woman $= \quad\quad 4$

$1 \cdot$ man $+ \quad 2 \cdot$ couple $+ \quad\quad 1 \cdot$ woman $= \quad\quad 7$

$1 \cdot$ man $+ \quad 0 \cdot$ couple $+ \quad (-1) \cdot$ woman $= \quad -1.$

Exercise 8.11 Determine at least four place invariants for the Petri net shown in figure 8.7(a) using the incidence matrix.

Calculating Transition Invariants A *transition invariant* represents several transition occurrences that yield a cycle in the reachability graph. A transition invariant assigns to each transition the concrete number of occurrences in the cycle. We defined a transition invariant for a Petri net with n transitions $t_1, \ldots, t_n$ as

$$z_1 \cdot t_1 + \cdots + z_n \cdot t_n.$$

The values z_i specify how often a transition t_i must fire to return to a marking m. Actually, $z_1, \ldots, z_n$ define a Parikh vector

$$\underline{x} = \begin{pmatrix} z_1 \\ \vdots \\ z_n \end{pmatrix}.$$

The Parikh vector is an element of the Petri net state equation:

$$\mathbf{C} \cdot \underline{x} = \underline{m} - \underline{m}_0.$$

The state equation specifies the Parikh vector of transition occurrences from the initial marking m_0 to any marking m. As a transition invariant should not change the marking, we rewrite the state equation to

$$\mathbf{C} \cdot \underline{x} = \underline{0}.$$

For a Petri net with k places and n transitions, the incidence matrix is a $k \times n$ matrix, and the Parikh vector is an $n \times 1$ matrix. The product is, consequently, a column vector— that is, a $k \times 1$ matrix.

We illustrate this equation with the Petri net in figure 8.17. Let the Parikh vector be

$$\underline{x} = \begin{pmatrix} \text{marriage} \\ \text{divorce} \end{pmatrix} = \begin{pmatrix} z_1 \\ z_2 \end{pmatrix}. \text{ We obtain}$$

$$\begin{pmatrix} -1 & 1 \\ 1 & -1 \\ -1 & 1 \end{pmatrix} \cdot \begin{pmatrix} z_1 \\ z_2 \end{pmatrix} = \begin{pmatrix} 0 \\ 0 \\ 0 \end{pmatrix}$$

$$\begin{pmatrix} -z_1 + z_2 \\ z_1 - z_2 \\ -z_1 + z_2 \end{pmatrix} = \begin{pmatrix} 0 \\ 0 \\ 0 \end{pmatrix}.$$

We obtain three equations, one for each place. Each equation calculates the sum of the weighted effects of all transitions on a particular place:

$$\begin{aligned} -z_1 &+ z_2 &= 0 \\ z_1 &- z_2 &= 0 \\ -z_1 &+ z_2 &= 0. \end{aligned}$$

A solution for one of these equations ensures that the number of firings of the transitions does not change the number of tokens in a particular place. A solution for all three equations is, hence, a transition invariant. Possible solutions are:

z_1	z_2
0	0
1	1
12	12

The first solution is the trivial solution, which is a transition invariant for any Petri net. The second solution shows that firing both transitions once returns the net to its initial state. As any linear combination of invariants is again an invariant, there are typically infinitely many transition invariants. As shown, we can multiply the second invariant by 12 and obtain another invariant.

Exercise 8.12 Determine at least four transition invariants of figure 8.7(a) using the incidence matrix.

Automated Invariant Calculation The incidence matrix of a Petri net enables us to obtain an equation system whose solutions are place or transition invariants of the net. Clearly, for large nets we cannot solve such an equation system by hand. In particular, as all linear combinations of invariants are again invariants, the number of invariants is typically infinite. There are linear algebraic techniques to calculate a basis from which all other invariants can be obtained. There are also techniques to obtain the most interesting invariants—that is, *minimal semipositive invariants*. A place invariant is *semipositive* if, for all places p, the weight z of p is greater than or equal to zero. If all weights are zero, we call the invariant *trivial*. If all weights are greater than zero, then the place invariant is a *positive place invariant*. A semipositive invariant i is *minimal* if there does not exist any other semipositive invariant i' that is nontrivial while covering a subset of the places covered by invariant i. We only consider transition invariants that are semipositive. Unlike for place invariants, negative weights do not make sense for transition invariants, as this would correspond to firing backward.

Example 8.9 For the Petri net in figure 8.17, we calculated two transition invariants: marriage + divorce and $12 \cdot$ marriage + $12 \cdot$ divorce. The former invariant is minimal; the latter is not. We can also compute the following two place invariants for this net: man + $2 \cdot$ couple + woman = 7 and man − woman = −1. The former is a minimal semipositive invariant. The latter is not semipositive, because the weight of place woman is negative.

There are standard techniques to solve systems of linear equations, for example, Gaussian elimination. For this, we refer to standard textbooks on linear algebra (Poole 2010; Strang 2009). For applying invariants it is not essential to understand linear algebra, as there are tools, such as Woflan (Verbeek, Basten, and Aalst 2001) and ProM (Aalst, Dongen, et al. 2007), that calculate invariants for Petri nets.

Applying Invariants for Analysis We can use invariants in three ways. First, we can verify whether previously determined (invariant) properties indeed apply. Second, we can derive invariants and later check which properties they represent. With place invariants, we can derive preservation laws. We can use place invariants, for example, to prove the preservation of products, information, and tools. Place invariants can be used to investigate safety aspects. For example, we can prove with a place invariant that the two traffic lights are safe. For the Petri net in figure 8.18, we can show that at least one traffic light is red. Using transition invariants, we can investigate (among other things) whether the modeled system can return to the initial state.

The third application of invariants is the analysis of standard properties of Petri nets. The number of properties that can be analyzed is, however, restricted. As with proving nonreachability, invariants provide only sufficient or necessary conditions for Petri net standard properties. The following properties hold:

- If a marking m is reachable from the initial marking m_0 and i is a place invariant of the net, then i holds in m—that is, $i \cdot m = i \cdot m_0$.
- Every place p is bounded if there is a semipositive place invariant i that assigns a positive weight to p.
- If there is a positive place invariant i that assigns a positive weight to all places, then the net is bounded for any initial marking.
- If the net is live and bounded, then it has a positive transition invariant that covers each transition.

The first property directly follows from the definition of place invariant. The proofs of the other properties are out of the scope of this book.

Exercise 8.13 Consider the four properties. Does the converse hold for each property? If not, give a counterexample.

8.4 Simulation-Based Analysis

The next analysis technique that we discuss is *simulation*. By simulation, we mean imitating reality by repeatedly executing a model. Using simulation, we can conduct various experiments. We illustrate this with an example.

8.4.1 Introduction
Simulation enables us to experiment by using an executable model. We apply simulation whenever real experiments are too costly or dangerous. For example, checking the automotive aerodynamics of a new car design is usually studied first by a simulation of a computer model, because wind tunnel tests are expensive and require a prototype of the car. To investigate the reliability of the operation of a nuclear power station,

one does not perform real experiments to see under which circumstances the nuclear reactor melts down. The results of such an experiment would be too dangerous.

Example 8.10 A taxi company has a gas station where the company's drivers can fill up their taxis with fuel. It is the company's policy that drivers who are not busy must take their taxis to the gas station and wait for their turn. At the gas station, there is only one gas pump, and there is waiting space for exactly three taxis. Filling up a taxi takes between two and five minutes. If there are already three taxis waiting, the driver is allowed to fill up at another gas station.

The business booms, and the company is growing. Additional taxis have been added, drivers have been hired, and the number of rides has increased. Recently, it turned out that about 8 percent of the gas refills are not done at the company's station. The management suspects that the drivers violate the rule to save time and, in this way, create a cost problem. About fifteen taxis arrive on average each hour for a refill at the gas station. The average time between two successive arrivals is thus four minutes.

By running a simulation experiment, taxi company management wants the following questions to be answered:

- Is the rule circumvented on some scale?
- The drivers complain that waiting times of more than ten minutes are the rule rather than the exception. Is this true?
- There are several alternatives to invest in the gas station: the waiting space could be enlarged, a second pump could be purchased, or a faster pump could replace the present pump. What is the effect of the three alternatives?

In this chapter, we consider simulation in the sense of experimenting with a CPN representing a system or a business process. The reliability of a simulation study succeeds or fails with the quality of the model. A poor representation of reality does not lead to reliable simulation results. This applies to all other analysis techniques discussed in this chapter.

A run of a CPN is a sequence of transitions such that we can reach a marking m from the initial marking m_0. We compare a simulation experiment with a run of the CPN model. A simulation experiment is a *simulation run*. A simulation run can be seen as a random walk in the reachability graph of the CPN starting in the initial node. A simulation run of the taxi company model is a sequence of consecutive states. Whenever a taxi arrives or is served, the taxi company, viewed as a discrete dynamic system, jumps to a next state.

The description of the taxi company process says that filling up a car takes between two and five minutes, and that the time between two successive arrivals is on average four minutes. For a simulation, these data are not sufficient. It is not clear, for example, whether two arrivals close together are possible. We can specify these changing

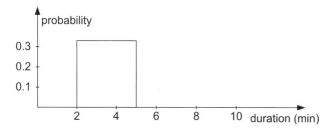

Figure 8.21
A uniform distribution of probability for service durations.

durations by a probability distribution that defines how probable a possible duration is.

In this chapter, we do not assume detailed knowledge of stochastic methods. However, to specify delays in a simulation model, we must discuss the concept of probability distribution.

For the example of the taxi company, we assume that the service duration (the time that it takes to refill a gas tank) is *distributed uniformly* between two and five minutes. That means we use a distribution of probability that allocates an equal probability to each duration between two and five minutes. A service duration of four minutes is, hence, as probable as a service duration of 2.567893 minutes. Figure 8.21 depicts the uniform distribution of probability (between two and five minutes). The average service time is $(2 + 5)/2 = 3.5$ minutes.

The time between two successive arrivals is on average four minutes, but the arrival times are irregular. It is possible that there are only two seconds between two successive arrivals, but it is also possible that there is one-half of an hour between successive arrivals. Assuming that the probability that two successive arrivals are close to each other (e.g., with a duration of one minute) is much larger than the probability that they are far apart (e.g., thirty minutes), we use a *negative-exponential* probability distribution, as shown in figure 8.22.

The uniform and the negative-exponential distribution are just two examples of random distribution functions. As discussed in section 6.6.3, CPN Tools provides a wide range of stochastic functions to model durations and choices.

During simulation, we can measure waiting times, throughput times, service levels, and utilization, for instance. To determine the reliability of the measurements, the simulation run is typically divided into several *subruns*. Furthermore, the simulation run typically starts with a *start run* (i.e., an initialization run to bring the model into steady state). Such a start run should take care that eventual start-up effects have disappeared before the first measurements are made. Because each subrun is separately measured, we get an impression of the reliability of these measurements.

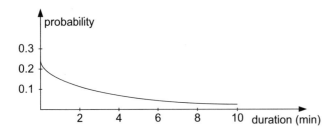

Figure 8.22
A negative-exponential probability distribution for the time in between two arrivals.

Table 8.1
The Average Waiting Time for Each Subrun

Subrun	Average waiting time (minutes)
1	2.25
2	7.63
3	6.23
4	8.23
5	2.34
6	3.45
7	6.34
8	5.87
9	4.67
10	2.99

Exercise 8.14 A supermarket has four cash registers. In the peak hours, these cash registers cannot handle the flow of customers. There are regularly large queues with dissatisfied customers. The administrator of the supermarket wonders whether the problems can be solved using an extra cash register.

1. This question can be answered by placing an extra cash register to experimentally determine whether the problems are solved by adding an extra cash register. Is this a sensible approach?
2. We can also simulate the present and future situation. Why is a start run desirable in this case?
3. After a simulation of ten subruns, we obtain the results of table 8.1. In this table, the average waiting time for each subrun is given. Assuming these results, we could conclude that the average waiting time is five minutes. Is this a valid conclusion?

8.4.2   Modeling the Taxi Company

After introducing some of the basic simulation concepts, we now model the gas station of the taxi company. We start with modeling the present situation according to the top-down approach sketched in chapter 7. First, we identify the interface between the gas station and its environment. The exchange between the gas station and the environment is limited to the arrivals and departures of taxis. Taxis that arrive are served, or they drive on, because there is no space.

Figure 8.23 depicts page main. This page models the gas station (substitution transition gas_station) and the environment (substitution transition environment). A token in place arrive corresponds to an arriving taxi, a token in place drive_on corresponds to a taxi not being served, and a token in place depart corresponds to a taxi that has been refueled.

We map substitution transitions environment and gas_station onto pages. Figure 8.24 depicts page environment. Transition create models a simple counter that creates taxis. These taxis arrive via port arrive at the gas station. Taxis are generated according to a negative-exponential probability distribution exponential(1.0/4000.0). Hence, the average time between two subsequent arrivals is four minutes. To get meaningful results, we represent one minute by 1,000 time units. Such a conversion is needed, because CPN Tools uses integer values for time stamps. A token in place arrive is a pair consisting of a string car_i, where i is the current counter value, and an integer IntInf.toInt(time()) specifying the creation time of the taxi. Transitions record_drive_on and record_depart consume the token from ports drive_on and depart. They will be used to monitor the simulation. Similarly, transition measure monitors the percentage of served cars. Later in this section, we discuss how one can add monitors to extract measurements without extending the model.

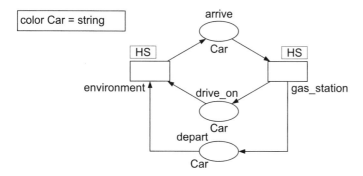

Figure 8.23
Page main modeling the gas station and its environment.

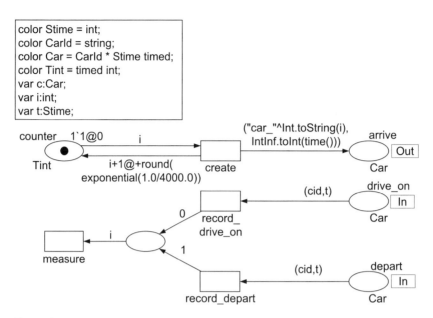

Figure 8.24
Page environment modeling the gas station and its environment.

We map substitution transition gas_station onto a page with the same name; see figure 8.25. This page has one input port and two output ports. Taxis that need to be refueled enter at port arrive and leave from port drive_on or port depart. Place queue serves as a store for waiting taxis. This place is of color Queue, and a token in this place corresponds to a list of taxis. Initially, place queue has one token with value [] (i.e., the empty list). Place fill_up models a taxi being refueled. Each token in place pump_free represents a pump available for service. As there is only one pump, initially place pump_free contains one token. As the identity of the pump does not matter, color set Pump is of type `unit` (i.e., the type with only one value: `()`).

Taxis that arrive at port arrive either queue or drive on. Transitions put_in_queue and drive_on model this choice. If fewer than three cars are waiting ([len(q)<3]), then transition put_in_queue fires. Otherwise ([len(q)>=3]), transition drive_on fires. Transitions start and end represent the start and end of the service at the pump. Transition start consumes the token from place queue, takes the head of the list, and produces the tail in place queue. In addition, it produces a token in place fill_up with a value equal to the head of the list and a delay of two to five minutes. We assume this delay is taken from a uniform distribution between 2,000 and 5,000 time units. CPN Tools provides a library of stochastic functions; see section 6.6.3. Transition start can fire only if there is a token in pump_free, and the token in queue is a nonempty list. The latter condition is enforced by the arc inscription c::q referring to a list with head c and tail q.

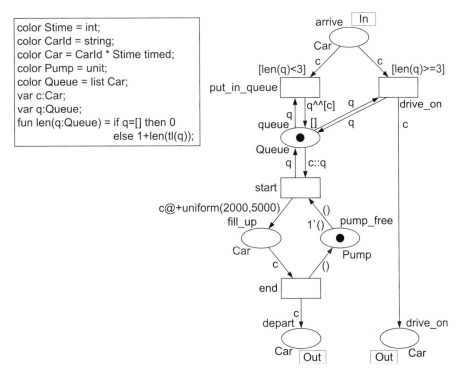

```
color Stime = int;
color CarId = string;
color Car = CarId * Stime timed;
color Pump = unit;
color Queue = list Car;
var c:Car;
var q:Queue;
fun len(q:Queue) = if q=[] then 0
                   else 1+len(tl(q));
```

Figure 8.25
Page gas_station.

8.4.3   Simulating the Base Scenario Using CPN Tools

We modeled the taxi company as a hierarchical CPN model. Using CPN Tools, we simulate this model. To answer the questions of the taxi company's management, we concentrate on the following properties:

- What is the average number of taxis in the waiting queue?
- What is the utilization of the pump?
- What is the average time to fill up a taxi?
- Which percentage of the arriving taxis are served?

To analyze these properties, we must reformulate them in terms of the CPN model in figure 8.23. For the first question, we need to know the average number of tokens in place queue. For the second question, we need the average number of tokens in places fill_up and pump_free. The time to fill up a taxi is the model time after filling up the taxi minus the creation time of the taxi. To calculate the average times, we need to sum up the times of all individual taxis and divide this time by the number of taxis that have been filled up. The fourth question can be answered by counting the tokens passed on via places drive_on and depart.

We do not need to program complicated functions to extract this information from the model during the simulation runs, because CPN Tools offers the concept of a *monitor*. The idea of a monitor is to collect data from markings that are reached and bindings that are enabled during the simulation runs. A *marking size monitor* counts the number of tokens in a place. A *data collection monitor* extracts data from bindings of a certain transition. To activate a data collection monitor, we must define a *predicate function* specifying when the monitor should collect data and an *observation function* specifying what data the monitor should collect. For each monitor, CPN Tools calculates statistics at the end of a simulation run. For more details on monitors in CPN Tools, we refer to the manual (see <http://www.cpntools.org>) and the book of Jensen and Kristensen (2009).

For the taxi company in figure 8.23, we use a total of six monitors; see figure 8.26. We measure the average number of tokens in places queue, fill_up, and pump_free with three marking size monitors—one for each place. More precisely, because place queue is of type list, we use a list length data collection monitor. The other three monitors are of type data collection, and we add them to monitor transitions record_drive_on, record_depart, and measure. The first two monitors count the number of firings of

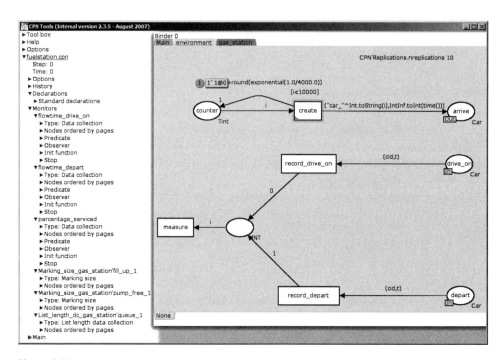

Figure 8.26
Screenshot of CPN Tools showing the six monitors defined for analyzing the simulation results.

Table 8.2
Statistics of the Colored Petri Net Model in Figure 8.23 for a 90 Percent Confidence Interval

queue	fill_up	free_pump	depart	measure
0.889 ± 0.013	0.797 ± 0.003	0.203 ± 0.003	$7,394 \pm 49$	0.912 ± 0.003

transitions record_drive_on and record_depart. In addition, the monitor of transition record_depart calculates the time to fill up a car. As each token in place depart carries a time stamp, the monitor subtracts the time stamp t (which defines the time when this token has been created) from the current model time IntInf.toInt(time()). The monitor of transition measure counts the average number of served taxis.

We simulated the model of the taxi company by using CPN Tools. In our first experiment, we generated ten subruns. In each subrun, we created 10,000 taxis. Table 8.2 lists the statistics provided by CPN Tools.

8.4.4 Subruns and Confidence Intervals

To interpret the results shown in table 8.2 correctly, we need to understand how confidence intervals are computed based on subrun results. To explain these concepts, we first formalize notions, such as *sample mean* and *sample variance*.

During simulation, there are repeated *observations* of quantities such as waiting times, run times, processing times, or stock levels. Suppose we have k consecutive observations $x_1, x_2, \ldots, x_k$ also referred to as a *random sample*. The mean of a number of observations is the *sample mean*. We represent the sample mean of observations $x_1, x_2, \ldots, x_k$ by $\bar{x}$. We can calculate the sample mean $\bar{x}$ by adding the observations and dividing the sum by k:

$$\bar{x} = \frac{\sum_{i=1}^{k} x_i}{k}.$$

The sample mean is only an estimate of the true mean. The variance of a number of observations is the *sample variance*. This variance is a measure for the deviation from the mean. The smaller the variance, the closer the observations will be to the mean. We can calculate the sample variance s^2 by using the following formula:

$$s^2 = \frac{\sum_{i=1}^{k} (x_i - \bar{x})^2}{k - 1}.$$

This is the unbiased estimator of the population variance, meaning that its expected value is equal to the true variance of the sampled random variable.

In a simulation experiment, we can determine the sample mean and the sample variance of a certain quantity. We can use the sample mean as an estimate for the expected true value of this quantity (e.g., waiting time), but we cannot determine how reliable this estimate is. The sample variance is not a good indicator of the reliability of the results. Consider, for example, the sample $\bar{x}_a$ and sample variance s_a^2 obtained from a long simulation run. We want to use $\bar{x}_a$ as a predictor for a performance indicator (e.g., waiting time). If we make the simulation experiment ten times as long, we will obtain new values for the sample mean and the sample variance—say, $\bar{x}_b$ and s_b^2—but these values do not need to be significantly different from the previous values. Although it is reasonable to assume that $\bar{x}_b$ is a more reliable predictor than $\bar{x}_a$, the sample variance will not show this. Actually, s_b^2 may be greater than s_a^2. This is the reason to introduce subruns, as mentioned earlier.

If we have *n independent subruns*, then we can estimate the reliability of estimated performance indicators. There are two approaches to create independent subruns. The first approach is to take one long simulation run and cut this run into smaller subruns. This means that subrun $i+1$ starts in the state left by subrun i. As the subruns need to be independent, the final state of a subrun should not strongly correlate with the final state passed on to the next subrun. An advantage is that start-up effects only play a role in the first run. Hence, by inserting a single start run at the beginning, we can avoid incorrect conclusions due to start-up effects. The second approach is to restart the simulation experiment n times. As a result, the subruns are by definition independent. A drawback is that start-up effects can play a role in every individual subrun. When simulating a process model with CPN Tools, it is easiest to use the latter approach. By executing the command *"CPN'Replications.nreplications n"*, CPN Tools simulates the model n times. Each of the n replications runs until it reaches the end of the simulation; that is, until it reaches a final marking or an explicit breakpoint.

There are two types of behavior that are considered when conducting simulation experiments: *steady-state* behavior and *transient* behavior. When analyzing the steady-state behavior, we are interested in long-term effects and performance indicators. For example, we may consider two different supply chain designs and analyze the differences with respect to average shipping costs and lead times in the next five years. When analyzing the transient behavior, we are interested in short-term effects and performance indicators. For example, if there are currently many backorders, we may want to know how many additional resources we need to temporarily deploy to handle these orders. When analyzing transient behavior, we are interested in the short-term effects. By using the command *"CPN'Replications.nreplications n"*, we can investigate both types of behavior, but the time per subrun will be very different. If we investigate steady-state behavior, the simulation runs need to be long, and we may want to discard the initial part of the simulation. When analyzing transient behavior, the simulation runs are short, and the initial part is most relevant. In the remainder of this section, we concentrate on the steady-state behavior and assume that each run is long enough to make start-up effects insignificant. Hence, we do not need to add start runs to remove initial measurements.

Suppose we have executed n subruns and measured a result y_i for each subrun i. Each result y_i serves as an estimate for a performance indicator. We assume that there exists a true value μ that each result y_i approximates. We want to derive assertions about μ from the values y_i. For example, y_i is the mean waiting time measured in subrun i and μ the true mean waiting time that we could find by conducting a hypothetical simulation experiment of infinite length. Instead, we might consider the mean variance of the waiting time, the mean occupation rate of a server, or the mean length of a queue. We must be certain that the values y_i are mutually independent for all subruns. This can be ensured by choosing a long enough subrun length or by using independent replications. Given the results $y_1, y_2, \ldots, y_n$, we derive the sample mean

$$\bar{y} = \frac{\sum_{i=1}^{n} y_i}{n}$$

and the sample variance

$$s_y^2 = \frac{\sum_{i=1}^{n} (y_i - \bar{y})^2}{n - 1}.$$

The sample standard deviation is $s_y = \sqrt{s_y^2}$. The sample mean and the sample variance for the results of the subruns should not be confused with the mean and the variance of a number of measures *within* one subrun. We can consider the sample $\bar{y}$ as an estimate of the true value μ. The value $\bar{y}$ can be seen as a sample from a random variable $\bar{Y}$, the *estimator*. Now $\frac{s_y}{\sqrt{n}}$ is an indication of the reliability of the estimate $\bar{y}$. If $\frac{s_y}{\sqrt{n}}$ is small, it is a good estimate.

If there is a large number of subruns, we can consider the estimator $\bar{Y}$ (because of the central limit theorem (Rice 2006)) as normally distributed. We will, therefore, treat the situation with more than 30 subruns as a special case.

Given a large number of independent subruns (say, $n \geq 30$), we can easily determine a *confidence interval* for the quantity to be studied. Because the sample mean $\bar{y}$ is the average of a large number of independent measures, we can assume that $\bar{y}$ is approximately normally distributed. From this fact, we deduce the probability that the true value μ lies within a confidence interval. Given the sample mean $\bar{y}$ and the sample standard deviation s_y, the true value μ conforms with confidence $(1 - \alpha)$ to the following equation:

$$\bar{y} - \frac{s_y}{\sqrt{n}} z\left(\frac{\alpha}{2}\right) < \mu < \bar{y} + \frac{s_y}{\sqrt{n}} z\left(\frac{\alpha}{2}\right)$$

where $z(\frac{\alpha}{2})$ is defined as follows: if Z is a standard normally distributed random variable, then the probability that random variable Z is greater than $z(x)$ is x. Table 8.3 shows for five values of x, the value $z(x)$. The value α represents the unreliability; that is, the probability that μ does not conform to the equation. Typical values for α range from 0.001 to 0.100. The interval

Table 8.3
The Probability That Standard Normally Distributed Random Variable Z Is Greater Than $z(x)$ is x—that is, $\mathbb{P}[Z > z(x)]$.

x	z(x)
0.001	3.090
0.005	2.576
0.010	2.326
0.050	1.645
0.100	1.282

$$\left[\overline{y} - \frac{s_y}{\sqrt{n}} \, z\left(\frac{\alpha}{2}\right), \overline{y} + \frac{s_y}{\sqrt{n}} \, z\left(\frac{\alpha}{2}\right) \right]$$

is known as the $(1 - \alpha)$-*confidence interval* for the estimated value μ.

Given a smaller number of independent subruns (say, $n \leq 30$), we need to make more assumptions about the distribution of the individual subrun results. A common assumption is that the individual subrun results are normally distributed. This is a realistic assumption when the subrun result itself is calculated by taking the average over a large set of independent measurements (see the central limit theorem, which states that, as the sample size increases, the distribution of the sample average of these random variables approaches the normal distribution irrespective of the shape of the common distribution of the individual terms). By using this assumption, we can deduce—given n subruns with a sample mean $\overline{y}$, sample deviation s_y, and reliability $(1 - \alpha)$—the following confidence interval:

$$\left[\overline{y} - \frac{s_y}{\sqrt{n}} \, t_{n-1}\left(\frac{\alpha}{2}\right), \overline{y} + \frac{s_y}{\sqrt{n}} \, t_{n-1}\left(\frac{\alpha}{2}\right) \right]$$

where $t_v(x)$ is the critical value of a *student's t distribution* with v degrees of freedom. Table 8.4, shows, for several values of v and x, the critical value $t_v(x)$.

Contrary to the method discussed earlier, we can also determine the confidence interval in the previous way if only a limited number of subruns (say, ten) is at our disposal. If we have a larger number of subruns, it is better to apply the $(1 - \alpha)$ confidence interval, even if we are convinced that the subrun results are normally distributed. For small numbers v, we have $t_v(x) > z(x)$. As v increases, the value of $t_v(x)$ decreases and, in the limit, we obtain $t_v(x) = z(x)$.

Exercise 8.15 Assume we have conducted a simulation experiment involving n subruns. We are interested in the response times to customers. For each subrun i, we collected a set of measurements and calculated the average of these measurements and recorded this average as y_i. This way, we obtained subrun results $y_1, y_2, \ldots, y_n$.

Table 8.4
The Critical Values for a Student's t distribution with v Degrees of Freedom

$t_v(x)$	$x =$ 0.100	0.050	0.010	0.001
$v = 1$	3.08	6.31	31.82	318.31
2	1.89	2.92	6.96	22.33
3	1.64	2.35	4.54	10.21
4	1.53	2.13	3.75	7.17
5	1.48	2.02	3.37	5.89
6	1.44	1.94	3.14	5.21
7	1.41	1.89	3.00	4.79
8	1.40	1.86	2.90	4.50
9	1.38	1.83	2.82	4.30
10	1.37	1.81	2.76	4.14
15	1.34	1.75	2.60	3.73
20	1.33	1.72	2.53	3.55
25	1.32	1.71	2.49	3.45
50	1.30	1.68	2.40	3.26
100	1.29	1.66	2.35	3.17
∞	1.28	1.64	2.33	3.09

1. How do we calculate the confidence intervals if $n = 10$? What assumptions are needed?
2. How do we calculate the confidence intervals if $n = 100$? What assumptions are needed?

CPN Tools makes these computations when the command "*CPN'Replications.nrepli-cations n*" is executed. First, it collects results for each of the n subruns. Second, it calculates confidence intervals for all subruns. We obtained the results shown in table 8.2 in this manner (based on ten independent subruns each involving 10,000 taxis).

8.4.5 Comparing Alternatives Using Simulation

Let us return to the simulation of the taxi company: table 8.2 shows that 0.889 cars were on average in place queue, 0.797 cars were on average in place fill_up, and 0.203 tokens were on average in place pump_free. That means, almost 80 percent of the time, the pump has been used. The average throughput for taxis being filled up is 7,394 time units. This is about 7.4 minutes. Finally, the last column illustrates that about 91.2 percent of the cars could be served. Based on this simulation experiment, it is hardly imaginable that there are regular waiting times of more than ten minutes. Nevertheless, almost 9 percent of the taxis could not be served.

The results of the previous simulation clearly show that the situation at the gas station can be improved. For this reason, the management considers investing in the gas station. Possibilities are:

• The extension of the waiting space with three extra places;
• The purchase of a second pump of the same type; and
• Replacing the present pump with a 30 percent faster model (filling up would then only take between 1.4 and 3.5 minutes).

These investments should reduce the number of taxis driving on without refueling when they arrive at the company's gas station. In addition, the average throughput time should be shortened if possible.

Next, we extend the model of figure 8.25 by taking into account the specifications of management. Then we simulate each model using CPN Tools. With the simulation results, we can compare the three proposed investments.

To extend the waiting space, we must enlarge the queue. To do this, we must change the guard of transition put_in_queue to [len(q)<6] and the guard of transition drive_on to [len(q)>=6]. In the case of purchasing a second pump, we must change the initial marking of figure 8.25 and put two tokens in place pump_free. For the third investment, we must change the inscription of arc (start, fill_up) from c@+discrete(2000,5000) to c@+discrete(1400,3500).

If we simulate the three resulting models using CPN Tools, we obtain the results as presented in table 8.5. From table 8.5, we derive the following details. Adding extra parking places increases the waiting time from seven minutes in the original model to more than ten minutes. As a benefit, almost 97 percent of the taxis can be served, and the average utilization of the pump increases as well. In case of a second pump, we obtain a waiting time of only four minutes, and 99.6 percent of the taxis can be served. The weakness of this approach is the low average utilization of the pumps. About 1.127 pumps are on average not used. By using a faster pump, the average

Table 8.5
Statistics of the Three Alternative Investments (90 Percent Confidence Interval).

Investment option	queue	fill_up	free_pump	depart	measure
Original	0.889 ± 0.013	0.797 ± 0.003	0.203 ± 0.003	$7,394 \pm 49$	0.912 ± 0.003
Extra places	1.73 ± 0.039	0.846 ± 0.005	0.154 ± 0.005	$10,646 \pm 125$	0.968 ± 0.002
Second pump	0.108 ± 0.003	0.873 ± 0.006	1.127 ± 0.006	$3,936 \pm 14$	0.996 ± 0.0003
Faster pump	0.388 ± 0.01	0.6 ± 0.005	0.4 ± 0.005	$4,033 \pm 32$	0.978 ± 0.002

waiting times can be reduced to four minutes and about 97.8 percent of the cars can be served.

If we compare the alternatives, then buying a second pump has the biggest effect, because almost every taxi can be served. The weak point is the low average utilization of the pumps. Buying a faster pump results in a high average utilization of the pump, and the number of served taxis is about 98 percent. Extending the waiting space results in the lowest percentage of served taxis and the highest waiting time but the highest average utilization of the pump. With these simulation results, the management can make a decision about which investment is preferable.

8.4.6   Simulation versus Verification

We introduced two techniques to support design-time analysis: verification and simulation. We describe their advantages and disadvantages in this section.

A strong point of simulation is its flexibility as an analysis technique. Simulation is useful in almost every situation. This is in contrast to other analysis techniques. For example, place invariants can only be used for answering specific questions. An advantage of simulation is that it can analyze a multitude of properties. The disadvantages of simulation are that it can be time-consuming, sometimes long simulation runs are necessary to get reliable results, and simulation does not provide a formal proof; that is, simulation can only analyze the presence of an error but never its absence. As noted before, a simulation run is a walk through the reachability graph of the Petri net model. We assume that such a walk is representative of the behavior of the modeled system, but this may not be true. For example, we can simulate the working of a nuclear power station several times. If no meltdown occurs during these simulations, we could assume that a meltdown will never occur. However, it is possible that, if we simulate the nuclear power station again, a meltdown occurs.

The advantage of verification is that, unlike simulation, it proves properties of the model and, hence, can analyze the absence of errors. There are many verification techniques. Whereas reachability analysis suffers from the state explosion problem, structural analysis is restricted to a few properties. Much progress has been achieved for verification over the last decades, and many success stories exist (Grumberg and Veith 2008) of safety critical systems having been (partially) verified. However, it is unrealistic to assume that large software systems, such as SAP ERP or Windows, can be verified completely.

Analysis is a complicated task and requires much experience in modeling and the analysis techniques used. For example, if we choose an inadequate statistical distribution for our simulation model, the results of the simulation run will be not representative. The same is true for verification, where we typically need to combine certain techniques to alleviate the state explosion problem.

8.5   Process Mining

In section 8.1.2, we explained the need for analysis at runtime and mentioned techniques originating from the field of data mining. In this section, we concentrate on process mining. We provide a brief overview of the process mining spectrum and then introduce a simple process-mining algorithm, the α-algorithm.

8.5.1   The Process Mining Spectrum

Information systems record more and more information about their business processes. This information is in the form of event logs. IT systems are becoming more and more intertwined with these business processes, resulting in an explosion of available data that can be used for analysis. Today's information systems already log enormous amounts of events. Classical WfMSs (e.g., FileNet, TIBCO iProcess Suite, and Global 360), ERP systems (e.g., SAP and Oracle), case handling systems (e.g., BPM|one), PDM systems (e.g., Windchill), CRM systems (e.g., Microsoft Dynamics CRM and Sales-Force), middleware (e.g., IBM's WebSphere and Cordys), and hospital information systems (e.g., Chipsoft and Siemens Soarian) provide detailed information about the activities that have been executed. Moreover, more and more devices are connected to the Internet today, and objects (i.e., products and resources) are tagged and monitored, thus allowing for unprecedented streams of data.

Because we are interested in analyzing business processes based on the data recorded, we concentrate on *events* that can be linked to relevant activities. The order of such events is important for deriving the actual business process. Fortunately, most events have a time stamp or can be linked to a date. Hence, the event data needed for business-process-based analysis is omnipresent.

Process mining techniques attempt to extract nontrivial and useful information from event logs. One aspect of process mining is *control-flow discovery*— that is, automatically constructing a process model (e.g., a Petri net or BPMN model) describing the causal dependencies between activities. The basic idea of control-flow discovery is simple. Given an event log containing a set of traces, automatically construct a suitable process model describing the behavior seen in the log. Such discovered business processes have proven to be useful for the understanding, redesign, and continuous improvement of business processes.

Control-flow discovery is just one aspect of process mining. Before providing an overview of the process-mining spectrum, we consider a small fragment of a larger event log shown in table 8.6. Only two traces are shown, both containing four events. Each event has an identifier and several properties. For example, event 35654423 is an instance of activity *a* that occurred at 11:02 a.m. December 30, 2009; was executed by John; and cost 300 euros. The second trace starts with event 35655526 and also refers

Table 8.6

A Fragment of an Event Log: Each Line Corresponds to an Event

Case ID	Event ID	Properties				
		Time stamp	Activity	Resource	Cost	...
x123	35654423	30-12-2009:11.02	a	John	300	...
x123	35654424	30-12-2009:11.06	b	John	400	...
x123	35654425	30-12-2009:11.12	c	John	100	...
x123	35654426	30-12-2009:11.18	d	John	400	...
x128	35655526	30-12-2009:16.10	a	Ann	300	...
x128	35655527	30-12-2009:16.14	c	John	450	...
x128	35655528	30-12-2009:16.26	b	Pete	350	...
x128	35655529	30-12-2009:16.36	d	Ann	300	...
...	...	...	...	...	...	...

to an instance of activity *a*. Each trace corresponds to a *case*—that is, a completed process instance. Table 8.6 provides information about just two cases, *x123* and *x128*.

Table 8.6 depicts the typical event data that can be extracted from today's information systems. To make the example more manageable, we now only consider the activities and their time stamps. Table 8.7 shows a bigger example, in which each line corresponds to a business process instance; for example, the first trace $\langle a^{02}, a^{06}, c^{12}, d^{18} \rangle$ refers to a business process instance *x123* where activity *a* was executed at time 2, activity *b* was executed at time 6, activity *c* was executed at time 12, and activity *d* was executed at time 18. The first two traces in table 8.7 correspond to the fragment shown in table 8.6. (We simplified the time stamps.)

Using existing process mining techniques, it is possible to extract a business process model from the events of table 8.7. For example, by applying the α-algorithm (Aalst, Weijters, and Maruster 2004), we obtain the business process model shown in figure 8.27. This Petri net describes the business process that starts with activity *a* and ends with activity *d*. In between activities *a* and *d*, either activity *e* or activities *b* and *c* are executed (in any order).

Figure 8.28 is an extension of figure 2.1. It shows the three basic types of process mining:

• *Discovery*. There is no a priori process model; that is, based on an event log, a process model is constructed. For example, the α-algorithm can discover a process model based

Table 8.7
A Simplified Event Log: Each Line Corresponds to a Trace Represented as a Sequence of
Activities with Time Stamps

Case ID	Activity sequence
x123	$\langle a^{02}, b^{06}, c^{12}, d^{18} \rangle$
x128	$\langle a^{10}, c^{14}, b^{26}, d^{36} \rangle$
x131	$\langle a^{12}, e^{22}, d^{56} \rangle$
x132	$\langle a^{15}, b^{19}, c^{22}, d^{28} \rangle$
x142	$\langle a^{18}, b^{22}, c^{26}, d^{32} \rangle$
x145	$\langle a^{19}, e^{28}, d^{59} \rangle$
x148	$\langle a^{20}, c^{25}, b^{36}, d^{44} \rangle$

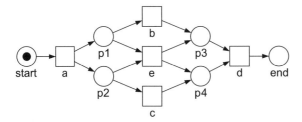

Figure 8.27
A process model discovered from table 8.7 using the α-algorithm.

on raw events only. The Petri net in figure 8.27 was discovered by using the α-algorithm
and the event log in table 8.7.

• *Conformance.* There is an a priori process model. This model is used to check whether
reality, as recorded in the log, conforms to the process model, and vice versa. For example, there may be a process model indicating that purchase orders of more than one
million euros require two checks. Another example is the checking of the four-eyes
principle. Using conformance checking, we may detect deviations, locate and explain
these deviations, and measure the severity of these deviations. The conformance
checking algorithm described by Rozinat and Van der Aalst (2008) is an example.

• *Extension.* There is an a priori process model. This model is extended with a new aspect or perspective; that is, the goal is not to check conformance but to enrich the
model. An example is the extension of a process model with performance data; that is,
some a priori process model is used on which bottlenecks are projected. For example, the
time stamps shown in table 8.7 can be used to calculate the waiting time distributions
for the activities in figure 8.27. The decision-mining algorithm introduced by Rozinat

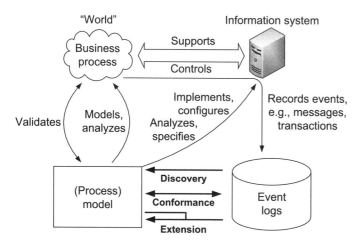

Figure 8.28
Three types of process mining: (1) discovery, (2) conformance, and (3) extension

and Van der Aalst (2006) is another example. This algorithm extends a given process model with conditions for each decision.

Orthogonal to the three types of process mining, there are at least three views. First, the *process view* concentrates on the ordering of activities (i.e., the control-flow). The goal of mining this view is to find a good characterization of all possible transition sequences—for example, expressed in terms of a Petri net or some other notation, such as EPCs, BPMN, and UML activity diagrams. Second, the *organizational view* concentrates on information about resources hidden in the log; that is, which performers are involved and how they are related. The goal is to structure the organization either by classifying people in terms of roles and organizational units or to show some social network. Process and organizational views of a model were introduced in section 2.3 when illustrating business process modeling tools. The third view, the *case view*, concentrates on properties of cases. Cases can be characterized by their path in the process or by the originators working on a case, but they can also be characterized by the values of the corresponding data elements. For example, if a case represents a replenishment order, it may be interesting to know the supplier or the number of products ordered.

In the remainder of this section, we investigate control-flow discovery and present a particular algorithm.

8.5.2 Process Discovery

After providing an overview of process mining, we now introduce a specific algorithm. The α-algorithm, as developed by Van der Aalst, Weijters, and Maruster (2004), constructs a Petri net based on an event log. To explain this algorithm, we first need to formalize the notion of an event log and the notion of a workflow net. We also need to understand the notion of a *case*, also referred to as *process instance* or *trace*. To learn a process model from an event log, we need to consider an operational business process in which the same business process is executed again and again. For example, the business process to handle customer orders is executed for all incoming orders. Each order is a case and is handled in a particular manner. We concentrate on the trace of events describing how a case is handled. For example, a case can be described by the trace $\sigma = \langle a_1, a_2, \ldots, a_n \rangle$ where a_i refers to the i-th activity executed for this case. Such a trace corresponds to one training sample. The α-algorithm learns a process model from these training samples. This is the only way to deduce a process model.

Definition 8.11 (Event log)   Let A be a set of activities. A sequence $\sigma \in A^*$ of events is a *trace*, and a multiset $L \in A^* \to \mathbb{N}$ of traces is an *event log*.

We need to consider a multiset of traces, because multiple cases may have the same trace. With $L(\sigma)$, we represent the number of times trace σ occurs in event log L. For the basic α-algorithm, only the presence and not the frequency of particular patterns is relevant, but more advanced algorithms use the frequencies of patterns to deal with noise (i.e., exceptional or incorrectly recorded behavior) and incompleteness (i.e., not all possible runs of the business process are recorded in the log). For process discovery, we look at business processes that are instantiated multiple times; that is, the same business process is executed for multiple cases. For example, the business process of handling insurance claims may be executed for thousands or even millions of claims. Such business processes have a clear starting point and a clear ending point. Therefore, the following subclass of Petri nets (WF-nets) is most relevant for process discovery.

Definition 8.12 (Workflow net)   A Petri net $N = (P, T, F)$ is a *workflow net* (WF-net) if and only if:

1. *Object creation*: N contains an input place i (the source place) such that $^\bullet i = \emptyset$.
2. *Object completion*: N contains an output place o (the sink place) such that $o^\bullet = \emptyset$.
3. *Connectedness*: Every node in N is on a path from i to o.

Figure 8.27 shows an example of a WF-net. Place start is the unique source place, place end is the unique sink place, and every node is on a path from start to end.

Not every WF-net represents a correct business process. For example, a business process represented by a WF-net may exhibit errors, such as deadlocks, activities that can never become active, livelocks, and garbage being left in the process after termination. Therefore, we define the following correctness criterion.

Definition 8.13 (Soundness)   Let $N = (P, T, F)$ be a WF-net with input place i and output place o. N is *sound* if and only if:

1. *Option to complete*: For any reachable marking m, it is possible to reach the marking $[o]$.
2. *Proper completion*: The only reachable marking that contains a token in place o is the marking $[o]$.
3. *Absence of dead activties*: There are no dead transitions.

The WF-net in figure 8.27 is sound. Soundness can be verified using standard Petri-net–based analysis techniques. Van der Aalst (1998) proved that soundness corresponds to liveness and safeness of the corresponding short-circuited net (i.e., the net that results from adding one transition, which has o as its input place and i as its output place). That way, we can apply efficient algorithms and tools to verify soundness. An example of a tool tailored toward the analysis of WF-nets is Woflan (Verbeek, Basten, and Aalst 2001). This functionality is also embedded in the process mining tool ProM (Aalst, Dongen, et al. 2007). Fahland et al. (2009) report results of a case study on verification of soundness of more than 700 industrial business process models using three different verification techniques. After introducing events logs and WF-nets, we can define the main goal of process discovery.

Definition 8.14 (Process discovery)   Let L be an event log over the set A of activities, that is, $L \in A^* \to \mathbb{N}$. A *process discovery algorithm* is a function $\gamma(L) = (N)$ that maps any event log L onto a Petri net system $N = (P, T, F, m_0)$. Ideally, N is a sound WF-net, and all traces in L correspond to possible runs of N.

The goal is to find a process model that can replay all cases recorded in the event log; that is, all traces in the log are possible runs of the discovered WF-net. Assume an event log $L_1 = [5 \cdot \langle a, b, c, d \rangle, 8 \cdot \langle a, c, b, d \rangle, 9 \cdot \langle a, e, d \rangle]$. In this case, the WF-net in figure 8.27 is a good solution. All traces in L_1 correspond to runs of the WF-net and vice versa. It may be possible that some of the runs of the discovered WF-net do not appear in the log. This is acceptable, as one cannot assume that all possible runs have been observed. For example, if there is a loop, the number of possible runs is infinite. As illustrated in section 4.3, even if the model is acyclic, the number of possible runs may be enormous due to choices and concurrency.

Process models may be discovered through process mining but may also already exist. The coexistence of event logs and process models raises an interesting question.

Question 8.15   Does the event log conform to the process model and vice versa?

There is not a simple answer to this question. There are various metrics to define the quality of a (discovered) process model given some event log. Rozinat and Van der

Aalst (2008) introduced various metrics, such as fitness (the event log may be the result of the business process modeled) and appropriateness (the model is a likely candidate from a structural and behavioral point of view). In this section, we do not formalize these metrics and simply refer to Occam's razor. Occam's razor is a logical principle attributed to the medieval philosopher William of Occam. The principle states that "one should not increase, beyond what is necessary, the number of entities required to explain anything." This principle suggests that we should look for a simple process model to explain behavior. The model should not be overfitting, should only encode the behavior recorded in the log, and should not generalize too much and allow for behavior unrelated to the event log.

8.5.3   The α-Algorithm

The α-algorithm is not intended as a practical process-mining technique, because it has problems dealing with noise, infrequent and incomplete behavior, and complex routing constructs. Nevertheless, it provides a good introduction to the topic of process mining. The α-algorithm is simple, and many of its ideas have been embedded in more complex and robust techniques. Moreover, it was the first algorithm to really address the discovery of concurrency.

The α-algorithm scans the event log for particular patterns. For example, if activity a is followed by activity b, but activity b is never followed by activity a, then it is assumed that there is a causal dependency between activities a and b. To reflect this dependency, the corresponding Petri net should have a place connecting transitions a and b. We distinguish four log-based ordering relations that attempt to capture relevant patterns in the log.

Definition 8.16 (Log-based ordering relations)   Let L be an event log over a set A of activities, that is, $L \in A^* \to \mathbb{N}$. Let $a, b \in A$ be activities. Define the following four *log-based ordering relations*:

- $a >_L b$ if and only if there is a trace $\sigma = \langle t_1, t_2, t_3, \ldots, t_n \rangle$ and $i \in \{1, \ldots, n-1\}$ such that $\sigma \in L$ and $t_i = a$ and $t_{i+1} = b$;
- $a \to_L b$ if and only if $a >_L b$ and $b \not>_L a$;
- $a \#_L b$ if and only if $a \not>_L b$ and $b \not>_L a$; and
- $a \|_L b$ if and only if $a >_L b$ and $b >_L a$.

Consider event log $L_1 = [5 \cdot \langle a, b, c, d \rangle, 8 \cdot \langle a, c, b, d \rangle, 9 \cdot \langle a, e, d \rangle]$ again. Because activity d directly follows activity c in trace $\langle a, b, c, d \rangle$, $c >_{L_1} d$. However, $d \not>_{L_1} c$ because activity c never directly follows activity d in any trace in the event log. $>_{L_1} = \{(a, b), (a, c), (a, e), (b, c), (c, b), (b, d), (c, d), (e, d)\}$ contains all pairs of activities in a directly follows relation. Because sometimes activity d directly follows activity c and never the other way around ($c >_{L_1} d$ and $d \not>_{L_1} c$), $c \to_{L_1} d$. Causality relation

$\rightarrow_{L_1} = \{(a, b), (a, c), (a, e), (b, d), (c, d), (e, d)\}$ contains all pairs of activities such that the first element is directly followed by the second but not the other way around. Sometimes activity c follows activity b and sometimes the other way around; that is, $b\|_{L_1}c$ because $b >_{L_1} c$ and $c >_{L_1} b$. $\|_{L_1} = \{(b, c), (c, b)\}$. $b\#_{L_1}e$ because $b \not>_{L_1} e$ and $e \not>_{L_1} b$. $\#_{L_1} = \{(a, a), (a, d), (b, b), (b, e), (c, c), (c, e), (d, a), (d, d), (e, b), (e, c), (e, e)\}$. For any event log L over A and activities $x, y \in A$: $x \rightarrow_L y$, $y \rightarrow_L x$, $x\#_L y$, or $x\|_L y$.

The log-based ordering relations can be used to discover patterns in the corresponding process model, as is illustrated in figure 8.29. If activities a and b are in sequence, the log will show $a \rightarrow_L b$. If, after activity a, there is a choice between activities b and c, the log will show $a \rightarrow_L b$, $a \rightarrow_L c$, and $b\#_L c$, because activity a can be followed by activities b and c, but activity b will not be followed by activity c, and vice versa. The logical counterpart of this XOR-split pattern is the XOR-join pattern, as shown in figures 8.29(b) and 8.29(c). If $a \rightarrow_L c$, $b \rightarrow_L c$, and $a\#_L b$, then this suggests that, after the occurrence of either activity a or b, activity c should happen. Figures 8.29(d) and 8.29(e) show the AND-split and AND-join patterns. If $a \rightarrow_L b$, $a \rightarrow_L c$, and $b\|_L c$, then it appears that after activity a, activities b and c can be executed in parallel (AND-split pattern). If $a \rightarrow_L c$, $b \rightarrow_L c$, and $a\|_L b$, then it appears that activity c needs to synchronize activities a and b (AND-join pattern).

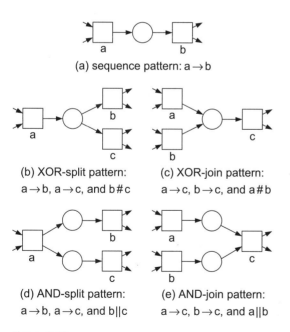

(a) sequence pattern: a → b

(b) XOR-split pattern: a → b, a → c, and b # c

(c) XOR-join pattern: a → c, b → c, and a # b

(d) AND-split pattern: a → b, a → c, and b||c

(e) AND-join pattern: a → c, b → c, and a||b

Figure 8.29
Typical process patterns and the footprints they leave in the event log.

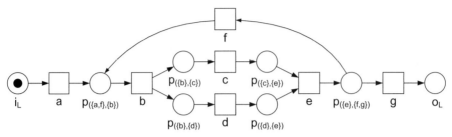

Figure 8.30
WF-net N_2 derived from $L_2 = [\langle a, b, c, d, e, f, b, d, c, e, g \rangle, \langle a, b, d, c, e, g \rangle, \langle a, b, c, d, e, f, b, c, d, e, f, b, d, c, e, g \rangle]$.

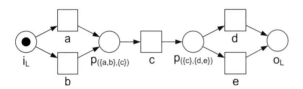

Figure 8.31
WF-net N_3 derived from $L_3 = [45 \cdot \langle a, c, d \rangle, 42 \cdot \langle b, c, d \rangle, 38 \cdot \langle a, c, e \rangle, 22 \cdot \langle b, c, e \rangle]$.

Figure 8.29 shows only simple patterns and does not present the additional conditions needed to extract the patterns, but the figure nicely illustrates the use of log-based relations to discover patterns in the corresponding process model.

Consider, for example, WF-net N_2 depicted in figure 8.30 and the event log $L_2 = [\langle a, b, c, d, e, f, b, d, c, e, g \rangle, \langle a, b, d, c, e, g \rangle, \langle a, b, c, d, e, f, b, c, d, e, f, b, d, c, e, g \rangle]$. The α-algorithm constructs WF-net N_2 based on L_2. The patterns in the model indeed match the log-based ordering relations extracted from the event log. Consider for example the business process fragment involving activities b, c, d, and e. This fragment can be constructed based on $b \rightarrow_{L_2} c$, $b \rightarrow_{L_2} d$, $c \|_{L_2} d$, $c \rightarrow_{L_2} e$, and $d \rightarrow_{L_2} e$. The choice following activity e is revealed by $e \rightarrow_{L_2} f$, $e \rightarrow_{L_2} g$, and $f \#_{L_2} g$.

Figure 8.31 depicts another example. WF-net N_3 can be derived from $L_3 = [45 \cdot \langle a, c, d \rangle, 42 \cdot \langle b, c, d \rangle, 38 \cdot \langle a, c, e \rangle, 22 \cdot \langle b, c, e \rangle]$. In this example, there are two start and two end activities. These can be detected easily by looking for the first and last activities in traces.

After illustrating the general concept, we formalize the α-*algorithm*.

Definition 8.17 (α-algorithm)   Let L be an event log over T. Then, $\alpha(L)$, is defined as follows:

1. $T_L = \{t \in T \mid \exists_{\sigma \in L}\ t \in \sigma\}$;
2. $T_I = \{t \in T \mid \exists_{\sigma \in L}\ t = first(\sigma)\}$;

3. $T_O = \{t \in T \mid \exists_{\sigma \in L}\ t = last(\sigma)\}$;

4. $X_L = \{(A, B) \mid A \subseteq T_L\ \wedge\ A \neq \emptyset\ \wedge\ B \subseteq T_L\ \wedge\ B \neq \emptyset\ \wedge\ \forall_{a \in A}\forall_{b \in B}\ a \to_L b$
   $\wedge\ \forall_{a_1, a_2 \in A} a_1 \#_L a_2\ \wedge\ \forall_{b_1, b_2 \in B}\ b_1 \#_L b_2\}$;

5. $Y_L = \{(A, B) \in X_L \mid \forall_{(A', B') \in X_L} A \subseteq A'\ \wedge B \subseteq B' \implies (A, B) = (A', B')\}$;

6. $P_L = \{p_{(A,B)} \mid (A, B) \in Y_L\} \cup \{i_L, o_L\}$;

7. $F_L = \{(a, p_{(A,B)}) \mid (A, B) \in Y_L\ \wedge\ a \in A\} \cup \{(p_{(A,B)}, b) \mid (A, B) \in Y_L\ \wedge\ b \in B\}$
   $\cup \{(i_L, t) \mid t \in T_I\} \cup \{(t, o_L) \mid t \in T_O\}$; and

8. $\alpha(L) = (P_L, T_L, F_L)$.

In the definition, L is an event log over some set T of activities. In step 1, the event log L is checked for activities that appear. Each activity will correspond to a transition of the generated WF-net. T_I is the set of start activities—that is, all activities that appear first in some trace (step 2). T_O is the set of end activities—that is, all activities that appear last in some trace (step 3). Functions *first* and *last* provide the first and last element of a sequence, respectively. Step 4 and step 5 form the core of the α-algorithm. The challenge is to find the places of the WF-net and their flow relation. We attempt to construct places named $p_{(A,B)}$ such that A is the set of input transitions ($^\bullet p_{(A,B)} = A$) and B is the set of output transitions ($p^\bullet_{(A,B)} = B$).

Figure 8.32 illustrates the basic idea for finding $p_{(A,B)}$. All elements of A should have causal dependencies with all elements of B; that is, for any $(a, b) \in A \times B$: $a \to_L b$. Moreover, the elements of A should never follow any of the other elements; that is, for any $a_1, a_2 \in A$: $a_1 \#_L a_2$. A similar requirement holds for B.

Let us consider event log $L_1 = [5 \cdot \langle a, b, c, d \rangle, 8 \cdot \langle a, c, b, d \rangle, 9 \cdot \langle a, e, d \rangle]$. Clearly $A = \{a\}$ and $B = \{b, e\}$ meet the requirements stated in step 4. Also $A' = \{a\}$ and $B' = \{b\}$ meet the same requirements. X_L is the set of all such pairs that meet the requirements just mentioned. In this case, $X_{L_1} = \{(\{a\}, \{b\}), (\{a\}, \{c\}), (\{a\}, \{e\}), (\{a\}, \{b, e\}), (\{a\}, \{c, e\}),$

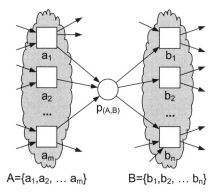

A=$\{a_1, a_2, \dots a_m\}$ B=$\{b_1, b_2, \dots b_n\}$

Figure 8.32

Place $p_{(A,B)}$ connects the transitions in set A to the transitions in set B.

$(\{b\}, \{d\}), (\{c\}, \{d\}), (\{e\}, \{d\}), (\{b, e\}, \{d\}), (\{c, e\}, \{d\})\}$. If one inserted a place for any element in X_{L_1}, there would be too many places. Therefore, only the maximal pairs (A, B) should be included. For any pair $(A, B) \in X_L$, nonempty set $A' \subseteq A$, and nonempty set $B' \subseteq B$, it is implied that $(A', B') \in X_L$. In step 5, all nonmaximal pairs are removed. So $Y_{L_1} = \{(\{a\}, \{b, e\}), (\{a\}, \{c, e\}), (\{b, e\}, \{d\}), (\{c, e\}, \{d\})\}$.

Every element of $(A, B) \in Y_L$ corresponds to a place $p_{(A,B)}$ connecting transitions of A to transitions of B. In addition, P_L also contains a unique source place i_L and a unique sink place o_L (see also step 6).

In step 7, the flow relation is generated. All start transitions in T_I have i_L as an input place, and all end transitions T_O have o_L as an output place. All places $p_{(A,B)}$ have A as input nodes and B as output nodes. The result is a Petri net $\alpha(L) = (P_L, T_L, F_L)$ that describes the behavior seen in event log L.

Thus far, we have presented three logs and three WF-nets. Clearly $\alpha(L_2) = N_2$ and $\alpha(L_3) = N_3$. In figures 8.30 and 8.31, the places are named based on the sets Y_{L_2} and Y_{L_3}. Moreover, $\alpha(L_1) = N_1$ where N_1 is the Petri net shown in figure 8.27 (modulo renaming of places). These examples show that the α-algorithm can indeed discover WF-nets from event logs.

Question 8.18 Consider event log $L_4 = [2 \cdot \langle a, b, e, f \rangle, 3 \cdot \langle a, b, e, c, d, b, f \rangle, 2 \cdot \langle a, b, c, e, d, b, f \rangle, 4 \cdot \langle a, b, c, d, e, b, f \rangle, 3 \cdot \langle a, e, b, c, d, b, f \rangle]$. Apply the α-algorithm to this log and describe the resulting model.

Figure 8.33 shows the WF-net N_4 derived from L_4; that is, $\alpha(L_4) = N_4$.

Van der Aalst, Weijters, and Maruster (2004) showed that the α-algorithm can discover a large class of WF-nets if one assumes that the log is *complete* with respect to the log-based ordering relation $>_L$. This assumption implies that, for any event log L, $a >_L b$ if activity a can be directly followed by activity b. If the log is incomplete, the α-algorithm may produce incorrect models. Moreover, the α-algorithm cannot

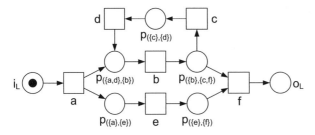

Figure 8.33
WF-net N_4 derived from $L_4 = [2 \cdot \langle a, b, e, f \rangle, 3 \cdot \langle a, b, e, c, d, b, f \rangle, 2 \cdot \langle a, b, c, e, d, b, f \rangle, 4 \cdot \langle a, b, c, d, e, b, f \rangle, 3 \cdot \langle a, e, b, c, d, b, f \rangle]$.

handle noise and makes assumptions about the underlying model. For a more detailed presentation of the α-algorithm and its limitations, see work of Van der Aalst, Weijters, and Maruster (2004).

Exercise 8.16   From some enterprise information system, the following event log consisting of seven traces is extracted:

```
a d e f h
a e d f h
g h
a b c d f h
a c b d f h
a b d c f h
a c d b f h
```

1. Derive the $\rightarrow_L$ relation.
2. Use the eight steps of the α-algorithm to construct the corresponding Petri net and draw the Petri net (delivering all of the intermediate results is not necessary, only the resulting Petri net is required).
3. If possible, give a possible trace according to the discovered model but not (yet) observed in the log.

Exercise 8.17   The following event log consisting of three traces was extracted from an enterprise information system:

```
a b c d e f b d c e g
a b d c e g
a b c d e f b c d e f b d c e g
```

1. Derive the $\rightarrow_L$ relation.
2. Use the eight steps of the α-algorithm to construct the corresponding Petri net and draw the Petri net (delivering all of the intermediate results is not necessary, only the resulting Petri net is required).
3. If possible, give a possible trace according to the discovered model but not (yet) observed in the log.

8.6   Tool Support

We introduced several techniques to analyze Petri nets both at design time and at runtime. Petri net analysis is usually not done by hand; instead, tools are used. In this section, we give an overview of the main features of CPN Tools, ProM, and LoLA. There are many more tools for analyzing Petri nets. For a comprehensive overview

of existing tools, we refer to the Petri net Web page <http://www.informatik.uni
-hamburg.de/TGI/PetriNets>.

8.6.1 CPN Tools

CPN Tools was developed in Kurt Jensen's group at the University of Aarhus, Denmark.
It contains a collection of tools for modeling and analyzing CPNs. CPN Tools offers
verification techniques and simulation. We can construct the reachability graph of a
CPN (if possible) and verify the standard Petri net properties, which we introduced in
section 8.2.2. Fairness of CPN transitions (see section 8.2.3) can be analyzed as well.
CPN Tools reports the analysis results as a text file. To alleviate the state explosion problem, several verification techniques have been implemented in CPN Tools that try to
verify properties on a reduced version of the reachability graph. However, CPN Tools is
not a core model checking tool and therefore is not as powerful as model checkers such
as LoLA. Currently, the ASCoVeCo State space Analysis Platform (ASAP) is developed
to provide more powerful verification capabilities in the context of CPN Tools.

In addition to verification, CPN Tools supports the simulation of CPNs. Simulation
in CPN Tools is quite fast compared to many other simulation packages. To extract
information from the simulation runs, CPN Tools provides monitors (see section 8.4.3)
and calculates statistical information about the simulation runs.

CPN Tools has proven itself as a modeling and analysis tool in many industrial applications. More than 10,000 organizations in over 140 countries are using CPN Tools. For
more details on CPN Tools, refer to the tool's Web page (<http://www.cpntools.org>)
and the book of Jensen and Kristensen (2009).

8.6.2 ProM

The ProM tool was developed in Wil van der Aalst's group at Eindhoven University of
Technology, the Netherlands. ProM focuses on business process analysis in the broadest
sense—that is, both design-time analysis and runtime analysis. It is an open source
framework that provides a plug-in infrastructure. Version 5.2 of ProM provides 286
plug-ins: 47 mining plug-ins, 96 analysis plug-ins, 22 import plug-ins, 45 export plug-
ins, 44 conversion plug-ins, and 32 filter plug-ins. Each plug-in is a program running
within the context of the ProM framework. For example, the plug-in that implements
the α-algorithm is one of the 47 mining plug-ins. ProM also supports various types
of models, for example, organizational models, social networks, decision trees, and a
wide variety of business process notations, including Petri nets, CPNs, YAWL, EPCs,
WS-BPEL, and heuristic nets.

ProM supports most of the analysis techniques described in this chapter. For example,
ProM can calculate place and transition invariants, reachability graphs, and coverability
graphs and has dedicated plug-ins to check for soundness of WF-nets. ProM does not
support simulation, but process models in ProM can be converted into CPNs and then

exported to CPN Tools for simulation. Although ProM provides many design-time analysis techniques, it is best known for its runtime analysis techniques involving event logs stored in MXML format. In figure 8.28, we showed that there are three basic types of process mining: discovery, conformance, and extension. ProM provides plug-ins for all three types.

There are many plug-ins for discovery. One of the plug-ins implements the α-algorithm, but more refined process discovery techniques have also been implemented—for example, based on genetic algorithms, region theory, and heuristics. From a practical point of view, the heuristic miner and the fuzzy miner are most relevant. Discovery is not limited to the process view; it also includes data and resource views (i.e., the data and the organizational view). For example, it is possible to extract social networks.

There are fewer plug-ins for conformance checking. A model given in terms of a Petri net or a set of rules can be compared with the behavior captured in the event log. Various checkers expose these differences; for example, it can be shown which rules are frequently violated, and parts of the process model where many deviations occur can be highlighted.

Version 5.2 of ProM provides considerable support for extending models by adding information extracted from logs. For example, it is possible to extract simulation models that cover the process, data, and organizational views. These models can be simulated by using CPN Tools.

ProM has been downloaded 30,000 times (estimate), and hundreds of organizations have used ProM's process-mining capabilities to analyze their actual business processes. For more information on process mining and ProM, refer to the process-mining Web page <http://www.processmining.org>. ProM can be downloaded from this Web site.

8.6.3 LoLA

The tool LoLA (Wolf 2007), Low Level Petri Net Analyzer, is a model checker to verify Petri nets. LoLA was developed by Karsten Wolf. He and his research group at the University of Rostock, Germany, maintain LoLA.

The strengths of LoLA include the fast calculation of reachability and coverability graphs for Petri nets and the verification of standard Petri net properties (see section 8.2.2), as well as more advanced properties specified in temporal logic. To alleviate the state explosion problem, LoLA implements several dedicated verification techniques. Another strength of LoLA is the calculation of a short run to a marking that violates a certain property (also referred to as *witness*). LoLA can analyze colored Petri nets if the color sets are finite. To this end, the tool automatically transforms the colored Petri net into a Petri net. For purposes of efficiency (i.e., speed and memory consumption), LoLA does not have a graphical user interface. Parts of LoLA have been embedded within the ProM framework.

LoLA has been successfully used in several case studies, including verification of asynchronous hardware and of process models, exploration of biochemical networks, and validation of a Petri net–based semantics for the process modeling language WS-BPEL. For more details on LoLA, refer to the tool's Web page, <http://service-technology .org/lola>.

8.7 Test Yourself

8.7.1 Solutions to Exercises

8.1   Examples of qualitative questions are:

- Can a customer with a negative balance withdraw money?
- Can the money in a cash dispenser run short?
- Is the new connection safe—meaning, can no one withdraw money without it being charged to an account?
- Is the withdrawn money charged to the right account under all circumstances?
- Is a stolen check card always confiscated?

Examples of quantitative questions are:

- How many customers can the cash dispensers handle in one hour?
- What is the average service time of a customer?
- How many customers can we serve within one month?
- What is the occupancy rate of each cash dispenser?
- What is the average waiting time of a customer?
- How often do failures occur?

8.2   The infinite run $\langle t1, t2, t1, t2, \ldots \rangle$ witnesses that place p3, and, hence, the net is unbounded. From the existence of this infinite run, we can also conclude that the net is not terminating. The net is live, deadlock free, reversible, has no dead transitions, and every reachable marking is a home-marking.

8.3   Transitions t1 and t2 are impartial, because in every infinite run they are fired infinitely often. Existence of the infinite runs $\langle t1, t2, t1, t2, \ldots \rangle$ and $\langle t4, t1, t2, t1, t2, \ldots \rangle$ proves that transitions t3 and t4 are not fair, because they are continuously enabled but do not fire.

8.4   Figure 8.34 depicts the coverability graph. There is more than one coverability graph. To calculate figure 8.34, we fired transition t4, t1, and t2 first. The net does not have dead transitions because all four transitions appear in the coverability graph. Place p3 is unbounded, and all other places are safe.

8.5   Figure 8.35 depicts the coverability graph. Place number is safe, but it contains in every reachable marking a different integer value. As for bounded nets, the reachability

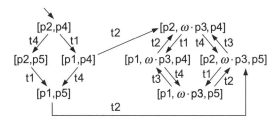

Figure 8.34
Coverability graph of figure 8.8.

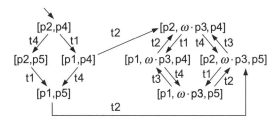

Figure 8.35
Coverability graph of figure 8.15.

graph and the coverability graph are identical; both graphs have infinitely many nodes. The example illustrates that the coverability graph is limited to representing unbounded nets in a finite manner. It cannot abstract from data values.

8.6   The place invariant is $woman - man = 1$. To verify that it is a place invariant, we check the effect that the firing of transitions marriage and divorce has. If transition marriage fires, a token is consumed from place man and from place woman, and the invariant still holds. If transition divorce fires, a token is produced in place man and in place woman. In this case the invariant also holds.

This place invariant shows that, in the Petri net of figure 8.17, there is always one unmarried man less than the number of unmarried women; that is, always at least one woman is unmarried.

8.7
1. $free + busy + docu = 1$ is a place invariant, because none of the three transitions can change the total number of tokens in places free, busy, and docu. This invariant proves that the specialist is always in one of the three mentioned states.
2. $wait + inside + done = 4$ is a place invariant. It proves that no patients disappear.
3. $free + 2 \cdot busy + docu = 1$ is not a place invariant, because the firing of transition start or change changes the weighted token sum. The marking in figure 4.6 has a weighted token sum equal to one. After transition start has fired, this weighted token sum is equal to two.
4. $free + 2 \cdot busy + docu + wait + done = 5$ is a place invariant. This invariant has no natural interpretation in this context.

5. busy $-$ inside $= 0$ is a place invariant. It indicates that there is only a patient inside, when the specialist is busy, and vice versa. In other words, there are two possibilities: the specialist is busy and there is one patient inside, or the specialist is not busy and there is no patient inside.

8.8 It is not a transition invariant, because, after transitions start_production and end_production fired once, the number of tokens in place product is increased by one. If transitions start_production, end_production, start_consumption, and end_consumption all fire once, we reach the initial marking again. Consequently, start_production + end_production + start_consumption + end_consumption is a transition invariant.

8.9 We order the transitions in the incidence matrix as follows: start_production, end_production, start_consumption, and end_consumption. We present the places in the order: free, producer, product, wait, and consumer:

$$
C = \begin{pmatrix}
-1 & 1 & 0 & 0 \\
1 & -1 & 0 & 0 \\
0 & 1 & -1 & 0 \\
0 & 0 & -1 & 1 \\
0 & 0 & 1 & -1
\end{pmatrix}.
$$

8.10 We obtain

$$
C \cdot \underline{x} = \underline{m} - \underline{m}_0
$$

$$
\begin{pmatrix}
-1 & -1 & 0 & 0 & 1 \\
1 & 0 & -1 & 0 & 0 \\
0 & 1 & 0 & -1 & 0 \\
0 & 1 & 1 & 0 & -1 \\
1 & 0 & 0 & 1 & -1
\end{pmatrix}
\cdot
\begin{pmatrix}
t1 \\ t2 \\ t3 \\ t4 \\ t5
\end{pmatrix}
=
\begin{pmatrix}
0 \\ 1 \\ 1 \\ 0 \\ 0
\end{pmatrix}
-
\begin{pmatrix}
1 \\ 0 \\ 0 \\ 0 \\ 0
\end{pmatrix}.
$$

The resulting equation system has the integer solution
$$
\begin{pmatrix}
t1 \\ t2 \\ t3 \\ t4 \\ t5
\end{pmatrix}
=
\begin{pmatrix}
1 \\ 1 \\ 0 \\ 0 \\ 1
\end{pmatrix}.
$$

8.11 We obtain

$$
(p1 \quad p2 \quad p3 \quad p4 \quad p5) \cdot C = \underline{0}
$$

$$(p1 \quad p2 \quad p3 \quad p4 \quad p5) \cdot \begin{pmatrix} -1 & 0 & 0 & 0 & 0 & 1 \\ 1 & 1 & -1 & 0 & 0 & 0 \\ 1 & 0 & 0 & 1 & -1 & 0 \\ 0 & -1 & 1 & 0 & 0 & -1 \\ 0 & 0 & 0 & -1 & 1 & -1 \end{pmatrix} = \underline{0}.$$

From the solutions of this equation system, we derive the following place invariants:

$$p1 + p2 + p4 = 1$$

$$p1 + p3 + p5 = 1$$

$$2 \cdot p1 + p2 + p3 + p4 + p5 = 2$$

$$6 \cdot p1 + 5 \cdot p2 + p3 + 5 \cdot p4 + p5 = 6.$$

8.12   We obtain

$$C \cdot \underline{x} = \underline{0}$$

$$\begin{pmatrix} -1 & 0 & 0 & 0 & 0 & 1 \\ 1 & 1 & -1 & 0 & 0 & 0 \\ 1 & 0 & 0 & 1 & -1 & 0 \\ 0 & -1 & 1 & 0 & 0 & -1 \\ 0 & 0 & 0 & -1 & 1 & -1 \end{pmatrix} \cdot \begin{pmatrix} t1 \\ t2 \\ t3 \\ t4 \\ t5 \\ t6 \end{pmatrix} = \begin{pmatrix} 0 \\ 0 \\ 0 \\ 0 \\ 0 \end{pmatrix}.$$

From the solutions of this equation system, we derive the following transition invariants:

$$t1 + t3 + t5 + t6$$

$$t2 + t3$$

$$t4 + t5$$

$$t1 + t2 + 2 \cdot t3 + t4 + 2 \cdot t5 + t6.$$

8.13   The statement "if $i \cdot m = i \cdot m_0$, for a place invariant i and markings m_0 and m, then m is reachable from m_0" (i.e., the converse) does not hold. Consider the place invariant man $-$ woman $= -1$ for the net in figure 8.17. For the initial marking m_0, we calculate $2 - 3 = -1$, and for the nonreachable marking [man, couple, $2 \cdot$ woman], we also calculate $1 - 2 = -1$.

The statement "if a place is bounded, then it occurs in a positive place invariant" (i.e., the converse) does not hold. It is trivial to provide a net with a dead initial marking and no positive place invariant. Figure 8.36 provides a more interesting counterexample. The net is live and bounded if $m_0 = [p1]$, but there is no positive place invariant.

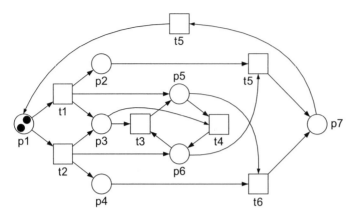

Figure 8.36
An unbounded Petri net without positive place invariant.

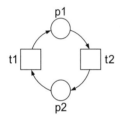

Figure 8.37
Although all transitions are covered by a transition invariant, the net is not live.

Moreover, if $m_0 = [2 \cdot p1]$, then the net suddenly loses all of its nice properties. For example, place p3 is unbounded, and the net may deadlock. This shows that, even though the structure did not change, properties such as boundedness may change when the initial marking changes.

The statement "if the net is bounded for any initial marking, then there exists a positive place invariant i that assigns a positive weight to all places" (i.e., the converse) does hold. Hence, it is not possible to give a counterexample.

The statement "if the net has a positive transition invariant that covers each transition, then it is live and bounded" (i.e., the converse) does not hold. Figure 8.37 provides a counterexample. A positive transition invariant is $t1 + t2$, but the net is not live. The problem is that transition invariants are independent of the initial marking.

8.14
1. This question can be answered by purchasing a new cash register and installing it. The administrator can, after some time, determine whether the problems are solved

with the extra cash register. However, this is an expensive solution if it turns out that this solution does not work.

One could also make a model of the supermarket with the extra cash register. By simulating this model, we could investigate in a cheaper way whether the suggested solution works.

2. A simulation run of the supermarket will probably start with an empty supermarket. The first four customers who go to a cash register find a free cash register. The waiting times of the first four customers are, thus, per definition equal to zero. That means there is a start-up effect, because the initial state clearly deviates from the average state.

3. If we sum the average waiting times and divide them by ten, we see that the average waiting time over all subruns is close to five minutes. If we compare the subruns with each other, we see that there are large differences. In the first subrun, the waiting time is, on average, 2.25 minutes and, in the second, 7.63 minutes. On the basis of these numbers, we cannot make a reliable statement about the average waiting time of a customer. The average waiting time can be three minutes, but also six minutes.

8.15

1. If we have only ten subruns ($n = 10$), we calculate the confidence interval using the critical value of a student's t distribution. Given n subruns with a sample mean $\bar{y}$, sample deviation s_y, and reliability $(1 - \alpha)$, the following confidence interval is computed:

$$\left[\bar{y} - \frac{s_y}{\sqrt{n}} \, t_{n-1}\left(\frac{\alpha}{2}\right), \bar{y} + \frac{s_y}{\sqrt{n}} \, t_{n-1}\left(\frac{\alpha}{2}\right) \right].$$

It is essential that the subrun results are mutually independent. Moreover, it is also assumed that the individual subrun results are normally distributed.

2. If we have 100 subruns ($n = 100$), we calculate the $(1 - \alpha)$ confidence interval as follows:

$$\left[\bar{y} - \frac{s_y}{\sqrt{n}} \, z\left(\frac{\alpha}{2}\right), \bar{y} + \frac{s_y}{\sqrt{n}} \, z\left(\frac{\alpha}{2}\right) \right].$$

Again, it is essential that the subrun results are mutually independent, but we no longer need to assume that individual subrun results are normally distributed. We can also use the Student's t distribution, if we assume that individual subrun results are normally distributed; for large integers n, the difference is negligible.

8.16

1. $>_L = \{(a, b), (a, c), (a, d), (a, e), (b, c), (b, d), (b, f), (c, b), (c, d), (c, f), (d, b), (d, c), (d, e), (d, f), (e, d), (e, f), (f, h), (g, h)\}$. Hence, $\rightarrow_L = \{(a, b), (a, c), (a, d), (a, e), (b, f), (c, f), (d, f), (e, f), (f, h), (g, h)\}$.

2. Figure 8.38 shows the discovered model.

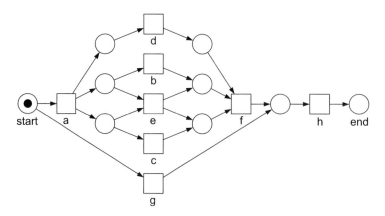

Figure 8.38
The Petri net discovered by the α-algorithm of exercise 8.16.

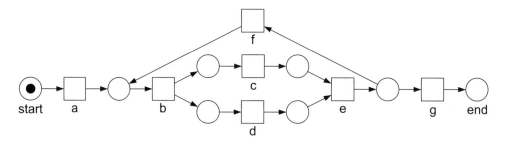

Figure 8.39
The Petri net discovered by the α-algorithm of exercise 8.17.

3. There are nine possible traces according to the discovered model. Seven are already given as input. The two missing ones are $\langle a, d, b, c, f, h \rangle$ and $\langle a, d, c, b, f, h \rangle$.

8.17
1. $\rightarrow_L = \{(a, b), (b, c), (b, d), (c, e), (d, e), (e, f), (e, g), (f, b)\}$.
2. Figure 8.39 shows the discovered model.
3. Trace $\langle a, b, c, d, e, g \rangle$ is the shortest trace possible according to the model but is not present in the event log.

8.7.2 Further Exercises
Exercise 8.18   Consider the Petri net system in figure 8.40.

1. Construct the coverability graph.
2. Does every path in the coverability graph correspond to a run?

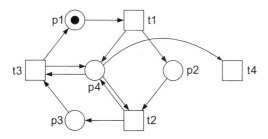

Figure 8.40
The Petri net system of exercise 8.18.

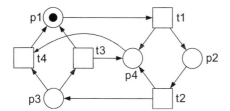

Figure 8.41
The Petri net system of exercise 8.19.

3. Determine for each transition whether it is impartial, fair, or just (or satisfies no fairness property).

Exercise 8.19   Consider the Petri net system in figure 8.41.

1. Construct the coverability graph.
2. Does any path in the coverability graph correspond to a run? If so, is this a coincidence or not? In other words, is it always the case that any path in the coverability graph corresponds to a run?
3. Determine for each transition whether it is impartial, fair, or just (or satisfies no fairness property).

Exercise 8.20   Consider the Petri net system in figure 8.42.

1. Does the net have a deadlock?
2. Is the net unbounded?
3. Is the net safe?
4. Is the net reversible?
5. Is the net live?
6. Give a place invariant assigning a positive weight to all bounded places.

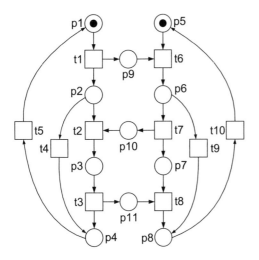

Figure 8.42
The Petri net system of exercise 8.20.

7. Give two nontrivial transition invariants.
8. Determine for each transition whether it is impartial, fair, or just (or satisfies no fairness property).

Exercise 8.21   Consider the Petri net system in figure 8.43.

1. Give an initial marking such that the Petri net is live and bounded.
2. If possible, give an initial marking such that the Petri net is bounded but not live.
3. If possible, give an initial marking such that the Petri net is not bounded but live.
4. Give a place invariant that shows which places are bounded independent of the initial marking.
5. Give a transition invariant that assigns a positive weight to all transitions.

Exercise 8.22   The following event log consisting of six traces was extracted from an enterprise information system:

```
a b c d f
a c b d f
a b d c f
a c d b f
a d e f
a e d f
```

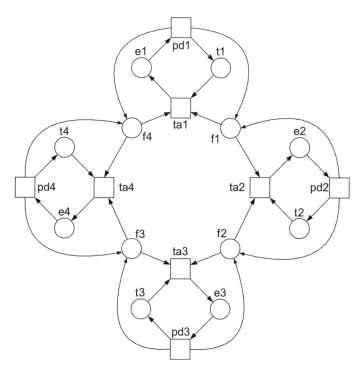

Figure 8.43
The Petri net of exercise 8.21.

1. Derive the $\rightarrow_L$ relation.
2. Use the eight steps of the α-algorithm to construct the corresponding Petri net and draw the Petri net (delivering all of the intermediate results is not necessary only the resulting Petri net is required).
3. If possible, give a possible trace according to the discovered model but not (yet) observed in the log.

8.8 Summary

One of the main purposes of a process model is to gain insight into the modeled system or business process. To this end, the process model must be analyzed. Analysis can be used to discover design flaws and errors but also to predict performance. If we specify process models as Petri nets, then a wide range of analysis techniques is available. In this chapter, we distinguished between design-time analysis and runtime analysis.

At design time, we attempt to analyze the process model. We introduced two types of analysis: verification and simulation. Verification can prove that the process model conforms to its specification. To verify a Petri net, we can explore the reachability graph and check whether the specification holds in every reachable marking, or we analyze the structure of the Petri net. Simulation explores only a part of the reachability graph but is particularly useful for performance analysis.

At runtime, we analyze the running system. We introduced process mining as a novel analysis technique. The goal of process mining is to extract information from the event logs recorded by the system. Event logs allow us to automatically generate a process model (process discovery), to analyze whether the running system conforms to its specification (conformance checking), and to extend the process model with runtime information (extension) to enable, for example, the construction of a simulation model.

Analyzing process models is a nontrivial task that requires much experience with the analysis technique and a model that is tailored toward the analysis goal. Analysis is not necessarily fully automated but is supported by tools. All analysis techniques described in this chapter are supported by tools such as CPN Tools, ProM, and LoLA. These tools are freely available and can be used to put the techniques to work in industrial applications.

After studying this chapter you should to be able to:

- Explain the difference between qualitative and quantitative questions.
- Calculate the reachability graph and the coverability of a Petri net and answer analysis questions by inspecting these graphs.
- Determine whether a net is terminating, bounded, safe, deadlock free, live, or reversible.
- Determine whether a transition is impartial, fair, or just.
- Explain the concepts "place invariant," "transition invariant," and "incidence matrix."
- Determine and interpret place and transition invariants for a simple Petri net.
- Explain the difference between simulations and verifications and their advantages and disadvantages.
- Build simple simulation models using CPN Tools.
- Understand the need for subruns and confidence intervals.
- Provide an overview of the process-mining spectrum and explain the concepts of process discovery, conformance checking, and extension.
- Construct a Petri net based on an event log by applying the α-algorithm.

8.9 Further Reading

In this chapter, we described various analysis techniques related to design-time analysis (validation, verification, and performance analysis) and runtime analysis (process mining).

Verification of Petri nets is related to the more general problem of *model checking*; that is, the task of deciding whether a system model conforms to a specification (Clarke, Grumberg, and Peled 2000). A model checker is a tool that uses a model and a specification as its input and verifies whether the model conforms to the specification. Model checking is a research discipline that has attracted much attention in the last 30 years (Grumberg and Veith 2008). There are many techniques and tools. All of these approaches verify a model while trying to alleviate the state explosion problem by avoiding the calculation of the complete state space. There are two main trends. *Explicit techniques* try to prove conformance of the model with its specification on a reduced state space. Partial order reduction (Valmari 1991; Godefroid 1991; Peled 1993) is one example technique. *Symbolic techniques* aim at data structures for a possible small representation of the state space. The textbooks of Clarke, Grumberg, and Peled (2000), Berard et al. (2001), Holzmann (2003), and Baier and Katoen (2008) give a good introduction to model checking.

Although Petri nets may have an infinite state space, most properties are decidable. The coverability graph illustrates this. Karp and Miller (1969) developed the classical coverability graph algorithm, but there are many variations of this algorithm. In this chapter, we constructed the coverability graph. Reisig and Rozenberg (1998), Reisig (1985), and Murata (1989) first constructed the coverability tree and then folded the tree into a graph. This has the advantage that the result is deterministic, but the graph may be larger. Finkel (1993) and Geeraerts, Raskin, and Van Begin (2007) provide techniques to further minimize the coverability graph.

State space analysis of Petri nets can be made more efficient using partial order reduction techniques or other dedicated techniques (Valmari 1998; Wolf 2007). Standard properties of Petri nets, such as liveness, boundedness, and safeness are described in any textbook on Petri nets (Desel and Esparza 1995; Desel, Reisig, and Rozenberg 2004; Girault and Valk 2002; Murata 1989; Peterson 1981; Reisig 1985; Reisig and Rozenberg 1998). Jensen and Kristensen (2009) describe the fairness notions calculated by CPN Tools. Lehmann, Pnueli, and Stavi (1981) and Clarke, Grumberg, and Peled (2000) introduce the classical fairness notions, such as weak and strong fairness.

There are many textbooks on simulation—for example, Bratley, Fox, and Schrage (1983), Kelton, Sadowski, and Sturrock (2003), Kleijnen and Groenendaal (1992), and Ross (1990). These books typically focus on the statistical analysis or on a particular simulation tool. Simulation is mainly used at design time, but Rozinat, Wynn, et al. (2009) showed that it can also be applied in an operational sense. Rozinat, Mans, et al. (2009) discuss the relation between simulation and process mining in detail.

In addition to simulation, analytical techniques can be used for performance analysis (Buzacott 1996; Bernardo and Hillston 2007). There is also an elegant relationship between stochastic Petri nets—that is, Petri nets extended with probabilities and stochastic timing—and Markov chains (Marsan et al. 1995; Haas 2002; Haverkort 1998).

This relationship is supported by tools, such as GreatSPN <http://www.di.unito.it/greatspn>.

In this chapter, we presented an overview of process mining and zoomed in on the challenge of process discovery by presenting the α-algorithm (Aalst, Weijters, and Maruster 2004). We have chosen this discovery algorithm because of its simplicity and because it forms the basis for many other discovery algorithms. However, there are much more sophisticated process discovery techniques that can deal with noise and incompleteness. The genetic miner (Alves de Medeiros, Weijters, and Aalst 2007) uses genetic algorithms, and the fuzzy miner (Günther and Aalst 2007) uses a variety of quantitative measures to decide whether a particular causal dependency exists or not. Process mining is not limited to discovery of the process view. For example, Rozinat and Van der Aalst (2008) showed that an event log can be used to quantify the quality of a model. They extended in (Rozinat and Aalst 2006) process models with decision rules learned from historical data. We refer to <http://www.processmining.org> and survey papers (Aalst, Reijers, et al. 2007) for more information on process mining.

9 Concluding Remarks

This book deals with the development and analysis of operational business processes and their information systems. The focus is on modeling business processes, as the main challenge is to realize enterprise information systems that are well aligned with the business processes and to support the further improvement of these business processes. In this concluding chapter, we first summarize the main objectives of this book (section 9.1) and then show how the various chapters contributed to these objectives (section 9.2). Finally, we reflect on the approach chosen in this book (section 9.3).

9.1 Lessons Learned

In the previous chapters, we provided a comprehensive introduction to the modeling and analysis of business processes and information systems. As a modeling technique, we presented Petri nets extended with data, time, and hierarchy. After reading this book, you should be able to:

1. Describe the functionality of characteristic classes of information systems.
2. Understand the role of models in the design, configuration, and analysis phase.
3. Explain the relation between business processes and information systems.
4. Describe the role of process-aware information systems and process modeling.
5. Translate informal requirements into explicit models.
6. Model complex business processes and information systems as Petri nets (extended with color, time, and hierarchy).
7. Analyze Petri nets (and the corresponding business processes and information systems) using reachability analysis and invariants.
8. Have a basic understanding of simulation and process mining.
9. Suggest redesigns for a business process.

Again, modeling business processes and information systems and analyzing these models are nontrivial tasks that require a lot of experience. It is, unfortunately, not possible to give a detailed recipe for making suitable models. Modeling is an art rather than a science. The wit and cunning of the model designer is imperative to the accuracy, efficiency, and usefulness of the model. This cannot be captured in the form of an algorithm or a procedure. However, we think that the large number of exercises in this book provides a good overview of this topics. Experience can be gained only by continuously applying the techniques presented in this book.

9.2 Summary

This section links the nine objectives of the previous section to the individual chapters.

In chapter 1, we introduced information systems and business processes and gave an overview of the different types of information systems and their roles in organizations (first objective). We further presented a life cycle model of information systems, which is depicted again in figure 9.1, and highlighted the importance of models and their role in this life cycle (second objective). The relation between business processes and information systems (third objective) was explained in chapter 2. We showed that most information systems are process aware. Process-aware information systems are configured on the basis of process models (fourth objective).

Chapters 3 to 7 were dedicated to introduce how business processes and information systems can be modeled as Petri nets (fifth objective), hence investigating the design

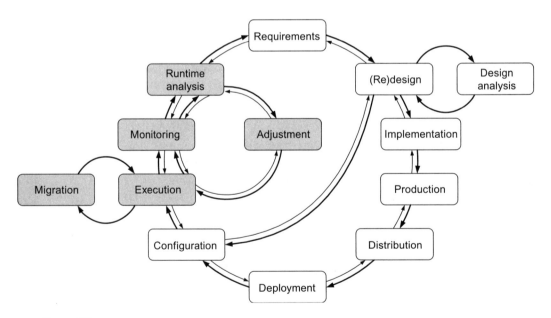

Figure 9.1
The life cycle model of an enterprise information system.

phase in the life cycle model in figure 9.1. In chapter 3, we presented the basic concepts of Petri nets. Chapter 4 provided an overview of how to map a business process or an information system onto a Petri net. We presented several modeling constructs that frequently appear in practice and showed how they can be modeled as Petri nets. In chapter 5, Petri nets were extended with data and time to adequately model all aspects of a business process or an information system. Color allows us to describe data in the model, and the extension with time makes it possible to model the length of time that activities take. In chapter 6, we introduced the CPN language—a concrete syntax to describe Petri nets extended with color and time (CPNs)—and CPN Tools to model and analyze CPNs. To facilitate the hierarchical design of CPNs, chapter 7 presented hierarchical CPNs (sixth objective).

Chapter 8 concentrated on the design analysis phase and the runtime analysis phase of figure 9.1. We exemplified two verification techniques—state space analysis and structural analysis (seventh objective)—and introduced performance analysis using simulation (eighth objective). Finally, we provided an introduction to process mining as an example of a runtime analysis technique. We showed how analysis results can be interpreted, thereby providing suggestions to redesign a model (ninth objective).

9.3   Discussion

The focus of this book is very different from most books on information systems. Typically, the focus is either on a concrete modeling language such as UML or BPMN or on high-level concepts and case studies. The drawback of selecting a concrete (industrial) modeling language is that the focus shifts to syntactical elements rather than basic concepts. Moreover, industrial languages tend to come and go and change all the time. For example, BPMN is now widely advocated as a language for business process modeling, but this language is very recent and subject to change. Moreover, BPMN provides many concepts that are rarely used and whose semantics are subject to multiple interpretations. Another example is the industry standard WS-BPEL. WS-BPEL has been around a bit longer, but it is clearly a compromise between different vendors and too complicated for end users. Moreover, the language seems to have lost much of its momentum and is likely to be superseded. UML and other industrial languages suffer from similar problems. Therefore, this book does not advocate a particular technique, but concentrates on the *foundations of business process modeling and analysis*. The focus on process modeling is justified by the increasing awareness that information systems development should start from the process view rather than the data view. The primary goal of any enterprise information system is to support business processes. Clearly, data modeling is important, but only in the context of a given business process.

To conclude this book, we discuss why Petri nets were chosen as a process modeling technique and why much emphasis was put on the analysis of process models.

There are at least six reasons for using Petri nets as a process modeling technique:

- Petri nets have a mathematical foundation.
- Petri nets offer a graphical notation.
- Petri nets can compactly represent the state space of a business process.
- Petri nets are able to naturally model concurrency and locality.
- Petri nets support a wide range of analysis techniques.
- There are many tools that support the modeling and the analysis of Petri nets.

The formal foundation of Petri nets allows us to model a business process in a precise and unambiguous manner and to apply various analysis techniques. This is in contrast to many industrial process modeling languages, which typically lack a formal semantics. The graphical notation of a Petri net makes this formalism accessible for non-experts. As industrial process models tend to become large in size, a compact model notation is advantageous. Concurrency becomes more and more important, because the step from monolithic information systems to service-oriented systems results in smaller systems that are running concurrently. Petri nets naturally support the modeling of such systems. The firing of a transition influences only the surrounding places. If two transitions in a Petri net are not directly connected with each other, concurrency is possible. This facilitates process modeling and analysis. In chapter 8, we introduced various analysis techniques for Petri nets and tools that support these analysis techniques. These considerations show that Petri nets are a formalism that captures modeling, analysis, and tool support.

Petri nets are an ideal language for explaining *foundational concepts of process modeling and analysis*. Petri nets have existed for more than four decades, whereas particular industrial languages come and go. There is a huge number of industrial process-modeling languages. These languages support different modeling constructs and also differ in their graphical notations. In contrast, the basic constructs, such as causality, concurrency, synchronization, and mutual exclusion, which we presented in section 4.3, will be supported by any language. Moreover, the expressiveness of CPNs allows us to model any business process and information system that can be modeled with any industrial modeling language.

As mentioned in section 2.3, contemporary model-based analysis tools are typically limited to simulation of process models. Verification and runtime analysis, such as process mining, are hardly supported. The important role process models play in information systems will further increase. More and more information systems are configured by process models. To this end, process models must be correct, precise, and unambiguous. Given the complexity of industrial process models, tool support for analyzing process models is indispensable. As a consequence, analysis techniques and tools supporting these techniques will play a more prominent role in the future. The wide acceptance of process-aware information systems (e.g., business process management systems and workflow management systems) will make such analysis techniques more accessible. For example, simulation is now rarely used because of the efforts required to make an accurate model and the difficulties associated with using simulation in an operational sense. This will change as simulation models are generated and parameterized based on historical and current data. Also, runtime analysis techniques such as process mining are becoming increasingly important. The availability of event data and sophisticated process-mining techniques enables organizations to get a better view on the real business processes. This will make the work of managers, consultants, and auditors more analytical. Given these developments, we emphasize the role of analysis in this book. Chapter 8 provides an overview of the various analysis techniques.

Finally, the existence of open source tools—such as CPN Tools, ProM, and LoLA—that support the modeling and analysis of Petri nets allows users to directly apply all concepts and techniques presented in this book, which is in strong contrast to many contemporary industrial process modeling languages that are not supported by such tools or that require large investments to get started.

Appendix A: Solutions

A.1   Solutions to Chapter 1

1.9   This question can be answered by looking up definitions 1.3 and 1.5.

1.10   See the discussion on the types of information systems in section 1.2.

1.11   See the explanation of the life cycle model in section 1.3.

1.12   Figure A.1 shows the state-transition diagram of the transition system of the washing machine.

1.13   In the description of the washing machine, no distinction is made between the rinse after the pre-wash and the rinse after the main wash. The system can, therefore, move from state pre-wash to state rinse to state main_wash to state rinse, or stop directly after the first turn of rinse. We can solve this problem by replacing state rinse by two states: prewash-rinse (after the pre-wash) and main wash-rinse (after the main wash). The state space changes to:

$S = \{$off, defective, whiz, main_wash,
   pre-wash, prewash-rinse, main wash-rinse$\}$.

Figure A.2 depicts the transition relation TR.

1.14   We can describe each state of the T-junction by a triple $(1, 2, 3)$ where each of the three numbers denotes the respective traffic light of figure 1.6. The set of states can be described by

$S = \{$(Rn, R, R), (G, R, R), (O, R, R), (R, Rn, R), (R, G, R),
   (R, O, R), (R, R, Rn), (R, R, G), (R, R, O)$\}$.

State Rn denotes which traffic light turns green next. That way, we can distinguish the three states in which all lights are red. Figure A.3 depicts the transition relation.

1.15   We can describe each state of the T-junction by a quintuplet (1S, 1R, 2, 3S, 3L) where each of the five values denotes the respective traffic light of figure 1.7. The basic

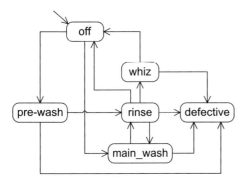

Figure A.1
A state-transition diagram for the washing machine.

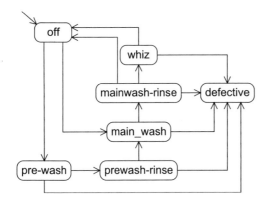

Figure A.2
Improved state-transition diagram for the washing machine.

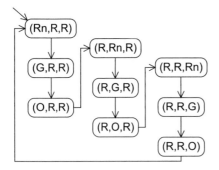

Figure A.3
State-transition diagram for the T-junction in figure 1.6.

observation is that the traffic lights 1S, 1R, and 3S can be green at the same time. The same holds for 1R and 2 and for 3L. The set of states can be described by:

$$S = \{(Rn, Rn, R, Rn, R), (G, G, R, G, R), (O, G, R, O, R),$$
$$(R, G, R, R, R), (R, G, G, R, R), (R, O, O, R, R),$$
$$(R, R, R, R, Rn), (R, R, R, R, G), (R, R, R, R, O)\}.$$

State Rn denotes which traffic light turns green next. That way, we can distinguish state (R, R, R, R, Rn) from state (Rn, Rn, R, Rn, R). The former encodes that, in the next state, traffic light 3L will turn green and not 1S, 1R, and 3S as in state (Rn, Rn, R, Rn, R). Figure A.4 depicts the transition relation.

1.16   We can describe the state space by:

$$S = \{(0-0), (15-0), (30-0), (40-0), (30-15), (40-15), (40-30),$$
$$(0-15), (0-30), (0-40), (15-30), (15-40), (30-40), (15-15),$$
$$(30-30), (40-40), (A-40), (40-A), (1-0), (0-1)\}.$$

State $(1-0)$ denotes that the first player has won the match, and state $(A-40)$ denotes that the first player has an advantage. Figure A.5 depicts the transition relation.

1.17

1. Customers can be in eight states: Initially, they are about to enter the restaurant (initial). They then enter the restaurant (entered), are assigned to a table (table), get the menu (menu), order (order), receive the food (food), ask for the check (check), pay (payment), and finally leave the restaurant (initial). (We could also model the latter situation by using an explicit state left.) We have the following set of states:

$$S = \{\text{initial, entered, table, menu, order, food, check, payment}\}.$$

Figure A.6(a) depicts the transition relation. In state food, customers can return to state menu to order additional food.

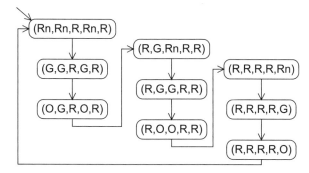

Figure A.4
State-transition diagram for the T-junction in figure 1.7.

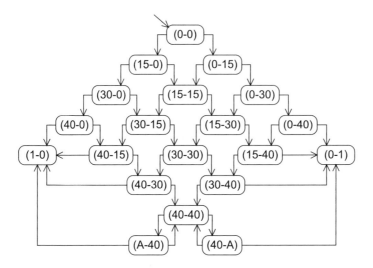

Figure A.5
State-transition diagram for the scoring in a tennis match.

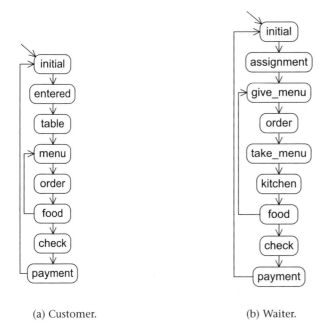

(a) Customer.   (b) Waiter.

Figure A.6
State-transition diagrams for the customer and the waiter.

A waiter can be in the following nine states: Initially, the waiter is waiting (initial). If customers enter the restaurant, the waiter assigns them a table (assignment), gives them the menu (give_menu), receives the order (order), takes the menu (take_menu), delivers the order to the kitchen (kitchen), delivers the food (food), delivers the check (check), receives the money (payment), and finally returns to state initial to wait for the next customers. As the last state is not specified, other modeling decisions are possible (e.g., the waiter remains in state payment). We can therefore describe the set of states by:

$$S = \{\text{initial}, \text{assignment}, \text{give\_menu}, \text{order}, \text{take\_menu},$$
$$\text{kitchen}, \text{food}, \text{check}, \text{payment}\}.$$

Figure 9.6(b) depicts the transition relation.

2. The state changes of the customer and the waiter are synchronized sequentially; that is, only one of the two can perform a state change at the same time. As a consequence, the state-transition diagram modeling the behavior of the customer and the waiter contains the sum of the two single state spaces: $8 + 9 = 17$ states. If, in contrast, both actors could change state independently, there would be $8 \cdot 9 = 72$ states.

1.18   Depending on the particularities of the TV considered, the answers may be different.

1. The system is dynamic. If we use the remote control, the system changes state. Pushing the off button, the mute button, or a place selection button leads to an instantaneous change. Considering the volume button, it is not clear whether it triggers a discrete or a continuous change. As in the case of an alarm clock, we can assume, however, that this change happens in discrete steps. Consequently, we deal with a discrete dynamic system.

2. The first possible state is off. When the TV is turned on, we can describe a state by the triple (channel, mute, volume) where channel is a number between 1 and 6, mute has value on or off, and volume is represented by a number—for example, on a scale from 0 to 20. We must represent mute separately, because off is not the same as turning the volume down to 0. When we switch the sound on again, it starts with an initial volume setting. Other assumptions are possible. We can, for example, think of a TV that, when switched on again, returns to the state it was in when it was switched off the last time. This TV must remember its state when turned off. We can model that as a quadruplet (power, channel, mute, volume).

3. The TV is typically turned on by choosing a channel. The values of mute and volume then become standard values—for example, on and 8. We therefore obtain six transitions of the form (off, n, on, 8). Pushing the volume button, when the TV is off,

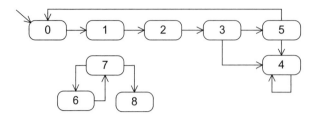

Figure A.7
A state-transition diagram of exercise 1.19.

has no effect. So we have a transition (off, off). The volume button is the most interesting button. Pushing the volume control on the side labeled "+" increases the TV's volume, except when the volume is already maximal. This gives the transitions: $((on, n, on, x), (on, n, on, x + 1))$ for $x < 20$ and transition $((on, n, on, 20), (on, n, on, 20))$. With the mute button, we may turn on the sound again. This results in transitions such as $((on, 3, off, 8), (on, 3, on, 8))$. As a consequence, changing the volume while the sound is muted is not possible.

1.19
1. Figure A.7 depicts the state-transition diagram.
2. The states reachable from state 0 are 0, 1, 2, 3, 4, and 5.
3. Assuming the initial state 0, examples of transition sequences are: $\langle 0, 1, 2, 3, 4, 4 \rangle$, $\langle 0, 1, 2, 3, 5, 4, 4, 4, 4 \rangle$, and $\langle 0, 1, 2, 3, 5, 0 \rangle$.
4. State 8 is a terminal state, because no arrows start here (state 8 is, however, not reachable). State 4 is not a terminal state, although it is not possible to escape from this state.

A.2   Solutions to Chapter 2

2.2   Business processes and information systems interact with each other. It is possible to model business processes, and it is also possible to model the information system. Moreover, there is typically an overlap between models of business processes and models of the corresponding information systems. Information systems are typically driven by process models that essentially describe the intended business processes.

2.3   The four trends are: (1) from data orientation to process orientation, (2) from programming to assembling, (3) from programming to configuration, and (4) toward redesign and organic growth.

2.4   The answer is given in definition 2.3.

2.5   The functionality of the various tools:
• Business process modeling tools: modeling business processes;
• Model-based analysis tools: analysis of business processes;
• Business process enactment tools: implementation or configuration of an information system based on a business process model, enactment; and
• Tools for analyzing running business processes: analysis and diagnosis of running business processes.

2.6   Examples of tools:
• Business process modeling tools: ARIS Business Architect, Process Designer (BPM|one), and Business Modeler (WebSphere);
• Model-based analysis tools: ARIS Business Architect, BPM|one, and Business Modeler;
• Business process enactment tools: BPM|one, Tibco, WebSphere, SAP ERP, Oracle's JD Edwards EnterpriseOne, Sage Pro ERP, and Microsoft Dynamics; and
• Tools for analyzing running business processes: BPM|one, ARIS Business Simulator, and IBM WebSphere Business Monitor.

2.7   The role of models in tools:
• Business process modeling tools: modeling and specification;
• Model-based analysis tools: analysis;
• Business process enactment tools: enactment and configuration; and
• Tools for analyzing running business processes: monitoring, performance analysis, data mining, process mining, and recommendations.

2.8   Figure A.8 depicts the UML class diagram. The example has 10 classes. Classes SolidProduct and LiquidProduct inherit from class Product, and classes Tanker and Cargo inherit from class Trailer. As specified, a tanker trailer can load at most one liquid product (i.e., multiplicity "0..1"), whereas a cargo trailer can load an arbitrary number of solid products. A shipment concerns zero or one order, because trucks sometimes drive without any load.

A.3   Solutions to Chapter 3

3.10   This question can be answered by looking up definitions 3.9 and 3.10 and by using the formalization described in section 3.4.

3.11   After renaming the places p1, p2, p3, p4, p5, p6, and p7 by r1, g1, o1, x, g2, o2, and r2, respectively, and after renaming the transitions t1, t2, t3, t4, t5, and t6 by rg1, go1, or1, rg2, go2, and or2, respectively, the resulting net should be identical to figure 3.17.

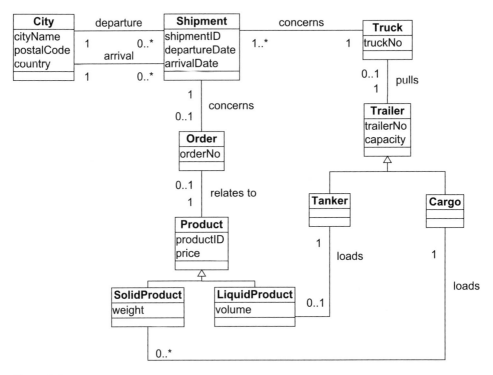

Figure A.8
UML class diagram of exercise 2.8.

3.12
1. We obtain $P = \{p1, p2, p3, p4\}$, $T = \{t1, t2, t3\}$, $F = \{(p1, t1), (t1, p2), (p2, t2), (t2, p4),$ $(t2, p3), (p3, t3), (t3, p4), (p4, t3), (p4, t1)\}$, and $m_0 = [p1, p3, 2 \cdot p4]$.
2. We obtain $^\bullet t1 = \{p1, p4\}$, $t1^\bullet = \{p2\}$, $^\bullet t2 = \{p2\}$, $t2^\bullet = \{p3, p4\}$, $^\bullet t3 = \{p3, p4\}$, and $t3^\bullet = \{p4\}$.
3. Transitions t1 and t3 are enabled at m_0, because each of their respective input places contains at least one token. Transition t2 is not enabled at m_0, because its input place p2 does not contain a token.
4. The initial marking is $m_0 = [p1, p3, 2 \cdot p4]$. The firing of transition t3 yields marking $[p1, 2 \cdot p4]$. Afterward, transitions t1, t2, and t3 can subsequently fire, yielding markings $[p2, p4]$, $[p3, 2 \cdot p4]$, and $[2 \cdot p4]$. If transition t1 fires in m_0, we reach marking $[p2, p3, p4]$. In this marking, transition t3 can fire, yielding marking $[p2, p4]$ (the reachable markings of this marking have been already given). Otherwise, if transition t2 fires in marking $[p2, p3, p4]$, the net reaches marking $[2 \cdot p3, 2 \cdot p4]$, and by firing transition t3 twice, we reach markings $[p3, 2 \cdot p4]$ and $[2 \cdot p4]$.

5. The only reachable terminal marking is $[2 \cdot p4]$.

6. At marking $[p1, p3, 2 \cdot p4]$, transitions t1 and t3 are enabled; at marking $[p2, p3, p4]$, transitions t2 and t3 are enabled.

7. If we remove place p1, then we have an infinite firing sequence: $\langle t1, t2, t1, \ldots \rangle$. As each firing of transition t2 produces a token in place p3, we can reach infinitely many different markings, meaning that the number of markings increases. In contrast, removing place p3 reduces the number of reachable markings. The firing of transition t3 does not change the marking, although this was the case in the presence of place p3.

3.13
1. We obtain $P = \{p1, p2, p3\}$, $T = \{t1, t2, t3, t4\}$, $F = \{(p1, t2), (t2, p2), (p2, t1), (t1, p1),$ $(p2, t3), (t3, p3), (p3, t4), (t4, p2), (p2, t4)\}$, and $m_0 = [p2, p3]$.
2. We obtain ${}^{\bullet}t1 = \{p2\}$, $t1^{\bullet} = \{p1\}$, ${}^{\bullet}t2 = \{p1\}$, $t2^{\bullet} = \{p2\}$, ${}^{\bullet}t3 = \{p2\}$, $t3^{\bullet} = \{p3\}$, ${}^{\bullet}t4 =$ $\{p2, p3\}$, and $t4^{\bullet} = \{p2\}$.
3. Transitions t1, t3, and t4 are enabled at m_0, because each of their respective input places contains one token. In contrast, transition t2 is not enabled at m_0, because its input place p1 does not contain a token.
4. The initial marking is $[p2, p3]$. The firing of transition t1 yields marking $[p1, p3]$. By firing transition t2, m_0 is reached again. The firing of transition t3 in m_0 yields marking $[2 \cdot p3]$. The firing of transition t4 in m_0 yields marking $[p2]$. If we continue with the firing of transition t3, we reach marking $[p3]$. Firing transitions t1 and t2 subsequently in marking $[p2]$ yields marking $[p1]$ and then marking $[p2]$ again.
5. There are two reachable terminal markings: $[p3]$ and $[2 \cdot p3]$.
6. At marking $[p2, p3]$, transitions t1, t3, and t4 are enabled; at marking $[p2]$, transitions t1 and t3 are enabled.
7. If we remove place p1, the postset of transition t2 is the empty set; that is, transition t2 has no input places. As a consequence, transition t2 is now, in any reachable marking, enabled, because definition 3.9 trivially holds (note that the definition of an enabled transition—"all input place of transition t2 contain at least one token" is equivalent to— "there is no input place of transition t2 that contains less than one token"). So transition t2 can subsequently fire infinitely often, thus producing an infinite number of tokens in place p2. Accordingly, infinitely many markings are reachable in the modified net.

3.14 If place p is an input place of transition t but no output place of t, then $m'(p) =$ $m(p) - 1$. If place p is an output place of transition t but no input place of t, then $m'(p) = m(p) + 1$. The third case is less obvious. If place p is either (1) no input and also no output place of transition t or (2) input and output place of t, then we have $m'(p) =$ $m(p)$. Clearly, if p is neither input nor output place of t, the number of tokens does not change. Likewise, the number of tokens does not change if t produces a token in place p and consumes a token from p. Formally, we have

$$m'(p) = \begin{cases} m(p) - 1, & \text{if } p \in {}^\bullet t \setminus t^\bullet, \\ m(p) + 1, & \text{if } p \in t^\bullet \setminus {}^\bullet t, \\ m(p), & \text{if } (p \in {}^\bullet t \wedge p \in t^\bullet) \vee (p \notin {}^\bullet t \wedge p \notin t^\bullet). \end{cases}$$

As the third condition is fulfilled only if the first and second conditions are not fulfilled, we can simplify the formalization as follows:

$$m'(p) = \begin{cases} m(p) - 1, & \text{if } p \in {}^\bullet t \setminus t^\bullet, \\ m(p) + 1, & \text{if } p \in t^\bullet \setminus {}^\bullet t, \\ m(p), & \text{otherwise.} \end{cases}$$

3.15   The transition system (S, TR, s_0) can be specified as follows. The set S of states is the set M of all markings of the Petri net system in figure 3.12. The initial state is equal to the initial marking, and the transition relation TR contains all transitions that can occur from any of the states in S.

1. We obtain $S = \{(0, 0, 0), (1, 0, 0), (0, 1, 0), (0, 0, 1), (1, 1, 0), (1, 0, 1), (0, 1, 1), \ (1, 1, 1)\}$, $s_0 = (1, 0, 0)$, and $TR = \{((1, 0, 0), (0, 1, 0)), ((0, 1, 0), (0, 0, 1)), ((0, 0, 1), (1, 0, 0)), ((1, 1, 0), (1, 0, 1)), ((1, 0, 1), (0, 1, 1)), ((0, 1, 1), (1, 1, 0))\}$.
Note that, with the restriction of the number of tokens in a place to at most one, transitions like $((1, 1, 1), (0, 2, 1))$ are not possible.
2. We can formalize the states as $S = \{(x, y, z) \mid x, y, z \in \mathbb{N}\}$. The initial state s_0 is equal to the initial marking $m_0 = (1, 0, 0)$. The transition relation can be specified by the union of the following three sets:

$$TR = \{((x + 1, y, z), (x, y + 1, z)) \mid x, y, z \in \mathbb{N}\}$$
$$\cup \{((x, y + 1, z), (x, y, z + 1)) \mid x, y, z \in \mathbb{N}\}$$
$$\cup \{((x, y, z + 1), (x + 1, y, z)) \mid x, y, z \in \mathbb{N}\};$$

the first, the second, and the third set contains all possible states that can be reached by firing transition start, change, and end, respectively.

3.16   We model each event by a transition and each state by a place. Figure A.9 depicts the corresponding Petri net system. The production of the next item starts only after the previous item has been sent (event "send") or discarded (event "negative"). To avoid that transition g is enabled before one of these transitions has fired, we model this state of the production process as a place free. The second state of the production process, busy, need not be explicitly modeled, because it is incorporated in the state of the product. Recall that we used a similar construction for the X-ray machine; see place free in figure 3.6.

3.17   We model each event as a transition and each state as a place. Figure A.10 depicts the corresponding Petri net system. The modeling is straightforward. Observe that we

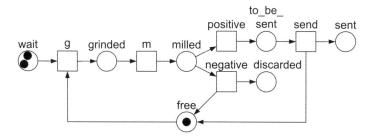

Figure A.9
The Petri net system of exercise 3.16.

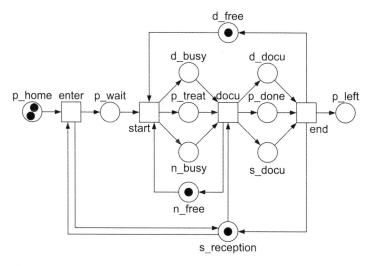

Figure A.10
The Petri net of exercise 3.17.

model the step when a patient enters the practice and registers at the reception desk by consuming the token from place s_reception and by producing the token in place s_reception, because the secretary does not change her state.

A.4 Solutions to Chapter 4

4.15 These terms are explained in sections 4.3, 4.4, and 4.6.

4.16 The network structure of a Petri net is fixed; that is, the number of places and transitions is constant. Because the number of patients in a hospital is variable, it is not wise to represent a patient as a place or a transition. Also, if we look at the role that a place or a transition plays in a Petri net, then it does not seem natural to represent a patient as a place or as a transition. Accordingly, we can represent a patient best as a token.

4.17
1. We distinguish three events: (1) taking two black balls, (2) taking two red balls, and (3) taking a red and a black ball. We model each event as a transition. The model, therefore, has transitions bb (two black balls), rr (two red balls), and rb (a red and a black ball).
2. The state of the game depends on the number of red and black balls in the bowl. There are two places: one to store red balls (red) and one to store black balls (black). We represent each ball as a token in these places. Figure A.11 depicts the resulting model.

In the initial marking, there are as many tokens in place red as there are red balls. The same applies to place black. Note that it is not correct to simplify the connections between place black and transition bb to only one arc connecting place black to transition bb. In this case, transition bb could fire if place black contains only one ball, which is against the rules of the game.

4.18 Figure A.12 depicts the model of the fairy tale. Let us first separately consider the states a frog can be in. A frog can be on the bridge, in the stream, on bank1, or on bank2. We model each of these states as a place. There are five events: the frog jumps from the

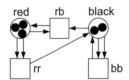

Figure A.11
A Petri net modeling red and black balls in a bowl.

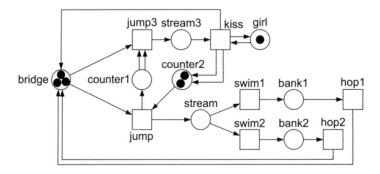

Figure A.12
The Petri net of exercise 4.18.

bridge ("jump"), swims to one of the banks ("swim1" and "swim2"), or hops from the respective bank back on the bridge ("hop1" and "hop2"). We model each event as a transition. To model the girl, we need a place and a token in this place (state girl) and an event "kiss" modeled as a transition kiss. To ensure that the girl picks up every third frog, we added transition jump3 and place stream3. After transition jump fires twice, transition jump3 is enabled. This is guaranteed by places counter1 and counter2. When the girl kisses the frog and puts it back on the bridge (i.e., transition kiss fires), then two tokens are produced in place counter2, and the next two frogs can jump using transition jump.

4.19   Figure A.13 depicts the unfolded Petri net system. As place free has a capacity of two, the unfolding has three places: free_0, free_1, and free_2. A token in place free_0 simulates zero tokens in place free, a token in free_1 simulates one token in place free, and a token in place free_2 simulates two tokens in place free. Likewise, the unfolding has places in_stock_0, in_stock_1, and in_stock_2. In the net with place capacities, transition deliver is enabled if there is either one token in place free (and hence one token in place in_stock) or two tokens in place free (and hence no token in place in_stock). Therefore, we need to unfold transition deliver into transitions deliver_12 and deliver_01. Likewise, we unfold transition take into transitions take_12 and take_01. The former transition simulates that the number of tokens in place free increases from one to two and the latter transition simulates that the number of tokens in place free increases from zero to one.

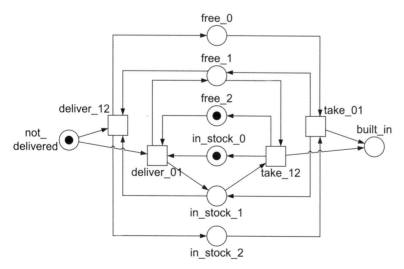

Figure A.13
The Petri net system of exercise 4.19.

This construction shows that place capacities do not increase the expressiveness of Petri nets, because there is always an unfolding that simulates the net with place capacities. Instead, the use of place capacities results in a more compact and readable process model. Note that it is also possible to unfold a Petri net with arc multiplicities into a Petri net without arc multiplicities.

4.20

1. Figure A.14 depicts the Petri net modeling this business process. Place p0 collects the incoming claims. We model the decision whether a claim is simple or complex by a nondeterministic choice (transitions simple and complex). For simple claims, checking the insurance policy of the insured party for validity (transition s_check) and retrieving the statement of a local authority (transition s_retrieve) is performed concurrently. The result is checked against the policy. As this check may have two outcomes, positive and negative, two transitions (s_check_p and s_check_n) model the decision by a nondeterministic choice. In the complex case, three events are executed concurrently: checking the insurance policy of the insured party for validity (transition c_check), retrieving the statement of a local authority (transition c_retrieve), and asking for two witness statements (transition ask_w). The two witness statements can be received concurrently (transitions w1 and w2). Afterward, the results are checked against the policy. Again, this is modeled by a nondeterministic choice (transitions c_check_p and c_check_n). Finally, transitions pay and send_letter model the payment (if the previous check was positive) and sending the letter of rejection (if the previous check was negative). We join the two alternative branches, because, after the check against the policy, both kinds of claims are processed in the same way.

2. To model the new procedure, we add transition validity_check. The firing of this transition takes a claim from place p0 and puts it in place p14, from which the payment can be arranged. Transition validity_check should be enabled only if the system is processing more than 150 claims. To model this, we make use of place capacities and introduce places claims and max. Place claims counts the number of claims that are in processing. It is an output place of transitions simple and complex and an input place of transitions s_check_p, s_check_n, c_check_p, and c_check_n. Place max ensures that place claims has a capacity of at most 150 tokens. To this end, place max contains in the initial marking 150 tokens. That way, transitions simple and complex are only enabled if place max contains at least one token; that is, the number of claims in processing has not yet exceeded 150. To guarantee that transition validity_check is enabled only if the number of claims in processing exceeded 150, this transition has to consume 150 tokens from place claims and to produce the same number of tokens in this place. As the sum of tokens in places claims and max is equal to 150, place max contains only 150 tokens (and thus enables transition validity_check) if the system is processing 150 claims. Figure A.15 illustrates the construction.

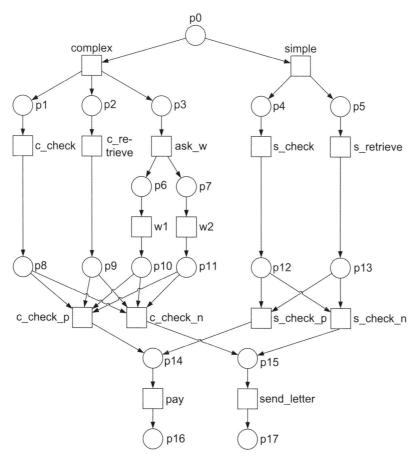

Figure A.14
The Petri net of exercise 4.20(1).

3. Modeling that transition simple is only enabled if more than 150 claims are being processed is easy. We add a place claims (see figure A.15) that counts the number of claims. Transition simple must then consume 151 tokens from place claims and produce the same number of tokens in place claims. We need to ensure that transition complex is only enabled if place claims contains less than or equal to 150 tokens. As we do not know the maximum number of claims being processed at the same time, we do not have a place capacity of place claims. Theoretically, place claims may contain infinitely many tokens. Consequently, we cannot unfold this place, as this would result in an infinite number of places, violating the requirement stated in definition 3.4. Hence, this choice cannot be modeled as a Petri net (using place capacities and arc multiplicities). Note that we can model the business process if we assume some upper bound for the number of customers.

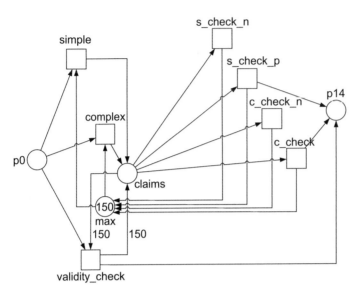

Figure A.15
The Petri net of exercise 4.20(2).

4.21

1. Figure A.16 depicts the business process model. Place p0 collects the traffic offenses. The offenses are then registered (transition register). After registration, two procedures are performed concurrently. The first branch models the judgment of the traffic offense. A nondeterministic choice of transitions normal and severe models the decision whether the traffic offense is normal or severe. If the traffic offense is normal, there is only a single judgment step (transition judge); otherwise, there are temporary and final judgment steps (transitions t_judge and f_judge). The second branch investigates the history (transition investigate_history). Information about earlier traffic offenses (transition earlier_offenses) and about other offenses committed by the offender (transition other_offenses) are collected. Then the fine is determined (transition determine). We model the evaluation of the fine again as a nondeterministic choice (transitions no_fine and fine). In the case of a fine, first a letter is sent (transition send), and then the traffic offense is archived (transition archive). If no fine is determined, the traffic offense is immediately archived, and a token is produced in the input place of transition archive.

2. As in exercise 4.20(2), we add two places, offenses and max, to the Petri net in figure A.16. Place offenses is an output place of transition register and an input place of transition archive. It counts the number of traffic offenses being processed at the same time. Place max ensures that offenses contains at most 100 tokens. To this end, it is an input place of transition register and an output place of transition archive. That way,

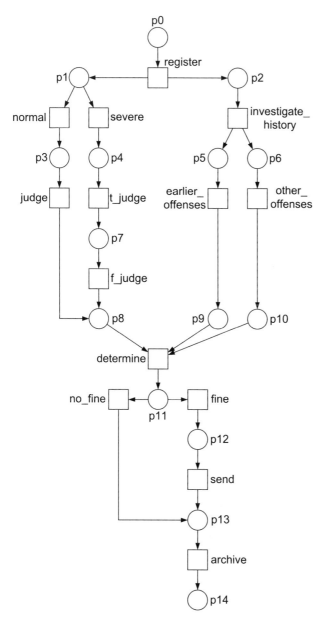

Figure A.16
The Petri net of exercise 4.21(1).

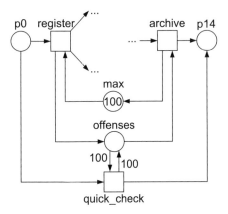

Figure A.17
The Petri net of exercise 4.21(2).

transition register is only enabled if the number of traffic offenses being processed is less than 100; that is, if there is at least one token in place max. To model the new procedure, we add a transition quick_check. Place p0 is an input place, and place p14 is an output place of this transition. In addition, this transition consumes 100 tokens from place offenses and produces 100 tokens in place offenses. By the construction of places max and offenses, transition quick_check is only enabled if there are 100 traffic offenses being processed. Figure A.17 sketches this construction.

4.22
1. Figure A.18 depicts the Petri net modeling the business process. Each assembly step consists of two events, "start" and "end"; each machine is either in state busy or in state free. To start an assembly step, the corresponding machine must be free, and the assemblies must be available. If the assembly step ends, then the machine involved changes to state free and the corresponding product is produced. A token in place sp1 and sp2 represents an assembled semi-product_1 and semi-product_2, respectively.
2. The run ⟨start_step1, end_step1, start_step2, end_step2, start_step3, end_step3⟩ yields a marking where place bike contains a token. Note that, afterward, several places still contain unused parts.

4.23   Figure A.19 is an example of a solution. Each transition in the reachability graph corresponds to a transition in figure A.19. The reachability graph also illustrates that transitions c and d can happen in any order. Hence, these transitions can occur concurrently in figure A.19.

The reachability graph in figure 4.36 illustrates that concurrency cannot be explicitly modeled as a transition system. In contrast, the Petri net in figure A.19 explicitly shows that transitions c and d are concurrent.

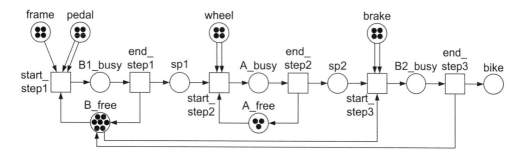

Figure A.18
The Petri net of exercise 4.22.

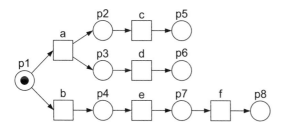

Figure A.19
The Petri net of exercise 4.23.

A.5 Solutions to Chapter 5

5.12 These concepts are described in sections 5.2, 5.4, and 5.5.

5.13
1. There are two events, "deposit" and "withdraw." We model each event as a transition. Furthermore, we need a place database modeling the customer database and two places, d_order and w_order. A token in d_order models a deposit of an account holder, and a token in w_order models a withdrawal of an account holder. Figure A.20 depicts the colored Petri net model.
Places d_order and w_order are of type AA = Account × Amount, and place database is of type AB = Account × Balance. The guard of transition withdraw ensures that the amount is less than 5,000 euros and that the transaction does not lead to a negative balance. Variable a is of type Account, variable x of type Amount, and variable y of type Balance.
2. Place database is of type BankAccount, and places d_order and w_order are of type Transaction × BankAccount. That way, a token in place database is a triple (accountNo, balance, charge). A token in places d_order and w_order is a pair ((accountNo, amount), (accountNo, balance, charge)).

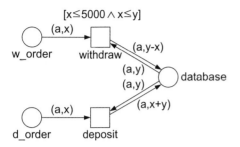

Figure A.20
A colored Petri net model of the banking system.

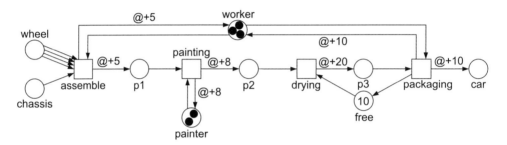

Figure A.21
The model of the production process.

5.14

1. Figure A.21 depicts the Petri net model extended with time. Transitions assemble, painting, drying, and packaging model the four steps. For each of the objects (wheel, chassis, painter, and production worker), we add a place. The intermediate products are stored in places p1, p2, and p3. Place car contains all produced toy cars. Place p3 models the room where the painted cars dry. This place has a capacity of ten tokens. The capacity has been realized by adding place free. Initially, place free contains ten tokens, and it is connected in such a way that the sum of tokens in places free and p3 is always equal to ten. Transition assemble consumes four tokens from place wheel, one token from place chassis, and one token from place worker. Furthermore, it produces a token with delay of five time units in place worker and in place p1. That way, we ensure that the worker token and the product token are not available for the next five time units. The same approach is used to model the other production steps. In the initial marking shown in figure A.21, there are three workers, two painters, and ten places in the drying room available.

2. As the resulting model should be an uncolored Petri net, we need to copy transitions painting and drying and their intermediate place. Figure A.22 shows the respective

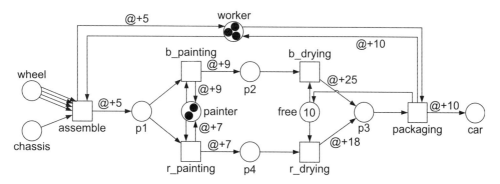

Figure A.22
The model of the modified production process.

model. Note that place free must be connected to transitions b_drying and r_drying to ensure the capacity of ten tokens for place p3.

5.15

1. Figure A.23 depicts the model. We model each of the four events "prepare," "garnish," "waiter serves," and "cook serves" as transitions. These transitions are connected to places order, p1, p2, and served of type Number. A token in each of these places models the status of an order, and the token value specifies the number of guests. Places cook and waiter serve as a store for cooks and waiters. These places are of type Cook and Waiter, respectively. The guard of transition prepare specifies that only orders with more than ten guests are accepted. Each transition consumes the employee tokens needed to pass the respective step. The consumed employee tokens are returned to the respective places waiter and cook. The delay added to these tokens avoids the respective employee working on different things during this delay. The same delay is also added to the token representing the order status. Note that we do not round the delay to an integer. The marking shown models that the catering company employs five cooks and two waiters.

2. We need to merge transitions c_serve and w_serve in figure A.23 into a transition serve, because one cook and two waiters together serve the meal. As two waiters must serve a meal, we need to consume two tokens from place waiter, and these two tokens also need to be produced in this place. We use the multiset notation [v,w] and [v@+n/10,w@+n/10] to denote that two tokens v and w of type Waiter must be consumed and produced, respectively. Furthermore, we add the delay of the cook to the order status, because it is the maximum delay. Figure A.24 depicts the resulting Petri net model.

5.16   According to the specification, we have two events: "create numbers" and "sieve numbers." We model each event as a transition. In addition, we need two places. Place trigger serves as a trigger for creating numbers, and place numbers models the store

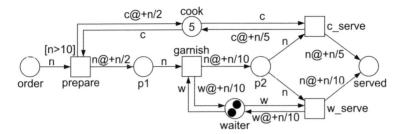

Figure A.23
The Petri net model of the catering company.

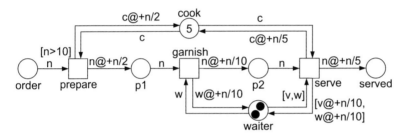

Figure A.24
The Petri net model of the modified catering company.

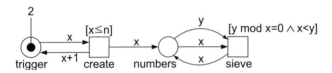

Figure A.25
The colored Petri net modeling the sieve of Eratosthenes.

of the numbers to be sieved. Both places are of type Number. Figure A.25 depicts the colored Petri net model. The guard of transition create ensures that the highest number that is created is equal to n. The guard of transition sieve ensures that the value of variable y is an integer factor of the value of variable x and that the value of variable x is less than the value of variable y.

5.17
1. Figure A.26 depicts the model of four philosophers as a Petri net. Note that philosopher $ph4$ uses fork $f4$ and $f1$, thus making the model circular. It is easy to see how to extend figure A.26 to more philosophers (e.g., five).

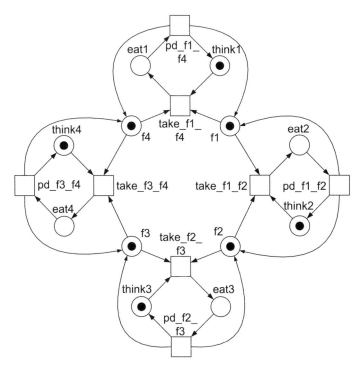

Figure A.26
Four philosophers modeled as a Petri net.

2. Figure A.27 depicts the colored Petri net model of the five philosophers. We need only three places (think, eat, and forks) and two transitions (take and putdown). The type of each place is Number. The size of the network structure is independent of the number of philosophers. Note the use of the modulo mod operator: 1 mod 5 = 1, 2 mod 5 = 2, . . . , 5 mod 5 = 0.

3. Figure A.28 models the situation in which the philosophers take their forks in two steps (first right, then left). The model can deadlock. For example, if each philosopher takes his right fork, then the colored Petri net deadlocks, because no philosopher can take a second fork, and no philosopher can put down a fork.

A.6   Solutions to Chapter 6

6.11
1. Figure A.29 models the railway as a Petri net. Because of the repetitive nature of the model, only a part of the model is shown. The model is linear in the number of tracks and trains. For example, if we double the number of tracks, the network structure gets twice as large.

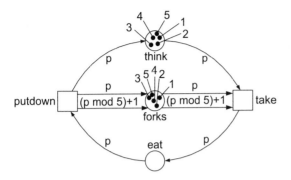

Figure A.27
A colored Petri net model of the five philosophers taking both forks at the same time.

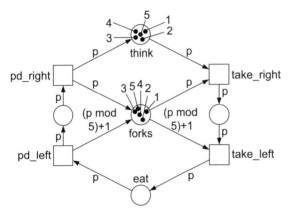

Figure A.28
A colored Petri net model of the five philosophers taking the right fork first.

2. Figure A.30 models the railway as a CPN with limited use of token colors. Because of the repetitive nature of the model, again, only a part of the model is shown. The model is smaller but still linear in the number of tracks; however, unlike the model in (1), the size is independent of the number of trains.

3. Figure A.31 models the railway also using colored tokens for the location of the train and empty sectors. In comparison to the models in (1) and (2), the model in figure A.31 is very compact. The network structure does not change if we add new sectors or trains.

6.12   Figure A.32 depicts the CPN model. Each of the three events "submit article," "add author," and "query articles" is modeled as a transition. A database entry (i.e., a

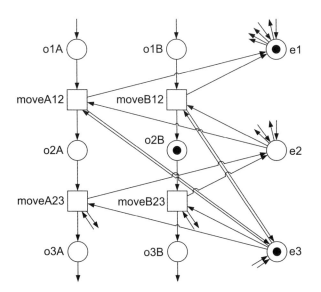

Figure A.29
The railway system modeled as a Petri net.

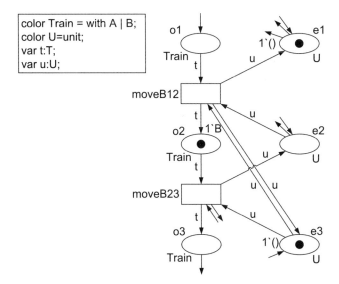

Figure A.30
The railway system modeled as a colored Petri net using color set Train.

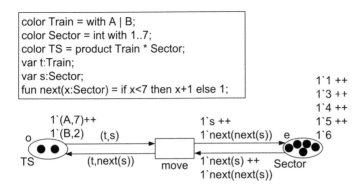

Figure A.31
The railway system modeled as a colored Petri net using test color sets: Train and Sector.

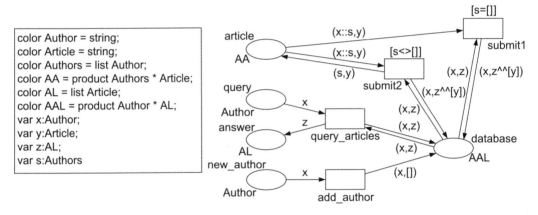

Figure A.32
An author's database colored Petri net model of the banking system.

token in place database) consists of an author name and a list of articles of this author. Transition add_author adds for a given author a database entry consisting of the author's name and an empty list of articles. Transition query_articles passes the name of an author to the database and gets the corresponding list of articles in return. More involved is the submission of new articles, because articles may have multiple authors. Transitions submit1 and submit2 peel off the list of authors. If there is just a single author, transition submit1 is enabled; however, if there is a second author, transition submit2 removes the first author and produces the remaining list in place article.

6.13
1. `fun f(a:INT,X:LINT) = a::X;`

2. The function is a recursive function. The base is the empty list, and the inductive step is the nonempty list. In the inductive step, we need to distinguish whether element a is less than or equal to the head of the list. If this condition holds, then we can include element a as the new head of the list; otherwise, we need to check whether element a can be included at the second position of the list, and so on.

```
fun f(a:INT,X:LINT) = if X=[] then [a]
                      else if a<=hd(X) then a::X
                          else hd(X)::f(a,tl(X));
```

3. In addition to (2), we need to check whether an element of the same value is already contained in list X. In this case, the list can be returned.

```
fun f(a:INT,X:LINT) = if X=[] then [a]
                      else if a<hd(X) then a::X
                          else if a=hd(X) then X
                              else hd(X)::f(a,tl(X));
```

Note that we assume that initially list X is already sorted.

6.14   Figure A.33 depicts the resulting CPN model. We need two transitions, bid and nextObject, to model the bidding for and the selling of an object. Place bids contains all bids and place sold all sold objects. Place auction stores all products to be sold. This place is of type DB. Initially, each element of DB identifies the object, the owner, and the price.

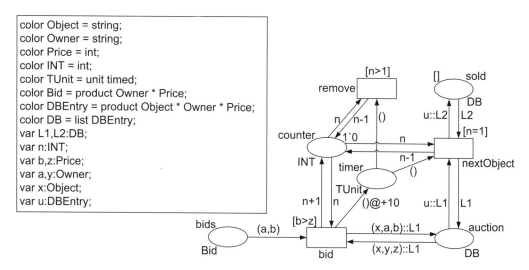

Figure A.33

A colored Petri net model of the auction service.

Let us ignore the time constraint for a moment. Bidding is modeled by increasing the price of the first object of the DBEntry list in place auction. Furthermore, the name of the bidder replaces the name of the object's owner. The guard at transition bid ensures that each bid increases the price of the previous bid. If the current object is sold, then it is removed from the list in place auction and added to the list of sold objects in place sold. In the model, we assume that all bids in place bids are for the current object.

Let us now consider the modeling of the time-out. Each bid produces a token with ten time units' delay in place timer. If there is no other bid submitted within the next ten time units, then transition nextObject is enabled. If there is another bid within this delay, then the previously produced timed token has to be removed. This is, however, not possible, because this token, due to the delay, is not available. Therefore, figure A.33 has a place counter. Each bid also increments this counter. If a timed token is available, then the guards of transitions remove and nextObject check whether the counter is equal to one (i.e., the current bid is the only one that has been submitted during the last ten time units). In this case, transition nextObject is enabled; otherwise, transition remove is enabled. Both transitions decrement the counter by one and consume the timed token.

6.15

1. Figure A.34 depicts the CPN model. In addition to the four interface places create_event, request, reject, and confirm, which have been given by the specification, a place database has been added. Furthermore, there are three transitions modeling the three possible events. For place database, which is of type EventData, the declarations have been extended. Each token in this place specifies for a single event the event ID, the number of free seats, and a list of reserved seats. The model is straightforward: transition create_event adds an event (together with 1,000 free seats and an empty list of taken seats) to the database. If a customer requests an event that is sold out (i.e., no free seats are available), a token is produced in place reject. If there is at least one free seat, then this seat is removed from the list of free seats, the name and the seat number are added to the list of taken seats, and a token is produced in place confirm.

2. Figure depicts the modified CPN model.

The three newly added transitions reject_payment, confirm_payment, and print model the three respective events. Places pay, reject_payment, confirm_payment, print_tickets, and tickets model the interface to the environment. In the declarations, we added a Boolean Paid to each taken seat, indicating whether this seat has been paid for. If a customer books a ticket, then this Boolean is initially set to false. Consider now the three events. If customers have paid for their ticket (i.e., for a given name and event ID, there is no reserved seat which has not been paid), then this payment request is rejected. Otherwise, this entry is removed from list TakenSeats. In addition, a new list containing only the seat information of the requester (where the Boolean Paid is true)

```
color Name = string;
color Event = string;
color Seat = int with 1..1000;
color NxE = product Name * Event;
color NxExS = product Name * Event * Seat;
color FreeSeats = list Seat;
color TakenSeat = product Seat * Name;
color TakenSeats = list TakenSeat;
color EventData = product Event * FreeSeats * TakenSeats;
fun seats() = Seat.all();
var n:Name;
var e:Event;
var s:Seat;
var fs:FreeSeats;
var ts:TakenSeats;
```

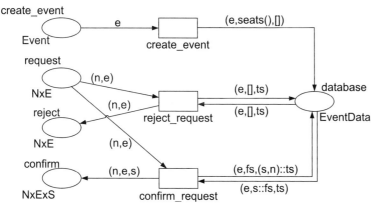

Figure A.34

A colored Petri net model of the reservation office.

and list TakenSeats are concatenated. In this case, the successful payment is confirmed. To print the tickets for an event, the respective database entry is taken, and the free and reserved seats are removed from this database entry. That way, we make sure that all future requests for this event will be rejected. In addition, function create filters from list TakenSeats all elements where customers have paid and produces this list in place tickets.

6.16   Figure A.36 depicts the CPN model.

The sequence of transitions start_accept_order, end_accept_order, start_deliver_order, and end_deliver_order on the left of the figure models the acceptance and the delivery of an order. Place free_resource contains all available employees. The two sequences on the right of the figure model the making of a drink (transitions start_make_drink and end_make_drink) and of food (transitions start_make_food and end_make_food), respectively. The guard of transition start_make_drink ensures that the order is a drink and that the drink is only prepared by a resource of type drinks or food. Likewise, the

```
color Name = string;
color Event = string;
color Seat = int with 1..1000;
color NxE = product Name * Event;
color NxExS = product Name * Event * Seat;
color LNxExS = list NxExS;
color FreeSeats = list Seat;
color Paid = bool;
color TakenSeat = product Seat * Name * Paid;
color TakenSeats = list TakenSeat;
color EventData = product Event * FreeSeats * TakenSeats;
fun seats() = Seat.all();
fun isEl(x,[]) = false |
    isEl(x,y::xs) = (x=y) orelse isEl(x,xs);
fun del(x,[]) = [] |
    del(x,y::xs) = if x=y then del(x,xs) else y::del(x,xs);
fun create(e,[]) = [] |
    create(e,(s,n,true)::ts) = (n,e,s)::create(e,ts) |
    create(e,(s,n,false)::ts) = create(e,ts);
var n:Name;
var e:Event;
var s:Seat;
var fs:FreeSeats;
var ts:TakenSeats;
```

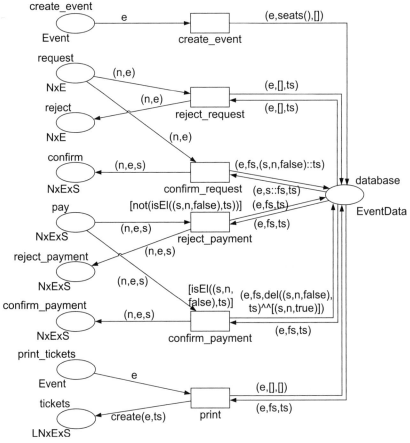

guard of transition start_make_food ensures that the respective order is food and the resource preparing the food is of type food. Note that the arc inscriptions server and food are constants.

6.17   Figure A.37 depicts the CPN model. There are three kinds of places: places modeling the position of a CityCat are of type CC, places modeling whether a stop is free are of type `unit`, and places modeling the FCFS queues are of type CClist. The network structure of this model extends the one of the Petri net model in figure 4.34 by adding six places for modeling the FCFS queues. Place BtoAL models the downstream queue between stops B and A and place AtoBL the upstream queue between these stops. Likewise, places CtoBL, BtoCL, CtoDL, and DtoCL model the respective queues between stops B and C and between C and D. A queue is modeled as a list of CityCats, hence ensuring that CityCats cannot overtake each other (see the third requirement). To distinguish individual CityCats (see the first requirement), each CityCat is identified by a number. Function d(c) implements the time CityCats need to move from one stop to the next. The time is a delay assigned to the respective CityCat token when moving from one stop to the next one (see the second requirement). Transition from_DtoC can fire if the corresponding downstream queue BtoCL is empty, and transition from_CtoB can fire if place AtoBL contains the empty list. That means that all CityCats moving upstream have to pass before a CityCat moving downstream can continue its service (see the fourth requirement). Finally, when a CityCat moves to a stop, a delay of five time units is assigned to it. This models the time necessary to let passengers embark or disembark (see the fifth requirement). In the initial marking, expression CC.all() generates the ten CityCats in place X, each of the free places (e.g., A_free) contains a token indicating that no CityCat docks at any of the four stops, and the queues are empty.

A.7   Solutions to Chapter 7

7.9   This exercise can be answered by inspecting figure 7.7 and by reading section 7.3.

7.10   To flatten the net, we replace each substitution transition by a copy of the corresponding subpage until all transitions are elementary. As this is rather straightforward, we omit the corresponding flat CPN model. The flat CPN model has 23 transitions and 35 places.

7.11   The modified version of page customer-b in figure A.38 models the customer if we assume lost sales with partial shipments. As long as there is at least one product left, it is delivered.

Figure A.35 (facing page)
A colored Petri net model of the modified reservation office.

```
color Customer = string timed;
color Product = coffee | tea | beer | fish | chips timed;
color Order = product Customer * Product timed;
color OrderNo = int;
color Request = product OrderNo * Customer * Product timed;
color InOrder = product OrderNo * Product timed;
color Resource = with server | drinks | food;
color IOxR = product InOrder * Resource timed;
fun isEl(p,[]) = false |
    isEl(p,p2::xs) = (p=p2) orelse isEl(p,xs);
var c:Customer;
var p:Product;
var ord:Order;
var n:OrderNo;
var r:Resource;
```

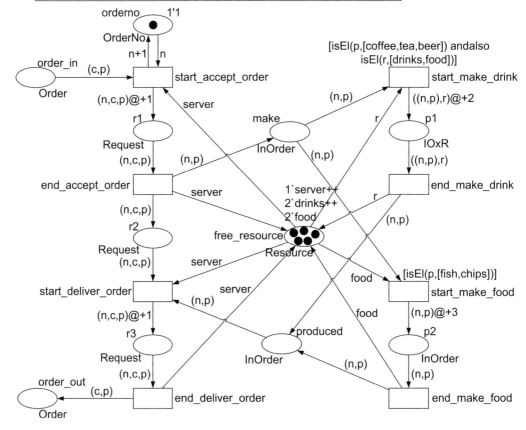

Figure A.36
A colored Petri net modeling the business process of a restaurant.

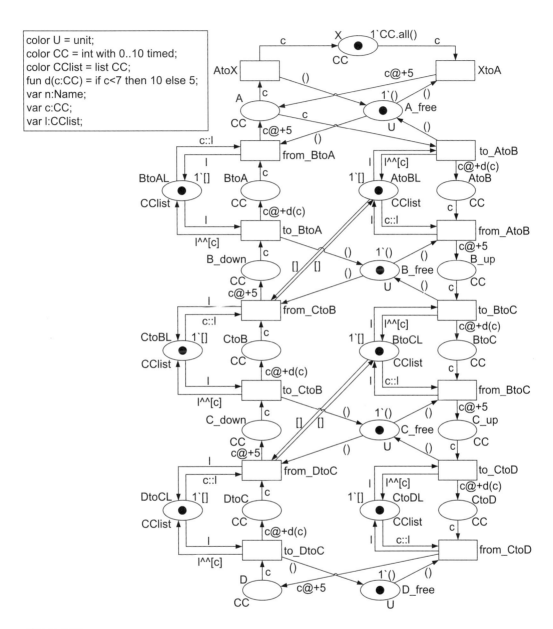

Figure A.37
A colored Petri net modeling the Brisbane CityCat system.

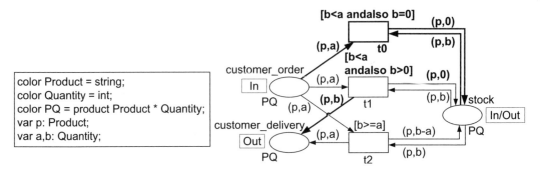

```
color Product = string;
color Quantity = int;
color PQ = product Product * Quantity;
var p: Product;
var a,b: Quantity;
```

Figure A.38
Page customer-b-part with partial shipments.

```
color Product = string;
color Quantity = int;
color PQ = product Product * Quantity;
var p: Product;
var a,b,c: Quantity;
```

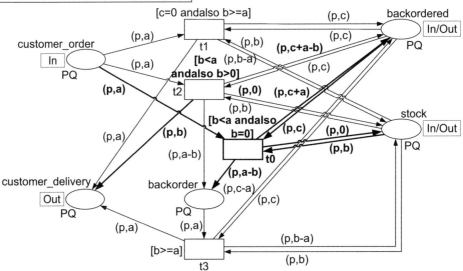

Figure A.39
Page customer+b-part with partial shipments.

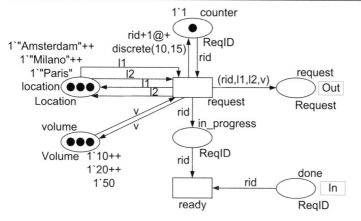

Figure A.40
Page environment.

7.12   The modified version of page customer+b in figure A.39 models the customer if we assume backordering with partial shipments. As long as there is at least one product left, it is delivered, whereas the remainder is backordered.

7.13   Figure A.40 depicts page environment. Transition request models the sending of a request to the routing system. A request is of type Request. To generate a request identifier, every firing of transition request increments the counter in place counter. The token produced in place counter has a delay of discrete(10,15) time units according to the specification. Transition ready models the receipt of the acknowledgment message, which is identified with the identifier.

   Figure A.41 depicts page routing_system. Place available contains initially all trucks. This place is of type TruckInfo and specifies for each truck the capacity, the current volume, and the current request identifier. Each truck has, according to the specification, a capacity of $100m^3$, is initially empty, and an identifier equal to zero. Places available, pending_commands, and executed_commands model the possible states of a truck. If a request arrives, transition load_command chooses an available truck and orders it via place command to the start location. The respective truck changes to state pending_commands (i.e., the truck is on the way to a location), and the request together

```
color Truck = int with 1..10 timed;
color Capacity = int;
color Volume = int;
color Location = string;
color ReqID = int timed;
color Action = with load | offload;
color Request = product ReqID * Location * Location * Volume timed;
color Command = product Truck * Location * ReqID * Action timed;
color TruckInfo = product Truck * Capacity * Volume * ReqID timed;
color TRequest  = product Truck * ReqID * Location * Location * Volume timed;
var t:Truck;
var a:Action;
var c:Capacity;
var v,v0:Volume;
var l0,l1,l2:Location;
var rid,rid0:ReqID;
```

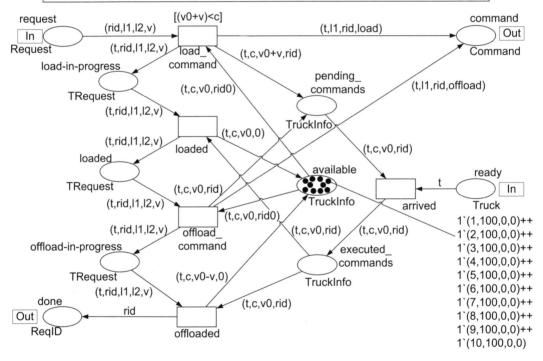

Figure A.41
Page routing_system.

with the truck chosen is stored in place load-in-progress. The latter place is of type TRequest—that is, the product of types Truck and Request. The guard of load_command ensures that the truck has the capacity to load the goods.

We model a truck that arrives at its location by a token in place ready. The firing of transition arrive changes the state of the truck from place pending_commands to place executed_commands; that is, the truck is loaded or unloaded. Transition loaded models the loading of the truck. After the loading, the truck is available. The firing of transition offload_command models that the truck driver gets the command to drive to his destination. Similar to transition load_command, the state of the truck changes from available to pending_commands. If the truck arrives at its destination, a token is produced in place ready. If transition arrived fires, then the state of the truck is updated to executed_commands. The truck can be offloaded by firing transition offloaded, thereby updating the volume of the truck. Afterward, the truck is again available.

Figure A.41 allows a truck to perform multiple subsequent actions. If transitions load_command and offload_command have the same enabling time, then goods of another request can be loaded on the truck. As we do not model a sophisticated scheduling system, the current location of a truck is irrelevant and for this reason not stored in the places of type TruckInfo.

Figure A.42 depicts page trucks. Place location stores for each truck its location. The initial location of each truck is "nowhere." The firing of transition start takes the respective truck from its current location l0. After a delay of delay(l0,l), transition complete fires, modeling that the truck reaches its destination l. As a delay, we chose a discrete distribution.

A.8   Solutions to Chapter 8

8.18
1. Figure A.43 depicts the coverability graph.
2. No; see, for example, the run $\langle t1, t2, t3, t4, t4, t4, t4 \rangle$, which is possible according to coverability graph, but which is not a run of the net in figure 8.40.
3. Transitions t1, t2, and t3 are impartial, because it is not possible to construct an infinite run in which not all of these transitions appear infinitely often. If we stop executing one of these transitions, the net deadlocks after a while. Transition t4 has no fairness, because the infinite run $\langle t1, t2, t3, t1, t2, t3, \ldots \rangle$ witnesses that t4 remains enabled but never fires.

8.19
1. Figure A.44 depicts the coverability graph.
2. In this case, all paths in the coverability graph correspond to a run of the net, because the number of tokens in place p4 is increasing in each cycle, and no transition is ever

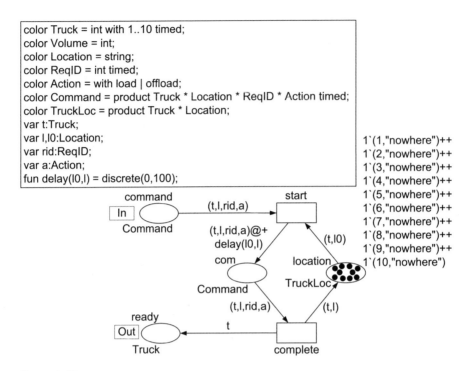

Figure A.42
Page trucks.

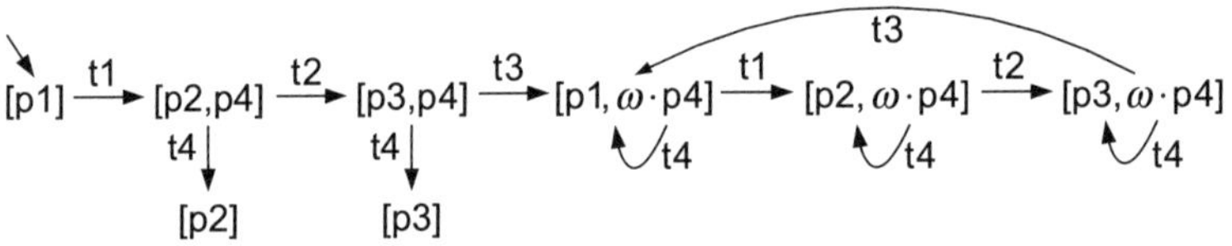

Figure A.43
The coverability graph of the Petri net in figure 8.40.

Figure A.44
The coverability graph of the Petri net in figure 8.41.

blocked because of the number of tokens in this place. In general, this does not need to be the case. Even markings tagged ω may correspond to markings where the place is empty at some point in time. The symbol ω specifies that this place is unbounded, but this does not imply that the number of tokens is always greater than zero. It is also easy to construct Petri nets where an unbounded place always has an even or uneven number of tokens or where the difference between the token number in two places is always within a certain range; see figure 8.14. In such nets, typically not all paths in the coverability graph correspond to a run.

3. Transitions t1 and t2 are impartial, because it is not possible to construct an infinite run in which not all of these transitions appear infinitely often. If we stop executing one of these transitions, the net deadlocks after a while. Transitions t3 and t4 are not impartial or fair, because the infinite runs $\langle t1, t2, t3, t1, t2, t3, \ldots \rangle$ and $\langle t1, t2, t4, t1, t2, t4, \ldots \rangle$ witness that t4 and t3 do not need to fire infinitely often even when they are enabled infinitely often. As there is no infinite run that enables transitions t4 and t3 continuously, they are just (one will disable the other one).

8.20

1. The net has no deadlocks. Always one of the transitions t1, t2, t3, t4, or t5 is enabled (as there is always one token in place p1, p2, p3, or p4).

2. There is an infinite run $\langle t1, t4, t5, t1, t4, t5, \ldots \rangle$ that witnesses that place p9 and, hence, the net is unbounded.

3. The net is not safe, because place p9 is unbounded.

4. There is always one token in one of the places $\{p1, p2, p3, p4\}$ and one token in one of the places $\{p5, p6, p7, p8\}$ (see also place invariants). The number of tokens in place p7 is always equal to the total number of tokens in places p10, p3, and p11. Hence, tokens can only accumulate in place p9. Assume that there are k tokens accumulated in place p9. These tokens can be removed to return to the initial marking. As long as there are tokens in place p9, the transitions t6, t9, and t10 can be executed, removing the k tokens one by one. These insights show that the net can indeed return to the initial marking from any reachable marking. Hence, the net is reversible.

5. The net is live, because it is reversible, and any transition can be enabled from the initial marking.

6. Examples of place invariants are

$$p1 + p2 + p3 + p4 = 1$$
$$p5 + p6 + p7 + p8 = 1$$
$$p10 + p3 + p11 - p7 = 0$$
$$p1 + p2 + 2 \cdot p3 + p4 + 2 \cdot p5 + 2 \cdot p6 + p7 + 2 \cdot p8 + p10 + p11 = 3.$$

The fourth invariant is the sum of the first three invariants (counting the second one twice). It covers all places except p9, which is unbounded.

7. Examples of transition invariants are

$$t1 + t4 + t5 + t6 + t9 + t10$$
$$t1 + t2 + t3 + t5 + t6 + t7 + t8 + t10.$$

8. As indicated before, there is an infinite run $\langle t1, t4, t5, \dots \rangle$. For each transition in the right part of the net, there is a marking that enables this transition continuously in this infinite run. For example, marking $[p4, p11, p7]$ is reachable and enables transition t8. Hence, all five transitions t6, t7, t8, t9, and t10 are unfair (i.e., not just). It is easy to see that there cannot be an infinite firing sequence without infinitely many executions of transitions t1 and t5. For this reason, both transitions are impartial. The remaining three transitions (i.e., t2, t3, and t4) do not need to occur infinitely often. Transition t3 occurs infinitely often in every infinite run where it is enabled infinitely often. Hence, transition t3 is fair. Transitions t2 and t4 are not fair, because, even if they are enabled infinitely often, they do not need to occur infinitely often. These two transitions are just; that is, it is not possible to continuously enable them in any infinite run. To summarize, transitions t1 and t5 are impartial, transition t3 is fair, transitions t2 and t4 are just, and transitions t6, t7, t8, t9 and t10 have no fairness.

8.21
1. There must be a token in each t and f place.
2. An example would be the empty marking.
3. This is not possible (see next answer).
4. There are two place invariants:

$$e1 + t1 + e2 + t2 + e3 + t3 + e4 + t4 = 4$$
$$e1 + f1 + e2 + f2 + e3 + f3 + e4 + f4 = 4.$$

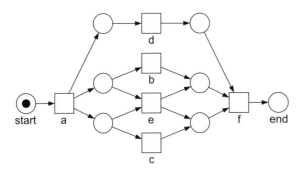

Figure A.45
The Petri net of exercise 8.22 discovered by the α-algorithm.

The first place invariant shows that all e and t places are bounded. The second invariant proves that the f places are bounded also. All places are bounded.

5. Assign to each transition a weight of one.

8.22

1. $>_L = \{(a,b),(a,c),(a,d),(a,e),(b,c),(b,d),(b,f),(c,b),(c,d),(c,f),(d,b),(d,c),(d,e),(d,f),(e,d),(e,f)\}$ and $\rightarrow_L = \{(a,b),(a,c),(a,d),(a,e),(b,f),(c,f),(d,f),(e,f)\}$

2. Figure A.45 shows the discovered model.

3. Traces $\langle a,d,b,c,f \rangle$ and $\langle a,d,c,b,f \rangle$ are possible according to the model but not present in the event log.

Bibliography

Aalst, W. M. P. van der. 1998. The application of Petri nets to workflow management. *The Journal of Circuits, Systems and Computers* 8 (1):21–66.

———. 2009. Process-aware information systems: Design, enactment and analysis. In *Wiley encyclopedia of computer science and engineering*, 2221–2233. Hoboken, NJ: Wiley & Sons.

Aalst, W. M. P. van der, B. F. van Dongen, C. W. Günther, R. S. Mans, A. K. Alves de Medeiros, A. Rozinat, V. Rubin, M. Song, H. M. W. Verbeek, and A. J. M. M. Weijters. 2007. ProM 4.0: Comprehensive support for real process analysis. In *International Conference on Application and Theory of Petri Nets and Other Models of Concurrency (ICATPN 2007)*, ed. J. Kleijn and A. Yakovlev, Lecture Notes in Computer Science 4546: 484–494. Berlin: Springer-Verlag.

Aalst, W. M. P. van der, and K. M. van Hee. 2004. *Workflow management: Models, methods, and systems*. Cambridge, MA: MIT Press.

Aalst, W. M. P. van der, A. H. M. ter Hofstede, B. Kiepuszewski, and A. P. Barros. 2003. Workflow Patterns. *Distributed and Parallel Databases* 14 (1): 5–51.

Aalst, W. M. P. van der, H. A. Reijers, A. J. M. M. Weijters, B. F. van Dongen, A. K. Alves de Medeiros, M. Song, and H. M. W. Verbeek. 2007. Business process mining: An industrial application. *Information Systems* 32 (5): 713–732.

Aalst, W. M. P. van der, A. J. M. M. Weijters, and L. Maruster. 2004. Workflow mining: Discovering process models from event logs. *IEEE Transactions on Knowledge and Data Engineering* 16 (9): 1128–1142.

Allen, Sharon, and E. Terry. 2005. *Beginning relational data modeling*. 2nd ed. New York, NY: Apress.

Alonso, G., F. Casati, H. Kuno, and V. Machiraju. 2003. *Web services: Concepts, architectures and applications*. Berlin: Springer-Verlag.

Alter, S. 2002. *Information systems: Foundation of e-business*. 4th ed. Reading, MA: Prentice Hall.

Alves, A., A. Arkin, S. Askary, C. Barreto, B. Bloch, F. Curbera, M. Ford, Y. Goland, A. Guízar, N. Kartha, C. K. Liu, R. Khalaf, D. König, M. Marin, V. Mehta, S. Thatte, D. van der Rijn, P. Yendluri, and A. Yiu. 2007. Web services business process execution language version 2.0 (OASIS Standard). WS-BPEL TC OASIS. <http://docs.oasis-open.org/wsbpel/2.0/wsbpel-v2.0.html>.

Alves de Medeiros, A. K., A. J. M. M. Weijters, and W. M. P. van der Aalst. 2007. Genetic process mining: An experimental evaluation. *Data Mining and Knowledge Discovery* 14 (2): 245–304.

Baeten, J. C. M., T. Basten, and M. A. Reniers. 2009. *Process algebra: Equational theories of communicating processes*. Cambridge Tracts in Theoretical Computer Science. 1st ed. Cambridge: Cambridge University Press.

Baier, C., and J.–P. Katoen. 2008. *Principles of model checking*. Cambridge, MA: MIT Press.

Berard, B., M. Bidoit, A. Finkel, F. Laroussinie, A. Petit, L. Petrucci, and P. Schnoebelen. 2001. *Systems and software verification: Model-checking techniques and tools*. Berlin: Springer-Verlag.

Bergstra, J. A., A. Ponse, and S. A. Smolka, eds. 2001. Handbook of process algebra. New York: Elsevier Science.

Bernardo, M., and J. Hillston, eds. 2007. Formal methods for performance evaluation, international school on formal methods for the design of computer, communication, and software systems (SFM 2007). Lecture Notes in Computer Science 4486. Berlin: Springer-Verlag.

Boehm, B. W. 1988. A spiral model of software development and enhancement. *Computer* 21 (5): 61–72.

Bratley, P., B. L. Fox, and L. E. Schrage. 1983. *A guide to simulation*. Berlin: Springer-Verlag.

Brauer, W., and W. Reisig. 2009. Carl Adam Petri and "Petri nets." *Fundamental Concepts in Computer Science* 3: 129–139.

Buzacott, J. A. 1996. Commonalities in reengineered business processes: Models and issues. *Management Science* 42 (5): 768–782.

Chen, P. P. 1976. The entity-relationship model: Towards a unified view of data. *ACM Transactions on Database Systems* 1: 9–36.

Cheng, A. M. K. 2002. *Real-time systems: Scheduling, analysis, and verification*. Hoboken, NJ: Wiley-Interscience.

Clarke, E. M., O. Grumberg, and D. A. Peled. 2000. Model checking. Cambridge, MA: MIT Press.

Desel, J., and J. Esparza. 1995. Free choice Petri nets. Cambridge Tracts in Theoretical Computer Science 40. Cambridge: Cambridge University Press.

Desel, J., and G. Juhás. 2001. What is a Petri net? In *Unifying Petri Nets, Advances in Petri Nets*, ed. H. Ehrig, G. Juhás, J. Padberg, and G. Rozenberg. Lecture Notes in Computer Science 2128: 1–25. Berlin: Springer-Verlag.

Desel, J., W. Reisig, and G. Rozenberg, eds. 2004. Lectures on concurrency and Petri nets, Advances in Petri nets. Lecture Notes in Computer Science 3098. Berlin: Springer-Verlag.

Diaz, M., ed. 2009. Petri nets: Fundamental models, verification and applications. London: Wiley-ISTE.

Dijkstra, E. W. 1971. Hierarchical ordering of sequential processes. *Acta Informatica* 1: 115–138.

Dumas, M., W. M. P. van der Aalst, and A. H. M. ter Hofstede. 2005. Process-aware information systems: Bridging people and software through process technology. Wiley & Sons.

Fahland, D., C. Favre, B. Jobstmann, J. Koehler, N. Lohmann, H. Völzer, and K. Wolf. 2009. Instantaneous soundness checking of industrial business process models. In *International Conference on Business Process Management (BPM 2009)*, ed. U. Dayal, J. Eder, J. Koehler, and H. A. Reijers. Lecture Notes in Computer Science 5701: 278–293. Berlin: Springer-Verlag.

Finkel, A. 1993. The minimal coverability graph for Petri nets. In *Advances in Petri Nets 1993*, ed. G. Rozenberg. Lecture Notes in Computer Science 674: 210–243. Berlin: Springer-Verlag.

Fokkink, W. 2010. *Introduction to process algebra*. Berlin: Springer-Verlag.

Geeraerts, G., J.–F. Raskin, and L. Van Begin. 2007. On the efficient computation of the minimal coverability set for Petri nets. In *International Symposium on Automated Technology for Verification and Analysis (ATVA 2007)*, ed. K. S. Namjoshi, T. Yoneda, T. Higashino, and Y. Okamura. Lecture Notes in Computer Science 4762: 98–113. Berlin: Springer-Verlag.

Genrich, H. J., and K. Lautenbach. 1981. System modelling with high-level Petri nets. *Theoretical Computer Science* 13: 109–136.

Girault, C., and R. Valk. 2002. *Petri nets for systems engineering: A guide to modeling, verification, and applications*. Berlin: Springer-Verlag.

Glabbeek, R. J. van. 1993. The linear time–branching time spectrum II. In *International Conference on Concurrency Theory (CONCUR 1993)*, ed. E. Best. Lecture Notes in Computer Science 715: 66–81. Berlin: Springer-Verlag.

———. 2001. The linear time–branching time spectrum I; The semantics of concrete, sequential processes. In *Handbook of Process Algebra*, ed. J. A. Bergstra, A. Ponse, and S. A. Smolka, 3–99. Amsterdam: Elsevier.

Glabbeek, R. J. van, and W. P. Weijland. 1996. Branching time and abstraction in bisimulation semantics. *Journal of the ACM* 43 (3): 555–600.

Godefroid, P. 1991. Using partial orders to improve automatic verification methods. In *International Workshop on Computer Aided Verification (CAV 1990)*, ed. E. M. Clarke and R. P. Kurshan. Lecture Notes in Computer Science 531: 176–185. Berlin: Springer-Verlag.

Grumberg, O., and H. Veith, eds. 2008. 25 years of model checking–History, achievements, perspectives. Lecture Notes in Computer Science 5000. Berlin: Springer-Verlag.

Günther, C. W., and W. M. P. van der Aalst. 2007. Fuzzy mining: Adaptive process simplification based on multi-perspective metrics. In *International Conference on Business Process Management (BPM 2007)*, ed. G. Alonso, P. Dadam, and M. Rosemann. Lecture Notes in Computer Science 4714: 328–343. Berlin: Springer-Verlag.

Haas, P. J. 2002. *Stochastic Petri nets: Modelling, stability, simulation.* Springer Series in Operations Research. Berlin: Springer-Verlag.

Halpin, T., and T. Morgan. 2008. *Information modeling and relational databases.* 2nd ed. Amsterdam: Morgan Kaufmann.

Hamez, A., L. Hillah, F. Kordon, A. Linard, E. Paviot-Adet, X. Renault, and Y. Thierry-Mieg. 2006. New features in CPN-AMI 3: Focusing on the analysis of complex distributed systems. In *International Conference on Application of Concurrency to System Design (ACSD 2006)*, 273–275. Los Alamitos, CA: IEEE Computer Society.

Hammer, M., and J. Champy. 1993. *Reengineering the corporation.* London: Nicolas Brealey Publishing.

Harrington, J. 1991. *Business process improvement: The breakthrough strategy for total quality.* New York, NY: McGraw-Hill.

Haverkort, B. R. 1998. *Performance of computer communication systems: A model-based approach.* New York, NY: Wiley.

Hee, K. M. van. 2009. *Information systems engineering: A formal approach.* 1st ed. Cambridge: Cambridge University Press.

Hoberman, S. 2009. *Data modeling made simple: A practical guide for business and IT professionals.* 2nd ed. Take IT With You(r) Series. Bradley Beach, NJ: Technics Publications.

Hofstede, A. H. M. ter, W. M. P. van der Aalst, M. Adams, and N. Russell. 2010. *Modern business process automation: YAWL and its support environment.* Berlin: Springer-Verlag.

Hohpe, G., and B. Woolf. 2003. *Enterprise integration patterns.* Reading, MA: Addison-Wesley Professional.

Holzmann, G. J. 2003. *The SPIN model checker: Primer and reference manual.* Boston, MA: Addison-Wesley Professional.

Hopcroft, J. E., and J. D. Ullman. 1979. *Introduction to automata theory, languages and computation.* Cambridge: Addison-Wesley.

Hull, E., K. Jackson, and J. Dick. 2004. *Requirements engineering.* 2nd ed. Berlin: Springer-Verlag.

Jablonski, S., and C. Bussler. 1996. *Workflow management: Modeling concepts, architecture, and implementation.* London: International Thomson Computer Press.

Jensen, K. 1997a. *Coloured Petri nets: Basic concepts, analysis methods and practical use.* Vol. 1, *Basic concepts.* Monographs on Theoretical Computer Science. Berlin: Springer-Verlag.

———. 1997b. *Coloured Petri nets: Basic concepts, analysis methods and practical use.* Vol. 2, *Analysis methods.* Monographs on Theoretical Computer Science. Berlin: Springer-Verlag.

———. 1997c. *Coloured Petri nets: Basic concepts, analysis methods and practical use.* Vol. 3, *Practical use.* Monographs on Theoretical Computer Science. Berlin: Springer-Verlag.

Jensen, K., and L. M. Kristensen. 2009. *Coloured Petri nets: Modelling and validation of concurrent systems*. Berlin: Springer-Verlag.

Karp, R. M., and R. E. Miller. 1969. Parallel program schemata. *Journal of Computer and System Sciences* 3 (2): 147–195.

Kelton, D. W., R. Sadowski, and D. Sturrock. 2003. *Simulation with Arena*. New York, NY: McGraw-Hill.

Kleijnen, J., and W. van Groenendaal. 1992. *Simulation: A statistical perspective*. New York, NY: John Wiley & Sons.

Kummer, O., F. Wienberg, M. Duvigneau, J. Schumacher, M. Köhler, D. Moldt, H. Rölke, and R. Valk. 2004. An extensible editor and simulation engine for Petri nets: Renew. In *International Conference on Applications and Theory of Petri Nets and Other Models of Concurrency (ICATPN 2004)*, ed. J. Cortadella and W. Reisig. Lecture Notes in Computer Science 3099: 484–493. Berlin: Springer-Verlag.

Lehmann, D. J., A. Pnueli, and J. Stavi. 1981. Impartiality, justice and fairness: The ethics of concurrent termination. In *International Colloquium on Automata, Languages and Programming (ICALP 1981)*, ed. S. Even and O. Kariv. Lecture Notes in Computer Science 115: 264–277. Berlin: Springer-Verlag.

Leymann, F., and D. Roller. 1999. *Production workflow: Concepts and techniques*. Upper Saddle River, NJ: Prentice-Hall PTR.

Marsan, M. Ajmone, G. Balbo, G. Conte, S. Donatelli, and G. Franceschinis 1995. *Modelling with generalized stochastic Petri nets*. Wiley Series in Parallel Computing, New York, NY: Wiley.

Milner, R. 1989. *Communication and concurrency*. Prentice-Hall International Series in Computer Science, Upper Saddle River, NJ: Prentice-Hall.

Milner, R., M. Tofte, R. Harper, and D. MacQueen. 1997. *The definition of Standard ML*. Cambride, MA: MIT Press.

Muehlen, M. zur. 2004. *Workflow-based process controlling: Foundation, design and application of workflow-driven process information systems*. Berlin: Logos.

Murata, T. 1989. Petri nets: Properties, analysis and applications. *Proceedings of the IEEE* 77 (4): 541–580.

Object Management Group. 2003. *UML 2.0 Object Constraint Language (OCL) specification*. Needham, MA: Object Management Group.

———. 2005. *Unified Modeling Language 2.0 specification*. Needham, MA: Object Management Group.

———. 2009. *Unified Modeling Language, infrastructure and superstructure (version 2.2)*. OMG Final Adopted Specification. Needham, MA: Object Management Group.

Olivé, A. 2007. *Conceptual modeling of information systems*. 1st ed. Berlin: Springer-Verlag.

Oppel, A. 2009. *Data modeling: A beginner's guide*. 1st ed. Ney York, NY: McGraw-Hill Osborne Media.

Papazoglou, M. P. 2007. *Web services: Principles and technology*. Essex: Pearson–Prentice Hall.

Park, D. 1981. Concurrency and automata on infinite sequences. In *GI–Conference on Theoretical Computer Science*, 167–183. Berlin and London: Springer-Verlag.

Paulson, L. C. 2010. *ML for the working programmer*. 2nd ed. Cambridge: Cambridge University Press.

Peled, D. 1993. All from one, one for all: On model checking using representatives. In *International Conference on Computer Aided Verification (CAV 1993)*, ed. C. Courcoubetis. Lecture Notes in Computer Science 697: 409–423. Berlin: Springer-Verlag.

Peterson, J. L. 1981. *Petri net theory and the modeling of systems*. Englewood Cliffs, NJ: Prentice-Hall.

Petri, C. A. 1962. *Kommunikation mit Automaten*. Schriften des IIM Nr. 2, Bonn: Institut für Instrumentelle Mathematik.

Ponniah, P. 2007. *Data modeling fundamentals: A practical guide for IT professionals*. 1st ed. Hoboken, NJ: Wiley-Interscience.

Poole, D. 2010. *Linear algebra: A modern introduction*. 3rd ed. Florence, KY: Brooks Cole.

Reisig, W. 1985. *Petri nets: An introduction*. EATCS Monographs on Theoretical Computer Science, vol. 4. Berlin: Springer-Verlag.

———. 1998. *Elements of distributed algorithms: Modeling and analysis with Petri nets*. Berlin: Springer-Verlag.

———. 2010. *Petrinetze–Modellierung, Analyse, Fallstudien*. Leitfäden der Informatik. Wiesbaden: Vieweg-Teubner.

Reisig, W., and G. Rozenberg, eds. 1998. Lectures on Petri nets I: Basic models, Advances in Petri nets. Lecture Notes in Computer Science 1491. Berlin: Springer-Verlag.

Rice, J. A. 2006. *Mathematical statistics and data analysis*. 3rd ed. Pacific Grove, CA: Duxbury Press.

Ross, S. M. 1990. *A course in simulation*. New York: Macmillan.

Royce, W. 1970. Managing the development of large software systems. In *Proceedings IEEE Wescon*, 1–9.

Rozinat, A., and W. M. P. van der Aalst. 2006. Decision mining in ProM. In *International Conference on Business Process Management (BPM 2006)*, ed. S. Dustdar, J. L. Fiadeiro, and A. Sheth. Lecture Notes in Computer Science 4102: 420–425. Berlin: Springer-Verlag.

———. 2008. Conformance checking of processes based on monitoring real behavior. *Information Systems* 33 (1): 64–95.

Rozinat, A., R. S. Mans, M. Song, and W. M. P. van der Aalst. 2009. Discovering simulation models. *Information Systems* 34 (3): 305–327.

Rozinat, A., M. Wynn, W. M. P. van der Aalst, A. H. M. ter Hofstede, and C. Fidge. 2009. Workflow simulation for operational decision support. *Data and Knowledge Engineering* 68 (9): 834–850.

Rumbaugh, J., I. Jacobson, and G. Booch. 1998. *The Unified Modeling Language Reference Manual*. Reading, MA: Addison Wesley.

Scheer, A. W. 1994. *Business process engineering: Reference models for industrial enterprises*. Berlin: Springer-Verlag.

Simsion, G., and G. Witt. 2004. *Data modeling essentials*. 3rd ed. San Francisco, CA: Morgan Kaufmann.

Strang, G. 2009. *Introduction to linear algebra*. 4th ed. Wellesley, MA: Wellesley Cambridge Press.

Ullman, J. D. 1998. *Elements of ML programming, ML97 edition*. 2nd ed. Upper Saddle River, NJ: Prentice Hall.

Valk, R. 2004. Object Petri nets: Using the nets-within-nets paradigm. In *Lectures on Concurrency and Petri Nets*, ed. J. Desel, W. Reisig, and G. Rozenberg. Lecture Notes in Computer Science 3098: 819–848. Berlin: Springer-Verlag.

Valmari, A. 1991. A stubborn attack on state explosion. In *International Workshop on Computer Aided Verification (CAV 1990)*, ed. E. M. Clarke and R. P. Kurshan. Lecture Notes in Computer Science 531: 156–165. Berlin: Springer-Verlag.

———. 1998. The state explosion problem. In *Lectures on Petri nets I: Basic models, Advances in Petri nets*, ed. W. Reisig and G. Rozenberg. Lecture Notes in Computer Science 1491: 429–528. Berlin: Springer-Verlag.

Verbeek, H. M. W., T. Basten, and W. M. P. van der Aalst. 2001. Diagnosing workflow processes using Woflan. *The Computer Journal* 44 (4): 246–279.

Wang, J. 1998. *Timed Petri nets: Theory and application*. Norwell, MA: Kluwer Academic Publishers.

Weske, M. 2007. *Business process management: Concepts, languages, architectures*. Berlin: Springer-Verlag.

Witten, I. H., and E. Frank. 2005. *Data mining: Practical machine learning tools and techniques*. 2nd ed. San Francisco, CA: Morgan Kaufmann.

Wolf, K. 2007. Generating Petri net state spaces. In *International Conference on Applications and Theory of Petri Nets and Other Models of Concurrency (ICATPN 2007)*, ed. J. Kleijn and A. Yakovlev. Lecture Notes in Computer Science 4546: 29–42. Berlin: Springer-Verlag.

Index